TURNING POINTS IN
AFRICAN
DEMOCRACY

T0373269

TURNING POINTS IN
AFRICAN
DEMOCRACY

EDITED BY
ABDUL RAUFU MUSTAPHA
& LINDSAY WHITFIELD

JAMES CURREY

James Currey
an imprint of
Boydell & Brewer Ltd
PO Box 9
Woodbridge
Suffolk
IP12 3DF
www.boydell.co.uk
and of
Boydell & Brewer Inc.
668 Mt Hope Avenue
Rochester
NY 14620 USA
www.boydellandbrewer.com

Copyright © Contributors 2009
First published 2009
Transferred to digital printing and reprinted in paperback 2011

British Library Cataloguing in Publication Data
Turning points in African democracy.
1. Decentralization in government--Africa, sub-Saharan--
Case studies. 2. Democratization--Africa, Sub-Saharan--Case
studies. 3. Africa, Sub-Saharan--Politics and government--
1960- --Case studies.
I. Mustapha, Abdul Raufu. II. Whitfield, Lindsay, 1978-
321.8′0967-dc22

ISBN 978-1-84701-317-0 (James Currey cloth)
ISBN 978-1-84701-316-3 (James Currey paper)

Typeset in 10/11pt Photina
by Long House, Cumbria

For Gavin

Contents

List of Tables & Figures   x
Foreword by Laurence Whitehead   xi
Notes on Contributors   xv
Abbreviations   xvii

1

African Democratisation
The Journey So Far
ABDUL RAUFU MUSTAPHA
& LINDSAY WHITFIELD

1

2

Senegal since 2000
Rebuilding Hegemony in a Global Age
TARIK DAHOU
& VINCENT FOUCHER

13

3

Côte d'Ivoire since 1993
The Risky Reinvention of a Nation
FRANCIS AKINDÈS

31

4

Ghana since 1993
A Successful Democratic Experiment?
LINDSAY WHITFIELD

50

5
Nigeria since 1999
*A Revolving Door Syndrome
or the Consolidation of Democracy?*
    ABDUL RAUFU MUSTAPHA   71

6
Kenya since 2002
The More Things Change the More They Stay the Same
    NIC CHEESEMAN   94

7
Zambia since 1990
Paradoxes of Democratic Transition
    MILES LARMER   114

8
South Africa since 1994
Who Holds Power after Apartheid?
    JEREMY SEEKINGS   134

9
Mozambique since 1989
Shaping Democracy after Socialism
    ERIC MORIER-GENOUD   153

10

Rwanda & Burundi since 1994
An End to the Discriminatory State?
PATRICIA DALEY   167

11

Zimbabwe since 1997
Land & the Legacies of War
JOCELYN ALEXANDER   185

12

Conclusion
The Politics of African States
in the Era of Democratisation
LINDSAY WHITFIELD   202
& ABDUL RAUFU MUSTAPHA

Index   229

List of Tables & Figures

Tables

1.1	How African Leaders Left Office, 1960-2007	2
1.2	Freedom House Indicators for selected African Countries	3
4.1	Governments of Ghana, 1957-2008	51
5.1	Governments and Leaders of Nigeria, 1976-2008	71
5.2	Trends in Shares of Federation Account 1998-2007 (Nigeria)	78
5.3	Trend Indicators for Nigerian Democracy 1999-2005 (%)	90
9.1	Elections Results 1994 (Mozambique)	156
12.1	Freedom House Categorisation of Sub-Saharan Africa, 1989 and 2007 (%)	226

Figures

6.1	The structure of patron-client networks in Kenya	96
6.2	*Harambee* contributions per year (KSh), inflation adjusted	104
6.3	Constituency Development Fund project submission flow-chart	106

Foreword

LAURENCE WHITEHEAD

Broadly speaking, democratisation came to much of sub-Saharan Africa after about 1990. In some cases, this was a *re*-democratisation, where independence initially transmitted sovereignty to a competitive multi-party system. The statement is a rough approximation. (Botswana was durably democratised following decolonisation in 1966, while Nigeria failed to make democratisation durable both before and again after 1990, for instance.) But as a generalisation applying to a large region, the claim is as defensible as most others of its kind. The more interesting questions are what this abrupt and extensive regional 'wave' of democratisation really signifies in the African context? Is it the same as in other large regions? Does it matter to ordinary people? How long do we need to assess either its significance or its durability?

This volume looks back on the processes of the 1990s from the perspective of 2008. The cut-off date is, of course, arbitrary, and may distort our perception of the underlying trends. Recent news from Zimbabwe, but also from Kenya, Somalia, and Mauritania among others, indicates the counter-currents to any over-generalised claims about 'waves'. The book demonstrates the diversity of outcomes across the region, and investigates how far theories and models developed elsewhere require modification in this context. Democratisation matters in Africa, as elsewhere. People struggle and suffer for it, some show great inventiveness in devising ways to enhance its significance and durability. But each national context matters as well. Historical memories, group loyalties, political economy issues, including aid dependence, and geopolitical realities all affect how any particular democratisation process turns out. A generation may not be long enough to determine the final outcome in every case. So this volume is an interim report, a first approximation, a survey of the field that raises as many questions as it answers.

The eleven countries studied here display a striking diversity of political trajectories. Ghana, Senegal and South Africa are all currently rated as 'free' by Freedom House, but if so they arrived at this condition from very different starting points and experienced strongly divergent 'modes of transition'. In addition, as the relevant chapters clearly demonstrate, they all still display important limitations, both from normative assessments of the 'quality' of democracy, and on empirical evidence available about citizen satisfaction with these outcomes. At the other extreme, Côte d'Ivoire, Rwanda and Zimbabwe are all currently rated 'not free' by Freedom House. Yet they too have each been affected by the region-wide shift to democratisation. Indeed, the Rwandan chapter even refers to the 1994 genocide as 'the culmination of a democratisation process gone wrong' (p. 176), and the perverse and disastrous courses adopted by the rulers of Côte d'Ivoire and Zimbabwe are also partly to be understood as responses by autocratic rulers to the threats they associated with democratic uncertainty. In between, we have the mixed assortment of Burundi, Kenya, Nigeria and Zambia, all currently rated as 'part free,' although the Kenyan case must currently be under review. Again, this cluster displays an impressive diversity of socio-historical contexts and institutional responses. The military are critical in the first and third, while the legacies of one-party dominance still cast a long shadow over the other two. Aid dependence is crucial in Ghana and Zambia, in contrast to oil dependence in Nigeria. Burundi can hardly be understood in isolation from the experience of neighbouring Rwanda, and Zambia's history is also entangled with that of Zimbabwe. In synthesis, a comparison of these case studies uncovers a multiplicity of contrasts and distinctions that impede the formulation of robust middle-range generalisations.

And yet this volume also brings out common patterns that justify the examination of all these experiences in parallel. A recurrent theme is the weight of executive dominance, and of top-down styles of political control, which clash with democratic normative assumptions about civic rights and at least formal political equality. Another is the highly constrained scope for policy choice, given economic scarcity and international pressures. A third is the prevalence of survival strategies as the most pressing preoccupations motivating large segments of the electorate. The 'collapse of the middle class' is another recurrent topic (highlighted in the chapters on Côte d'Ivoire, Nigeria, Zambia and Zimbabwe, for example). Democratisation is unlikely to prove well-supported, durable or satisfying in such conditions. Interestingly, the volume also records a few instances where the middle class has not so evidently collapsed – or may perhaps even be gaining cohesion– especially in South Africa, but perhaps also in Ghana, and maybe even in Kenya and Senegal. Could it be that these are relatively favourable conditions for a gradual deepening of democracy? Although this proposition merits a tentative assent, it is only one among a series of partial and provisional interpretations that can be extracted here. These are significant and well-delineated patterns, but they all fall far short of the uni-causal and predictive models favoured by a dominant school of social science technicians. This volume provides a solidly argued antidote to such reductionism.

That is as it should be. Not only in Africa, but also in most other large world regions, experience since 1990 should have taught us to be cautious in our assessments of what democratisation signifies for ordinary people; of how well it 'takes'; and of how each specific national process is to be characterised and understood. It should have taught us that there is no single reliable template or definition, no unambiguous consolidated end-state. These processes matter, but they vary. They share some family resemblances, but each is also highly distinctive. If they are durable and significant, that is also because they are complex and long-term, and also often quite open-ended since the basic processes and patterns of democratisation may also be subject to distortion, deviation and even reversal in particular high-stress contexts. Ideas about national unity, the rights of minorities, the place of religion, the status of women, and the accountability of leaders, will evolve within each country, and perhaps diverge between them. Different viewpoints about what counts as a successful and definitive outcome will therefore remain in contention. All this can be detected in the eleven country studies covered in this volume.

Given the spread of cases under review here, does it make sense to treat sub-Saharan Africa as a unitary large region? Or would it be more appropriate to bracket Nigeria with Indonesia, Zimbabwe with Myanmar, and South Africa with Brazil? Suitably selected cross-regional paired comparisons can certainly be of interest, and may highlight regularities that might otherwise pass unobserved. But there is also a case for differentiating Africa from other large regions, each with their own characteristic political 'style' and democratic impetus.

Thus, for example, although ethnic politics in 'divided societies' can be found elsewhere (notably in Guyana or Sri Lanka, for instance) the prevalence of this type of group alignment and inter-group conflict is far greater and more widespread in sub-Saharan Africa. Similarly, although there are 'weak' and 'failing' states in Europe (such as Bosnia) and the Americas (Haiti, for instance) and in Asia (as in East Timor), such problems are more prevalent in Africa, and have more spill-over effects for neighbouring countries. And there is a more generalised consciousness of the potential for praetorianism in this large region than elsewhere (this was one of the justifications for one-party regimes prior to 1990). In large swathes of sub-Saharan Africa the term 'praetorianism' hardly does justice to the scale of the prevalent disorder and insecurity. This is largely a reflection of the independence struggles and subsequent prolonged civil wars that engulfed huge territories after colonialism was withdrawn. The Cold War may have flooded many areas with small arms, but the fighting soon lost any ideological focus, as unemployed young men fuelled a spiral of banditry and predation. Of course, this is not a situation that is unique to Africa, nor is it uniformly spread. But in contrast to other large regions, the new states of Africa were more vulnerable.

Demographic and environmental pressures, and health crises symbolised by the AIDS epidemic, aggravated these tendencies. In quite a few countries such conditions have prevailed for so long that it is hard to envisage a sustained recovery, let alone the building of fully democratic regimes. But there are also elements of the African political tradition that are quite favourable to a certain style of democratisation. Perhaps the failings of public administration have a compensating benefit in terms of self-organisation and the activism of non-governmental organisations; colonial legacies include educational, media, and judicial traditions that can potentially be directed towards democratic advancement. The landed oligarchs of Latin America, or the hereditary power structures of the Gulf of Arabia, or the political dynamics of South Asia lack African counterparts of equivalent weight. Although gender inequalities are severe here, as elsewhere, the womenfolk of Africa play a decisive role in managing the informal economy – more so than in the Middle East or much of South Asia, and so they have potential political leverage.

Overall, piecing together these disparate features of a distinctively African political style (together with other characteristics that can be extracted from the case studies in this volume), one arrives at a mixed, but by no means entirely negative, prognosis for the future of democracy in sub-Saharan Africa. The type of political regime that can be stabilised in conditions such as this is unlikely to match universal models of liberal political democracy. But there is a collective understanding of what more accountable and responsive regimes should look like (as reflected in the *Afrobarometer* survey data), and there is a widespread desire to move that way. Despite the generally very low level of per capita incomes, and the region's great failings in the areas of education, basic healthcare and job creation, there are considerable societal resources that can be mobilised in favour of such aspirations. The biggest impediments may concern administrative capacities rather than the veto power of entrenched interests. Fortunately, the citizens of these countries are fully conscious of the limitations of their existing states. The excessive popular expectations that have been known to destabilise democratic experiments in other large regions are less of a problem here.

The authors have made an effort to circle back from their specific analyses to the general issues raised by the comparative study of democratisation processes. In this way, the volume serves to enrich the general level of an analysis, without impoverishing its coverage of the highly specific political realities of each country. If there is a normative thread linking these studies, it concerns the need for tolerance, pluralism, and open-endedness when analysing the political predicaments facing democrats in contemporary Africa. There are few pre-fabricated answers, and outsiders should hesitate to substitute their heavy-handed certainties for the delicate tasks of persuasion and adaptation that only those directly and permanently involved can undertake.

Nuffield College, Oxford

Notes on Contributors

FRANCIS AKINDÈS is Professor of Economic and Political Sociology and Head of the Department of Anthropology and Sociology at the University of Bouaké, Côte d'Ivoire. He is also an Associate Researcher at the IRD (Institut de Recherche pour le Développement) in Paris. He has written several books and articles in the fields of economic sociology, political change, and poverty reduction policies.

JOCELYN ALEXANDER is Professor of Development Studies at the University of Oxford. She has published widely on the history and politics of Zimbabwe. Her books include *Violence and Memory: One Hundred Years in the 'Dark Forests' of Matabeland* (2000) (with JoAnn McGregor and Terence Ranger), and *The Unsettled Land: State-making and the Politics of Land in Zimbabwe, 1893-2003* (2006). She is currently working on a history of crime and punishment in Zimbabwe.

NIC CHEESEMAN is University Lecturer in African Politics, Oxford University and Hugh Price Fellow, Jesus College. His research interests include the one-party state, African political parties, comparative democratisation, and the politics of Kenya and Zambia. He has published on subjects such as the structure of Kenya's colonial legacy and the impact of opinion polling in Africa's new democracies.

TARIK DAHOU is an anthropologist at the Institut de Recherche pour le Développement (IRD) and is associated with the Centre d'Etudes Africaines de l'Ecole des Hautes Etudes en Sciences Sociales (EHESS), Paris. His former work is about liberalisation policies in Senegal and their impact on clientelism and corruption. His recent research deals with the public sphere and environmental policies with a comparative perspective between West Africa and North Africa.

PATRICIA DALEY is a University Lecturer in Human Geography and a Fellow of Jesus College, University of Oxford. She researches and teaches on warfare, peace and post-conflict reconstruction, forced migration, and environmental issues in Africa; and on African communities in Britain. Her recent publications include *Gender and Genocide in Burundi: The Search for Spaces of Peace in the Great Lakes Region of Africa*, (2007) (Oxford: James Currey).

VINCENT FOUCHER, a senior researcher at the Centre National de la Recherche

Scientifique, is based at the Centre d'étude d'Afrique noire, Bordeaux. He obtained a PhD in political science from the School of Oriental and African Studies, London University in 2002, researching the origins of the separatist movement in Casamance, Senegal. His research has since analysed the war and peace process in Casamance, as well as other aspects of Senegalese politics. He is the editor in chief of *Politique africaine*.

MILES LARMER is a Lecturer in International History, University of Sheffield. He was previously a Lecturer in Post-1945 Global History at Sheffield Hallam University in the United Kingdom. He is the author of numerous articles on Zambian history and politics, as well as on the role of social movements in Southern Africa as a whole. His book, *Mineworkers in Zambia: Labour and Political Change in Post-Colonial Africa*, was published by I.B. Tauris in 2007.

ERIC MORIER-GENOUD is a Lecturer in African and Imperial History, Queen's University, Belfast. He was previously research fellow at the Oxford Research Network on Government in Africa (OReNGA), University of Oxford. He has published widely on religion and politics in Mozambique and South Africa. He is currently working on issues of war commemoration and memory. He is co-editor of the journal *Social Sciences and Missions* (Leiden: Brill).

ABDUL RAUFU MUSTAPHA is a University Lecturer in African Politics and Kirk-Greene Fellow at St. Antony's College, University of Oxford. He is a member of the Scientific Committee of the Council for the Development of Social Science Research in Africa (CODESRIA), and the Senior Researcher for West Africa at the Centre for Research on Inequality, Human Security and Ethnicity (CRISE), at Queen Elizabeth House, University of Oxford. He has published extensively on Nigerian politics, ethnicity and identity politics, and the politics of rural societies. His recent publications include *Gulliver's Troubles: Nigeria's Foreign Policy after the Cold War* (edited with Adekeye Adebajo), University of Kwazulu Natal Press, 2008. His current research focuses on the implications of third-wave democratisation for rural communities in the north of Nigeria, the management of ethnic diversity by the Nigeria state, and the nature of the state in Africa.

JEREMY SEEKINGS is Professor of Political Studies and Sociology at the University of Cape Town. His books include *The UDF: A History of the United Democratic Front in South Africa, 1983-2001* (2000) and *Class, Race and Inequality in South Africa* (co-authored with Nicoli Nattrass, 2005). His current research concerns the politics of welfare state-building in developing countries, and the reproduction of inequalities in South Africa and elsewhere.

LINDSAY WHITFIELD was a research fellow at the Global Economic Governance Programme, University of Oxford (2005–8) and is now a research fellow at the Danish Institute for International Studies, Copenhagen. She completed her doctorate in Politics at the University of Oxford in 2005, researching the impacts of foreign aid on democracy in Ghana. Her current research interests focus on the intersection between African politics and foreign aid and on African elites and economic policymaking. She has also edited and contributed to *The Politics of Aid: African Strategies for Dealing with Donors* (Oxford University Press, 2008).

Abbreviations

AC	Action Congress
AD	Alliance for Democracy
ADEP	*Alliance pour la Démocratie, l'Equité et la Progres*
AFDL	*Alliance des Forces Démocratiques pour la Libération du Congo*
AFP	*Alliance des Forces du Progrès*
AIDS	Acquired Immune Deficiency Syndrome
AIG	Assistant Inspector General
ALR	*Armée de Liberation Rwanda*
ANC	African National Congress
ANPP	All Nigerian Peoples' Party
APP	All Peoples' Party
APRM	African Peer Review Mechanism
BEE	Black Economic Empowerment
CCI	*Centre de commandement intégré*
CDD	Centre for Democracy and Development
CDF	Constituency Development Fund
CEDEAO	*Communauté Economique des Etats de l'Afrique de l'Ouest* (ECOWAS in English)
CFA Franc	*Communauté Financière Africaine*
CNCR	Council for Intra-Rural Dialogue
CNDD/FDD	*Conseil National pour le Défense de la Démocratie / Forces pour le Défense de la Démocratie*
COSATU	Congress of South African Trade Unions
DA	Democratic Alliance
DCE	District Chief Executive
DP	Democratic Party
DPA	Democratic Peoples' Alliance
DRC	Democratic Republic of the Congo
ECA	Economic Commission for Africa
ECOWAS	Economic Community of West African States (CEDEAO in French)
EFCC	Economic and Financial Crimes Commission
FAO	Food and Agriculture Organisation
FAR	*Forces Armée Rwandaise*

FDLR	*Armées pour la Libération du Rwanda*
FESCI	Students' and Scholars' Federation of Côte d'Ivoire
FIDH	*Fédération Internationale des Ligues des Droits de L'Homme*
FIRS	Federal Inland Revenue Service
FORD	Forum for the Restoration of Democracy
FPI	*Front Populaire Ivoirien*
FRODEBU	*Front pour la Démocratie au Burundi*
Frolina	*Parti pour la Libération National*
G8	Group of Eight leading industrialised countries
GDP	Gross Domestic Product
GEAR	Growth, Employment and Redistribution
HIV	Human Immunodeficiency Virus
HRW	Human Rights Watch
ICG	International Crisis Group
ICPC	Independent Corrupt Practices Commission
ID	Independent Democrats
IMF	International Monetary Fund
INEC	Independent National Electoral Commission
IPAC	Inter-Party Advisory Committee
KANU	Kenya African National Union
LDP	Liberal Democratic Party
LIPRODHOR	League for the Promotion and Defence of Human Rights
MASSOB	Movement for the Actualisation of the Sovereign State of Biafra
MDC	Movement for Democratic Change
MDR	*Mouvement Démocratique Republicain*
MEND	Movement for the Emancipation of the Niger Delta
MMD	Movement for Multiparty Democracy
MNRDD	National Republican Movement for Democracy and Development
MPCI	*Mouvement Patriotique de Côte d'Ivoire*
MPLA	*Movimento Popular de Libertacao de Angola*
MRC	Movement for the Rehabilitation of Citizens
MRND	*Mouvement Revolutionnaire National pour le Développement*
MRND(D)	*Mouvement Revolutionnaire National pour le Développement (Démocrate)*
MSP-Inkinzo	*Mouvement Socialiste Panafricaniste-Inkinzo y'Ijambo ry'Abarundi*
MUZ	Mineworkers' Union of Zambia
NAFDAC	National Administration for Food and Drugs Administration and Control
NaRC	National Rainbow Coalition
NCC	National Constitutional Conference
NDC	National Democratic Congress
NDDC	Niger Delta Development Commission
NDI	National Democratic Institute
NDLEA	National Drugs Law Enforcement Agency
NEEDS	National Economic Empowerment and Development Strategy
NEITI	Nigerian Extractive Industries Transparency Initiative
NEPAD	New Partnership for Africa's Development
NGO	Non-Governmental Organisation

NLC	Nigeria Labour Congress
NNP	New National Party
NP	National Party
NPP	New Patriotic Party
NPRC	National Political Reforms Conference
NURC	National Unity and Reconciliation Commission
OAU	Organisation of African Unity
OCHA-IRIN	UN Office for the Coordination of Humanitarian Affairs-Integrated Regional Information Networks
ODM	Orange Democratic Movement
OMPADEC	Oil Mineral Producing Areas Development Commission
OPC	O'odua People's Congress
Palipehutu/FNL	*Parti pour la Libération du Peuple Hutu /Forces National de Libération*
PARENA	*Parti pour le Redressement National*
PDC	*Parti Démocrate Chrétien*
PDCI	*Parti Démocratique de la Côte d'Ivoire*
PDM	People's Democratic Movement
PDP	People's Democratic Party
PDR-UBuyanja	*Parti Démocrate pour le Renouveau*
PDS	*Parti Démocratique Sénégalais*
PF	Patriotic Front (Zambia)
PIT	*Parti Ivoirien de Travailleurs*
PL	*Parti Libéral*
PNC	People's National Convention
PNDC	Provisional National Defence Council
PRONACO	Pro National Conference Organisation
PRSP	Poverty Reduction Strategy Paper
PS	*Parti Socialiste*
PSD	*Parti Social Démocrate*
PSI	*Parti Socialiste Ivoirien*
RCD-Goma	*Rassemblement Congolais pour la Démocratie* – Goma
RDR	*Rassemblement des Republicains*
RPA	Rwandese Patriotic Army
RPF	Rwandese Patriotic Front
SACP	South African Communist Party
SEEDS	State Economic Empowerment and Development Strategy
SNC	Sovereign National Conference
TAC	Treatment Action Campaign
TI	Transparency International
UN	United Nations
UNAR	*Union National de Rwanda*
UNDP	United Nations Development Programme
UNIP	United National Independence Party
UNSC	United Nations Security Council
UPRONA	*Union Pour le Progrès National*
URD	*Union pour le Renouveau Démocratique*
Zanu(PF)	Zimbabwe African National Union (Patriotic Front)
Zapu	Zimbabwe African People's Union

1

African Democratisation
The Journey So Far

ABDUL RAUFU MUSTAPHA
& LINDSAY WHITFIELD

Introduction: How Has Democratisation Affected African Countries?

The 1989 National Conference in Benin opened the era of political liberalisation and re-democratisation in sub-Saharan Africa, an era marked with such optimism that Claude Ake (2000) characterised it as Africa's 'second independence'. A combination of internal and external factors created effective pressure for political change which culminated in the introduction of multi-party elections in most African countries in the 1990s (Nolutshungu 1992; Rijnierse 1993). Democracy, understood as institutionalised and competitive elections, along with respect for civil and political liberties, was once again on the agenda of many countries that had hitherto suffered from the suffocating yoke of one-party rule or outright military dictatorships. Public opposition to the authoritarian regimes arose out of a steady accumulation of discontent over many years, accentuated by economic hardship and deepening social divisions of ethnicity, religion, class and region. This opposition included a variety of groups and interests: marginalised politicians, businessmen who lacked or had lost the favour of government, people from regions which they felt had been left out or discriminated against by governments, workers and trade unions, students, women's organisations, religious organisations and human rights activists (Ake 2000).

The agitations of these groups represented a resurgence of normative values, particularly of freedom and economic well-being that had long been repressed by authoritarian post-colonial regimes. Many local actors within specific African countries hoped that democratisation would bring greater political inclusion, the demilitarisation of politics, greater economic and social opportunities, and a loosening of presidential authoritarianism. Amidst an unprecedented crisis of legitimacy within African states, public protest contained a multiplicity of demands and expectations, often contradictory, and did not necessarily possess a consensus on what should replace the resented regimes.

A range of external pressures for democratisation supported the internal longing for change. These included the increasing policy control of fiscally weakened African states by international financial institutions and allied bilateral agencies of industrialised countries. Following the end of the Cold War, Western powers also shifted away from tolerance of, and complicity with, some authoritarian African regimes. These two-pronged external pressures were exacerbated by liberalising processes unfolding in Eastern Europe. Within the international community, the wave of democratisation brought with it expectations of economic and political liberalisation in Africa, as well as greater integration of the continent into the neo-liberal global economic system. This international context accounts for the simultaneity and similarity of calls for political liberalisation and multi-party elections across so many African states (Chabal 1998; Joseph 1997).

Almost two decades after these events, this book considers the extent to which local and international expectations of African democratisation have been met. It examines the major trends and patterns in the politics of African states in the era of democratisation, and then assesses *what* these trends and patterns mean for the process of democratisation. It approaches these twin tasks through a comparative study of eleven countries: Senegal, Côte d'Ivoire, Ghana, Nigeria, Kenya, Zambia, South Africa, Mozambique, Zimbabwe, Rwanda and Burundi.

In such an enterprise, two lines of enquiry must be separated. The first task is to understand the actual processes of change and continuity that have taken place. The second task is to evaluate these processes of change and continuity against normative ideas of democracy. The first raises questions about 'what is', while the second asks 'what ought to be?' In practice they are interrelated, as democracy is a contested concept (Whitehead 2001) and debates over the meaning of democracy shape its actual implementation. Yet it is critical not to confound the empirical with the normative, but to see them separately and clarify their relationship. At the empirical level, democratisation has led to some 'tectonic movements' in African politics (Bratton *et al.* 2005: 14). One indicator of this is its effect on the way African leaders get into power and leave office. As Table 1.1 suggests, the number of leaders leaving office via coups has reduced, particularly after 2000, while the number leaving voluntarily or through electoral defeats has increased since 1990. The process of leadership recruitment in sub-Saharan African countries is beginning to be affected by constitutional changes which stipulate presidential term limits and by the 'proliferation of elections' (Villalon & Huxtable 1998: 15).

Table 1.1 How African Leaders Left Office, 1960–2007

	1960–69	1970–79	1980–89	1990–99	2000–07
Overthrown in coups	27	30	22	22	7
Retired voluntarily	1	2	5	9	10
Lost elections	0	0	1	12	7

Data from 1960-2003 adapted from Hyden (2006: 19).

A second indicator of change is the effect of democratisation on the rights and liberties enjoyed by ordinary African citizens, as illustrated by Table 1.2. A comparison of the 1989-95 mean figures for political rights from the Freedom

Table 1.2 Freedom House Indicators for selected African Countries

	Political Rights				Civil Liberties			
	Mean 1989-95	Mean 1996-2000	Mean 2001-06	2007	Mean 1989-95	Mean 1996-2000	Mean 2001-06	2007
Burundi	6.67	6.60	5.17	4	6.17	6.60	5.33	5
Côte d'Ivoire	6.00	6.00	5.83	7	4.50	4.40	5.33	6
Ghana	5.50	3.20	1.83	1	4.83	3.40	2.50	2
Mozambique	5.50	3.00	3.00	3	5.17	4.00	3.30	4
Kenya	5.50	6.40	4.17	3	5.83	5.60	3.83	3
Nigeria	5.83	6.20	4.00	4	4.83	5.20	4.33	4
Rwanda	6.17	7.00	6.50	6	5.83	6.00	5.33	5
Senegal	4.00	4.00	2.33	2	3.67	4.20	3.33	3
South Africa	4.67	1.00	1.00	2	4.00	2.00	2.00	2
Zambia	3.67	4.60	4.33	3	4.00	4.00	4.00	4
Zimbabwe	5.33	5.20	6.33	7	4.33	5.00	5.83	6
Mean	5.35	4.95	3.05	3.81	4.83	4.58	3.21	4

Source: Freedom House. All values on a scale of 1 to 7, with 1 representing the highest degree of freedom and 7 representing the lowest.

House data set and the 2007 figures shows that political rights have improved in nine out of eleven of our case-study countries and worsened in two. Similarly, over the same period, civil liberties have improved in eight countries, remained constant in one, and deteriorated in two. Although there are ebbs and flows in the figures, the general trend suggests an improvement in the freedoms and liberties enjoyed by ordinary citizens of sub-Saharan Africa under democratisation.

However, the era of democratisation has been characterised not only by processes of change, but also by continuities with past political practices. In many countries, democratisation has been halting, incomplete, and frequently reversible. In others like Côte d'Ivoire and Zimbabwe (see figures in Table 1.2), things seem to have worsened in the era of democratization as stable semi-authoritarian political regimes became less stable and more authoritarian. The inchoate nature of the democratisation process has bred disappointment. Joseph (1998) uses the term 'virtual democracies' to describe the admixture of democratic forms and illiberal practices that still characterise many democratising countries in Africa. The euphoria of the early 1990s has been replaced since the late 1990s by a pessimistic outlook (Herbst 2001). Is this pessimism any more justified than the earlier euphoria? It would seem that the answer to this question is influenced by the methodological approach adopted by the researcher.

Studying African Democratisation

The study of democracy in Africa since the 'third wave' has been dominated by the democratisation school, which sought to determine whether a political system is democratic or not, how it moves from being non-democratic to democratic (transition to democracy), and how likely it is to stay a democracy (the extent to which democracy is consolidated). Some of these approaches were excessively normative in orientation, often confusing 'what ought to be' with 'what is', as, for example, in the rosy theorisation of 'civil society' within the process of democratisation. There was also a teleological tendency in some studies: all countries are necessarily moving toward the full institutionalisation of elections and related processes and can be located on a linear continuum. Thus democratisation studies often point to the 'obstacles' stymieing a process that would otherwise operate unfettered (O'Donnell 1996). The democratisation school also presupposes a generic and somewhat idealised view of established democracies as their yardstick for normative comparison. They compare African countries with a liberal democratic model, judging African political systems by how much they deviate from this ideal. This is despite the fact that some 'mature' democracies sometimes fall short of these same standards. For example, some have argued that in the 'mature' democracies in the West the right to vote is perhaps seen more as a symbol of equality than as in any sense an influence on public policy (Young 1993). African experiences are thus judged, not so much by what they really are, but by what it is presumed they should be. It is hardly surprising that many of such studies took a pessimistic turn from the late 1990s.

Against this background, it is understandable that Herbst challenges us to conduct empirical research and comparative analysis, exhorting us to 'begin to analyze what is actually happening' (2001: 360). He calls for the identification of clear and defined indicators through which the process of democratisation in Africa can be monitored and evaluated. These challenges have been robustly taken up in the quantitatively-driven works of Bratton *et al.* (2005) and Lindberg (2006).

Bratton *et al.* see the consolidation of the political regimes that have developed within the democratisation process in Africa as a function of the mutually reinforcing processes of institutionalisation, at the macro level of the state, and legitimation, at the micro level of the individual. They therefore 'explore the sub regime of public opinion, explicitly deriving measures of regime legitimacy and institutionalization from mass perceptions' (2005: 29). Using the regression analysis of *Afrobarometer* surveys in twelve selected African countries, it is argued that 'an individual's *cognitive awareness* is the principal source of demand for democracy' (ibid.: 274). The ability of the elites and the political regime to respond to this demand determines the level of regime and democratic consolidation. Based on this approach, Bratton *et al.* nevertheless come down on the pessimistic side of the debate about African democratisation:

> within the one dozen countries in the Afrobarometer sample, fewer than half (five) are moving in the direction of democratic consolidation, while the quality of democracy in the remaining seven is deteriorating. Since the Afrobarometer represents countries that are Africa's most aggressive reformers, we can only conclude that the prospects for the consolidation of democracy in other parts of Africa are probably even more austere. (ibid.: 342)

Using the same quantitative method, but a different sub-regime – continent-wide data on elections – Lindberg contradicts the conclusion reached by Bratton *et al.* Starting from the premise that 'democratic behavior produces democratic values and not the other way around', he argues that the inception of multiparty elections and the repetition of these elections 'instigate liberalization' measured in terms of increases in political participation, competition, and legitimacy (2006: xi-xii). He suggests that generalisations from continent-wide data on elections 'convey a measured optimism' about African democratisation (ibid.: 143). In some countries, electoral experiences have led to a regression in democratic quality, 'but two-thirds are slowly and steadily moving forward' (ibid.: 144).

While the turn towards the quantitative method has improved our understanding of the processes at work, it has not provided a clear answer to the vexed question of the quality and trajectory of African democratisation. Furthermore, the quantitative method has been condemned by some commentators and qualified by others. 'Culturalist' scholars such as Chabal and Daloz are adamant about the 'unreliability of statistical evidence' and the 'untrustworthiness of questionnaires, opinion polls and surveys' in the African context (2006: 14). In their view, 'the key to making sense of ... politics lies in an analysis of the cultural context within which ... power is exercised' (ibid.: 14–15). However, even if we were to agree with this primacy of 'culture', it is still possible that Chabal and Daloz have a challengeable understanding of African cultural dynamics (cf. Meagher 2006; Mustapha 2006). For his part, Hyden cautions against 'relying on quantitative data analysis alone'; he suggests that data sets 'are a simplification of reality' and relying on cross-sectional surveys 'is never enough' because of 'the importance of a historical perspective on the present' (2006: 4). Even from within quantitative traditions of research, Heath *et al.* (2005) have raised questions about the validity of international opinion surveys. While they recognise *Afrobarometer* as one of the better surveys, the authors note problems of bias and non-comparability across countries, arising from varying non-response rates, cultures of deference, and the inappropriateness of an individualistic rational-choice framework for representing what are often group processes.

In this volume, we are interested in investigating the consequences of democratisation for the politics of African states. Is democratisation a turning point away from the old politics of authoritarianism as the optimistic view suggests, or are the pessimists correct in suggesting that the more things change, the more they stay the same? Or are we on safer ground in emphasising the inconclusive and mixed outcomes of the democratisation process? Turning point in this context is quite similar to the concept of 'critical juncture': a period of significant change, likely to produce distinct legacies, yet combining contradictory tendencies of transformation and preservation of elements of the old order (Villalon & Huxtable 1998: 6–8). We agree with Bratton *et al.* (2005: 320) that 'country characteristics matter', and that the 'prospects for regime consolidation are also best apprehended from a macrolevel "country" perspective'. And we are deliberately eclectic methodologically, as we are not averse to calling on culture, history, structuralism or data sets, where appropriate and applicable, to explore the country dynamics under democratisation. Our central concern is the *processes* of change and continuity in our selected countries. We look at competing ideas and policies through which change has happened in Africa since the early 1990s. We are also concerned with the institutional expressions of these ideas, the agency of individuals and groups in promoting or resisting change, and with the intended and unintended consequences of the change process. As Gavin Williams noted, democracy is not a state, it is a process:

> ...a *continuing battle* to hold those in power accountable, to protect the liberties of citizens and residents, to secure effective political representation, and to give people a say over the ways they are governed and the decisions which affect their lives. It

involves defining, defending and creating the institutions and the cultures which promote these goals and facilitate debates about public issues, including the nature and condition of democratic politics. (Williams 2003: 343)

In analysing the experiences of the countries examined in this volume, we use a conceptual approach which emphasises structural constraints, while not underplaying the significance of individual agency and choices. We propose a framework for achieving a balanced assessment of democratisation in Africa by combining a range of approaches which draw on different criteria. The first approach is to draw on concepts developed in empirically informed theoretical work on democratisation. Diamond and Morlino (2005) identify eight dimensions on which democracies vary in quality. Here we place emphasis on the various means to achieve *accountability* – the obligation of elected political leaders to answer for their political decisions – as one of the highest expectations people attach to democracy. Vertical accountability is that which citizens as electors can demand from their officials in the course of campaigns and elections, and which political and civil society actors can exercise at moments of political controversy. Peruzzotti and Smulovitz (2006) use the concept of societal accountability to capture the efforts of civic associations, social movements, religious movements, ethnic associations, NGOs, think tanks and the mass media to hold governments accountable in between elections. Horizontal accountability refers to office-holders being answerable to other institutional actors who have the expertise and legal authority to control and sanction their behaviour, usually independent government agencies. In contrast to vertical and social accountability, horizontal actors are more or less political equals. These three concepts of accountability are particularly useful in describing and assessing the state politics of contemporary African countries: to what extent are African democracies accountable to their citizenry?

A second approach is the comparative method. We seek to compare the situation in each country before and after the purported trigger for democratic change. Was the resulting change substantive? Or were the forces of continuity stronger than those of change, despite the 'trigger event'? Another dimension of our comparative method is to compare across African countries. Comparing across Africa points us in the direction of commonly shared problems which may help us better comprehend the continent's collective experience of democratisation.

In sum, the methodology of evaluating democracy in this volume is a case-study approach, examining different countries' experiences since democratisation across time. Then it compares across these experiences, highlighting concepts gleaned from democracy studies as well as themes and trends emerging from the countries and their populations' expectations. A case-study approach allows us to avoid generalising for all of Africa, a huge and diverse continent, using stylised facts from selected countries which results in over-extended generalisations. The historical institutionalism which informs our studies allows for limited generalisations about political institutions within a grounded historical context (Hall & Taylor 1996). Furthermore, this approach builds on an established tradition in the study of African politics (Dunn 1978; Cruise O'Brien *et al.* 1990; Nnoli 1998).

Though we do not make a claim for representativeness, our eleven case studies are chosen to reflect the variety of state traditions and forms within sub-Saharan Africa. Firstly, there are states from all the colonial traditions in sub-Saharan

Africa – British, French, Portuguese, Belgian; settler and non-settler. Secondly, the cases cover all the sub-regions within sub-Saharan Africa. Thirdly, the cases span the whole range of experiences of democratisation. Diamond (2002) identified five categories of political regimes in sub-Saharan Africa by 2001 and each is represented in our cases: Liberal democracy (South Africa); electoral democracy (Ghana and Senegal); ambiguous regimes (Mozambique, Nigeria and Zambia); liberal autocracy (Côte D'Ivoire, Kenya and Zimbabwe); and unreformed autocracies (Burundi and Rwanda). This comprehensive range of cases makes it possible for us to compare across experiences.

Each of these countries' experience is explored in a separate chapter, except for Rwanda and Burundi which are analysed together. And each chapter revolves around an important 'trigger event' or process in the country's political trajectory. While some of these 'trigger events' ushered in significant changes, others did not. Each chapter takes a persepective centred on local perceptions within each country in examining the politics of democratisation, with the emphasis on the *process* of change. The contributing authors also come from a variety of disciplines – history, politics, anthropology, sociology, and geography and the different disciplinary perspectives also provide rich and varied insights.

The countries are grouped into five pairs, three of which are based on an intuitive historical reading of African politics: Senegal and Côte d'Ivoire, Ghana and Nigeria, and Kenya and Zambia. South Africa and Mozambique are paired, because both countries started the process of democratisation by breaking out of a radically different political orientation, apartheid and socialism respectively. Zimbabwe is compared with Rwanda on the one hand, and Burundi on the other, because the three countries share a particularly authoritarian tendency in their political systems.

There are few works on democracy in Africa in recent years that undertake a comparative analysis based on a large number of in-depth country studies. The work that most closely resembles the objectives and methodological approach employed here is the volume edited by Leonardo Villalon and Peter VonDoepp (2005), *The Fate of Africa's Democratic Experiments: elites and institutions*. The country studies overlap in only two cases, and thus the two volumes should be seen as complementary. The ten countries selected by Villalon and VonDoepp constitute those that appeared to make successful democratic transitions in the early 1990s, based on the typology by Bratton and van de Walle (1997). They are concerned to track the fate of these initially successful democratic experiments. In contrast, the eleven countries in this volume fall across the Bratton and van de Walle typology. Thus, rather than just explaining why initial success has been consolidated or not, this volume seeks to explain movements in various directions across the spectrum of African experiences in the 1990s and 2000s.

Four Key Questions in African Democratisation

Our case studies raise four questions as key to understanding African democratisation:

(1) what has happened to the pervasive presidentialism of the authoritarian era?;
(2) have there been any changes in the pattern of political mobilisation and clientelist politics?;

(3) what has replaced the developmentalist social contract of the immediate post-colonial state and what are the consequences for the public sphere?; and
(4) what is the new meaning of elections in democratising Africa?

The answers to these questions in any specific case will determine the extent to which democratisation has affected the process of accountability.

The ugly phenomenon of the President-for-life was one of the distinctive elements of authoritarian post-colonial Africa. Even where this was not explicit in the Constitution, sit-tight presidents achieved the same objective through their unchallenged longevity in office. Many of these presidents were not only above the law, in some cases they were even out-laws! If democratisation is to mean anything, it has to address this pervasive and over-bearing executive authority. Hyden (2006: 105) asks 'whether it is possible to rein in the powers of the Big Man and make him subject to the law of the land'. In addressing this challenge to democratisation, we are confronted by important conceptual issues raised about the notions of 'neopatrimonialism' and 'personal rule', which are the dominant prisms through which executive authoritarianism in Africa is often understood.

In their important study of African democratisation, Bratton and van de Walle (1997: 61) emphasise the Weberian concept of a patrimonial political system, one in which

> an individual rules by dint of personal prestige and power, ordinary folk are treated as extensions of the 'big man's' household, with no rights or privileges other than those bestowed by the ruler. Authority is entirely personalized, shaped by the ruler's preferences. Modern African state systems are patrimonial to the extent that they retain in modified form many of the characteristics of patrimonial rule'. (1997: 62)

Customs and practices of patrimonial rule co-exist with and suffuse the rational legal institutions of the state. This neopatrimonialism may include aspects of prebends, patronage, and clientelism, all subsumed under the 'patrimonial logic'. From this perspective, agency is crucially exercised almost exclusively by the 'big men'. As Cammack (2007: 600) bluntly states, decisions are made by 'big men' and their cronies.

We nuance this conception of neopatrimonialism in two important respects. As Crook (1989) and Cheeseman (2006) argue, we need to nuance the concept of African presidentialism to include not just the personal and capricious (with emphasis on the person of the executive), but also the systemic and the organisational (with emphasis on system-wide structures of control and coordination). We also think it is important to see agency as a function not just of elites but also of non-elites. The critical questions then are the extent to which democratisation has tamed presidential prerogatives by making the office more accountable to elites (horizontal) and non-elites (vertical and social)? And to what extent have these changes been institutionalised into structures of systemic control and coordination which may begin to transcend the importance of the individual leader? While Table 1.1 suggests that more African leaders are leaving office voluntarily or via democratic means, can this be regarded as a positive shift away from authoritarian presidentialism?

The second key question is whether democratisation has affected the patterns of political mobilisation and clientelist politics that characterised the authoritarian era. Political scientists have distinguished between different forms of clientelism in Africa: patronage, prebends and tribute (Lemarchand 1988).

Nicolas van de Walle (2001, 2007) argues that clientelist politics in Africa has been dominated by prebendalism, a form of elite clientelism in which an individual is given a public office in order for him/her to gain personal access to state resources. Prebendalism is usually mediated not through political parties, but through the executive branch of government, and it is typically a feature of authoritarian states. Patronage, on the other hand, is the practice of using state resources to provide jobs and services for political clients, and it is used to gain support for the patron who dispenses it. Patronage has typically been a characteristic of mass electoral politics all over the world, being dispensed by political parties in order to gain votes at elections. While prebends and patronage do overlap, the distinction is still significant.

Van de Walle (2007) argues that, in a context of low levels of economic development, inadequate national integration, a history of authoritarian politics, and few organisational resources available to them, African leaders typically used state resources to co-opt different ethnic elites to maintain political stability. The resulting clientelism, he claims, was not redistributive and generally benefited only a relatively small proportion of the population – the elites. Some nationalist parties at independence did create patron-client networks resembling political machines seen in the early period of mass party politics in industrial countries, but African countries lacked the resources to keep these political machines going. However, the end of multiparty politics with the establishment of one-party states and military regimes also brought about the demise of these cliental networks with societal depth, as they are only necessary for electoral politics. By this account, it would seem that political mobilisation in the authoritarian era was based on the co-optation of a narrow elite and the perpetration of electoral fraud or political violence against the bulk of the population. How adequate is van de Walle's notion of elite clientelism in explaining the process of political mobilisation in authoritarian post-colonial Africa? And what changes have taken place since the re-introduction of multiparty elections?

The third key question is whether democratisation has affected the tangible and affective links between the citizen and the state in Africa. In short, what social contract undergirds the process of democratisation in contemporary African states? In using the term social contract, we are drawing loosely on J.J. Rousseau, and our central concerns are the grounds on which the individual commits to being part of the body politic and accepts the legitimacy of the state. These questions are important for historical and contemporary reasons. Historically, nationalists rallied African peasants and the urban poor into the anti-colonial movement with the promise of making their lives better. In most African countries, the end of colonialism was followed by a massive expansion in access to education, health facilities, and other social infrastructure. The legitimacy of the state and African rulers became tied to the notion of 'bringing development' to the people (Williams 2003). However, this 'nationalist project', founded on Keynesian economics and an entitlement ethos, was a top-down elitist process open to political abuse and opportunism. In many countries, debates between technocrats and politicians were an important intra-elite aspect of development planning and policymaking in this period (see Fahnbulleh 2005), even if the politicians most often won (see Tignor 2006). Many African nationalist leaders like Nkrumah had economic visions, even if these visions eventually succumbed to the exigencies of domestic politics and the international economy. State controls on the economy were not necessarily introduced in order to provide rent-seeking opportunities, but rather as solutions to perceived macro-economic problems of development. Indeed, some of the institutions of state intervention, like the marketing boards, were put in place in the colonial period. However, they were often maintained past their utility, once other less honourable outcomes and opportunities became apparent.

In the contemporary period, democratisation took place in the context of economic decline, political decay, and unprecedented pressure from the international system. Most countries signed up to structural adjustment programmes under the tutelage of the World Bank and the IMF, replacing the 'nationalist' ethos of entitlement with a demand-driven, market-friendly vision of social and economic relationships (cf. Hutchful 2002). User fees and cost recovery in health, education, and other services became a cornerstone of social policy, ostensibly to rationalise resource use and increase access. Philosophically, there was a move from the universalism of social provision embedded in the Keynesian/nationalist vision to one of means-testing and safety-nets (Townsend 2004) In reality, however, cost recovery amounted to little more than the regulation of access, and a very substantial section of the poor were thereby denied access to basic health and education (Townsend 2004; Adesina 2007). The safety-nets that were expected to mitigate the impact on the vulnerable poor often failed to live up to expectations (Mustapha 2000). The legitimacy crisis of incumbent regimes starting in the period of economic crisis, became exacerbated under adjustment. The social impacts of structural adjustment programmes undermined the little legitimacy that some regimes had left, and loans from the World Bank and IMF created the impression that key decisions were made by foreigners. Furthermore, even where it was 'successful', as in Ghana and Mozambique, structural adjustment had a polarising effect on the wellbeing of social groups and ethnic and regional communities. As a consequence, democratisation happened in the context of an upsurge in the challenge to the state by organised and semi-organised groups in society (Beckman 1992). The shape of the state and its relationship to social groups were called into question in various contexts (Villalon & Huxtable 1998). It was therefore imperative that, under democratisation, 'issues of leadership, civic culture and trust have to be re-negotiated between the state and the citizens' (Norberg & Obi 2007: 7). Has this re-negotiation taken place? Has a new social contract emerged through the process of democratisation?

Our final question deals with the meaning of elections in democratising Africa. Authoritarian one-party states had differing degrees of electoral credibility, some allowing limited, controlled competition, particularly for parliamentary seats, while others merely engaged in electoral charades which returned 99 per cent of the votes in favour of the incumbent president. As Table 1.1 suggests, democratisation restored some credibility to the electoral system; otherwise, incumbents would not have lost power. However, after the fraudulent Nigerian elections of April 2007, the fiasco of the December 2007 Kenyan elections, and the farcical 'slow motion' of the Zimbabwean elections of March/April 2008, the question arises, what do elections really mean within contemporary African democratisation?

Some have denounced African elections as 'choiceless elections' in which the electorate are voting without choosing (Mkandawire 1999). In the same vein, Norberg and Obi (2007: 6) suggest that in some war-torn African countries, elections have been used 'as an exit strategy' by the international community, without due consideration for the important question of impunity in arriving at trade-offs between the objectives of war termination and peacebuilding, on the one hand, and democracy, on the other. However, Villalon and Huxtable (1998: 18) suggest that elections in Africa may have a deeper significance. They argue that elections are only an *initial* response to the pressures for change within African societies; elections and the wider debates within which they occur are 'only the beginning of the deeper processes of change that African states appear to be undergoing'. For their part, Bratton *et al.* (2005: 312) argue that just participating in voting affects mass opinion by increasing democratic values within the system as a whole. This point of view is strongly endorsed by Lindberg (2006: xi), who argues that in Africa 'elections improve the quality of a democracy'. Using a quantitative analysis of more than 200 elections in Africa since the 'third wave of democratisation' and Freedom House data on civil liberties, he suggests that an uninterrupted series of competitive elections, regardless of their relative freeness and fairness, have a positive impact on human freedoms and democratic values. He argues that the general trend is for repeated elections to change actors' behaviour, which in turn reinforces and improves the democratic qualities of subsequent elections. Our various case studies examine the regularity and significance of elections.

To different degrees, our case studies explore these four key questions in the context of the specific concerns and debates of the individual countries in question. Analytical gaze and intensity are dictated, in every case, by the issues thrown up by the actual country-specific process at play. In the concluding chapter we return to these questions in the light of the comparative experience of our eleven country studies.

References

Adesina, Jimi O. 2007. Social Policy and the Quest for Inclusive Development: Research Findings from Sub-Saharan Africa. Paper No. 33. Geneva: United Nations Research Institute for Social Development (UNRISD).

Ake, Claude. 2000. *The Feasibility of Democracy in Africa*. Dakar: CODESRIA.

Beckman, Bjorn. 1992. Empowerment or Repression? The World Bank and the Politics of African Adjustment. In *Authoritarianism, Democracy, and Adjustment: The Politics of Economic Reforms in Africa*, eds Peter Gibbon, Yusuf Banura, and Arve Ofstad. Uppsala: Scandinavian Institute of African Studies.

Bratton, Michael and Nicholas van de Walle. 1997. *Democratic Experiments in Africa: Regime Transition in Comparative Perspective*. Cambridge: Cambridge University Press.

Bratton, Michael, Robert Mattes and Emmanuel Gyimah-Boadi. 2005. *Public Opinion, Democracy and Market Reforms in Africa*. Cambridge: Cambridge University Press.

Cammack, Diana. 2007. The Logic of African Neopatrimonialism: What Role for Donors? *Development Policy Review* 25(5): 599-614.

Chabal, Patrick. 1998. A Few Considerations on Democracy in Africa. *International Affairs* 74(2): 289-303.

Chabal, Patrick and Jean-Pascal Daloz. 2006. *Culture Troubles: Politics and the Interpretation of Meaning*. London: Hurst & Company.

Cheeseman, Nicholas. 2006. The Rise and Fall of Civil-Authoritarianism in Africa: Patronage, Participation and Political Parties in Kenya and Zambia. D.Phil. thesis, Department of Politics and International Relations, University of Oxford.

Crook, Richard. 1989. Patrimonialism, Administrative Effectiveness and Economic Development in Côte D'Ivoire. *African Affairs* 88: 205-28.

Cruise O'Brien, Donal, John Dunn, and Richard Rathbone eds. 1990. *Contemporary West African States*. Cambridge: Cambridge University Press.

Diamond, Larry. 2002. Thinking About Hybrid Regimes. *Journal of Democracy* 13(2): 21-35.

Diamond, Larry, and Leonardo Morlino. 2005. Introduction. In *Assessing the Quality of Democracy*, eds

Larry Diamond and Leonardo Morlino. Baltimore, MD: Johns Hopkins University Press.

Dunn, John ed. 1978. *West African States: Failure and Promise*. Cambridge: Cambridge University Press.

Fahnbulleh, Miatta. 2005. The Elusive Quest for Industrialisation in Africa: a comparative study of Ghana and Kenya, 1950-2000. London School of Economics and Political Science, University of London.

Hall, Peter and Rosemary Taylor. 1996. Political Science and the Three New Institutionalisms. *Political Studies* 44(5): 936-57.

Heath, Anthony, Stephen Fisher and Shawna Smith. 2005. The Globalization of Public Opinion Research. *Annual Review of Political Science* 8: 297-333.

Herbst, Jeffrey. 2001. Political Liberalization in Africa after Ten Years. *Comparative Politics* 34: 357-75.

Hutchful, Eboe. 2002. *Ghana's Adjustment Experience: The Paradox of Reform*. Oxford: James Currey.

Hyden, Goran. 2006. *African Politics in Comparative Perspective*. Cambridge: Cambridge University Press.

Joseph, Richard. 1997. Democratization in Africa after 1989: Comparative and Theoretical Perspectives. *Comparative Politics* 29: 363-82.

—— 1998. Africa, 1990-1997: From *Abertura* to Closure. *Journal of Democracy* 9(2): 3-17.

Lemarchand, René. 1988. The State, the Parallel Economy, and the Changing Structure of Patronage Systems. In *The Precarious Balance: State and Society in Africa*, eds Donald Rothchild and Naomi Chazan. Boulder, CO and London: Westview Press.

Lindberg, Staffan. 2006. *Democracy and Elections in Africa*. Baltimore, MD: Johns Hopkins University Press.

Meagher, Kate. 2006. Cultural Primordialism and the Post Structuralist Imaginaire: Plus ça Change .... *Africa* 76(4): 590-97.

Mkandawire, Thandika. 1999. Crisis Management and the Making of 'Choiceless Democracies'. In *State, Conflict and Democracy in Africa*, ed. Richard Joseph. Boulder, CO and London: Lynne Rienner.

Mustapha, Abdul Raufu. 2006. Rethinking Africanist Political Science. In *The Study of Africa: Disciplinary and Interdisciplinary Encounters*, ed. Paul Tiyambe Zeleza. Vol.1. Dakar: CODESRIA.

—— 2000. The Politics of Economic Reforms: Implications for Institutions and Poverty in the Rural African Setting. In *The Institutional Context of Poverty Eradication in Rural Africa*, eds K. J. Havnevik with E. Sandstrom. Uppsala: Nordiska Afrikainstitutet.

Nnoli, Okwudiba ed. 1998. *Ethnic Conflicts in Africa*. Dakar: CODESRIA.

Nolutshungu, Sam. 1992. Africa in a World of Democracies: Interpretation and Retrieval. *Journal of Commonwealth and Comparative Politics* 30(3): 316-34.

Norberg, Carin and Cyril Obi (eds). 2007. *Reconciling Winners and Losers in Post- Conflict Elections in West Africa: Political and Policy Imperatives*. Uppsala: Nordiska Afrikainstitutet.

O'Donnell, Guillermo. 1996. Illusions About Consolidation. *Journal of Democracy* 7(2): 34- 51.

Peruzzotti, Enrique and Catalina Smulovitz, eds. 2006. *Enforcing the Rule of Law: Societal Accountability in New Latin American Democracies*. Pittsburgh, PA: Pittsburgh University Press.

Rijnierse, Elly. 1993. Democratisation in Sub-Saharan Africa? Literature Overview. *Third World Quarterly* 14(3): 647-63.

Tignor, Robert. 2006. *W. Arthur Lewis and the Birth of Development Economics*. Princeton, NJ: Princeton University Press.

Townsend, Peter. 2004. From Universalism to Safety Nets: The Rise and Fall of Keynesian Influence on Social Development. In *Social Policy in a Development Context*, ed. Thandika Mkandawire. Basingstoke: Palgrave Macmillan.

van de Walle, Nicolas. 2001. *African Economies and the Politics of Permanent Crisis, 1979-1999*. Cambridge: Cambridge University Press.

——. 2007. Meet the New Boss, Same as the Old Boss? The Evolution of Political Clientelism in Africa. In *Patrons, Clients, and Policies: Patterns of democratic accountability and political competition*, eds Herbert Kitschelt and Steven Wilkinson. Cambridge: Cambridge University Press.

Villalon, Leonardo and Philip Huxtable. 1998. *The African State at a Critical Juncture: Between Disintegration and Reconfiguration*. Boulder, CO and London: Lynne Rienner.

Villalon, Leonardo and Peter VonDoepp. 2005. *The Fate of Africa's Democratic Experiments: elites and institutions*. Bloomington, IN: Indiana University Press.

Whitehead, Laurence. 2001. *Democratization: Theory and Experience*. Oxford: Oxford University Press.

Williams, Gavin. 2003. Democracy as Idea and Democracy as Process. *Journal of African American History* 88(4): 339-60.

Young, Tom. 1993. Elections and Electoral Politics in Africa. *Africa* 63(3): 299-312.

2

Senegal since 2000
Rebuilding Hegemony in a Global Age

TARIK DAHOU
& VINCENT FOUCHER

Senegal is often seen as a model of democracy in Africa. The changing character of Senegalese political life since independence has been paralleled by just as many changes in the literature about it. Initially most work tended to focus on the long history and rooted character of Senegalese democratic culture. This was essentially an urban-based political history centred on the lives of an enlightened class of *évolués*, African elites with a French education. In various shades, subsequent authors described how the powerful Muslim brotherhoods functioned as mechanisms for political integration in the countryside: in exchange for agricultural services and other resources channelled to client marabouts, the party-state could count on the votes of the disciples attached to these marabouts (Copans 1980; Coulon 1981). Cruise O'Brien (1975, 1992) analysed this procedure as a way to bring the state back home to people. Towards the end of the 1970s, when authoritarianism was at an all-time high in Africa, Senegal brought the *de facto* one-party state to an end and returned to a limited version of competitive politics. This, coupled with the voluntary departure of President Senghor from office in 1980, replaced by his young Prime Minister Abdou Diouf, gave birth to the idea of a 'Senegalese success story' (Diop & Diouf 1990).

Senegal is therefore remarkable in the sense that it had a competitive political party system rooted in a democratic culture well before the 'third wave' of democratisation hit Africa from 1989. Another distinctive aspect of this reading of Senegalese politics was the emphasis on the stable mechanisms of incorporation which linked the peasant citizens to the state via the intermediary roles of the religious brotherhoods and the ruling *Parti Socialiste* (PS). Through this linkage, the state extracted resources from groundnuts production and passed down favours. Urban elites, marabouts and peasants constituted discreet parts of a functioning political system within this self-proclaimed 'peasant state'.

Nevertheless, this semi-democracy and the carefully prepared succession from Senghor to Diouf bore the imprint of external constraints on the post-colonial Senegalese state, along with economic difficulties caused by declining groundnut prices and drought. Popular discontent was also mounting as a result of declining economic opportunities, as was rural-urban migration. President Diouf and a new elite, a generation of 'technocrats', progressively took over from the older 'barons' of Senghor's PS. This reshuffle of the ruling class actually ended up in a reciprocal assimilation of elites (Diop & Diouf 1990). Ideologically, the regime broke away from *négritude* during the 1980s and took popular aspirations into account by affirming a 'traditionalist pluralism' that further strengthened the marabouts as political brokers (Diop & Diouf 1999).

Quickly, however, the transition ended in disappointment. The economic crisis of the 1980s, the implementation of structural adjustment, the decline in living standards, and the outbreak of conflict in Casamance, all led to a critical re-reading of Senegalese political life. Most research has moved away from a linear vision of political change and begun to focus on new themes, such as the crisis in the social contract, the survival strategies of the former single party and the societal break with totalitarianism (Diouf 1994). Critically appraising the extent of the changes brought about by Abdou Diouf, Fatton (1987) borrows Gramsci's notion of 'passive revolution' to describe the process of political liberalisation as very controlled and highly selective. Procedurally speaking, changes were few, and power was still used in very much the same way as under the single party, with a combination of co-option and coercion.

The erosion of the PS hegemony was aggravated by the 50 per cent devaluation of the CFA Franc in January 1994, a result of the general crisis of the clientelistic Francophone African states which had tied their currencies to the French Franc. Donors backed economic liberalisation policies and governance conditionalities which further weakened the clientelistic basis of the regime. With the dismantling of agricultural extension services and the privatisation of parastatals, the productive arenas linking the state to the general public could no longer serve as vehicles for mobilising political support.

The shift in the policy orientation of external players was combined with severe internal struggles within the PS itself. Two of its leading 'barons', Djibo Ka and Moustapha Niasse, chose to leave and to create their own parties, respectively the Union for Democratic Renewal (*Union pour le Renouveau Démocratique*, URD) and the Alliance of Forces for Progress (*Alliance des Forces du Progrès*, AFP). The former's good results in the legislative elections of 1998 demonstrated that Diouf's attempts at political 'decompression' – the co-optation of opposition figures and anti-corruption measures – had had little effect on voters. The persistent crisis of the groundnut economy and its liberalisation also strained the close relationship between the state and the marabouts, and it is typical of this evolution that the state failed in its attempts to use the development of irrigation-based agriculture in the Senegal River Valley Region in the same clientelistic way as it had done with groundnut cultivation (Dahou 2004). The economic and institutional foundations of Senegal's partial democratisation were coming under increasing strain. The weakening of the state's capacity to distribute patronage was key to Diouf's defeat in the 2000 election (Beck 2002). The presidential elections in February-March 2000 thus came at a time when the Abdou Diouf regime was on its last legs. The increasing untenability of the extant post-colonial model was therefore one of the fundamental triggers of increased democratisation in Senegal.

In February 2000, Abdoulaye Wade, the leader of the Senegalese Democratic Party (*Parti Démocratique Sénégalais*, PDS) and the main opponent of both Senghor and Diouf since the democratic opening of 1978, ran as the candidate of a coalition of opposition groups, including all the small but influential post-Marxist parties. With 30.1 per cent of the vote in the first round, he came second to Diouf (who obtained 41.3 per cent), but he rallied to his side Moustapha Niasse, who ranked third (with 16.8 per cent). In the second round of voting, on 30 March 2000, Wade was elected President with 58.5 per cent of the votes.

To their credit, Diouf and his entourage quickly accepted defeat. This smooth transition owed much to the massive mobilisation, particularly in the urban areas, which had been taking place in the run-up to the elections. Over the years, Diouf had had to give increasingly strong guarantees of transparency and fairness within the electoral institution. An independent National Observatory of Elections had been created for this purpose, and the opposition was united and efficient in its close watch on the electoral process, as were the press and civil society organisations. The press played a key part in transmitting the results straight from the polling stations. A unified opposition and an activist civil society and media were critical elements in the deepening of Senegalese democratisation. The resulting change in ruling party (*alternance*) has revived idealised linear readings of Senegalese political life, confirming the oft-quoted idea of 'Senegalese exceptionality' (see Gellar 2002; Hesse 2004).

By 2007, enthusiasm about the quality of Senegalese democracy had once again waned among local intellectuals, civil society activists and journalists as well as foreign analysts. Their disappointment seems as profound as the many hopes which *alternance* had raised. Many observers express concern about the authoritarian and patrimonial drift that has seeped into political life. The works of the journalist Abdou Latif Coulibaly (2003, 2005, 2006) are typical of this disappointment. Coulibaly's first book on Wade describes in scathing terms the clientelistic, personalised and amateuristic nature of the new regime. Described as 'the most important counter-hegemonic piece of work to have emerged out of Senegal since March 2000' (Diop 2004: 34), this book created a political storm. External observers have also been critical. Thus, in her analysis of the ambiguities of democratisation worldwide, Marina Ottaway (2003) describes Wade's Senegal as a case of semi-authoritarianism. Protests have intensified against Wade's governance. Yet, on 22 February 2007, Abdoulaye Wade was re-elected President with more than 55 per cent of the votes in the first round.

How can one make sense of the twists and turns in both the historiography and the politics of Senegal? How can one interpret Wade's 2000 election and his 2007 re-election? What do these tell us about trends within Senegalese democratisation? Behind the automatic celebration of *alternance*, what has changed – and what has stayed the same – since 2000? More cautious than most commentators, Diop and Diouf (2002) suggest that the change in ruling party would result in a new 'passive revolution', akin to the limited changes that marked the transition from Senghor to Diouf. Putting aside political scepticism and the tide of criticism against Wade, this chapter identifies the changes, both long-term and short-term, that have occurred in Senegalese society and politics since 2000 and their impact on the process of democratisation.

We argue that one important change has been the rebuilding of the Senegalese economy around migration, remittances and increased donor funding. Even though this reconfiguration around migration is not wholly beyond the reach of the state, it has contributed to the reduction of the grip of the Senegalese state on society. Notwithstanding this fact, the new regime has been able to gain unprecedented room for manoeuvre by playing its international cards well, and benefited from a rather favourable international economic and political climate before the economic difficulties of the 2008 credit crunch. This has allowed the PDS government to rebuild the hegemony that the PS had lost; democratisation since 2000 seems to have reconstructed the erstwhile foundations of dominant party rule, albeit with a different dominant party now in charge.

A Changing Political Economy

Migration is crucial to understanding the new political economy of Senegalese democratisation. Shortly before *alternance*, Senegalese sociologist Malick Ndiaye (1996 and 1998) described the figure of the *moodu-moodu*, the illiterate and pious informal migrant, wandering throughout the world with his bag of goods for sale, the symbol of the revenge of society against the once hegemonic state – home to the *évolué* and the *ku jang ekool* (Wolof for 'school-educated'). In today's Senegal, the indisputable triumph of the migrant has indeed challenged the centrality of the state, while never escaping its grip entirely. Furthermore, the Senegalese state itself, whose path has so often been determined by external forces, has found in this particular characteristic a source of renewed strength.

The Migrant Triumphant

Groundnuts have been central to the Senegalese economy since the colonial period, but have not recovered from the economic crisis that precipitated the introduction of structural adjustment in the 1980s and 1990s. Production, which had stood at around 1 million tons, has halved since 2000. Structural problems with the way the sector was organised have forced many producers to turn to food crops. The 'peasant state' remains unable to stimulate growth in the agricultural sector and continues to focus only on those crops from which export revenues can be guaranteed. Alternative crops, such as cotton and horticulture, struggle to make headway. The contribution of agriculture to GDP has fallen to less than 10 per cent in recent years. This persistent crisis is speeding up the rate of rural-urban migration. Urban population growth stood at 4 per cent in 2003, in a context of high population growth of 2.5 per cent per year.

Mineral extraction is not a viable alternative source of state revenue. The long anticipated extraction of iron, gold and petroleum still seems some distance away, though Mittal announced in 2007 that it would exploit ore in the Tambacounda region. Once an important source of export revenue and a pillar of Senegalese industry, phosphates have suffered a decline in their market share and are facing a major financial crisis. Furthermore, mounting prices of petroleum products have caused serious problems, notably in terms of the cost of electricity supply which affects the whole economy.

Nevertheless, economic growth remained fairly stable between 1995 and 2005, at around 5 per cent per year, but declined to about 3.6 per cent in 2006, to rebound at an estimated rate of 5 per cent in 2007. Despite the boost received from the 1994 devaluation of the CFA Franc, the other pillars of the Senegalese economy, the fishing industry and tourism, remain fragile in the medium term. Over-fishing has led to a declining trend in catch rates, and fishermen's unions are highly critical of the clientelism that pervades relations between Senegal and the European Union. Tourism, which amounted to 2 per cent of GDP between 2000 and 2004, has also seen a decline. Industrial production remains weak and investment scarce. The high cost of production factors has meant that foreign direct investment has remained low. Unsurprisingly, exports to the United States have not taken off despite Senegal's inclusion in the African Growth and Opportunity Act of 2002. In terms of general productive economic fundamentals, not much has changed from the declining days of the PS.

Consumption and distribution activities are now the prime movers of the economy and make up 80 per cent of growth. Consumption is critically stimulated by external financial inflows. One estimate puts migrant remittances at US$1 billion in 2004. Western Union alone has 400 branches in the country, a testimony to the scale of these financial flows. Vast sums are also transferred informally. These remittances are key to the dynamism of the services sector. Trade, in particular, benefits from migrants because of their role as (both legal and illegal) intermediaries between Senegal and the outside world, and because of the high levels of consumption that remittances generate in Senegal. The transport sector and the property market have also been booming as a result of remittances, particularly in the Dakar region where in 2003 alone the construction industry grew by 20 per cent.

Migrant remittances are one of the main engines of growth in the Senegalese economy today and they continue to grow. Historically rooted along the Senegal River and later in the groundnut basin in the heart of Murid country, international migration now affects the whole country and is no longer the preserve of the stereotypical ubiquitous *moodu-moodu*. Present estimates of the size of the Senegalese expatriate community often run in excess of 1 million, which is considerable given that the 2002 census put the Senegalese population at 10 million. Remittances are what keep the Senegalese economy afloat, and the nicknames *italien* and *américain* have replaced *évolué* as markers of achievement and metaphors of success and moral worth in contemporary Senegalese society (Havard 2001; Foucher 2007a).

The Politics of Migration. The transformation of the Senegalese economy around remittances has profoundly affected the political dynamics of democratisation. Already under Diouf, a ministry for Senegalese abroad had been set up and representatives of the migrants had been included in the Senate. Politicians have followed the marabouts in paying attention to the expatriate Senegalese communities. Notably, Wade launched his 2000 election campaign among the diaspora. This trend has continued unabated and Paris and New York are key sites for Senegalese politicians. More importantly, the disintegration of the state's near monopoly over the economy and the explosion of migration have consolidated the pluralism that started from 1978 with the introduction of the controlled multiparty system. The shift of the Senegalese economy from groundnuts to migration and its increasing dependence on resources generated abroad could be seen as the final stage in the process of ending the hegemony once enjoyed by the state over Senegalese society.

Caution, however, is advised with this hypothesis: 'globalisation' cannot be equated with the demise of the state. As has been shown at various levels by Boone *et al.* (1998) and Dahou (2004), privatisation and liberalisation during the Diouf era have been ambiguous, often working to the benefit of political elites. It could similarly be shown that opportunities for emigration do not escape the reach of the state. Scholarships for study abroad are still used by the government to control students (Zeilig 2004), and ever since the colonial period, the Hajj pilgrimage has been organised by the state and used as a reward for reliable partners. One could also cite the way the state tries to exert authority over the distribution of real estate which is the main target of migrant investment. Property investment projects are often targeted at migrants abroad and the state-owned Senegalese Bank for Habitat has opened a New York branch. There is, however, no doubt that this delocalisation of the economy stems from the erosion of the earlier Senegalese 'social contract' and that the Senegalese state is no longer the 'gatekeeper' it once was.

Migration is a blessing for the government on two other counts. For now, migration acts as a safety-net, injecting a new dynamism into the economy and providing an exit option for young Senegalese caught between non-employment-generating growth, on the one hand, and the increasing fragility of social services, on the other. At the heart of these migratory flows and the patterns of reinvestment associated with them stand organised social groups and networks, for example religious ones, which are intricately linked to the state (Riccio 2001). Through these brokers, strategies for political and economic accumulation connect the migratory processes and the state. The rapid rise of the Murid marabout Cheikh Béthio Thioune, who is very active in structuring migration, and his alliance with Wade, is a case in point.

However, migration does not come without its dangers for the state, and it is putting the Senegalese government's international standing at risk. Since 2005 and the tightening of controls in the Spanish enclaves in Morocco, Senegal has become a major departure point for West African migrants who have been gathering along its coastline to try and reach the Canary Islands by sea. Spain and the European Union have been exerting pressure on Senegal to repress these migrations. Dependence works both ways, however. Dakar has obtained some advantages, such as an increase in European (particularly Spanish) foreign aid as well as an opportunity to organise the flows through a quota of temporary work permits. With typical opportunism, Dakar announced a plan to encourage would-be migrants to go 'Back to Agriculture'. This is a somewhat dangerous gambit, as the repression of migrants and smugglers by the Senegalese police and the forced repatriation of Senegalese nationals have stirred up trouble on several occasions, with Senegalese would-be migrants protesting against this violation of their 'right to migrate'. But so far, the reputation of President Wade seems not to have been affected.

The Externally Driven State

In much the same way as it has used migration for its own ends, the state has been adept at playing on its external linkages with the outside world. And the Senegalese often refer jokingly to Abdoulaye Wade's taste for *tukki*, travel in the Wolof language. Born as an external creation, the Senegalese state has taken its externally oriented nature to new heights under President Wade, and aid has both increased and diversified. Wade has thus softened the budgetary constraints that played such a large part in his predecessor's defeat.

Wade has carefully raised his international profile. He mediated crises in Madagascar and Côte d'Ivoire and contributed troops to peacekeeping missions in the Democratic Republic of Congo, Côte d'Ivoire and Sudan. He has consistently taken pro-Western positions on key international questions, such as reparations for the Atlantic slave trade, the War on Terror, Zimbabwe and Darfur. On the war in Iraq, in order to cosy up to his traditional French allies as well as his American friends, Wade was reserved, tempering the initially very pro-American line of his entourage. Although he was not initially part of the continent-wide development initiative that gave birth to the New Partnership for Africa's Development (NEPAD), spearheaded by the Nigerian, South African and Algerian Presidents, he hurriedly put together his own 'Omega Plan' which got him on board the NEPAD founding team. Wade has earned invitations to the G8 meetings as a representative of Africa. He has also strengthened links with Morocco and the Gulf states, and Dakar hosted a summit of the Organisation of the Islamic Conference – an event regularly delayed but very profitable in terms of investments. In October 2005, Dakar decided to recognise China and break with Taiwan – a pure exercise in *Realpolitik* that seems to have borne fruit in gifts and loans totalling CFAF 337 billion.

Diplomatic weight has also given the Wade government additional leverage in its relations with the Bretton Woods institutions. Dakar has repeatedly, and with little consequence, refused to comply with their rules, for instance in connection with the planned privatisation of the electricity company, Senelec. The government's increased access to development aid is the other major factor stimulating consumption and growth in an otherwise unstable economic context. Senegal has a long tradition of being one of the largest recipients of aid to Africa. President Wade has maintained this status, for example by securing Senegal's inclusion in the Heavily Indebted Poor Country Initiative through its classification as a Least Developed Country in 2001. Senegal's external debt decreased from 69 per cent of GDP in 2000 to 38 per cent in 2005 (CFAF 1750 billion). The reduction in debt-servicing obligations has increased the state's budgetary latitude.

Wade has also benefited from the softening of the so-called 'Washington Consensus', as well as the post-September 11 turn towards 'state-building'. Worried about 'failed states' as grey zones harbouring terrorism, illegal immigration and humanitarian disasters, Western governments are now more willing to engage in 'state-building' projects, resume budgetary assistance and allow new loans. Playing on Senegal's image as a model country and its large set of contacts ranging from the Arab World to Europe, the United States and Japan, the Wade government has attracted more aid than Diouf. In 2003, official development assistance to Senegal stood at US$450 million, significantly higher than the average for sub-Saharan Africa. In 2004, aid reached US$1 bn, three times the African average.

Increases in aid flows, years of externally-driven economic growth, the long-run impact of the 1994 devaluation, combined with increases in tax revenue, have led to increases in the national budget since 2000. Between 1999 and 2006, state spending doubled, from CFAF 600 to 1,200 bn. And Senegal's credit rating has improved. With the tolerance of aid donors, the government's budget deficit, which had been suppressed in 2002, stood at 3 per cent of GDP in 2005 and 5.7 per cent in 2006.

During the 1990s, President Diouf had to give up the idea of creating any new posts in the 'structurally adjusted' civil service, where the number of civil servants stagnated at 65,000. By contrast, in 2003 President Wade launched a recruitment drive with the creation of 15,000 new posts spread over time in the health and education sectors and 1,000 in the judiciary. Between 2003 and 2004 alone, civil service staff numbers increased by more than 6 per cent to a new high of 71,694. State capacity and the latitude for patronage and clientelism have thereby improved since 2000.

It is not yet clear whether this injection of new money into the apparatus of the Senegalese state will improve its effectiveness. In spite of the notable improvements in national income and expenditure, the state's public performance remains problematic. Whatever the effect on the actual quality of public service delivery, this 'renaissance' of the state budget is certainly having an impact on the political sphere. As shown below, it has given the regime the means to pursue its hegemonic project. Even if Senegal remains dependent on the outside world, this external dependence has not necessarily weakened the state.

By 2000 the international legitimacy of the Diouf government had worn thin, even with the expert management of the economy by the former Prime Minister, Mamadou Lamine Loum. Under President Wade, Senegal is now one of the 'model students' of African democracy, and the relative scarcity of such models means that the international community over-invests symbolically and materially wherever it finds them, inverting, in part, relationships of dependence between Senegal and the donors.

Rebuilding the Hegemonic Bloc

Changes associated with democratisation in Senegal since 2000 have had the consequence of re-constituting the erstwhile foundations for a dominant party hegemony, but under the control of a party different from the PS. Wade's political charisma, his election, his diplomatic activism, the country's continued economic growth, the transformation of the aid paradigm and the new international context have all contributed to a strengthening and recentralisation of state power around the President. Borrowing from Diouf's well-worn carrot-and-stick tradition, the new regime has been trying to establish and guarantee its hegemony, whilst not quite achieving it fully. Frustrated by not being able to achieve the desired hegemony over a population captured by the spirit of nascent pluralism, the Wade government has grown impatient and has occasionally drifted towards authoritarianism. The political opposition and the press have focused on this authoritarian drift. But despite the mounting criticism of his governance, Wade seems sufficiently successful at establishing his hegemony; indeed, while he obtained only 31 per cent of the votes in the first round of the presidential election of 2000, he obtained 55 per cent in the election of 2007.

A Forever Shifting Bloc?

It is worth remembering that just before the PDS came to power in March 2000, the party was particularly weak. The successive comings and goings of Wade in and out of various PS governments had tarnished his image. The 1998 legislative elections were a disaster for the PDS. Lastly, many PDS notables had 'cross carpeted' to the PS or had set up their own political parties. The PDS victory in 2000 was only possible because of the creation of a broad opposition coalition, over which the PDS was only marginally dominant. This electoral majority subsequently fell apart, and since then, President Wade has struggled to re-establish a political bloc under his control.

As mentioned above, Wade's principal partner in the 2000 coalition was Moustapha Niasse. Niasse thus earned the job of Prime Minister in the new government. But the AFP was too much of a rival for the coalition to survive into the legislative elections of May 2001. The clear victory of the PDS in these elections gave the party a comfortable majority in the National Assembly, though this was as much a product of the bias of the electoral system; although the PDS gained less than 50 per cent of the popular votes, it obtained 75 per cent of the seats.

After the AFP left the government, small left-wing parties that had played an important role in the build-up to *alternance* followed suit. The Independence and

Workers Party, the Jëf-Jël Alliance and the Democratic League-Labour Movement all distanced themselves from the new government. Only And Jëf remained, but its leader Landing Savané felt that it was better for him to be replaced in government by fellow party members. To compensate for this erosion, Wade relied increasingly on traditional PS mechanisms for political and economic control. Senegalese democratisation seems to have gone full circle. Playing on the growing cleavages within the PS, Wade achieved the cross-carpeting, or what the Senegalese call *transhumance*, of major PS figures into the PDS fold and brought back former big chiefs in the PDS who had left the party in the 1980s and 1990s to join the PS. He also rallied together the smaller parties and created space for them in the government. Of note were Iba Der Thiam's Convention of Democrats and Patriots party and Djibo Ka's Union for Democratic Renewal. Discussions were also initiated with the PS.

All this has been happening at the same time as realignments and internal factionalism within each party, ending in schisms and further realignments or fusion. In Senegal as elsewhere in Africa, the proliferation of political parties suggests the existence of a fluid and unstable market in political goods where small-scale yet dynamic political entrepreneurs look to increase their market value in the eyes of bigger fish. The proliferation of ministries and presidential advisers with ministerial rank, the rapid succession of Prime Ministers (four in the last seven years), the even more numerous ministerial changes (six in just six years) stem in part from the need to weed out underperformers in a new political team, but above all from the necessity to constantly rebuild the coalition.

Back to the Future: Presidentialism Consolidated

Facing this uncertainty, President Wade embraced presidentialism, not only in his choice of institutions but also in how these institutions were run. This was yet another return to old PS ways. He disregarded widespread calls among his coalition partners for a change in the parliamentary system. The Senegalese constitutional tradition is presidential, and this tradition was not changed in the new Constitution adopted in 2001. In fact, the President now enjoys greater power to dissolve the National Assembly. The reduction of the seven-year presidential term to five years, an old demand of the opposition, was adopted, but it soon emerged that it would not apply to Wade's first mandate. The National Assembly remains weak and dependent, due to both French-derived institutional traits and persistent capacity problems. An example of the former is that, according to the constitution, the Assembly cannot pass legislation that increases the budget without working out a way to finance it, which is generally beyond its expertise. This virtually gives the executive a near-monopoly in the initiation of laws. An example of the latter is that members of the Assembly have little research capacity or training; a growing number do not even understand French, the working language of the state. Optimistic observers see the National Assembly as a 'liaison-type legislature' (Thomas & Sissokho 2005), but this liaison is more of a one-way street, with the Assembly functioning as a channel through which to legitimate projects decided upon by the executive (Samb 2004: 47).

But presidentialism has expanded outside the constitutional text as well. The Presidency and Prime Minister's Office have exerted a growing direct influence over the state bureaucracy and the budget, and procedural requirements are regularly circumvented. Furthermore, the President and Prime Minister have created and/or taken direct control of a number of state agencies, such as the

Agency for the Promotion of Investment and Public Works and the Agency for the Organisation of the Islamic Conference, thus increasing their autonomy vis-à-vis the bureaucracy. To take but one example, the Agency for the Organisation of the Islamic Conference and its significant funds coming from the Gulf countries are under the authority of the President's son, who works as an adviser to his father. In 2006, these agencies controlled about 10 per cent of the whole budget and about 20 per cent of the investment budget. The enhancement of presidential powers through the creation of parallel bureaucracies directly under executive control is another recurring theme within African democratisation.

Clientelism and Alternoce

In spite of good governance pronouncements, clientelism has remained at the heart of Senegalese political life since *alternance*. As seen above, Abdoulaye Wade has been in a much better position than his predecessor to play the game. The growth of the Senegalese economy, further increased by considerable international aid with few strings attached, has given the new government room for manoeuvre. Yet the reconstruction of a clientelist base has not been smooth or gone unchallenged, and many Senegalese deride *alternance* as *alternoce*, where *noce*, the French for 'wedding party' or 'ball', refers to the 'good life' that the victors are now enjoying. As far as clientelism is concerned, the actors may have changed but the show continues.

From March 2000 onwards, the new government began its campaign to capture the state apparatus and the parastatals that have traditionally served as loci for clientelism. It is significant that while, in the early 1980s, President Diouf had been increasingly keen on using army officers in the strategic parastatals, in an attempt at better technocratic governance, President Wade has been placing PDS figures in these positions, with all the potential negative economic consequences. The persistent difficulties faced by such key parastatal companies as the Senegalese National Society for the Marketing of Oilseeds, and the Senegalese National Lottery or Senelec, owe something to this PDS interference.

An even more glaring example of Wade's efforts to increase his client base is the failure to keep the commitments he had made in 2000 to keep the size of government down to 20 ministers and to do away with the Senate and the Economic and Social Council. While in April 2000 there were only 28 ministers, they were no fewer than 44 in September 2006. Even though the 2001 Constitution did abolish the Senate and the Economic and Social Council, a Council of the Republic was created in January 2004, a purely consultative body with about one hundred councillors whose appointments are largely controlled by the President and which is chaired by a former PS heavyweight who sided with Wade soon after the first round of the March 2000 elections. The distribution of perks to Assembly members and the increase in their number (from 120 to 140 and then to 150) follows the same logic of maximising hand-outs for political middlemen.

These strategies of clientelism are very similar to those used by Diouf, and there is little doubt that 'vote-buying' also played a part in the 2007 elections. As a means of political mobilisation, clientelism remains the strategy of choice, despite democratisation. One issue in which this has been particularly clear is the separatist conflict in Casamance, where initial pretences at change and a quick solution soon gave way to a well-worn policy of co-optation. This policy, a revamped Senegalese army, and the mounting unhappiness of the population with the separatist movement have combined to bring the conflict to a standstill, but the insurgency has not disappeared (Foucher 2003, 2007b).

The composure with which Senegalese politicians publicly assert their clientelistic practices, and the seriousness with which the local media report them, show just how much clientelism remains at the heart of Senegalese political life (see Blundo 1998, 2000). However, in spite of the new resource base of the state, it is no longer simply a case of triumphant clientelism as during the PS 'single party' era; even within continuity, there are some elements of change. The uncertainties unleashed by *alternance* have opened up a phase of competitive clientelism, where allegiances are no longer fixed as in the seemingly unending reign of the PS. With the strengthening of local government that resulted from the 1996 law of decentralisation, and the support which aid donors provide to NGOs and local organisations, opportunities for patronage are now less concentrated. This dispersal of resources, which had been key in bringing about *alternance* in the first place, persists, despite the PDS government's resolute attempts to concentrate resources under its control. At all levels, economic and political entrepreneurs tap their own resources to mobilise clients, whom they use in turn to bargain for influence and advantages further up the political chain. Democratisation has led, not to programmatic accountability, but to a competitive clientelistic system.

The Return of 'Urban Bias'?

The attack on the 'urban bias' characteristic of post-colonial African states by scholars like Michael Lipton and Robert Bates in the late 1970s and early 1980s softened the intellectual ground for the anti-statist arguments that ultimately led to structural adjustment policies. Most economic and political liberalisation policies are premised on an implicit assumption that adjustment would lead to improvements in rural lives by reversing the 'urban bias'. Democratisation in Senegal would seem to be turning this logic on its head.

President Wade, because of the new-found solvency of the Senegalese state, has been able to use the politics of distribution to go beyond his immediate clients within the PDS and his own political coalition allies, and to reach out to other important strategic social actors. This was a feat which the PS was increasingly unable to achieve in the run-up to the 2000 elections. This broadening of the PDS clientelistic base was clearly apparent after a student strike in January 2001 went out of control. The Wade government quickly gave way to collective student demands, handing out some financial assistance and grants to the students. More discreet classic methods of co-optation were used as well, with some of the student leaders being provided with government scholarships for study abroad. In this way and for some time, the government was able to dissipate student protest (Zeilig 2004).

In the same way, a whole gamut of public policies can be interpreted as mechanisms for widening the scope of co-optation. The increase in the budget of the Press Fund from CFAF 100 million in 2000 to 300 million in 2003 is another example. The political potential of this measure is considerable, given the extreme financial fragility of the Senegalese press (Wittmann 2006). Other sectors of civil society, like the trade unions, have also been targeted. The pressures of competitive clientelism, in the context of increased state revenues, may be leading to an increasing concentration of group-based patronage on urban constituencies, in a very similar way to the political calculus of the immediate post-colonial regimes across much of Africa. Wade is favouring those classes in society that politically could do the most damage to his regime: the urban salaried workers. Unsurprisingly, therefore, civil servants have benefited most from improvements in their conditions. Particular attention has been paid to strategic constituencies: the highest ranks of the territorial administration, university staff, judges, customs officials, police officers and soldiers. Workers in the official private sector have not been forgotten, with the state obliging private-sector management to concede to one of the workers' main demands, the extension of the working age from 56 to 60 years. Group patronage is also targeted at the urban population as a whole through the reduction of tariffs on the import of basic staples, in spite of the fact that these measures have direct negative effects on the agricultural sector (Faivre-Dupaigre forthcoming).

We should also not forget that, because of the PS mechanisms for incorporating and controlling the peasantry, the arrival of the PDS in government was celebrated less in the countryside than in the towns, which had nurtured the hope that the opposition would defeat the PS. This urban-rural electoral divide is yet another feature which occurs in many African experiments with democratisation. Even if the rural areas did contribute to reversing the PS majority, the results of the 2000 election show that they were less of a major factor in Wade's actual victory. Wade has tried to break the PS patron-client networks in the countryside by weakening established peasant organisations through the creation of rival peasant movements. This strategy bore a striking resemblance to that of his PS predecessors. The denizens of the countryside can be forgiven for thinking that democratisation simply means the replacement of one patronage organisation by another!

The political manoeuvres of the PDS in the countryside created tensions, which were made even worse by the agricultural crisis which began with the 2002 drought. The Council for Intra-Rural Dialogue (CNCR) of the PS era organised a well-attended demonstration in Dakar to defend peasant rights, forcing the government to renew the dialogue with truly representative peasant organisations. This created a more favourable environment in which the Council could defend its interests within the government's rural development programme. Donor pressure also meant that it was included in the implementation of a number of development programmes, most of which were initiated as part of a poverty reduction strategy.

Despite these positive developments, problems between an organised peasant force and the state resurfaced with the introduction of a new law in 2004 on the future of the agricultural sector. The law fell short of what was expected of an agricultural policy and consisted merely of a list of growth targets dependent on support from local development institutions and extension services, insurance mechanisms, and land reform (Dahou & Ndiaye forthcoming). It radicalised positions among the peasantry, who asked for the land reform section to be removed on the grounds that any such initiative requires widespread consultations beforehand. The peasantry were concerned that the creation of a land agency would deprive local authorities of their right to control the allocation of land. The precedent of allocating extensive plots of land for agribusiness projects exacerbated these concerns. The CNCR set up a participatory negotiation process that went down to the local level. Land privatisation, which seemed to be the real motive behind the reform, poses a threat to the CNCR's grassroots base, most of whom are dependent on small family farms. The negotiation process blocked attempts at the hasty reform of the land ownership system. By demanding a nation-wide consultation on what was such an important question, the CNCR stymied the land privatisation process. In spite of the coherence of the arguments put forward by the peasant movement, their demands on the state have fallen on deaf ears. Although the PDS government may have overcome its initial mistrust of the peasantry, it is still a victim of its own technocratic vision of rural development and there is little inclination to engage in a serious dialogue with peasant representatives.

The Prince and the Marabouts: the Forging of a New Alliance?
As seen above, *alternance* owed something to the weakening of the links between the marabouts and the PS state. On this count too, Wade has been adept at reviving the old alliance, but in a transformed way. During the 1990s, the rules of the game between the state and the head khalifs of the main Sufi brotherhoods changed. The khalifs used to express open support for the government, while maintaining a subtle distance to preserve their legitimacy. Now they have withdrawn from politics for fear of undermining their legitimacy and the unity of the brotherhoods they lead, and they have grown increasingly reluctant to instruct their followers on how to vote. In so doing, they have opened up space for new politico-religious actors. In a context where struggles for succession are brewing within the brotherhoods, younger marabouts who hail from minor or controversial lineages within the Sufi hierarchies or may even not be from the original maraboutic descent lines, have embraced politics enthusiastically, to the point of creating their own parties or engaging directly in support of Wade's PDS. The Murid Modou Kara Mbacké and Cheikh Béthio Thioune, the Tijani Mamoune Niasse and Ahmed Khalifa Niasse are cases in point. All of them eventually sided with Wade in the 2007 elections, a powerful indication of the President's interest in these new religious brokers. As in other parts of Africa, in the uncertain context of electoral politics and changing religious hierarchies, the social capital of religion and religious movements is a coveted resource.

Wade has been more open than his predecessor about his religious affiliation, and has even toyed with the suppression of the principle of religious neutrality enshrined in the Constitution, harping on the growing intellectual influence of Islamic reformism. His pilgrimages to Mecca and his visits to the head khalif of his brotherhood, the Muridiyya, have been widely broadcast. This has stirred up controversy about the connections between the Wade government and the Muridiyya. The name of the Murid head khalif even made a brief appearance on a list of PDS candidates for the 2002 local elections. Among the Tijaniyya brotherhood, resentment has been expressed about the government's lack of impartiality. With discrete calls for support from the Muridiyya, Wade obtained no less than 84 per cent of the votes in the constituency of Mbacké, the Murid heartland, in the 2007 election. Conversely, in the largely Tijani constituency of Tivaouane, Wade had one of his poorest results, earning only 44 per cent of the votes, while his protégé turned arch opponent, Idrissa Seck, gained 29 per cent.

Wade has met with some success in his attempts to reorganise his government's relationship with Islam, co-opting a new generation of religious figures, whose largely urban followers are worth canvassing. While reformist Islam remains a minority current with an essentially intellectual appeal, tensions between and within the Sufi brotherhoods have a greater potential for future trouble.

Factionalism and the Personalisation of Power

With the recourse to presidentialism, clientelism, and the attempted recon-struction of a state/marabout linkage as means of managing power, Wade's PDS has basically been reconstructing the post-colonial state of the PS era under new conditions. But Wade has brought to new heights the personalisation of power already inherent in Senegalese politics. As the example of Houphouet-Boigny's Côte d'Ivoire shows, this personalisalisation is not without risk, particularly as the time of succession approaches. Just as the political strategies used by the PDS government resemble those of the PS, the problems facing both parties in government are also very similar. The intra-party factional pressures that were a strong feature of the old government have intensified within the new PDS government, despite its relative financial security. The same factional dualism that characterised the PS years in office is once again apparent. A study by Olivier Legros (2004) of electoral contests in Yeumbeul, a commune in the Dakar suburbs, clearly shows how within the presidential party two major tendencies are at war with each other. Factionalism is equally present at the higher echelons of the government, as is shown by the split between Abdoulaye Wade and his number two, Idrissa Seck. The expulsion of Seck from the PDS was not enough to put an end to the factional infighting. Initially considered a political light-weight within the PDS, Macky Sall replaced Seck as Prime Minister in 2004, but was in turn sacked in 2007, and replaced by Cheikh Hadjibou Soumaré, a technocrat with no known political affiliation. The growing publicised tensions between Sall and Karim Wade, the President's son, who is seen as a potential heir to his father, played a key part in this episode. Competition between factions in the PDS has on many occasions degenerated into violence and accusations of misappropriation of publics are frequently made.

Factionalism is closely related to clientelism, and it has reached alarming proportions under the new regime. The advanced age of President Wade, and speculations about his health, pose the question of succession in the context of an unconsolidated ruling elite. The heterogeneous nature of this elite is partly to blame: an unsteady coalition of Wade loyalists, former PDS activists who had switched camp to the PS and later returned to join the *alternance* bandwagon, young party supporters mobilised for the 2000 elections, PS carpet-crossers, enterprising marabouts and seasoned politicians of the small allied parties. A host of support movements, groups and associations have also grown both inside and on the margins of the PDS. They are all busy demonstrating and renegotiating their political weight within the coalition. This cuts a contrast to Diouf, who had used – and indeed created and sponsored – these kinds of para-partisan structures to develop a base *outside* the PS party structure so as to counter the PS *barons* and avoid too close an association with a discredited PS (Diop & Diouf 1990).

The situation has grown so complicated and the dangers of factionalism for the PDS so great that even local factional struggles can often be resolved only with the intervention of the President or the Prime Minister himself (Legros 2004). In order to avoid the outbreak of open factional warfare, positions in the PDS hierarchy have gone unchanged since 1996, and carpet-crossers and new militants have been incorporated through the designation of posts from above. Tensions within the PDS are so problematic that the legislative elections scheduled for April 2006 were postponed twice (to June 2007), so as to secure Wade's re-election prior to the PDS primaries.

In the case of the PDS as in that of KANU under Kenyatta, the factionalisation of the ruling party and the casting of the President as an arbiter in factional contests often led to the accretion of presidential powers and the increased personalisation of that power. This impetus to personalise power within the ruling party is indeed a long-standing characteristic of the Senegalese political system. President Senghor had needed personalisation to balance the complex coalition he put together in the late colonial era, and his heir Diouf used it to take over the PS apparatus. For Wade, it has been a way to rebuild the PDS and to take over the state. Classically, this personalisation also means that kinship is called on to play a part. Wade's two children, Karim and Sindiély, are important advisers, and his nephew, Doudou, presides over the PDS group in the National Assembly.

Whether or not Idrissa Seck, Wade's protégé and first PDS Prime Minister, was actually involved in attempts to hasten Wade's retirement is a moot point. His position in the PDS, his intimate knowledge of the party structures, the pressure he exerted to become Prime Minister, his efforts to guarantee his position as Wade's likely successor, and his attempts to build up his own independent networks earned him the sack. Dismissed in April 2004, Seck was arrested in July 2005, charged with corruption and with being a security threat to the state, and released after 200 days in jail. As in the immediate post-colonial regimes in Kenya and Senegal, ambitious deputies often fell foul of equally ambitious presidents.

The Authoritarian Temptation

Despite all the borrowings from the armoury of PS statecraft and governance, and the favourable international and fiscal climate, the PDS under Wade has yet to develop an unassailable hegemony. For reasons of the inchoate nature of the ruling group and the undimmed instinct of pluralism within society of which *alternance* itself was the most striking demonstration, the Wade government enjoys an incomplete hegemony marked by uncertainties. This has led to a tendency to adopt an authoritarian attitude, partly the result of the strong sense of legitimacy felt by the PDS leadership, born of their long struggle, as well as of the scale of their 2000 victory. Furthermore, President Wade does seem to bear the imprint of his beginnings in politics, in the 1950s and 1960s, times of nationalism, voluntarism and state intervention. But it is not only a question of political culture, for bouts of authoritarianism are a classic tool in the toolbox of Senegalese politics, present also under the PS.

In Senegal just as in Nigeria, the 'fight against corruption' has been used as an instrument for settling political scores rather than purely as a means of improving governance. Since the arrival of the new government, civil service and state company audits have been carried out and have played an important role in 'bringing round' those close to the PS and occupying strategic sites within the Senegalese economy. In this respect, Wade has behaved exactly like Abdou Diouf when he succeeded President Senghor (Diop & Diouf 1990). It would seem that changes in governmental leadership, even as a result of democratisation, call forth the use of underhand measures to secure power.

Apart from the punitive audits, the Justice Ministry plays an important role in the unfolding mode of domination and is the subject of tight control. Trouble-making politicians, public figures, and journalists have been subjected to unexpectedly high levels of pressure by the Wade government through a range of legal measures such as temporary closure of newspapers, suing for libel or for threatening the security of the state (according to Article 80 of the Penal Code) and police investigations. A number of journalists have received anonymous threats or have been victims of assaults about which little has usually been done (Havard 2004; Wittmann 2006). The official state media, which in 2000 had gained a little more room to report freely, have also been reined in. *Le Soleil*, the state daily, which tried to free itself from state control immediately after the change in ruling party, has subsequently become a praise-singing mouthpiece of the President. The Wade government has also been behind the creation of new so-called independent papers, like *Le Messager* and *Il est midi*, which are renowned for their particularly salacious line against opposition figures.

Though violence has always been part of Senegalese politics, the public sphere now seems to be much less pacified than before, and insults and threats are prominent political currencies under Wade. A law granting amnesty for political crimes and offences committed between 1983 and 2004 was passed in January 2005, guaranteeing total immunity for those found guilty. The stabbing of Talla Sylla, a famous opposition figure, in October 2003, of which some presidential aides were suspected, the raid in May 2005 against Idrissa Seck's Dakar home, the clashes in Fatick at the end of May 2006 between supporters of Mamoune Niasse (then an ally of Idrissa Seck) and PDS militants, are all evidence of the regime's nervousness. Many public figures have received death threats following their criticism of the government. The regime has allowed a climate of tension to develop or is deliberately creating it, as a way of dealing with the complexities of building its hegemony.

Conclusion

The defeat of the old PS order in 2000 offered the prospect of the deepening of Senegalese democratisation. What has happened, however, is the maintenance of the same mechanisms of control which the PS had perfected in its forty-year strangle-hold over Senegalese society and state. Overbearing presidentialism, clientelism, intermediation by the marabouts, and occasional violence and intimidation have continued despite democratisation. While *alternance* has given a formidable boost to the state and its budget, it could also be interpreted as a promise postponed, insofar as it has failed to institutionalise more democratic and pluralist norms within Senegalese state and society.

The February 2007 presidential election is the obvious epilogue for this chapter. It indicates unmistakably that criticisms of Wade's governance by a divided opposition and 'civil society' organisations do not make for real mass mobilisation. For reasons of the fiscal health of the state, the deployment of clientelism, and the successful manipulation of symbols of the political culture, mobilisation has been on Wade's side. While the electoral body had substantially increased from about 2.8 million in 2002 to 4.9 million in 2007, the turnout was around 70 per cent in 2007, and Wade won 55 per cent of the votes. Following the results, the opposition reiterated its criticism of the new electoral roll and denounced fraud and vote-buying. Whatever the truth in these accusations, and no doubt there is some, the vote did express the existence of support for Wade. This indicates the depth of the gap between the urban educated elites who took the lead in criticising Wade's governance and the broader electorate. This gap is confirmed by the defeat of all the old parties (the PS, AFP and the historical left-wing parties) and by the fact that it was the young

Idrissa Seck who, on his first candidacy, came second in the presidential race with about 15 per cent of the votes. But despite his age (he was born in 1926), it is Wade who still seems to be the best at connecting with the Senegalese youth: their revenge against the old elites, their hope for successful globalisation through migration, their support for marabouts. Lucky shifts in the global context (the growth of remittances and international assistance, a new aid paradigm) have been essential to Wade's success, since they have increased his room for manoeuvre well beyond his predecessor's wildest dreams, allowing him to refurbish the clientelistic state, placate strategic groups and fulfil some social commitments in the fields of health, education and roads. *Alternance* has thus allowed for a revamping of the mechanisms of political domination: a case of passive revolution.

Over the longer term, while there is no doubt that the Wade years have contributed to the embeddedness of elections as a procedure, of political pluralism as a system and of regime change as an acceptable outcome, it remains to be seen what the personalisation of power at the expense of institutionalisation, the increasingly direct participation of marabouts in politics, and the growing heterogeneity of political elites may produce. Will these tendencies ensure an increased connection of state and society? What will the quality of this connection be? The future of Senegalese democratisation will be decided by the answers to these questions.

References

Beck, Linda. 2002. Le clientélisme au Sénégal: un adieu sans regrets? In *Le Sénégal contemporain*, ed. Momar-Coumba Diop. Paris: Karthala.
Blundo, Giorgio. 1998. Elus locaux, associations paysannes et courtiers du développement au Sénégal. PhD thesis, University of Lausanne.
——. 2000. La corruption entre scandales politiques et pratiques quotidiennes. In *Monnayer les pouvoirs. Espaces, mécanismes et représentations de la corruption*, ed. Giorgio Blundo. Paris: PUF and Geneva: IUED.
Boone, Catherine, Momar-Coumba Diop and Ibrahima Thioub. 1998. Economic liberalization in Senegal: shifting politics of indigenous business interests. *African Studies Review* 41(2): 63-89.
Copans, Jean. 1980. *Les marabouts de l'arachide*. Paris: Le Sycomore.
Coulibaly, Abdou Latif. 2003. *Wade, un opposant au pouvoir. L'alternance piégée?* Dakar: Éditions Sentinelles.
——. 2005. *Sénégal. Affaire Me Sèye: un meurtre sur commande*, Paris: L'Harmattan.
——. 2006. *Une démocratie prise en otage par ses élites. Essai politique sur la pratique de la démocratie au Sénégal*. Dakar: Editions Sentinelles.
Coulon, Christian. 1981. *Le Marabout et le Prince. Islam et pouvoir au Sénégal*. Paris: Pédone.
——. 1992. 'Le "contrat social" sénégalais à l'épreuve'. In *Sénégal: la démocratie à l'épreuve*, ed. C. Coulon. *Politique africaine* 45: 9–20.
——. 2000. La tradition démocratique au Sénégal: histoires d'un mythe. In *Démocraties d'ailleurs. Démocraties et démocratisation hors d'Occident*, ed. Christophe Jaffrelot. Paris: Karthala.
Cruise O'Brien, Donal. 1971. *The Mourides of Senegal: the Political and Economic Organisation of an Islamic Brotherhood*. Oxford: Clarendon Press.
——. 1975. *Saints and Politicians. Essays in the Organisation of Senegalese Peasant Society*. London: Cambridge University Press.
——. 2004. *Symbolic Confrontations: Muslims Imagining the State in Africa*. London: Hurst.
Dahou, Tarik. 2004. *Entre parenté et politique. Développement et clientélisme dans le delta du Sénégal*. Paris: Karthala.
Dahou, Tarik, and Ndiaye, Abdourahmane. Forthcoming. Les enjeux d'une réforme foncière. In *Libéralisation et politique agricole au Sénégal*, ed. Tarik Dahou. Paris: Karthala & Dakar: Crepos and Enda-Graf.
Diop, Momar-Coumba. 2004. Essai sur l'art de gouverner le Sénégal. In *Gouverner le Sénégal. Entre ajustement structurel et développement durable*, ed. Momar-Coumba Diop. Paris: Karthala.
Diop, Momar-Coumba and Mamadou Diouf. 1990. *Le Sénégal sous Abdou Diouf. Etat et société*. Paris: Karthala.

——. 1999. Sénégal. Par delà la succession Senghor-Diouf. In *Les figures du politique en Afrique. Des pouvoirs hérités aux pouvoirs élus*, eds Momar-Coumba Diop and Mamadou Diouf. Dakar: CODESRIA and Paris: Karthala.

——. 2002. Léopold Sédar Senghor, Abdou Diouf, Abdoulaye Wade, et après? In *La construction de l'Etat au Sénégal*, eds D. B. C. O'Brien, M.-C. Diop and M. Diouf. Paris: Karthala.

Diouf, Mamadou. 1994. L'échec du modèle démocratique au Sénégal, 1981-1993. *Afrika Spectrum* 1: 47-64.

Ebin, Victoria. 1993. Les commerçants mourides à Marseille et à New York. Regards sur les stratégies d'implantation. In *Grands commerçants d'Afrique de l'Ouest. Logiques et pratiques d'un groupe d'hommes d'affaires contemporains*, eds Emmanuel Grégoireand Pascal Labazée. Paris: Karthala-Orstom.

Faivre-Dupaigre, Benoît. Forthcoming. Une économie politique du secteur agroalimentaire à la lumière des choix de politique commerciale. In *Libéralisation et politique agricole au Sénégal*, ed. Tarik Dahou. Paris: Karthala and Dakar: Crepos and Enda-Graf.

Fatton, Robert. 1987. *The Making of a Liberal Democracy: Senegal's Passive Revolution 1975-1985*. Boulder, CO: Lynne Rienner.

Foucher, Vincent. 2007a. Blue marches. Public performance and political turnover in Senegal. In *Theatre Politics in Asia and Africa: Subversion, Collusion or Control?*, ed. Donal Cruise O'Brien and Julia Strauss. London: I.B. Tauris.

——. 2007b. The resilient weakness of Casamançais separatists. In *African Guerillas. Raging against the Machine*, ed. Morten Boas and Kevin Dunn. Boulder, CO: Lynne Rienner.

——. 2003. Pas d'alternance en Casamance? Le nouveau pouvoir sénégalais face à la revendication séparatiste casamançaise. *Politique africaine* 91: 101-19.

Gellar, Sheldon. 2002. Pluralisme ou jacobinisme: quelle démocratie pour le Sénégal? In *Le Sénégal contemporain*. ed. Momar-Coumba Diop. Paris: Karthala.

Guèye, Cheikh. 2002. *Touba. La capitale des mourides*. Paris: Karthala and IRD and Dakar: ENDA.

Havard, Jean-François. 2001. Ethos 'Bul Faale' et nouvelles figures de la réussite au Sénégal. *Politique africaine* 82: 63-76.

——. 2004. De la victoire du 'sopi' à la tentation du 'nopi'? 'Gouvernement de l'alternance' et liberté d'expression des médias au Sénégal, *Politique Africaine* 96: 22-37.

Hesse, Brian J. 2004. The Peugeot and the Baobab: Islam, structural adjustment and liberalism in Senegal. *Journal of Contemporary African Studies* 22(1): 3-12.

Legros, O. 2004. 'Les tendances du jeu politique à Yeumbeul (banlieue est de Dakar) depuis "l'alternance". In Sénégal 2000-2004: l'alternance et ses contradiction, eds. T. Dahou and V. Foucher. *Politique africaine* 96: 59-77.

Ndiaye, Malick. 1996 & 1998. *L'éthique ceddo et la société d'accaparement ou les conduites culturelles des Sénégalais d'aujourd'hui*. 2 volumes. Dakar: Presses Universitaires de Dakar.

Ottaway, Marina. 2003. *Democracy Challenged: The Rise of Semi-Authoritarianism*. Washington DC: Carnegie Endowment for International Peace.

Riccio, Bruno. 2001. From 'ethnic group' to 'transnational community'? Senegalese migrants' ambivalent experiences and multiple trajectories, *Journal of Ethnic and Migration Studies* 27 (4): 583-99.

Samb, Moussa. 2004. La gouvernance publique: changement ou continuité. In *Gouverner le Sénégal. Entre ajustement structurel et développement durable*, ed. Momar-Coumba Diop. Paris: Karthala.

Seck, Assane. 2005. *Sénégal, émergence d'une démocratie moderne (1945-2005): un itinéraire politique*. Paris: Karthala.

Tall, Serigne Mansour. 1998. Un instrument financier pour les commerçants et émigrés mourides de l'axe Dakar-New York: Kara international foreign money exchange. In *Les opérateurs économiques et l'Etat au Sénégal*, ed. Leonard Harding, Laurence Marfaing and Mariam Sow. Hamburg: LIT Verlag.

Thomas, Melissa A., and Oumar Sissokho. 2005. Liaison legislature: the role of the National Assembly in Senegal. *Journal of Modern African Studies* 43(1): 97-117.

Touré, El Hajj Seydou Nourou. 2002. Tendances et perspectives de l'agriculture. In *La Société sénégalaise entre le local et le global*, eds Momar-Coumba Diop. Paris: Karthala.

Wittmann, Frank. 2006. La presse écrite sénégalaise et ses dérives: précarité, informalité, illégalité. *Politique Africaine* 101:181-93.

World Bank. 2006. *Sénégal. Développements récents et sources de financement du budget de l'Etat*. Report No. 36497-SN, Washington, DC: World Bank, September 18.

Zeilig, Leo. 2004. En quête de changement politique: la mobilisation étudiante au Sénégal, 2000-2004. *Politique Africaine* 96:39-57.

3

Côte d'Ivoire since 1993
The Risky Reinvention of a Nation

FRANCIS AKINDÈS

Côte d'Ivoire and Senegal were the jewels in the crown of the French colonial empire in West Africa. Both shared many colonial experiences based on the pan-territoriality of the colonial empire. The rivalry between African nationalist politicians in both countries was a feature of the decolonisation process. Senegal prided itself as the political and cultural centre of French West Africa, due to the cultural sophistication of its *évolué* elite and the fact that the Governor-General of all the territories was based in Dakar. Côte d'Ivoire, on the other hand, saw itself as the real power-house of the economy of the colonial empire. Importantly, however, the post-colonial settlements in both countries were radically different. Post-colonial Senegal had a greater institutionalisation of formal and informal threads connecting society to the state, while Côte d'Ivoire developed a more elitist, more ethnic, and more personalised post-colonial regime centred on the person of President Houphouet-Boigny. This difference was to have important ramifications for their experiences of democratisation. Both continued to depend heavily on France, while being held up as models of post-colonial development in Africa: Senegal for its tolerant, almost liberal political orientation, and Côte d'Ivoire as a haven of stability and an African economic 'miracle'. The trajectory of democratisation has been radically different in both countries. Senegalese democratisation is a gradual process of decompression, deliberately initiated from the top, starting in 1978. Ivorian democratisation, on the other hand, came about as a result of unanticipated shocks to the Houphouetist post-colonial paradigm. The interaction between these shocks and the structural features of Ivorian society informs the specific nature and trajectory of democratisation in that country and this process cannot be understood in isolation from an examination of the Houphouetist legacy.

The Côte d'Ivoire of Houphouet-Boigny's Dreams

The Ivorian civil war and the current political crisis reveal the monopolistic creative vision of one man, Félix Houphouet-Boigny, in the engineering of political and economic stability between 1960 and 1990. In the span of one generation, however, the sustainability of the social, political and economic network that he constructed was called into question. Democratisation was the

31

trigger and context for this re-examination, which has been characterised by violent contestation over citizenship and nationhood. The idea of the Ivorian nation was the result of the compromises made by Houphouet-Boigny. The Houphouetist compromise was a politico-economic mélange that drew its power from the synergy of three intimately linked principles: the centralised open-door economic policy, the creation of an indigenous bourgeoisie dependent on the state, and the paternalistic management of social and ethnic diversity. Each of these principles is described in turn.

Houphouet-Boigny inherited the colonial politics of controlling Ivorian territory and transformed these principles into a national policy of development. This inheritance included primarily the production of agricultural commodities (cocoa, coffee, cotton, rubber) as well as the procurement of a steady supply of manual labour from Upper Volta, what is today Burkina Faso. The adoption of a particularly attractive investment code after independence completed the economic institutional arsenal necessary to facilitate the dynamic mobilisation of foreign capital and expertise. This political economy facilitated the heavy concentration of immigrant populations on Ivorian soil: 26 per cent of the population according to the census of 1998.

Allied to this economic structure was the use of state-controlled patronage to build an elite loyal to the person of Houphouet-Boigny. The goal was to create a national bourgeoisie capable of acting as a class of local investors and entrepreneurs in an economy dominated by foreign, largely French, capital, often through the licit and illicit use of state resources. To this effect, the proliferation of parastatal organisations was an instrument for the promotion of a national bourgeoisie that was at the same time a political client, in a context of great confusion between the state, the nation, the single party and the President. There was also the confusion between public and private good. The dominant elite belonged to a single party, the PDCI (Democratic Party of Côte d'Ivoire), and were distinguished by their wealth and ostentatious consumption made possible by political protection. Côte d'Ivoire therefore lacked the type of informal institutions used in Senegal to tie the peasantry to the state through the marabouts. In Côte d'Ivoire, the legitimacy of the elitist politico-economic model rested on the ability of the system to 'trickle down' benefits to a wider cycle.

This entire politico-economic system was based on a particular management of ethnic diversity. To guarantee the longevity of his power, Houphouet-Boigny developed an ideology based on the myth of the legitimacy of members of the 'Akan' group to govern others. To support this myth it was necessary that the ideology should double as a way of managing the mosaic of more than sixty ethnicities, regrouped into four linguistic families: the Mandé (Malinké, Dan, Kweni), the Voltaïques today better known as the Gur (Sénoufo, Koulango, Lobi), the Kru (Wê, Bété, Dida, Bakwé, Néyo), and the Kwa, or Akan (Agni, Baoulé, Abron, Alladian, Avikam and other lagoon-based ethnicities). The Houphouetist ideology of the natural propensity of the Baoulé (a sub-group of Akans) to rule over others, which according to Memel-Foté (1999) was without any justification, also served to disqualify two other ethnicities from political power: the Dioula, a generic name for people from the north (either Mandé or Gur but always Muslim) and the Bété. According to this political ideology, the Bété and Dioula constitute a danger to the state and nation, the former because of their cultural incompatibility with presidential functions and the latter because they are potential propagators of Islam. These anthropological elements were used to define, through negation, the more dignified qualities of the ideal political class. These qualities are attributed only to Akans, and in particular to the Baoulé and the Agni, who subsequently came to dominate the political system. In Akan and especially Baoulé circles, the internalisation of this 'spontaneous anthropology' fuelled for many decades the political efficacy of an idea that one race was predestined to rule over others, an idea that was contested by these other groups while waiting for the occasion to prove the contrary. Democratisation provided such an opportunity.

Houphouet-Boigny's political and economic compromise had installed a carrot-and-stick arrangement. This political mechanism was based on a strong relationship with the ex-colonial power. Through accords with Paris, Houphouet-Boigny secured his regime in a West African environment that was politically unstable due to many military coups (McGowan 2003). France assured the development of Houphouet-Boigny's Côte d'Ivoire through military, financial and technical assistance. This negotiated independence produced formal and informal accords that guaranteed the interests of both parties. The result was a state-run capitalism that produced a unique prosperity and averaged 7 per cent growth per year between 1960 and 1980, leading to the so-called 'Ivorian miracle'.

But Côte d'Ivoire between 1960 and 1990 was not the product of a collective social imaginary but the dream of one man who thought of himself as the 'father of the nation' (Memel-Foté 1991). It was a personal project which, though not entirely devoid of nationalism, Houphouet-Boigny did not want to share with any other political contender (Amondji 1984). Côte d'Ivoire under Houphouet-Boigny did not have an oppositional figure with the stature and visibility of Senegal's Wade. Houphouet-Boigny realised his vision through the institutionalisation of a particular brand of the one-party state (Médard 1982). He wanted to turn Côte d'Ivoire into a model modern nation and believed that the best way to achieve this goal was for the country to open itself to external forces, to accept migrant labour and expatriate expertise, and to cultivate ties with France. However, his vision of Ivorian independence was at odds with the ideal held by the young Ivorian intellectual elite in the 1960s, moulded in leftist, nationalist, and resolutely anti-colonialist ideologies. This young elite preferred a radical and complete independence, which was the norm in many political circles in Africa. Houphouet-Boigny was concerned about what Africans would do with their independence if they cut themselves off completely from their colonial masters, and remarked to this young elite: 'You are the soft fruits of a colonialism from which you do not want your brothers to profit' (see Diabate's interview in Akindès et al. 2005).

While holding a monopoly on the political and economic vision of Côte d'Ivoire, Houphouet-Boigny invested in the education of a technocratic and apolitical elite that would above all remain loyal to himself. Participation in the realisation of his vision was open to all, provided that his policies and the system of political compromise that supported them were not challenged. Personal accounts by many who refused to play the game by Houphouet-Boigny's rules are eloquent demonstrations of the consequences of the carrot-and-stick politics of the Houphouetist model (see Diarra 1997; Koné 2003).

Until Houphouet-Boigny's death, Côte d'Ivoire retained its social cohesion due to the tools of construction held by its great lone engineer. In as much as this vision was personalised, the management and use of materials by this architect, in terms of internal and external policy, were personalised as well. The tools of this project were mainly informal, neither institutionalised nor constitutionalised. From 1960 to 1980, the economic fruits of development led to important investments in the socio-economic infrastructure and education. Resources were also used to maintain a clientelistic political system aimed at elite co-optation and control. Important and informal transfers of resources served to stabilise the socio-political front and particularly to neutralise any possible threat to this personal vision. The clientelist system was based on the regulation of opportunities for enrichment by Houphouet-Boigny and the one-party state. Clientelism was therefore a common feature of both Senghor's Senegal and Houphouet's Côte d'Ivoire, though the context in which this clientelism operated were radically different. This pragmatic philosophy was voiced under the slogan 'Who is crazy?': Who is crazy not to silence his critics and profit from the real or virtual possibilities of enrichment offered by the system? This left virtually every Ivorian with the hope of benefiting from the system one day.

In the context of economic growth, the abstract promise of socio-political gain for all those who 'played the game' by Houphouet-Boigny's rules generated a stable and self-regulating political market. The process of redistribution profited the young elite that had come to be known as the 'ranks of the nation'. These ranks were recruited according to their regional or ethnic origins, with an attempt at some measure of ethnic balancing, and were positioned in the most highly lucrative political and economic sectors. Ethnic balancing, seen as a temporary tool in managing local geopolitical issues, evolved into a national political culture and functioned as the official mechanism of social peace. This overt concern with ethnicity, not seen in Senegal, is shared with Nigeria. In fact, many of the resources from cocoa and coffee served, from this perspective, to mitigate regional rifts. The creation of multiple parastatals enlarged the field of distribution of political rents (Fauré 1982: 37). This form of politically capitalising on the fruits of economic growth created a privileged elitist class within the regime, but social investments in education and infrastructure also allowed the state to avoid political challenges through the informal subsidisation of social peace. The climate of economic growth and individual search for opportunities permitted Houphouet-Boigny to co-opt or silence his political opponents. Through a series of 'Ivorian dialogue' days, Houphouet-Boigny also created an open channel for the exchange of ideas that allowed him to anticipate and to regulate any possible social or political threat (Médard 1982).

Thanks to these mechanisms of socio-political regulation and a policy of profiting from relationships with Western countries, especially France, Houphouet-Boigny constructed a relatively prosperous country. Compared with other African countries, Côte d'Ivoire under Houphouet-Boigny posted undeniably impressive economic results, a relatively long period of political stability and social cohesion, and an inclusive, if hierarchical, social fabric. It was this convergence of factors that led to the academic debates over the 'Ivorian miracle'. Houphouet-Boigny's dream of collective wealth in a national space did not exclude solidarity in the sharing of the fruits of economic growth, a philosophy aptly illustrated by his policy of according dual citizenship to all West Africans who went to Côte d'Ivoire and aided in its development. However, as early as 1963 this inclusive philosophy was the target of intense scrutiny by fellow patriots who feared the loss of national control over their economic progress. From the beginning, the arrival of foreigners attracted by the economic promise of Côte d'Ivoire regularly provoked tensions between the native and immigrant populations (see Le Pape

1997). Sharing the fruits of prosperity was thus at odds with the nationalism at the heart of decolonisation, though this contradiction was always successfully subdued by Houphouet-Boigny. Democratisation was to renew the struggle over this contradiction; whereas out-migration re-defined the nature of the Senegalese state and its democratisation process, conflict over the status of immigrants was to do the same for Côte d'Ivoire.

From a Personalistic Vision to a Battle of Visionaries

From 1960 to the beginning of the 1980s, economic growth provided the favourable context for the informal redistribution of political patronage which led to widespread opportunities for individual access to rents through 'trickle-down' processes. This situation permitted the politico-anthropological ethnic myths of the Houphouetist model to function more or less discreetly (Crook 1989, 1990). Economic stability and growth justified the situation of unequal distribution of political and economic resources in favour of the dominant group. The first shock to the Houphouetist model was an economic crisis which shook the very foundations of the model. The first signs of economic recession started between 1983 and 1984 with the fall in the world market price of cocoa, the country's main export. The cocoa sector is the pillar of the economy, producing most of the export earnings and employing around 1.2 million peasant producers. The country's dependence on the international price of cocoa and the state's major role in the productive economy led to a deep crisis, which ran from 1980 to 1993 and exposed the frailty of the Ivorian economic model. Between 1978 and 1986, cocoa prices fell by 40 per cent and the deficit in the external trade balance started in 1979. At the same time, the level of public investments grew. According to the World Bank, public investments in 1981 were 40 per cent higher than the proposed investment in the previous five years. The resulting fiscal crisis had a direct impact on health and education expenditure. Access to schools, which had continuously increased in the 1970s, started to decrease in the 1980s despite an increase in the overall population. The share of education in the national budget fell from 31.4 per cent between 1981 and 1984 to 18.8 per cent between 1994 and 1998.

Between 1981 and 1993, the Ivorian state launched nine unsuccessful attempts at economic stabilisation. The public financial crisis and the government's weakening capacity to fund its patronage system led to the contraction of employment which shattered the faith many students and young men had in the automatic link between academic achievement and employment in important administrative posts. These increasingly volatile young people became a major factor later in the politics of contestation and violence. The economic crisis was soon followed by a second shock, the physical exhaustion of the ageing Houphouet-Boigny who was 88 years old. Not only was the economic foundation of the system failing to deliver 'trickle-down' effects', the principal engineer of this unequal system was also losing vitality. The first two shocks provided the context for the third: increasing external demands for democratisation.

Since the end of the 1980s, the economic crisis and the demands of structural reforms designed to correct macroeconomic imbalances and government deficits considerably affected the pillars of Houphouet-Boigny's political compromise. The country faced a conjuncture of three factors: (i) the weakening of the personal capacities of Houphouet-Boigny due to old age and ill health; (ii) economic crisis and public financial difficulties which forced the government to accept structural adjustment reforms and thus a reduction in resources available to invest in the system of clientelist politics; and (iii) strident injunctions from the Bretton Woods institutions and from Paris in favour of democracy. Unlike the gradualist democratisation that took place in Senegal, democratisation in Côte d'Ivoire was a result of the combined effects of internal crises and external pressures.

From 1990 on, many pillars of the Houphouetist model came under increasing reassessment. The major political concerns included the openness of the country to the external world, the idea of 'solidarity between Ivorian regions' based on the question of land (Yapi Diahou 2002) and the mythical legitimisation of the Akan as a governing group. Many opposition figures, including Laurent Gbagbo, have worked since then towards an alternative to the Houphouetist compromise. The system was thus forced to democratise, and many political candidates stepped into the arena to participate in the first pluralist election held in 1990 (Crook 1997). Even after the first multiparty elections took place on 30 April 1990, Houphouet-Boigny's party continued to govern as before, strengthened by the re-election of its leader over Laurent Gbagbo by a margin of 82 per cent.

In the aftermath of the introduction of the multiparty system, the opposition consisted of three political parties: Professor Francis Wodié's *Parti Ivorien de Travailleurs* or PIT (Ivorian Worker's Party); teacher Bamba Moriféré's *Parti Socialiste Ivoirien* or PSI (Ivorian Socialist Party); and Laurent Gbagbo's *Front Populaire Ivoirien* or FPI (Ivorian Popular Front). The latter had a relatively more important political base than the other two, although its political influence was modest as compared with the PDCI's. The FPI had a largely regional base and an ethno-regional character. It mobilised support mostly in its leader's region, the country's centre-West region, but also in the South-West (in the cities of Adzopé, Agboville and Divo). In these areas, immigrants and non-native Ivorians (Baoulé and Sahelian, especially Malians and Burkinabés) were historically strong. This presence started to foster resentment on the part of the native population because of a political order perceived as favourable to the 'outsiders'. The FPI had managed to capitalise on these frustrations by positioning itself as the spokesman for populations outside the Baoulé hegemony. In the first legislative elections in the multiparty era, the FPI won 9 seats out of 175, mostly in those regions.

The return to multiparty rule has since consecrated a system of parliamentary democracy and political debate. It has enlarged the horizon for reinventing an alternative Côte d'Ivoire and has allowed a reassessment of Houphouet-Boigny's model. But the complete absence of a culture of political debate has led to a hotbed of political violence as many visionaries sought to replace the Houphouetist vision with their own in a context of economic crises and diminishing legitimacy.

The Quest for Democracy

Ivorian democracy was born through a paradoxical weakening of state capacity simultaneously with the escalation of state violence. Renewed democratisation in 1990 might have led to multipartyism, but not to increased civic rights or respect for pluralist politics. Indeed, the recourse to violence is the common thread that connects all post-1990 governments. Successive governments mobilised the state's coercive instruments against populations or specific parts of the population, who in turn developed the means for organising themselves according to a violence of 'protest' or 'contestation' against the state (Braud 2005). Especially since 1993, Côte d'Ivoire is a nation reinventing itself at a high cost to human life. The growing brutality of political combat has led to the extreme politicisation of Ivorian society, the militarisation of politics, and the gradual desensitisation of society. In order to understand this persistence of violence from 1990, the phenomenon must be placed in the historical context of the ruptures and continuities which have characterised this period. In doing so, the analysis shows that, while the forms of violence have changed over time, the motives for them remain the same.

From 1990 to 1993, the Ivorian state was still being run by the ageing Houphouet-Boigny. In response to demands posed by ongoing economic reforms, he named Alassane Dramane Ouattara, a former IMF staff member, as Prime Minister. This tactic of using former IMF or World Bank staff for economic management is common to many democratising states in Africa. Ouattara's nomination triggered mass public protest, because he had not built his political base and experience within the domestic scene but from 'above'. He appeared as a political alien and a threat to the political base that local protagonists had fought to build over many years. Ouattara resorted to violence in order to impose his political will. Thus, pacifist marches and protests against the structural adjustment programmes were met with repression. The first victims were protesting students and soldiers, who were enlisted in an army considered to be 'disliked by the nation' and 'downgraded in Ivorian society as much in its role as in its status' (Bouquet 2005; Keiffer 2000). The political opposition profited quickly from this social disillusionment by aligning itself with the students' unions. A series of union demands were quickly supported by opposition parties such as the FPI and the PIT. FESCI (Students' and Scholars' Federation of Côte d'Ivoire), the first student movement in the country, opened a floodgate of democratic demands. Whether organised or not in political parties, parts of the population began to demand a more transparent form of governance.

As protests multiplied, the government resorted more frequently to violent suppression, which led in turn to more protests against a government that still ruled as if in a one-party state in what was supposedly a multiparty democracy. Government thugs broke up FESCI protests. The street, the traditional theatre of marches supporting the 'father of the nation' in the single-party era, became the venue for the expression of a pluralism of opinions and increasingly violent confrontations between protestors and forces of the state (Konaté 2003), the frequency of which engendered an escalation of violence within the polity. The stage for this cyclical violence was set as early as 1990, when a students' protest triggered the intervention of the army under the command of General Robert Guéï. Live bullets were fired at the protestors and a student in Adzopé was killed. These military forces were also allegedly responsible for the rape of numerous students in a punitive attack on the students' dormitories at Yopougon in 1991. In response to the increasingly repressive behaviour of the state, students who believed that they had nothing left to lose began to adopt more violent methods of response. Stone-throwing was quickly replaced by machetes and home-made grenades known as a *lacry-baoulé*.

One of the worst moments came in response to a march in February 1992, a moment seared in the newly pluralist Ivorian collective memory as Black Tuesday.[1] The march, directed by Laurent Gbagbo of the FPI and Francis Wodié of the PIT, degenerated into a riot. The state responded to the stick-wielding protestors with extreme violence. Cars were burned, shops and buildings ransacked, government and public administration buildings damaged. Acts of vandalism were recorded in towns across the country. Democratisation and economic reforms had led to increasing chaos and social disorganisation.

In the context of this madness rose the question of who would succeed the waning Houphouet-Boigny, with rumours pointing to his Prime Minister, Ouattara. Such a prospect drew attention to the ethnic tensions that had been suppressed by Houphouet-Boigny's manipulations. The vigour with which the government resisted popular demands for change was already leading sections of the media to describe the government as a 'Baoulé clan' that wanted to use violence to get rid of the opposition leader Laurent Gbagbo, a Bété.

One could arrange the tensions dominating Ivorian society at the end of Houphouet-Boigny's reign as a series of binaries: indigenous/foreigners, power/ opposition, inclusion/exclusion. The social bearers of these tensions began to express themselves whenever and wherever possible. Initially in the form of sporadic protests (marches, barricades, sit-ins) that had little social consequence, these expressions were followed by state-directed acts of violence (political assassination and the lethal use of force against protestors).

After the death of Houphouet-Boigny in December 1992, three presidents would succeed him: Henri Konan Bédié (1993-99), General Robert Guéï (1999-2000), and Laurent Gbagbo (since 2000). Throughout these three governments, the relationship between the state and Ivorian society continued to deteriorate, with violence as the dominant mode of political articulation. Le Pape (2003) has summarised the divisions inherent in this ongoing escalation of brutality and political violence, but it remains to look at the motives for this violence and how they were instrumentalised by the leading political figures that succeeded Houphouet-Boigny.

The Logic of Violence under Bédié and Guéï

Under Bédié, the Ivorian state continued to seek to assert its will against a reluctant population. Resistance to the institutionalisation of Baoulé ethnic hegemony, which Bédié was seen as representing, fuelled the spiral of violence between state and society. Henri Konan Bédié was President of the National Assembly in 1993 when Houphouet-Boigny died, a position he had held since 1980. According to the Constitution, he became the interim President until an election could be held within a period of ninety days. Bédié's rise to Head of State occurred not only at an extremely tense political moment, but also in the context of continuing economic recession, the closing of enterprises, and rising unemployment (Memel-Fotê 1997). In 1993 the World Bank classified Côte d'Ivoire as among the seventeen most indebted nations in the world, and its debt per capita ratio was the highest in the whole of Africa (Azam 1994). The Ivorian government was consequently forced once again by the International Monetary Fund and the World Bank to enact structural adjustment programmes. The poverty rate had skyrocketed from 10 per cent in 1985 to 32.3 per cent in 1993. Bédié thus found himself immediately sandwiched between social complaints regarding the declining standard of living and international pressures to continue further along the path of economic reform, especially after the devaluation of the CFA Franc in January 1994.

The situation for Bédié was further complicated because Houphouet-Boigny's demise triggered a crisis in the PDCI itself, including a struggle for succession between Bédié and the former prime minister Ouattara, who is a Malinké from the north. This struggle caused a schism in the party, leading to the formation of a new party, the RDR (*Rassemblement des Républicains*), which would henceforth divide the vote that would have gone to the PDCI. The RDR and Laurent Gbagbo's FPI were the serious challengers to the PDCI in the presidential election of October 1995 and together they formed an opposition alliance called the *Front Républicain* (Republican Front).

A key contentious element in the 1995 elections was the new electoral code enacted in December 1994, which stipulates that the president-elect must be born of Ivorian parents and must have resided in Côte d'Ivoire for five years prior to the election. This is the notorious policy of *Ivoirité* or 'Ivorianness'. While Gbagbo, a Bété, had been challenging Baoulé hegemony under Bédié, the enactment of this code was to introduce yet another schism into the complicated politics post-Houphouet-Boigny. This was because the electoral code was adopted by Bédié's PDCI specifically to disqualify Ouattara from running for president on the grounds that he was not Ivorian enough to occupy that office. At one stroke, contention over nationality and region joined the extant struggle against ethnic hegemony as a defining characteristic of the politics of democratisation in Côte d'Ivoire. The Republican Front demanded the revocation of the code and the introduction of a more transparent electoral system. When these demands were not met, it boycotted the 1995 elections. Bédié was allegedly elected with 96 per cent of the popular vote.

The political tension dissipated slightly when the two parties of the Republican Front decided to participate in the legislative and municipal elections, even though a RDR candidate was rejected because of questions over his nationality. Such conflict over the definition of membership of the political community and the rights attached to such membership has been an important aspect of politics in the era of democratisation in other African countries such as Rwanda, Burundi, Zimbabwe and South Africa. The legislative elections confirmed the domination of the PDCI which obtained 149 of the 175 seats; the two opposition parties each got 13 seats.

The political manipulation of citizenship and belonging by the elite found resonance within the wider population over the rights to land. Years of structural adjustment, state contraction, and unemployment put new value on access to land as a livelihood strategy, particularly for those increasingly marginalised in the urban areas. Inter-communal clashes broke out more and more over land in rural areas as questions were increasingly raised about 'foreigners' and 'outsiders' (Collett 2006). In 1998 a skirmish occurred in Fengolo between the Guéré and the Baoulé, leading to casualties. The National Assembly adopted a new law in December of that year which acknowledged the primacy of customary land rights and thus guaranteed the possession of land only to national citizens. The law reserves private property rights in land to Ivorians. Within 10 years, land holders must get a new certificate of ownership from the state, in the place of whatever existing land-rights documentation they may have. Non-Ivorian residents can only rent land from the state or from 'indigenous' owners. This law marked an end to the Houphouetist philosophy which preached that the earth belonged to whoever would make good use of it, and introduced a violent politics of nationality, indigeneity and regionalism at the grassroots of Ivorian society.

The elite rivalry between Bédié and Ouattara was soon overshadowed by the chain effects of rural violence set off by conflicts over the question of *Ivoirité*, or what constitutes being Ivorian. Conflicts over land between native and non-native groups flared, including a murderous confrontation between the native Kroumen community and non-native Burkinabés in October 1999. Bédié's leadership motivated land conflicts based on interethnic or xenophobic issues. It was in the midst of such strife that Bédié was overthrown by a coup d'état on 24 December 1999. Côte d'Ivoire's fabled stability was in tatters as the violent politics of democratisation, initiated by a state suffering from economic and legitimacy problems, seeped into wider society and ultimately sucked the army into direct governance. While military-prone Ghana to the east was moving from military rule towards a democratic system, 'democratic' Côte d'Ivoire was moving in the opposite direction. The election boycott in 1995 when Krou and Baoulé communities confronted each other over allegations of 'Baoulé hegemony', as well as the numerous subsequent land conflicts, constitute a turning point after which ethnic and religious communities began to participate more openly in the arenas of political struggle and ethnic identities became explicitly linked with political contestation.

Ivoirité led northern Ivorians to a collective reassessment of their place in Ivorian society because of the suspicion that the term works against the origins of these northern groups. This problem was heightened by the difficulties in differentiating Ivorian northerners from their ethnic kin from neighbouring countries to the north, specifically Burkina Faso and Mali. Both Ivorian and foreign northerners increasingly faced harassment at the hands of the police and petty administrators who defined them all as 'foreigners'. The fact that Ouattara was from the north led many people from this region to identify with him as potential victims of *Ivoirité*.

At the same time as *Ivoirité* was opening a nationality and regional breach within the Ivorian nation between the northern and southern halves of the country, the politics of democratisation was also exposing a festering ethnic divide within the south. Harking back to Houphouetist philosophy, Bédié considered the Krou people as unfit for leadership of the nation. He thus created two political enemies: the militants of the RDR, which were recruited in the north, and the Krou populations who felt continuously dominated by the Akan. The Krou easily rallied around Laurent Gbagbo, a western Ivorian of Bété ethnicity (a sub-group of the Krou) now based in the southern part of the country where land struggles were pronounced.

In December 1999, Bédié's rule was cut short by a bloodless coup led by General Guéï. The military junta complained about laws based on an arbitrary *Ivoirité* ideology that had divided citizens by law, installed a corrupt system that compromised economic recovery, and endangered the population by the untimely and abusive recourse to force. Keiffer (2000) argues that the officers who rebelled against Bédié belonged to all ethnic groups (Bété, Guéré, Yacouba, Sénoufo and Dioula) except the Akans. The coup was welcomed by a public that had grown apathetic towards the distorted process of democratisation (Akindès 2000). The end of this exclusionary principle of *Ivoirité* was the goal espoused by the leader of the coup, yet within three months in office, General Guéï had acquired a taste for power, aspired to be his own successor through 'democratic' elections, and had become lukewarm in his criticism of *Ivoirité*. In selling his candidature, he adopted the nationalist rhetoric of *Ivoirité*, but was extremely careful not to use the word. Despite the coup, *Ivoirité* had not been expunged from law or politics. Instead, the military had now become a contending party in the violent politics of democratisation.

The entrance of the military itself became a prelude to the disintegration of the army and the country. Unsuccessful attempts by Guéï to balance competing ethnic and regional claims within the junta and his further efforts at entrenching himself in power plus his flirtation with *Ivoirité* soon provoked a coup attempt on 17 May 2000 by militant soldiers badly disillusioned with the Guéï regime and disappointed by its adoption of the very ideology against which the original coup had been executed. This mutiny was cut short and drowned in bloodshed: soldiers were tortured, killed or vanished. The deleterious socio-political climate was exploited by the military which split into small autonomous paramilitary groups (Camora, Kamajor, Cosa Nostras, Red Brigade, and Puma). These militants, as if exacting revenge for years of social marginalisation, began using a heightened state of military security as a pretext for racketeering and pillaging local communities. This state of affairs led to yet another mutiny in July 2000, in which paramilitary soldiers stormed the streets in order to claim what they called their 'spoils of war'. Côte d'Ivoire had descended into a state of near anarchy.

The vortex of violence also sucked in the students. This period saw a change in the strategy and philosophy of FESCI, an important player in the Ivorian theatre of political violence. FESCI leaders had become divided along political lines and pledged their allegiance to different parties as the elections promised by Guéï drew near, splitting the Federation between partisans of the RDR and the FPI, the latter of which were now discreetly in alliance with General Guéï. FESCI was drawn into a tailspin of infighting that included violent confrontations regularly pitting these two factions against each other. Within the students' movement, regionalism and ethnic mobilisation had triumphed over democratisation.

In the election on 22 October 2000, the country was to return to 'democratic' rule. But General Guéï had succeeded in eliminating all of his major political adversaries from the race with the exception of Laurent Gbagbo. The electoral contest between Guéï and Laurent Gbagbo took place in a climate characterised by tension within the army. Guéï attempted to rig the elections and declared himself winner in the first round. Laurent Gbagbo claimed to be ahead in partial results and declared himself head of the Ivorian state. Protestors from Ouattara's RDR took to the streets on 25 October demanding the resignation of General Guéï. Protestors from the FPI also took to the streets as Gbagbo demanded 'resistance by all means' from his partisans. While both Ouattara and Gbagbo were opposed to Guéï's fictitious election, they were fundamentally divided in their demands: Ouattara, excluded from the election on *Ivoirité* grounds, demanded a new election, while Gbagbo rejected the call for another election, claiming that he had legitimately won the original contest. Thus, resistance to the electoral results came from two opposing sources and led to violent confrontation between the army, which supported the FPI, and the militant protestors of the RDR. Thousands were injured and 120 killed, including 57 in a mass grave in Yopougon, a district of Abidjan (FIDH 2000). This level of violence had not been reached since 1990. On 26 October, General Guéï fled, and Laurent Gbagbo became President of the Second Republic.

While Bédié tried to use violence and ethnic grandstanding to block his opponents and secure the Baoulé core of the Houphouetist philosophy around his power, Guéï borrowed the concept of *Ivoirité* from Bédié, principally as a weapon against Ouattara and the 'northern' threat. Guéï, however, was interested in ending Baoulé hegemony and replacing it with a non-Akan power configuration built principally around his personal power. Personal ambition, ethnicity, and regionalism all clashed in a process of democratisation in which violence was the principal means of articulating the various positions and interests.

From Political Violence to Civil War

Neither the election in October 2000 nor the assumption of office by Gbagbo led to the establishment of a more orderly government. Indeed, Côte d'Ivoire lurched from political violence and social conflict to civil war, further dramatising the unstable nature of its democratisation process. Conflict resolution, peace-building, and reconciliation have replaced democratisation as the principal objectives of public policy in a country once regarded as very stable. The reasons for the civil war are traceable to the vexed policy of *Ivoirité* and its physical manifestation, the identity card, that ubiquitous symbol of citizenship in francophone Africa.

Gbagbo became President in a political climate of general suspicion, and rumours of conspiracies and coups were common during his first two years. Each of at least twenty alleged plots to overthrow the newly installed government was responded to with arrests, torture, mutilation and death. Violence continued to be the preferred instrument of politics, revealing an almost systematic use of force by successive regimes in the face of equally violent incivilities from opponents. In 2001, as if to lower social and political tensions, the new government organised a Forum of National Reconciliation. This Forum proved to be an arena of post-Houphouetist catharsis, in which the nation's major political problems (questions of land, impunity, citizenship) were discussed. It seemed that reconciliation, consultation, and the respect for pluralism would replace violence as the principal mechanisms for political articulation. But this was not to be, as President Gbagbo refused to accept the Forum's conclusions, which included full acknowledgment of the citizenship of Ouattara, who had become a symbol of northern and mixed ethnicities' sense of exclusion from full citizenship and the political system. Like Bédié and Guéï before him, Gbagbo found the concept of *Ivoirité* useful in containing the 'northern threat', however defined.

The unresolved tensions soon degenerated into civil war and the partitioning of the country. On 19 September 2002, another mutiny broke out, involving simultaneous attacks in Abidjan, Bouaké and Korhogo by aggrieved factions of the army. While the insurgents were repelled at Abidjan, they managed to take the latter two towns. Man and Danané also fell to them subsequently. General Guéï was attacked in his home and killed, along with a government minister. Ouattara and Bédié, the two principal leaders of the opposition to Gbagbo, were forced to take refuge in the sanctuary of embassies. Gbagbo's FPI party refused all dialogue with the insurgents. The mutiny led to a full-fledged rebellion, and the country was from that moment divided in two. The northern regions were controlled by three insurgent groups organised into one rebel movement under the name MPCI (Patriotic Movement of Côte d'Ivoire), which was renamed the *Forces Nouvelles* (New Forces) during the negotiation of the Linas-Marcoussis accords in January 2003. At this point, Côte d'Ivoire resembled the Clausewitzian conception of war as the expression of political dialogue by other means.

Several actors got involved in searching for solutions to the Ivorian crisis.

Several negotiations and agreements reflected domestic and international interests in promoting peace. From the beginning of the crisis, in September 2002, France became involved in order to protect the large French population on Ivorian soil. However, asked by the Ivorian government to help defeat the rebels, France refused to implement its bilateral military agreements with Côte d'Ivoire, arguing that the crisis was purely an 'Ivorian' one that did not involve an external threat. Paris sent 2,500 troops under 'Licorne' and asked the Economic Community of West African States to send peace-keepers under the security wing of ECOWAS. After some delay, the Mission of ECOWAS in Côte d'Ivoire (composed of 1300 peace-keepers from Senegal, Ghana, Togo, Niger and Benin) replaced the French troops on the cease-fire line in March 2003. The following month this Mission was placed under UN command within the operation created by UN Security Council Resolution 1528. In parallel, ECOWAS created a 'contact group' in charge of setting up diplomatic initiatives. Laurent Gbagbo agreed with its creation after long negotiations and accepted to negotiate with the rebels. In October 2002, the Senegalese Minister of Foreign Affairs and the MPCI (Côte d'Ivoire's Patriotic Movement) signed a cease-fire agreement in Bouaké with the ECOWAS contact group. President Gbagbo then asked France to control the implementation of the cease-fire.

The contact group managed to lead the belligerents to political dialogue. These direct negotiations started in Lomé, Togo and were led by President Eyadéma of Togo. Over the course of two months, the government and rebel delegations exchanged views but could not find consensus. Unproductive, these negotiations ended in confusion with no official declaration. ECOWAS organised an extra-ordinary summit in Dakar on 18 December 2002, which most Heads of State in the region refused to attend. West African presidents grew increasingly indifferent for two sets of reasons. On the one hand, the tussle over the leadership issue in resolving the crisis between Presidents Wade and Eyadéma made the mediation process difficult. On the other, many regional governments were put off by the constant threats by the Ivorian government that West Africa faced a 'risk' should a decision be taken against its interests. With the failure of regional crisis management, France took over and organised a Round-Table in Linas-Marcoussis (France), headed by Pierre Mazeau (France) assisted by Kéba Mbaye (Senegal) and Ivorian former Prime Minister Seydou Diarra.

For the first time since the beginning of the crisis, the Marcoussis agreement set up consensual measures that dealt with major issues such as: (i) nationality, (ii) foreign people's identity and condition, (iii) the electoral regime, (iv) eligibility for running for the Presidency, (v) the agrarian regime, (vi) the media, (vii) human rights and liberties, (viii) disarmament and demobilisation, (ix) economic recovery and social cohesion. The core issues leading to the crisis were now dealt with without taboo. However, implementation of the agreement proved difficult because it put the political order, and many interests associated with it, at risk. Increasingly aware of this, the French government handed over – in the most discreet and smooth manner – the task of peace-making to the international community. To that effect, President Chirac organised the Kléber conference in Paris on 25–26 January 2003. With the UN General Secretary, multilateral donors, and Heads of State from Europe and Africa (such as South African President Thabo Mbeki) in attendance, this conference set up the institutional framework for implementing the Marcoussis agreement: the constitution of a national reconciliation government, power-sharing principles within the government, the appointment of a new Prime Minister, and the establishment of relationships between the government and the National Assembly.

The implementation of the Marcoussis agreement triggered tension, uncertainty and violence because the different parties (the government, the opposition and rebel factions) could not agree on the modalities. Only in Accra on 8 March 2003, during the Accra II summit organised by the Ghanaian President, who had by this time become ECOWAS President, did the New Forces and political parties agree on the distribution of ministries in the new government which met in Abidjan on 17 April 2003. However, the government and the rebels had different political conceptions of the Marcoussis agreement, and the political dialogue that followed was not constructive. President Gbagbo claimed to be operating in good faith, but insisted on the importance of the agreement's 'spirit', whereas the opposition wanted a strictly literal implementation of all its terms. Ministers coming from the rebel faction subsequently suspended their participation in the government, while Gbagbo excluded the ministers coming from the civilian opposition.

The mediation process returned to the African arena with Accra III in July 2004. This involved a wider spectrum of actors: President John Kufuor (Ghana) and then UN Secretary General Kofi Annan invited Presidents Thabo Mbeki (South Africa), Omar Bongo (Gabon), and Dos Santos (Angola). The presence of Alpha Oumar Konaré, President of the African Union Commission, gave a continental dimension to the event. All participants adopted a firm attitude towards Ivorian political actors in order to reaffirm the integrity of the Marcoussis agreement, but Gbagbo resisted the pressure. At the political level, he had little respect for various Heads of State of the ECOWAS countries, whom he considered as 'puschists': Kérékou (Benin), Bongo (Gabon), Compaoré (Burkina Faso), Obasanjo (Nigeria), Touré (Mali), and Eyadéma (Togo). At the economic and financial level, Côte d'Ivoire was the economic power-house of francophone West Africa. Gbagbo therefore felt that he had no lessons to learn from his West African counterparts. Moreover, he suffered from a persecution complex and blamed the West African leaders for not considering him as 'one of them'. According to the testimony of some members of the Ivorian delegation, Mbeki was the only President for whom Gbagbo had some respect. Accra III subsequently turned into Gbagbo-Mbeki bilateral negotiations, which guaranteed the summit's successful outcome. Accra III agreements contained commitments to peace and measures to implement the Marcoussis agreement. The Pretoria agreement signed under the supervision of Mbeki in April 2005 contributed to the end of the war and rebel disarmament, but also to the setting up of the eligibility conditions for running for the presidency.

During the mediation, the arguments of both the insurgents and the government were couched in the language of democracy. Conflict over the definition of rights inherent in a democratic system has been central to the instability that has engulfed Côte d'Ivoire under democratisation. The insurgents, reflecting the concerns of northerners, demanded justice, equal treatment in the army, a common citizenship and identity card, and respect for their right to land. The idea of nation and citizenship espoused by the rebellion is rooted in a nostalgia for the *vivre-ensemble* notion created by Houphouet-Boigny, but without the hierarchical separation between the Akans and the northerners. *Vivre-ensemble* loosely translates as 'social pact', meaning people living together according to an agreed set of principles and norms. This desire for a more inclusive *vivre-ensemble* is behind the rebels' attempt to impose justice and equal rights by force of arms. Reflecting the primacy of violence in democratising Côte d'Ivoire, the rebels justified taking up arms as the only means of forcing the government to create a political order that is more ethnically inclusive. That democratisation has been displaced by the politics of regionalism, nationality, and citizenship was aptly brought out by the arguments of the Leopard Company, an armed branch of the MPCI:

> If tomorrow all Ivorians have identity documents, this uprising will not be in vain – this step, even more than elections, will bring peace. ...The ensemble of players in this crisis prefers to neglect this aspect, preferring to focus on the date of elections. The root of this problem is much deeper. ... how can elections help a country when the problems are so deeply-rooted? Identity documents define a nation – national citizens define a nation. What good is organising elections if the basis of the nation is itself imprecise? That the state grants each citizen the right to exist, this is a struggle that, in the context of Côte d'Ivoire, justifies this war.[2]

The rebellion is therefore aimed at the destruction of all mechanisms of social and political exclusion connected with *Ivoirité*, that xenophobic by-product of democratisation.

On the other hand, the Gbagbo government denounced the rebellion for rejecting democratic institutions and trying to seize power by force. Respect for properly constituted authority is seen as the cornerstone of a democratic system. The government justified its right to defend itself against attack as its duty to restore the authority of the state and to protect the nation against the realisation of political designs that, while manifested by visible players (the rebels), were supported by players hidden in the shadows. These shadow enemies include Ouattara, suspected of having financed the rebellion; his primary ally Blaise Compaoré, President of Burkina Faso, who offered his territory as a support base for the rebellion; and France, which would have benefited politically from the instability in Abidjan and which made no secret of its desire to revise some of the terms of the military and economic accords between the two countries. Thus, the government viewed the rebellion as a failed coup and a 'dirty war' waged by those intent on opposing the process of 're-founding Côte d'Ivoire', a process that required the necessary redefinition of the lines of demarcation between inside and outside in order better to protect the political, social, economic and cultural rights of the 'true Ivorians'.

The network of conspirators against the Ivorian state was seen as hydra-headed: interior enemies, the rebels described as 'immigrants' sons' due to their origins near the northern border; and exterior enemies, including northern neighbouring countries such as Mali and Burkina Faso, as well as France. A more native-based defence of the notion of nation was central to this perception of conspiracy and justified the attacks by 'Young Patriots' on French contingents of UN forces who were maintaining the peace. Thus France and its peace-keeping force was hurled into an increasingly hostile situation (Akindès 2007). Having started this crisis in the role of arbiter, France quickly became part of the problem as both sides suspected it of neo-colonialism rooted in its historical connection with the Houphouetist system.

In sum, democratisation in Côte d'Ivoire degenerated initially into a socio-political crisis and subsequently into a politico-military one. Both the New Forces and the government camp justified their actions through reference to different conceptions of rights and democracy. The primary movement of resistance in defence of the government was called the Alliance of Young Patriots, organised around the FESCI. This group claimed the right to fight for the second independence of the homeland against France and other 'foreigners' (Banégas 2006). Self-determination and the sanctity of the national authority were cardinal principles for them. The rebels, on the other hand, claimed to be fighting for their rights as full citizens. Both groups fought in the name of patriotism and for the territory known as Côte d'Ivoire, but their objectives were mutually exclusive and force, rather than democratic dialogue, was the main mode of articulation. The artificial geographic division between north and south that arose after 2002 created a partition where there was none, but this division was not acknowledged by either side. Neither group wants to see the country split into two, but rather both groups dream of reunification *on their own terms*. For reunification to happen, the pro-government side seeks disarmament of the rebels, and for their part, the rebels sought official documentation conferring full citizenship rights.

Quite unexpectedly on 4 March 2007, President Laurent Gbagbo and leader of the opposition Guillaume Soro Kigbafori concluded an accord with the aid of President Compaoré of Burkina Faso, acting president of ECOWAS. Any kind of international mediation (France, ECOWAS, the UN) was de-emphasised: only President Compaoré, who had long been blamed for fuelling the rebellion, was allowed to take part. Laurent Gbagbo and Guillaume Soro signed the Ouaga-dougou political agreement, which hoped to end the crisis thanks to a new government and the departure of foreign troops, but also through the carrying out of major actions such as:

(1) resolving the problem of lack of identity and citizenship papers through a general identification of people;
(2) after this identification, preparing open, democratic and transparent presidential elections, in agreement with the Marcoussis, Accra and Pretoria agreements. To do so, it was agreed that the National Institute for Statistics with the technical unit for identification would register all voters, under the responsibility of the Independent Electoral Commission;
(3) restructuring and integrating the two armies – government and rebel – so as to set up new defence and security forces, attached to the principles of integrity and republican ethics. A special mechanism was created, and the two conflicting parties decided to unite into an integrated structure of command (*Centre de commandement intégré* or CCI);
(4) normalising the political and institutional situation in Côte d'Ivoire by restoring state authority and deploying the administration and public service delivery back on the whole national territory;
(5) reaching national reconciliation through a transitional government. This involved 33 ministries and included personalities from the presidential party, the *Forces Nouvelles* and the opposition. Laurent Gbagbo subsequently appointed Guillaume Soro Prime Minister;
(6) asking the UN Security Council, with the support of ECOWAS, to end the arms embargo against Côte d'Ivoire within three months after the presidential elections; to give the country special authorisation to import light arms so as to give CCI the means to accomplish its tasks; to ask Licorne and the UN operation to eliminate the buffer 'trust zone' in the central areas, which had separated north and south since late 2002; to put an end to the personal sanctions against the protagonists of the crisis; to set up a pro-

gramme for the return of displaced populations; to help create a new political environment in the country and avoid any partial or demagogic interpretation of the agreement.

Since this agreement was signed, Laurent Gbagbo and Guillaume Soro have multiplied signals of appeasement. They celebrated the 'restored peace' with the dismantlement of the 'trust zone'. In the centre and west of the country, the three first 'mixed brigades' (with government and rebel troops) were set up in order to replace the international forces. As the International Crisis Group noted, if the agreement 'has made an armed conflict less probable (...) it is only a first step'. Since the Ouagadougou agreement, a 'direct dialogue' between the belligerents has been established. Guillaume Soro, former 'enemy number one' of President Gbagbo, and still leader of the *Forces Nouvelles*, became Gbagbo's Prime Minister. This agreement has triggered various reactions. On 29 June 2007, Guillaume Soro's plane was attacked, presumably by his own side, at the Bouaké airport, leaving three aides dead. On the government side, disagreement between Gbagbo and the President of the National Assembly, Mamadou Koulibaly, is no secret in Abidjan. The latter describes the 'direct dialogue' as *Rebfondation*, a derogatory phrase referring to a mix between rebellion and *refondation*, and a regression from the re-foundation of the Ivorian state promised by Gbagbo's FPI. The agreement seems to have destroyed the consensus within both the government and the rebellion and their various supporters. The deadline of December 2007 for concluding the implementation of the agreement has come and gone; delays in re-establishing the state administration across the whole country and in dismantling the militias have cast some doubt on the will of the key actors.

However, it is too early to offer a prognosis on the chances of success in this attempt to jumpstart the nation, but should the government and rebel forces arrive at some sort of political reconciliation, it would go down as a major feat of reinvention in the blood-soaked annals of Africa's once most stable country.

Conclusion

Côte d'Ivoire demonstrates the path-dependence of democratisation in contemporary Africa. The issues, concerns, and even the methods used in the era of democratisation are deeply informed and structured by the terms of the immediate post-colonial settlement under Houphouet-Boigny. For thirty-nine years the idea of the nation, such as it was collectively lived from independence until 1990, was the vision of one man. But the compromise that guaranteed social cohesion was undermined when the economic promise that provided this adhesion began to fall apart, and when the architect began to age beyond the capacity to unify a society whose sociological mutations no longer accommodated such a vision.

This chapter has attempted to explain firstly how the military-political crisis that has paralysed Côte d'Ivoire since 2002 is the product of a larger effort to unhinge the political compromises at the base of Houphouet-Boigny's post-colonial policy. Secondly, it has tried to show how the dynamic struggle to reinvent the notion of an Ivorian nation, often in the name of democracy, led to a continuum of political violence, in which violence has became commonplace. For democratisation to proceed in a constructive manner in which conflicts are contained and domesticated, there has to be a common agreement on minimum basic rules and procedures, even if these are of non-democratic origin. Côte d'Ivoire lacked these rules as the Houphouetist template suffered economic and political shocks. At the best of times, these shocks would have tested the capacity and sagacity of the Houphouetist system to the limit. With the introduction of democratisation, clubs quickly became trumps, as contending groups sought to promote their interests in the context of the lack of guiding and effective rules. Instability, violence, and ultimately civil war have been the result. As in other African countries such as South Africa, Zimbabwe, Rwanda, and Burundi, establishing common rules over basic questions of citizenship, nationality, and land, is crucial for democratisation. The future of Côte d'Ivoire will depend on the extent to which these ground rules are re-established as pre-conditions for the return to a democratic order. As the leader of the Young Patriots puts it, 'if the Ouagadougou agreements pave the way for a lasting peace in Côte d'Ivoire, it will be a revolution in Africa'.

Notes

1. These marches were launched in protest against the President's refusal to take into account the conclusions of an enquiry into army brutality in May 1991, in a student quarter in Yopougon, a district of Abidjan. According to the investigation committee, soldiers had beaten and raped students; the committee members recommended the sanctioning of Robert Gueï, who had been promoted to the rank of General just after having authorised his soldiers to intervene in this very affair. In January 1992, President Houphouët-Boigny made this committee's findings public, but refused to sanction General Gueï, stating that he was a top-ranking military official whose removal would divide the army. He publicly reaffirmed his support of the General, thus granting him and other military leaders – despite its contradiction of Ivorian law – impunity from the acts of May 1991.
2. 'Conflict in Côte d'Ivoire: can war be avoided?' published on the Internet to commemorate the fourth anniversary of the rebellion. http://compagnie –guepard.chez-alice.fr/direct.htm#guerre19.

References

Amondji, Marcel. 1984. *Félix Houphouet et la Côte d'Ivoire.* Paris: Karthala.

Akindès, Francis. 2000. Les transitions démocratiques à l'épreuve des faits. Réflexion à partir des expériences des pays d'Afrique noire francophone. In *Bilan des Conférences nationales et autres processus de transition démocratique.* Paris: Organisation Internationale de la Francophonie, Editions Pedone.

——. 2007. Vue de Côte d'Ivoire. Le double jeu de Paris se retourne contre lui. *Alternatives Internationales* 34: 55-6.

Akindès, F. Diabaté Idriss and Dembélé Ousmake (eds). 2005. *Les intellectuels ivoiriens face à la crise.* Paris: Karthala.

Azam, Jean-Paul. 1994. *La faisabilité politique de l'ajustement en Côte d'Ivoire (1981-1990)* Paris: OECD.

Banégas, Richard. 2006. Cote D'Ivoire: Patriotism, Ethnonationalism and Other African Modes of Self-Writing. *African Affairs* 105 (421): 535-52.

Bouquet, Christian. 2005. *Géopolitique de la Côte d'Ivoire.* Paris: Armand Colin.

Braud, Philippe. 2005. La violence politique: repères et problèmes. In *Cultures et Conflicts.* Available at http://www.conflits.org/document.php?id=406.

Collett, Moya. 2006. Ivorian Identity Constructions: Ethnicity and Nationalism in the Prelude to Civil War. *Nations and Nationalism* 12: 613-29.

Crook, Richard. 1989. Patrimonialism, Administrative Effectiveness and Economic Development in Cote d'Ivoire. *African Affairs* 88: 205-28.

——. 1990. Politics, the Cocoa Crisis, and Administration in Cote d'Ivoire. *Journal of Modern African Studies* 28(4): 649-69.

——. 1997. Winning Coalitions and Ethno-Regional Politics: The Failure of the Opposition in the 1990 and 1995 Elections in Cote d'Ivoire. *African Affairs* 96: 215-42.

Diabaté, Lamine. 2005. Interview in *Intellectuels ivoiriens face à la crise* (eds). Francis Akindès, Diabaté Idriss and Dembélé Ousmane. Paris: Karthala.
Diarra, Samba. 1997. *Les faux complots d'Houphouet*. Paris: Karthala.
Fauré, Yves-André. 1982. Le complexe politico-économique. In *Etat et bourgeoisie en Côte d'Ivoire*, eds Yves-André Fauré and Jean-François Médard. Paris: Karthala.
FIDH. 2000. Côte d'Ivoire. Enquêtes sur le charnier de Yopougon du 26 Octobre 2000. Paris: Fédération Internationale des Ligues des Droits de l'Homme.
Kieffer, Guy-André. 2000. Armée ivoirienne: le refus du déclassement. *Politique africaine* 78: 26-44.
Kirwin, Matthew. 2006. The Security Dilemma and Conflict in Cote d'Ivoire. *Nordic Journal of African Studies* 15: 42-52.
Konaté, Yacouba. 2003. Les enfants de la balle. De la Fesci aux mouvements de patriotes. *Politique africaine* 89: 49-70.
Koné, Amadou. 2003. *Houphouet-Boigny et la crise ivoirienne*. Paris: Karthala.
Le, Pape, Marc. 1997. *L'énergie sociale. Economie politique de la ville en Afrique noire, 1930-1995*. Paris: Karthala.
Le Pape, M. 2003. Les politiques d'affrontement en Côte d'Ivoire. 1999-2003. *Afrique Contemporaine* 2(206): 29-39.
McGowan, Patrick J. 2003. African military coups d'état, 1956-2001: frequency, trend and distribution. *Journal of Modern African Studies* 41: 339-70.
Médard, Jean-François. 1982. La régulation socio-politique. In *Etat et bourgeoisie en Côte d'Ivoire*, eds. Yves-André Fauré and Jean-François Médard. Paris: Karthala.
Memel-Foté, Harris. 1991. Des ancêtres fondateurs aux pères de la nation. Introduction à une anthropologie de la démocratie. In *Conférences Marc Bloch*. Available at http://cmb.ehess.fr/document40.html.
——. 1997. De la stabilité au changement. les représentations de la crise politique et les réalités des changements. In *Le modèle ivoirien en questions. Crise, ajustements, recompositions*, eds. Bernard Contamin and Harris Memel-Foté. Paris: Karthala.
——. 1999. Un mythe politique des Akans en Côte d'Ivoire: le sens de l'Etat. Mondes akan. In *Identité et pouvoir en Afrique occidentale*, eds P. Valsecchi and F. Viti. Paris: L'Harmattan.
Yapi Diahou, Alphonse. 2002. De la composition et de la solidarité des régions en Côte d'Ivoire. In *Côte d'Ivoire. L'année terrible 1999-2000*, eds Marc Le Pape and Claudine Vidal. Paris: Karthala.

4

Ghana since 1993
A Successful Democratic Experiment?

LINDSAY WHITFIELD

Ghana became famous for being the first sub-Saharan African colony to gain independence in 1957, and then became infamous for its political instability and economic decline. Ghana under Kwame Nkrumah was often compared unfavourably with Côte d'Ivoire under Félix Houphouet-Boigny. While the latter was regarded as stable, successful, and 'capitalist' inclined, the former was characterised as unstable and 'socialist'. Starting with the military coup against the Nkrumah government in 1966 and ending with J.J. Rawlings' second coup at the close of 1981, Ghana experienced seven changes in Head of State and ruling coalition, four of which resulted from a coup d'état by sections of the military (see Table 4.1). Three republics were toppled, more than once to loud popular applause. It is ironic that whilst Côte d'Ivoire has descended into civil war, Ghana is once again famous on the continent, this time for the quality of its democratic governance.

Ghana returned to multiparty politics and constitutional government under the Fourth Republic in 1993. The common narrative of its democratisation experience goes something like the following. Rawlings, head of the authoritarian Provisional National Defence Council, set a timetable for a democratic transition under external and internal political pressure, but manipulated the process in order to remain in power as a dictator-cum-democrat. He won the presidential election in 1992, but the opposition parties argued that the election was not free and fair and boycotted the parliamentary elections held shortly thereafter. The result was *de facto* one-party rule by Rawlings' newly created National Democratic Congress (NDC). In 1996, Rawlings and the NDC won again. This time opposition parties participated, elections were generally regarded as free and fair, and the contending parties joined Parliament. In the 2000 election, Rawlings could not stand for president again, given the two-term constitutional limit. None of the presidential candidates received the 50 per cent plus one of the votes necessary to win, and a second round of voting between the two top candidates was held. The NDC lost its hold on power as the New Patriotic Party (NPP) presidential candidate J. Kufuor won, and the NPP barely took a majority in Parliament with the help of the smaller parties. While the NPP had come to power in 2001 largely with the support of the other opposition parties, as the incumbent ruling party it secured a more comfortable margin of votes over the NDC in the 2004 elections and retained power under the leadership of President Kufuor.

Table 4.1 Governments of Ghana, 1957–2008

Date	Government	Head of Government	Type
1957-60 1965–6	Convention People's Party (CPP)	K. Nkrumah	Civilian Parliamentary; *First Republic* One-party
1966-69	National Liberation Council (NLC)	E. Kotoka/ A.A. Afrifa	Military/police coup Military-bureaucratic
1969-72	Progress Party (PP)	K.A. Busia	*Second Republic* Civilian multiparty
1972-	National Redemption Council (NRC)	I.K. Acheampong	Military coup Military-bureaucratic
1975-	Supreme Military Council (SMC)		Military
1978-9	SMC II	F.W.K Akuffo	Military
04/06/1979	Armed Forces Revolutionary Council (ARFC)	J.J. Rawlings	Military
09/1979	People's National Party (PNP)	H. Limann	*Third Republic* Civilian multiparty
31/12/1981- 1993	Provisional National Defence Council (PNDC)	J.J. Rawlings	Military coup Military-bureaucratic
1993-2000	National Democratic Congress (NDC)	J.J. Rawlings	*Fourth Republic* Civilian multiparty
2001-8	New Patriotic Party (NPP)	J.A. Kufuor	Civilian multiparty

Source: Ninsin (1998) and updated by the author.

The literature evaluating democracy in Ghana has largely focused on the deficiencies of Rawlings as a democrat and on his National Democratic Congress as a political machine. Rawlings and the NDC governments were seen as authoritarians in transition, with observers wondering if Rawlings would leave office peacefully when his two terms were up. Another body of literature emphasises Rawlings' attempt to liberalise and reform the economy, the articulation of reforms under structural adjustment with the return to representative democracy, and whether one undermines the other. Since Rawlings left the political stage, there has been little published on the NPP in power. Is it because democracy has been consolidated with the alternation of the ruling party through the ballot box; because election processes are performed to near perfection and outcomes accepted by all participants; because Ghana has a cohesive and stable party system which provides a strong opposition and viable alternative to incumbent governments; and because Ghana has high ratings on political and civil liberties? Or does the lack of literature on the NPP governments stem from bewilderment that much has stayed the same, despite these achievements in democratic process? Corruption remains a widespread problem; political mobilisation remains significantly based on patronage; citizens have few tools with which to hold the government accountable; the executive branch of government dominates the political system and oversight functions of other agencies are weak; public access to information is still difficult; and education levels and literacy have not increased significantly.

Ghana's political history is characterised by chronic political instability, military intervention as a means of changing the ruling elite, and popular discontent with representative democracy in practice. This chapter re-examines Ghana's experience under the Fourth Republic using criteria derived from this political history. It asks how this latest experiment in representative democracy differs from previous republics, and whether it has led to fundamental changes in political practices. The main themes emerging from this assessment are discussed in the third section: elite integration, voting trends, the legacy of presidentialism, the experience of decentralisation and changes in the public sphere. Any analysis of contemporary Ghanaian politics must include the politics of aid dependency. The fourth section outlines the way aid dependence has developed over the last two decades, its political consequences and their implications for democracy. The chapter concludes by evaluating the significance of the alternation between parties in power.

Ending Political Instability

Control of the post-colonial African state enabled those in power to reap the benefits of office and to decide to which Africans to transfer resources. In Ghana, competition between different factions of the post-independence elites for control over the state led to military coups and repeated regime changes. Three factors contributed to this chronic political instability: (i) the role of the state in the economy, (ii) the degree of elite fragmentation and (iii) the way in which intra-elite competition at the national level intertwined with local politics.

This extreme disunity among Ghanaian political elites resulted from the historical context of elite production and the diversity in social status and background of elite generations (see Svanikier 2007). Intra-elite competition became more destabilising as it became tangled up with local struggles, particularly during periods of multiparty politics. Political parties stitched together national coalitions out of local elite followings. Patronage linked elites regionally, ethnically, and by lineage to their support base, and it could turn elite rivalries over the state into ones characterised by other emotionally charged identities and social conflicts. However, these support bases also made demands on public officials. Patronage networks gained their importance partly because a powerful central authority could be used to maximise returns to political access and partly because a majority of the electorate were socially and economically excluded rural producers and urban poor. Elections under the first three republics exhibited considerable consistencies in their purpose, patterns of competition, means of mobilisation, campaign methods and voting patterns (Chazan 1987).This period saw the crystallisation of two political traditions which emerged during the late colonial period and which represent the two main partisan affiliations in the country: the Nkrumahist tradition, which is perceived as ethnically and socially inclusive, broad-based, populist and left-wing, and the Busia/Danquah tradition which is perceived as elitist, ethnically exclusive, liberal-democratic and right-wing (Svanikier 2007: 130).

The pattern of elite circulation that emerged was particularly destructive to

Ghana's economy. Although most African countries suffered a similar economic fate at the end of the 1970s, Ghana's economic crisis was one of the most severe. Hutchful (2002) provides the most convincing explanation of its origins and the inability of successive regimes to halt the deepening crisis. He argues that a broad consensus emerged after independence on the fiscal and economic responsibilities and behaviour of the state in capital mobilisation and social welfare investment. The 'Nkrumahist bargain' was modernity and welfare provided by the state in return for increased state authority and centralisation of power, which ultimately led to state domination of most of the economic and political space. The outcome was a new form of state dependence and a culture in which political loyalty and the legitimacy of the state were defined in terms of instrumental expectations, with patronage constituting the basic glue of politics. In seeking to suppress autonomous centres of power outside the state, the Nkrumah regime generated alternative power centres within the state that became sources of political instability (ibid.).

The Nkrumahist social and fiscal paradigm remained intact after the 1966 coup. Subsequent regimes preserved this paradigm: the state sector was not significantly contracted and the social orientation of the state was retained. In explaining why, Hutchful (2002) argues that this paradigm represented a consensus on key issues of economic and social policy which largely transcended partisan and class identities. Although support for this fiscal paradigm was diffused throughout society, he notes that in practice it did not work equally in the interests of everyone. Those who benefited the most from the control systems were public institutions and individuals in the upper and middle-income groups who generally belonged to organised bodies in the public and semi-public sectors. Political resistance by the civil and military bureaucracies and other urban groups prevented the state from resolving its fiscal and economic crisis. Growing political instability and the increasing corruption and authoritarianism of successive regimes made it difficult to impose any reforms that called for significant popular sacrifice. It is within this context that Rawlings' 'accountability coups' in 1979 and 1981 must be understood.

Rawlings' 'revolution' at the end of 1981 aimed to halt the crisis. His Provisional National Defence Council (PNDC) confronted the statist-distributionist mode of governance and attempted to redesign the social contract in a more market-oriented way (Hutchful 2002). His economic solution worked, in the sense that it initiated economic recovery. Regardless of the legitimate critiques of structural adjustment programmes, many of the policies of the 1983 Economic Recovery Programme supported by the World Bank and IMF were needed. Average incomes increased by about 50 per cent by 2001, but this statistic obscures the extremely low point from which the economy had to recover: real per capita GDP in 2000 had only just recovered to the level achieved in 1960. The limited achievements of economic reforms, and the reasons behind their limited impact, have been discussed elsewhere (see Aryeetey *et al.* 2000; Hutchful 2002).

Rawlings' political solution, on the other hand, did not work. His stated intentions were to create a 'real democracy' in which ordinary Ghanaians participated meaningfully in the processes through which they were governed, as opposed to the ritualistic participation in elections and to the failed institutions of representative democracy. Rawlings' discourse resonated with many people, particularly in the rural areas. However, his attempt to provide a legitimate alternative by establishing a form of participatory democracy failed. The particular form which 'people's power' embodied was more destructive than constructive to achieving the benefits of participation. The People's and Workers' Defence Committees created as mechanisms of popular participation in political and economic decision-making were disastrous because their functions and operations were not clear or well-conceived, and they were not free from the capricious dictates of the PNDC which evolved their roles to fit its own purposes of staying in power (see Nugent 1995). The Defence Committees were subsequently disbanded because power shifted away from the ultra-radicals that were coordinating them and because they were economically and politically disruptive. To fulfil its promises on democracy and in response to pressure for a return to multiparty democracy, the PNDC introduced a decentralisation policy creating District Assemblies in 1988-89.

About this time, political opposition resurged, bridging the ideological divide that had previously paralysed it. The political opposition, although presenting itself as a broad-based national movement, was actually composed of the same urban-based, elite organisations that had rallied around multiparty government in the past. External pressure for political liberalisation came from the collapse of communist states and the new donor agendas around good governance. The National Commission for Democracy, instructed by the PNDC regime to gather public opinion on the future constitutional order, reported in 1991 that the majority of the population was not against political parties. As pressure mounted, Rawlings accepted a return to multiparty government, but through a process which he controlled and which provided renewed legitimacy for his rule. A new Constitution was promulgated by a Consultative Assembly and approved by referendum in 1992.

It is important to note that two ideas of democracy historically have battled to shape Ghana's political system, contributing to political instability (Hutchful 2002: 205-10). The radical/populist idea of democracy, which involves a change in the class character of the state and the relationship between state and society, continuously challenged the formal/legal idea of democracy, which includes the circulation of elites in power through elections and constitutional devices – a conflict that can be traced back to the bi-polar ideological divide within the nationalist movement during decolonisation. The formal/legal version of democracy did not have much attraction for the mass of Ghanaians, because it stressed the values of negative liberty and was not concerned with material needs or with placing democracy within a larger social project. Rawlings' 1981 coup embodied the pursuit of the populist idea of democracy, although this goal gave way to other imperatives such as revitalising the economy and securing his regime in power.

In the Fourth Republic, the struggle between popular and liberal democracy has dissipated. The 2002 *Afrobarometer* survey also concludes that Ghanaians attach a largely liberal meaning to democracy (democracy gives citizens a voice) as opposed to a utilitarian one (democracy is only worth having if it addresses basic economic needs) (Gyimah-Boadi & Mensah 2003). Perhaps this change is not surprising in the post-ideological global setting where it is accepted that there is no alternative to representative democracy. However, the endurance of the Fourth Republic does not imply that previous criticisms of representative democracy no longer apply. On the contrary, many past political practices have carried over. The rest of this chapter examines this change and continuity, as well as the factors underlying the durability of Ghana's latest democratic experiment.

Democratic Achievements and Deficits in the Fourth Republic

The NDC government appeared at first to be the PNDC regime by another name. Senior personalities in the government and the support base of the two governments were almost identical (Aubynn 2002). The NDC government continued its top-down approach to policy-making, decreeing reforms and avoiding public debate. Finally, the NDC government was characterised by competition between the old structures of the PNDC regime and new ones of the Fourth Republic, and by the resilience of old behaviour under the new institutions and the resistance of old institutions to their termination (Osei 2000). It was, however, gradually transformed during the 1990s in terms of its composition, actions and method of engagement with non-state actors. Although the NDC continued to reproduce political practices from the past, some of these practices cannot be attributed only to Rawlings and his party. The era of NPP government has demonstrated remarkable differences from as well as similarities with its predecessor.

From Elite Fragmentation to Elite Integration
Since the inauguration of the Fourth Republic the political elite have become more unified. What accounts for this shift from elite conflict to consensus? It is argued that the move from fragmentation to integration was not marked by a single event but was a gradual process that turned into a virtuous circle.

The National Commission for Democracy organised public platforms to hear opinions on its District Assembly concept and then on the future constitutional direction, but it did not engage in dialogue with its critics. This tendency to ignore political dissent and policy critique was a key feature of the PNDC regime and it allowed political disagreements to evolve into polarised positions, making cooperation between the different political factions almost impossible. The degree of polarisation between the PNDC and the political opposition led the latter to reject participation in the political institutions created by the former. The opposition called for a mass boycott of voter registration for District Assembly elections in 1988. The distrust between the ruling political elites of the PNDC and other elite factions reached a climax during the founding 1992 elections, when the opposition political parties boycotted the Parliamentary elections on the grounds that Rawlings' victory in the preceding presidential election was the result of fraudulent practices.

In an effort to establish dialogue between the NDC government and opposition parties, the Electoral Commission initiated the formation of the Inter-Party Advisory Committee (IPAC) in March 1994. During the following two years, IPAC provided a forum where disagreements, suspicions and fears were regularly addressed. Ninsin (1998) argues that the deliberations of IPAC were a major exercise in building trust among the political elites, because all political parties were incorporated and their leaders were involved in making decisions about the electoral system. Donors provided significant aid to the Electoral Commission to conduct the 1996 elections, which enhanced the technical capacity of the Commission to manage the elections and thus contributed to building trust in the

Commission and the electoral process. Before the 1996 elections took place, the political elite had thus forged the institutional bases necessary for a more stable democratic politics through negotiation.

Subsequent elections charted significant improvements to the electoral process which increased the perception of elections as free and fair among political party leaders as well as the electorate. Changes in the electoral procedure include the use of voter identity cards, transparent ballot boxes, opening the voter register for public inspection, and new rules of monitoring voting, counting votes and reporting results. Prior to voter registration for the 2004 election, the Electoral Commission compiled a fresh electoral register, conceding to criticisms that the register was bloated. New voter identification cards were also distributed, which contained the voter's photograph for the first time. At polling stations, the voting process and vote counting were well-organised and transparent. While many observers commented that the 2004 elections were not run as efficiently as in 2000, they were content that Ghana had carried out another near perfect election process. Since 1992, official aid agencies have supported the electoral process with significant financial contributions to facilitate these reforms and support the functioning of the Electoral Commission.

The Legacy of Presidentialism

As in Senegal and Nigeria, the concentration of powers in the executive branch of government has been a feature of Ghanaian democratisation. The 1992 Constitution significantly changed the political system, but it also allocated extensive powers to the executive branch in a hybrid parliamentary-presidential system, which was designed as a remedy against the gridlock that contributed to the demise of the Third Republic. Since 1993 the independence and power of some agencies of horizontal accountability have increased, such as the judiciary, the Electoral Commission and the Commission on Human Rights and Administrative Justice. The involvement of Parliament in lawmaking, deliberations over policy, scrutiny of international loans and agreements, and executive oversight also increased, but arguably has declined since the NPP came to power, as explained below.

The judiciary provides the most potent check on the power of the executive (APRM 2005). The legal profession has historically been the bastion of liberal democratic thought and advocates for representative democracy. The courts have asserted their independent powers of judicial review and their willingness to pronounce acts of the executive as unconstitutional. However, they remain financially and operationally dependent on the executive, leaving them weakened and short of resources (Mattes & Gyimah-Boadi 2005). The NPP government has avoided interfering blatantly with judicial independence, but there are cases of it avoiding judicial rulings through manoeuvrings that raise questions about the separation of powers (APRM 2005). For instance, in the so-called 'poultry case', the Poultry Farmers' Association took the government to court on grounds of its failure to implement its own law introduced to raise tariffs on imported poultry products. After the High Court granted a verdict to compel the government to implement the law, the government decided to fast-track a Bill by suspending the relevant standing orders that allowed it to repeal the law on an emergency basis – making the Court order otiose. Lastly, although the rule of law is a reality in Ghana, the judicial system is largely inaccessible to the majority of the population due to poverty.

The Commission for Human Rights and Administrative Justice is another potential agency of horizontal accountability. The mandate of this Commission is to investigate corruption, abuse of public power and human rights violations. It has taken action to address abuse of human rights by the state and its officials as well as cases arising from cultural practices. However, there is uncertainty over the status and enforceability of the Commission's decisions, and its pronouncements have not always been respected by the government (APRM 2005). The strength of the Commission comes from the origins of its mandate in the 1992 Constitution which gives it legitimacy and authority, unlike Nigeria's National Human Rights Commission which was established by a Military Decree that provides it with virtually no enforcement powers and little protection from executive interference (Cameron 2008). Ghana's Electoral Commission, discussed above, has achieved a significant degree of independence from the executive. It is often cited as a model for the continent. However, there are worries over its lack of adequate resources and sustainability, given that its budget is dependent on donor funds.

The Parliament is a unicameral legislature consisting of 230 members elected by plurality vote in single-member constituencies (the seats increased from 200 to 230 with the 2004 elections). While the 1992 Constitution accords the Parliament significant powers, it also fosters what Mattes and Gyimah-Boadi (2005) call a 'hegemonic' presidency that largely negates the checks and balances in it. The Constitution gives vast appointment powers to the President, which results in patronage and control. The President appoints members to the Council of State (advisory body to the President), parastatal boards and District Chief Executives (heads of District Assemblies) as well as one-third of District Assembly general members. The Constitution also instructs the President to appoint the majority of Ministers from Parliament, and Cabinet Ministers serve at the President's discretion. The effect is to significantly diminish the independence of the legislature and thus weaken its oversight role (APRM 2005). The parliamentary process of approving ministerial nominees is growing in importance, but the fusion of executive and legislative powers again undermines its ability to examine nominees critically, among other factors (CDD-Ghana 2005; Boafo-Arthur 2005).

Parliament's lawmaking function is further weakened by a constitutional provision which prohibits MPs from introducing Bills that impose taxes, charges or withdrawals from public funds. It can only reduce and not increase the allocations to a particular line item in the Executive budget proposal. There is disagreement over whether the Constitution allows Parliament to determine its own institutional budget, with different Articles being cited, but Lindberg (forthcoming 2009) also cites a 1993 Act which provides that administrative and operational expenses of the Parliamentary Service are not subject to control by the Ministry of Finance. In practice, however, this Ministry has always exerted this control. Thus, Parliament is dependent on the executive for what it receives. This dependence may be the reason why Parliament lacks the facilities, logistics and the support staff required to carry out its functions. It has also been unable to effectively scrutinise and control the budget process, partly because, in overseeing budget implementation, it neither receives nor demands systematic budget reports.

Despite the constitutional provisions limiting its power, the Parliament has a number of instruments to assert its autonomy and power. From its inception to around the first half of the third Parliament (1993-2002), the legislature was gradually and partially strengthened, taking some advantage of these instruments (Lindberg forthcoming 2009). However, it has not continued to evolve towards an autonomous institution and to develop its legislative and executive oversight functions, but rather regressed in its autonomy and willingness to use its power under Kufuor's NPP governments. Lindberg finds only part of the explanation for this decline to be the result of the limited resources of the legislature, the weak capacity of its parliamentary service, the high turnover among Members of Parliament, and the increasing demands for constituency service. He argues that the most important explanation is the quest for survival of a new government in power under conditions of high political competition. When the NPP first came to power, it barely had a majority in Parliament, unlike the NDC which had always had a strong majority. Furthermore, President Kufuor faced challenges within his own party (see Agyeman-Duah 2006).

These political conditions created incentives for President Kufuor and his administration to contain the legislature and co-opt MPs. The primary means of co-opting the legislature stem from the hybrid system: appointing MPs as Ministers, executive control over resources for constituency service, and creating seats on procurement boards for Ministries, Departments and Agencies (Lindberg forthcoming 2009). Ministerial portfolios not only provide a 50 per cent increase in salary and perks, but also put MPs in a better position to service constituents' demands. In 2005, the share of MPs holding ministerial or deputy ministerial positions was 24 per cent of total MPs and 43 per cent of NPP MPs (ibid). The Cabinet had expanded from 37 ministers under Rawlings to 55 under Kufuor at the beginning of his second term in office. President Kufuor also has used frequent Cabinet reshuffles to keep ministers in line. Control over the Speaker and Majority Leader has been another way in which President Kufuor has undermined the Parliament's autonomy. Although the power to appoint Speaker and Majority Leader are vested with the legislature, in practice the President nominates to these positions. The Speaker of the Third Parliament (2001-04) proved to be too independent-minded and tended to assert the autonomy of Parliament, including exercising its right to financial autonomy, so the President replaced him in the Fourth Parliament with a more 'loyal' NPP member who would toe the party line.

Thus, Lindberg concludes that currently the executive is for the most part unconstrained by Parliament. In this situation, there is the danger of unchecked corruption. After improving in the early 2000s, Ghana's score on the Transparency International Corruption Perception Index fell in 2006 to 3.3 (out of a corruption-free 10) – the same score received under Rawlings' government in 1999. The NPP government's actions on corruption have focused on improving its ability to police corruption internally, rather than increasing the ability of non-state actors to obtain information and investigate the conduct of public officials (Keith 2005). The NPP government has passed laws creating boards to oversee the financial functions of government agencies, but these institutions may fall prey to the same weaknesses plaguing the Serious Fraud Office, the Commission for Human Rights and Administrative Justice and the presidential Office of Accountability: under-funding and operational dependence on the executive. There is not yet a freedom of information law that would create a process for citizens to obtain public information, and the asset declarations of public officials are not made public.

Expanding the Public Sphere

Under the Fourth Republic, the public sphere became more open and the landscape of social organisations more diverse due to the 1992 Constitution which guarantees freedom of association and speech, as well as from increased foreign aid directly to Ghanaian organisations. These changes have had a significant impact on democratisation, but the achievements should not be overstated.

The media landscape has undergone major transformations. From a situation of no private daily newspapers or radio and television stations in the early 1990s, in 2004 there were approximately 12 newspapers (10 independently owned), 70 radio stations (68 are state-owned, with one in each region) and 4 television stations (3 independently owned) (Mattes & Gyimah-Boadi 2005: 253). The NDC governments, however, used an archaic colonial law of criminal libel, as well as other kinds of legislation and tactics, to constrain the exercise of free expression and break the will of journalists who challenged its authority (Tettey 2003). Nevertheless, the media played an instrumental role in monitoring state institutions and providing alternative channels for citizens to voice their opinions and for learning about and debating public issues. Since the NPP came to power, relaxed censorship, liberalisation of broadcasts, and repeal of the criminal libel law have helped to increase government accountability through the risk of exposure. However, the NPP government has also not shied away from using state intimidation against its opponents (ibid).

Ghana stands out as an exemplar of media freedom in Africa, but there are questions concerning the impact of these burgeoning media. The ability of the news media to promote accountability is limited by low levels of professionalism and integrity (see Hasty 2005). Furthermore, the media continue to be largely a space for the political expression of the elite and urban residents (Temin & Smith 2002). Print media circulate mostly in urban areas and are accessible only to the 53.4 per cent of the adult population that is literate; rural literacy stands at 39.8 per cent. Radio programming in local languages reaches the largest section of the population and is a staple source of information. However, 19 per cent of respondents in the 2002 *Afrobarometer* survey said they received news from television or radio a few times a month, if at all. Authors of the 2002 *Afrobarometer* report conclude that Ghanaian society remains basically illiterate in the sense that Ghanaians resort to aural and visual, rather than written, methods of acquiring and disseminating information generally, and particularly regarding politics (Gyimah-Boadi & Mensah 2003).

Freedoms granted by the Constitution also led to an explosion in the organisational landscape. This explosion had two sources. First, Ghanaian professionals who had fled during earlier military regimes returned to Ghana under the new democratic dispensation and set up think-tank types of organisations. Second, and more important, was a continued proliferation of service-delivery NGOs, which began in tandem with the implementation of structural adjustment in the second half of the 1980s, as a result of increased aid from donors and international NGOs channelled to non-governmental organisations. Third, the move by donors to promote 'civil society' also contributed to the mushrooming of Ghanaian NGOs, think-tanks and public policy advocacy networks.

The term *NGO* has become a homogenising façade for organisations with a wide range of origins, objectives and abilities. NGOs do not necessarily contribute to pushing the boundaries of political freedoms or enhancing democracy. NGOs can act both as a new type of patronage network and as an alternative site for political activism (Whitfield 2007). NGOs have become alternative employment opportunities to the public sector and sites of access to resources (computers, vehicles, foreign travel) partly because of structural adjustment, which has led to a reduction of the public sector, and partly because of the civil society paradigm that has channelled lucrative amounts of funding to 'civil society organisations'. These employment opportunities generate patronage networks linking rural to urban, private sector to public sector and donors to new elites. One could argue that the 'NGO sector', as it is often called, has produced a new class of elites, just as state patronage produced a political-administrative elite. Importantly, these patronage networks and the new class of elites are not dependent on the state and thus can be critical of it, but their funding by donors has mitigated their criticism of the government's financial and technical dependence on aid and the extent of donor participation in policy-making described below. Similar patterns occur in the assistance foreign NGOs provide to villages through intermediary Ghanaian NGOs.

NGOs can also serve as sites for political activism, a platform from which to challenge government policies. They can garner external resources, especially transnational leverage and financial support. They provide a vehicle through which political activists can channel their energies following the de-legitimisation of the Left and its ideologies with the adoption of structural adjustment. Students and intellectuals who were formerly members of the progressive organisations of the late 1970s and early 1980s can now be found working in the most outspoken advocacy NGOs such as the Integrated Social Development Centre and Third World Network-Africa. Linkages to global social movements and advocacy campaigns have been critical to the rise of advocacy NGOs in Ghana and the political activism they are leading, as illustrated in the anti-water privatisation campaign.

Despite these changes in the public sphere, have engagements between the public and political spheres changed? The PNDC strategy of excluding interest groups from participating in policy formulation gave way in the Fourth Republic to a more inclusive approach by the NDC government, which reconsidered several of its policies in light of public resistance and sometimes agreed to engage its critics in dialogue. More discussion over economic problems and policy options fostered a less polarised political environment in which trust could develop and political debate could cease to be always confrontational. Using the rhetoric and strategies of donor agencies, the NDC government consulted with various organised groups ('stakeholders') on specific government policies during the formulation stages and solicited their help and public support in implementation. As the language of civil society penetrated the African continent, organised groups donned the mantle of civil society to legitimise their bids to influence policy, or at least their right to be consulted (Whitfield 2003). The parameters of inclusion and the nature of engagement became the substance of political contestation. The opening of the policy platform to a wider body, along with the improvements to the electoral body, helped to bridge the old populist/liberal ideological divide.

Nevertheless, several problems have continued to plague public engagement with the political process under both the NDC and NPP governments. First, there is still a shortage of public information on government actions and policies. Second, the NPP government still reacts with hostility towards public criticism of its policies and perceives sources of such criticism as being opposed to the government, as was seen in the debates over the government's plan for urban water reform (Whitfield 2006). Third, given continuing poor levels of education, the ability of Ghanaian citizens to engage meaningfully in the public debate and political processes remains limited. The 2002 *Afrobarometer* survey found that nearly two-thirds of respondents say they find matters of politics and government too complicated to understand.

Decentralisation and Local Government

The District Assembly system introduced under the PNDC was incorporated into the 1992 Constitution without major changes (Ayee 1994). Seventy per cent of District Assembly members are elected by the district, with the remaining 30 per cent appointed by the President in consultation with chiefs and other interest groups, similar to the original two-thirds and one-third formula under PNDC law. District Secretaries were renamed District Chief Executives (DCEs), but remained the head of the Executive Committee responsible for the execution of Assembly decisions. DCEs are still appointed by the President, but they must be approved by two-thirds of Assembly members present and can be removed by a vote of two-thirds of all members. The most important innovation in the system is the creation of the District Assembly Common Fund, which provides the major source of revenue for District Assemblies. The non-partisan character of the Assembly was retained; candidates seeking election to a District Assembly or any sub-district structure must run as individuals and not as party candidates. The district sub-structures (Urban/Town/Area Councils and Unit Committees) were created to extend political participation to the lowest level. The Councils deliberate on issues and make recommendations to the District Assembly. They are not directly elected but consist of five Assembly members and the chairmen of Unit Committees in the area. The Unit Committees have fifteen members of whom ten are elected and five appointed by the DCE.

Not all of the elements of the local government system have been implemented and others do not function as intended. The general Assembly is supposed to serve as a representative organ, providing a voice for citizens in district-level decision-making through elected and appointed members. However, District Assemblies contain competing forms of representation – electoral, technocratic and central government representation. Electoral representation is the weakest among them, due to structural biases in the system, resource constraints of Assemblies and low levels of education among Assembly members relative to the political appointees and technocrats. The structure of authority in the District Assemblies is biased towards the DCE, who is the administrative and political head of the district and has more statutory power than the elected Presiding Member of the Assembly. The DCE presents national policies and programmes to the general Assembly and is paid by the central government, and the district civil servants are accountable to the DCE.

The Councils and Unit Committees are generally not functioning. When the Assembly system was introduced the NDC government did not make provision for the sub-district structures. Slowly elections for Unit Committees were held, but the physical establishment of buildings, paying for administrative staff and training of Committee members have been slow or non-existent. Assemblies are also under-resourced in terms of staff, skills, equipment and money. Both the NDC and NPP governments have been satisfied with waiting for external agencies to resource the local government structures. Donors and international NGOs provide human and financial resources to District Assemblies in selected districts, supporting their planning processes and increasing their budget. Districts without a patron do what they can with what they have. This situation raises the question of sustainability and of the government's commitment to decentralisation in the face of other pressures on the state purse.

Despite the resource constraints facing Assemblies, the NPP government created 28 new districts in 2004, increasing the total from 110 to 138 districts. President Kufuor claimed that the creation of additional districts was intended to deepen the decentralisation process and accelerate development, as each new district capital is to be provided with modern facilities. It is likely that the new districts were a political tool by the NPP to gain support before the December 2004 elections, because the central government will upgrade the small towns that become district capitals, increasing the access of local citizens to modern facilities and increasing their say over the use of resources allocated to the district level. In October 2007, President Kufuor approved the creation of a further 24 new districts, again on the grounds of deepening decentralisation and local governance at the grassroots level, but is it another strategic move ahead of the 2008 national elections?

Although the Assembly system increased the access of people living in previously neglected areas to government resources and institutions, initial enthusiasm has waned due to the inability of Assemblies to deliver public goods and services effectively. Voter turnout in District Assembly elections fell from 57.7 per cent in 1988-89 to 32.8 per cent in 2002 (statistics were not available on the most recent 2006 Assembly elections).[1] The increase in development projects has been marginal and often undertaken in collaboration with, or solely by, NGOs and donor agencies. The presence of aid agencies has also created legitimacy problems for District Assemblies, for even when they do carry out projects most local people mistakenly credit NGOs and donors (Ayee 2003). The Constitution encompasses a vision of decentralisation that provides a large degree of local control over resource allocation, but the state bureaucracy remains as centralised as before. Part of the reason stems from the lack of financial and manpower resources in the Assemblies and partly from contradictory legislation that keeps health and education staff under the control of their headquarters in Accra (ibid). In December 2007, the NPP government finally launched the long-awaited Local Government Service, which is supposed to decentralise control over resources and staff in government services, especially health and education. As in Senegal, decentralisation is an important context for the process of democratisation. In Ghana it is debatable if the process is leading to the empowerment of marginal communities or to the penetration of the periphery by the central state.

Elections: Electoral Spectacle or Democracy in Action?
The victories of Rawlings and the NDC in the 1992 and 1996 elections were the product of Rawlings' charisma, the party's support base forged from relationships with local elites through the decentralisation reforms, and the ability of Assembly members, revolutionary organs and other PNDC supporting groups to mobilise voters. Public investment in the rural areas was also an important factor. Donor aid projects enabled the PNDC to expand infrastructure and social amenities. Aubynn (2002) argues that the attractiveness of the NDC party was not ideology or policy programme, however, but pragmatism. Why did the NPP win in the

2000 elections? The NPP's victory is attributed to a combination of Rawlings' absence as a presidential candidate, the NDC national executives forcing candidates onto constituencies and leading some NDC members to stand as independent candidates, economic stagnation and high inflation, and innovations in the NPP's electoral campaign to cater to the urban youth vote (Nugent 2001).

These are the broad contours of political support that determined election results, but what factors determine the individual voter's electoral choice? Ghana's political system is marked by two features which stand out in the African context. First, voter alignment with political parties is not overshadowed by ethnic affinities or ethno-regional identities, although they do exist. Svanikier (2006) shows that the main cleavages in Ghanaian society are ethnic (Akan/non-Akan), class/status (elite/commoner), geographic (urban/rural) and religious (Christian/Muslim), with the latter being rather insignificant. I would add a second geographic cleavage between the northern and southern parts of the country. The underdevelopment of the north is present in the political consciousness of northerners and affects their electoral choice, evidenced by strong support for a third party, the People's National Convention (PNC), in certain areas.

There is a general overlap between region and ethnicity, similar to most African countries. Election results since 1992 show an ethno-regional pattern to voting. The three most northerly regions and the Volta region (all non-Akan) have consistently gone to the NDC, while the southern, Akan-dominant regions have gone to the NPP. Ethnicity actually plays out in voting patterns within regions, between Akan and non-Akan groups located near each other, with NPP supporters being largely Akan and NDC supporters largely non-Akan (Nugent 2005). This pattern also holds true within constituencies. If Akan is the dominant ethnicity, non-Akan are likely to vote for the NDC (Svanikier 2005). The NPP lost seats in Accra due to the Ga peoples, the majority ethnic group, feeling a sense of alienation from the dominantly Akan ruling elite. However, the NPP also failed to deliver on its promises of jobs and provision of basic amenities. The three northern regions and the northern part of the Volta region are the most impoverished regions in Ghana, which indicates that the NDC attracts the vote of the poor and the marginalised, overlapping ethnic factors with economic and status factors. Svanikier (2006) argues that the relative weights of the four cleavages wax and wane over time, and that party support is explained by three factors: (i) ethnic hegemony/ethnic marginalisation, (ii) social tensions among status groups, and (iii) the competition between existing and aspiring elites.

The second key feature of Ghana's political system is a high degree of party identification. Lindberg and Morrison (2005) show that about 82 per cent of the electorate are loyal party supporters, forming the *core* voters of each party. The remaining 18 per cent are *swing* voters who switch from one party to another and who effectively decide the fate of the election. Comparing Lindberg and Morrison's analysis of the 2000 election with Nugent's analysis of the 2004 election, we see clearly the core voter trend and the importance of the swing voters. The regional voting pattern in 2004 was similar to the 2000 elections. The NDC won its traditional strongholds in the three northern regions and the Volta region, thus holding on to its core voters, but the NPP increased the number of its parliamentary seats, indicating that it gained swing voters in these regions. The six other regions went to the NPP, but there was a swing towards the NDC in three of them, with the NDC increasing its share of the vote over its performance in 2000. In eight of the ten regions, both parties shared the votes almost equally, with Ashanti and Volta being the exceptions. In sum, a majority of voters come from ethnic backgrounds other than Ashanti and Ewe, do not vote as a bloc, and ultimately evaluate the two parties on factors other than ethnicity. It is this dynamic that makes Ghanaian elections unpredictable and discourages politicians from emphasising ethnicity (Fridy 2007).

The NDC put up a tough fight in the 2004 elections and still constitutes a viable alternative. Rawlings was very visible and vocal in the NDC electoral campaign, arguably overshadowing its presidential candidate J.A. Mills. There is debate within the party on whether Rawlings' loud presence is killing the party's chances of regaining power and whether the party can survive without Rawlings because he is crucial to mobilising votes.

One of the weaknesses of many African democracies is the absence of a cohesive and credible opposition. Ghana's strong opposition may be the result of its having been in government in the recent past and having benefited from access to the state purse. The Nkrumahist versus Danquah/Busia divide produced by the country's nationalist politics faded as these two political traditions found common ground in their opposition to Rawlings and the NDC in the 1990s. The Nkrumahist tradition also lost its cohesion, splintering into several parties, and largely lost the mantle of the populist/radical party which the NDC picked up. Thus, there are still two dominant parties divided ideologically into the social democrats (NDC) and the liberal-conservatives (NPP). However, this ideological divide has been tempered both by the extensive involvement of donors in policy-making and by the fact that both parties believe in an active role for the state in economic development (Whitfield & Jones 2009).

Ghana's two-party system looks likely to remain stable, despite the breakaway of key figures from both parties and their establishment of splinter parties in recent years.[2] These new parties do not look likely to take a significant number of members away from the NDC or NPP. Despite this recent splintering and internal divisions within the NPP and NDC, these parties still look stable and dominant. Perhaps the strength of Ghana's party system is that the two parties have managed for the most part to keep factional struggles within the parties, leading to a large degree of party consolidation as opposed to the continuous splintering of parties seen in other African countries such as Senegal.

In sum, Ghana has perfected the ritual of elections and its voting patterns are reassuring for representative democracy, but to what extent are elections institutions through which citizens can hold their leaders accountable? The link between party loyalty and political patronage is still salient. In rural areas, political relations are largely dominated by patron-client ties and unequal communication between politicians and sections of the electorate, especially in the three northern regions which are some of the poorest (van Walraven 2002). For this reason, incumbency has immense advantages, which include skimming off state resources into party coffers; blurring the line between the state and ruling party during electoral campaigns; and commanding allegiance because of the perception that development projects go to areas supporting the ruling party and loans, contracts and jobs go to individuals who are known supporters of the ruling government (CDD-Ghana 2004a,b).

The patronage-based politics of past multiparty eras persists, but it is weakening. While politics is still dominated by personalities and party manifestos are barely heard outside of Accra, voters are demanding socio-economic development in the form of generalised benefits for their community. Citizen-politician linkages have historically consisted of both representation and patronage to varying degrees. In Ghana, political parties are channels of representation, but they are weak channels. One reason is the limited ability of citizens to use their vote meaningfully in a situation of information shortage (a problem that is not Africa-specific). There is a general lack of information (or existence of misinformation) about the incumbent party's performance and about the contesting parties' policies and plans. This lack of information/misinformation results partly from limited public access to information about the incumbent government, partly from poor access to the media in rural areas and small towns, and partly from the high level of illiteracy.

A second reason that parties are weak channels is that voters may be demanding socio-economic development but they cannot translate these demands into effective pressure on politicians to deliver. In most parts of the country, parties are active only around election time, and they are not based on sustained political mobilisation but rather on transient activities designed to mobilise the votes necessary to win elections. The individual income-poor voter has limited means with which to exert pressure on parties or politicians to pursue issues or to hold them accountable. Lastly, in the current situation where official and private aid agencies provide (or are seen to provide) a large portion of basic goods and services, public attention is diverted away from holding politicians to account for these services and lessens the demand on local and central government to provide them.

The Politics of Aid Dependence

Since the mid-1980s, Ghanaian governments have relied on foreign aid to service the country's external debt burden and to finance a significant amount of its development expenditure. In 2005, official development assistance was equivalent to 10.6 percent of Gross National Income, fluctuating around that level since 1988.[3] Apart from their economic impact, these continuous large inflows of aid over the last two decades, and the operations of official aid agencies that go along with them, have had significant effects on the institutions and processes of governance as well as state-society relations. These political effects have produced another type of aid dependence, where official and private aid agencies are embedded within the state and society of the country. This embeddedness has thrown up new political dynamics, such that politics is the product of the multiple interfaces between the ruling elite, civil service, official aid agencies, Ghanaian organised interest groups and NGOs and international NGOs. These multiple interfaces increase the possible variations of alliances within and between these 'categories' of actors and the political leverage available to them. This embedded aid system has implications for democratic governance.

One side-effect of extensive donor involvement in policy-making processes is their attempts to reduce the inherently political process of economic development in general, and policy-making in particular, to technical administrative ones through the use of conditionality and technical assistance which claim to provide the 'right policies' and 'international best practices'. The NDC and NPP governments have attempted to maintain control over the policy agenda despite aid dependence in roughly the same ways, using strategies of non-implementation of conditions, reversing previously implemented conditions and producing policies and plans that are compromises between what donors want and what parts of the Ghanaian government want (Whitfield & Jones 2009). These strategies have resulted in the fragmentation of control over policy-making, allowing the government to externalise responsibility for policy and outcomes to donors when it wishes, thus blurring lines of accountability. With the country's improved economic fortunes in recent years (high growth rates, access to new sources of finance, discovery of oil), the second NPP government has taken more policy initiatives and is asserting its own vision of development. However, it currently remains dependent on aid from traditional donors.

Another side-effect is that donors create paradoxes as their attempts to support 'good governance' actually constrain and sometimes override institutions and processes of representative democracy (Whitfield 2005). Donors support the strengthening of democratic institutions like Parliament to play a larger role in governance, particularly in holding the executive to account, but the economic clout of donors and their position in the policy-making terrain also limit the role that representative institutions can play. Furthermore, aid practices accentuate the strong role of the executive and sideline Parliament through the creation of numerous arenas, attached to the constitutional and normal civil service processes, where donors and ministries negotiate policy. The complexity of the aid system makes it harder for Parliament to provide oversight of the donor-government relationship, and the under-resourced nature of Parliament has turned it into another hand seeking donor funds.

As mentioned earlier, access to information about government policies and actions is still difficult, even under the NPP. In one way, donors can serve as a source of information for citizens about government policies and as a mechanism through which citizens can put pressure on the government to be more transparent. On the other hand, donor interventions into policy debates can also exacerbate the lack of transparency and information on the part of the government.

Donors can act as partners to groups in Ghanaian society to push through policies or exert pressure on the government, but they can also act as competitors, competing for influence over the government and taking opposing positions on policies. Competition for influence often takes the guise of debates over who represents the interests of the poor. While some donors want to be seen as representing the interests of the poor only to legitimise their position, others actually believe themselves to represent the poor vis-à-vis the Ghanaian government. These claims come up against counter-claims by groups in Ghanaian society to represent the interests of the poor.

If the link between elections, representation, and accountability of the government was always doubtful in Ghana, it is even more so in the current situation where donors provide a large portion of the funding for these services and influence policies regarding them, and NGOs play a crucial role in delivering them. Citizens cannot demand more and better services from the government when it has ceded this role and when no formal accountability mechanisms link Ghanaian citizens with donors and NGOs. While the latter claim to have their own mechanisms for consultation and beneficiary participation, whether these mechanisms form accountability linkages is very doubtful. These relations among government, non-state actors and external agencies observed at the national level have parallels at the district level. Regional and district-based NGOs have sprouted to soak up resources flowing into the local development aid market.

Donors are pushing decentralisation and trying to build model local government institutions, but in the process replicating patterns of aid dependence in the District Assemblies.

Ghana resembles Senegal under President Wade in terms of the degree of aid dependence, but the political consequences of aid in Senegal appear to be different from those in Ghana. While resources from aid networks are intimately tied to patronage systems in both countries, the multilateralisation of aid sources to bring in American and Arab and Islamic sources seems to have served to weaken erstwhile French clientelism in Senegal, while at the same time bolstering Wade's personal power.

Conclusion

As in Senegal, the alternation of ruling parties after the 2000 Ghanaian elections was heralded as a sign of consolidating democracy. Standing back from theoretical assumptions and moving closer to politics on the ground since then, what has been the real significance of this alternation? On the positive side, it has further entrenched formal democratic procedures and elite acceptance of the possibility of losing power through elections. Some have argued that increased electoral competition may be changing the nature of patronage politics; pork-barrel politicking will continue in the near future but may increasingly take the form of providing widely shared goods rather than special privileges to politician's home towns (Booth *et al.* 2004). Under the NPP government, media freedom has increased and the extent to which people feared to criticise the government has significantly decreased; in Ghana there has not been a crackdown on the media as in Wade's Senegal.

The limits to alternation become clear when we look at how the NPP government has acted in similar ways to the previous NDC government. Presidentialism persists. One of the NPP's campaign promises in 2000 was to make the District Chief Executive an elected office, but the government has not yet done so nor does it look likely that it will. Furthermore, President Kufuor's attempts to shore up the NPP's control of Parliament and his own political support base in the party have weakened the legislative and oversight functions of Parliament. Second, local politics and elite competition over the state continue to be intertwined in ways that can produce political instability, as is the case with the Yendi crisis.[4] Third, relations between the government and the business community remain politicised. Some Ghanaian businesses have become associated with either the NDC or the NPP, and each party favours its allies and discriminates against those of its opponents when in power. While the NPP government named its rule the Golden Age of Business, the business community remains dominated by political favouritism with big contracts and investment opportunities swayed by perceptions of 'which side you are on' (Luckham *et al.* 2005). Finally, the NPP government is in the same situation of aid dependence, and it has, until very recently, reacted to the constraints and opportunities of the embedded aid system in much the same way.

An important change that has made elections work as a mechanism through which citizens choose a set of elites to govern the state is elite consensus. Political elites forged a consensus that elections are to play this role, agreed to improve the electoral process so as to make the outcomes credible and accepted the fact of alternating political parties in power. This achievement should not be underestimated, since it is yet to be achieved in many African countries, and it has brought political stability to a country devastated by instability in the past. This elite consensus did not automatically result from reintroducing multiparty elections, but rather from an intentional process associated with them. The factors compelling this process may have included the extent of economic decline witnessed during the late 1970s and 1980s and memories of personal repression under military governments. Economic reforms under structural adjustment and the extensive influence of foreign aid agencies decreased the prize at stake in contestations over control of the state. Furthermore, those on the political Left rejected revolution in return for the political and civil rights of liberal democracy. Representative democracy is accepted as the starting framework within which to push for issues on the agenda of social democrats and economic nationalists.

Further democratic achievements, however, are obstructed by several structural factors. As this chapter shows, some of these factors relate to the political system on paper, some to the way it works in practice, and some to the structure of Ghanaian society. A major obstacle to generating democratic accountability is socio-economic development. Ghanaians have begun to realise the significance of their voting power, but this cannot compensate for the lack of socio-economic development that would provide increased political equality between the social strata (van Walraven 2002: 198). Since the early 1980s, Ghana's economy has grown steadily, but this growth has not been accompanied by structural transformation and is not perceived to have delivered improved living standards or generated enough jobs (Aryeetey & Kanbur 2006). But if the country continues on the current path of rising GDP growth rate from 3.7 per cent in 2000 to 6.7 per cent in 2007, this growth may have significant effects on domestic politics. The Fourth Republic is a successful democratic experiment if evaluated from the perspective of past attempts and in comparison with the African continent as a whole, but it still faces many challenges.

Notes

1. 'Workshop on the Legal and Institutional Framework for District Level Elections', draft workshop report, unpublished.
2. Obed Asamoah broke away from the NDC and formed the Democratic Freedom Party in October 2006, after losing leadership of the national executive in December 2005 and feeling that the rift between him and Rawlings was too great to mend. Key members of the NPP broke away and established the Reformed Patriotic Democrats in October 2007, a move which seems to be motivated by a group of young NPP members feeling stifled by the older generation.
3. Source: OECD Development Assistance Committee development statistics, accessed at www.oecd.org/dac/statistics.
4. The Yendi crisis is the term given to the state of affairs since the paramount chief of the Dagomba kindom, whose palace is in Yendi (in the northern region), was murdered in 2002. It is linked to a dispute over the succession of the Yendi paramount chief that became enmeshed in party politics back in the 1950s. When the NPP won the 2000 elections, the side of the chieftancy dispute aligned with the Danquah/Busia tradition attacked and killed the chief who came from the other royal family. It is believed that high-level politicians in the NPP government were involved. No one has been arrested for the murder and, at the time of writing, the succession crisis had not been resolved. For more, see MacGaffey (2006) and Agyeman-Duah (2006).

References

Agyeman-Duah, Ivor. 2006. *Between Faith and History: A biography of J.A. Kufuor.* Banbury, UK: Ayebia Clarke Publishing.

(APRM) African Peer Review Mechanism. 2005. Country Review Report of the Republic of Ghana. Accessed at www.nepad.org.

Aryeetey, Ernest, Jane Harrigan, and Machiko Nissanke. 2000. *Economic Reforms in Ghana: The miracle and the mirage.* Oxford: James Currey.

Aryeetey, Ernest and Ravi Kanbur. 2006. Ghana's Economy at Half Century: an Overview of Stability, Growth and Poverty, Cornell University Working Paper 2006-04. Ithaca, NY: Department of Applied Economics and Management, Cornell University.

Aubynn, Anthony. 2002. Behind the Transparent Ballot Box: The Significance of the 1990s Elections in Ghana. In *Multi-party Elections in Africa*, eds Michael Cowen and Liisa Laakso. Oxford: James Currey.

Ayee, Joseph. 1994. *An Anatomy of Public Policy Implementation.* Aldershot: Avebury.

——. 2003. Local Government, Decentralization and State Capacity in Ghana. In *Critical Perspectives on Politics and Socioeconomic Development in Ghana*, eds Wisdom Tettey, Korbula Puplampu and Bruce Berman. Leiden: Brill.

Boafo-Arthur, Kwame. 2005. Longitudinal View on Ghana's Parliamentary Practices. In *African Parliaments: Between governance and government*, ed. M. A. M. Salih. New York: Palgrave Macmillan.

Booth, David, Richard Crook, Emmanuel Gyimah-Boadi, Tony Killick, and Robin Luckham. 2004. Drivers of Change in Ghana, Overview Report. Report for DFID Ghana for the country situation assessment based on a Drivers of Change analysis.

Cameron, Geoffrey. 2008. National Human Rights Commissions and Government Accountability in New Democracies: A comparative study of Ghana and Nigeria. MPhil. thesis, Department of Politics and International Relations, University of Oxford.

CDD-Ghana (Centre for Democratic Development-Ghana). 2004a. Abuse of Incumbency, State administrative Resources and Political Corruption in Election 2003-Part I. Briefing Paper Vol.6, No.4.

——. 2004b. Abuse of Incumbency, State administrative Resources and Political Corruption in Election 2003-Part II. Briefing Paper vol.6 no.5.

——. 2005. Appointment and 'Vetting' of Ministerial Nominees: constitutional and other challenges. Briefing Paper Vol.7 No.1.

Chazan, Naomi. 1987. The Anomalies of Continuity: Perspectives on Ghanaian Elections Since Independence. In *Elections in Independent Africa*, ed. F. Hayward. Boulder, CO and London: Westview Press.

Fridy, Kevin. 2007. The Elephant, Umbrella, and Quarrelling Cocks: Disaggregating partisanship in Ghana's Fourth Republic. *African Affairs* 106:281-305.

Gyimah-Boadi, Emmanuel and Kwabena Mensah. 2003. The Growth of Democracy in Ghana Despite Economic Dissatisfaction: A power alternation bonus?: Afrobarometer Working Paper No. 28, www.afrobarometer.org/abseries.html.

Hasty, Jennifer. 2005. *The Press and Political Culture in Ghana.* Bloomington, IN: Indiana University Press.

Hutchful, Eboe. 2002. *Ghana's Adjustment Experience: The paradox of reform.* Oxford: James Currey.

Keith, Adam. 2005. Invigorating Ghana's Lagging Anticorruption Agenda: Instruments for enhanced civic involvement. Accra: Center for Democratic Development-Ghana, *Briefing Paper* Vol.7, No.1.

Lindberg, Staffan with Yongmei Zhou. forthcoming 2009. The Rise and Decline of Parliament of Ghana. In *Legislatures in Emerging Democracies*, ed. Joel Barkan.

Lindberg, Staffan and Minion Morrison. 2005. Exploring Voter Alignments in Africa: Core and swing voters in Ghana. *Journal of Modern African Studies* 43 (4):565-86.

Luckham, Robin, with Emmanuel Gyimah-Boadi, William Ahadzie, and Nana Boateng. 2005. The Middle Classes and their Role in National Development, *Overseas Development Institute Policy Brief* No.3. London: Overseas Development Institute.

MacGaffey, Wyatt. 2006. Death of a King, Death of a Kingdom? Social pluralism and succession to high office in Dagbon, northern Ghana. *Journal of Modern African Studies* 44 (1):79-99.

Mattes, Robert and Emmanuel Gyimah-Boadi. 2005. Ghana and South Africa. In *Assessing the Quality of Democracy*, eds Larry Diamond and Leonardo Morlino. Baltimore, MD: Johns Hopkins University Press.

Ninsin, Kwame. 1998. Postscript: Elections, Democracy and Elite Consensus. In *Ghana: Transition to*

Democracy, ed. Kwame Ninsin. Dakar: CODESRIA.

———— (ed.). 1998. *Ghana: Transition to democracy*. Dakar: CODESRIA.

Nugent, Paul. 1995. *Big Men, Small Boys and Politics in Ghana: Power, ideology and the burden of history, 1982-94*. London: Pinter.

————. 2001. Winners, Losers and Also Rans: money, moral authority and voting patterns in the Ghana 2000 elections. *African Affairs* 100: 405-28.

————. 2005. Reading the 2004 Elections Results in Ghana: National swings and the dynamic in the Volta Region. Paper read at African Studies Association (US) Annual Conference, at Washington, DC. 17-20 November.

Osei, Philip, 2000. Political Liberalisation and the Implementation of Value Added Tax in Ghana. *Journal of Modern African Studies* 38 (2): 225-78.

Svanikier, Johanna. 2005. An Overview of Ghana's 2004 Elections. Paper presented to the African History and Politics seminar, University of Oxford.

————. 2006. 'Ghana's 2004 elections: Ethnicity, class and the legacy of Ghana's two dominant political traditions.' Paper presented at the African History and Politics Seminar, University of Oxford, 13 February.

————. 2007. Political Elite Circulation in Ghana: Implications for leadership diversity and democratic regime stability in Ghana. *Comparative Sociology* 6.

Temin, Jonathan, and Daniel Smith. 2002. Media Matters: Evaluating the Role of the Media in Ghana's 2000 Elections. *African Affairs* 101: 585-605.

Tettey, Wisdom. 2003. The Mass Media, Political Expression and Democratic Transition. In *Critical Perspectives on Politics and Socioeconomic Development in Ghana*, eds Wisdom Tettey, Korbula Puplampu and Bruce Berman. Leiden: Brill.

van Walraven, Klaas. 2002. The End of an Era: the Ghanaian elections of December 2000. *Journal of Contemporary African Studies* 20 (2):184-202.

Whitfield, Lindsay. 2003. Civil Society as Idea and Civil Society as Process: The Case of Ghana. *Oxford Development Studies* 31 (3):379-400.

————. 2005. Democracy as Idea and Democracy as Process: the politics of democracy and development in Ghana. D.Phil. thesis in Politics, University of Oxford.

————. 2006. The Politics of Urban Water Reform in Ghana. *Review of African Political Economy* 33 (109): 425-48.

————. 2007. Identity Construction in Development Practices: the government of Ghana, civil society, private sector and development partners. In *Professional Identities: Policy and practice in business and bureaucracy*, ed. Fiona Moore and Shirley Ardner. Oxford: Berghahn.

Whitfield, Lindsay and Emily Jones. 2009. Ghana: Breaking out of Aid dependence? Political and Economic Barriers to Ownership. In *The Politics of Aid: African strategies for dealing with donors*, ed. Lindsay Whitfield. Oxford: Oxford University Press.

5

Nigeria since 1999
A Revolving Door Syndrome
or the Consolidation of Democracy?

ABDUL RAUFU MUSTAPHA

In 1999 Nigeria returned to civilian rule after fifteen years of military dictatorship. Nigeria represents one of the most severe challenges to democratisation in Africa; the state struggles to control a complex and fractious society while also contending with democratic demands. The impetus for democratisation is embedded in popular aspirations and the political culture, even when the state has failed to provide adequate institutional anchors for the flourishing of democratic expression. Like Ghana, post-colonial Nigeria witnessed many destabilising coups, but, unlike Ghana, Nigeria also experienced very high levels of ethnic and religious conflict. Still, their political trajectories could be said to be relatively similar with repeated cycles of coups and re-civilianisation: the so-called revolving door syndrome. The main divergence between the two countries has come with the latest processes of democratisation. While Ghana is gradually consolidating its democratic system and institutions, Nigerian democratisation remains fraught with disputes over fundamental issues and mired in undemocratic methods of contestation. Despite the efforts of the judiciary since 2006, the rules of the game are neither clear nor are they generally accepted. Nigeria therefore represents a process of democratisation in which struggles over fundamental issues continue to generate, rather than resolve, uncertainty.

Table 5.1 Governments and Leaders of Nigeria, 1976-2008

Date	Head of Government	Regime Type
Feb. 1976-Sept. 1979	General Olusegun Obasanjo	Military
Oct. 1979-Dec. 1983	Shehu Shagari	Elected civilian
Jan. 1984-Aug. 1985	General Mohammadu Buhari	Military
Aug. 1985-Aug. 1993	General Ibrahim Babangida	Military
Aug. 1993-Nov. 1993	Ernest Shonekan	Unelected civilian
Nov. 1993-June 1998	General Sani Abacha	Military
June 1998-May 1999	General Abdusalami Abubakar	Military
May 1999-May 2007	Olusegun Obasanjo	Elected civilian
May 2007-	Umaru Musa Yar' Adua	Elected civilian

There are some unique features of the Nigerian state and society which inform this process of democratisation. Its size and diversity are not comparable with any other African country. With about 140 million citizens, over 300 ethno/linguistic groups, and entrenched religious, regional and cultural diversity, Nigeria represents the institutionalisation and politicisation of diversity. The differences have been wired into the structures of the state from colonial times, particularly the differences between the northern and southern halves which under colonialism had different educational, legal, local government, and land tenure systems. Unlike other large British colonies such as India and Sudan, which had single colonial administrations, Nigeria had two. Furthermore, even in the heat of anti-colonialism, Nigerian politicians never developed a single nationalist movement. Different ethno-regional blocs threw up competing movements and nationalist champions. Many years of military rule and the role of oil rents have further complicated matters. Democratisation in Nigeria has therefore been influenced by four major factors: competing ethno-regionalism; many years of military authoritarianism; the prominence of oil rents in state revenue; and economic crises which became manifest from the early 1980s.

Given this fractious context, many observers have characterised Nigeria as chaotic and even ungovernable, with little prospect for democratisation. Emphasis is placed in such analyses on the high levels of corruption and intractable 'patrimonialism', the growing role of ethnic militias in various parts of the country, the collapse of public order in the Niger Delta, and the farcical elections of 2007. Others, like Chabal and Daloz (2006) even suggest that the ungovernability of Nigerian society is deeply rooted in cultural norms. While most Nigerians will recognise the dysfunctional features alluded to in these analyses, they do not approach their country or its democratic prospects with the same pessimism (cf. Lewis & Bratton 2000: 8). Nigerians are keenly aware of the continuing capabilities of their errant state. To date, Nigeria has not been overwhelmed by its social conflicts, as is the case with Côte d'Ivoire or Sudan. Repeated forecasts of the imminent disintegration of the country have come to naught precisely because the state has always been able to see off challenges to its core interests. Through the use of superior force, and political and constitutional devices like federalism, ethnic balancing, the manipulation of the party system, and a majoritarian presidency, the Nigerian state continues to dominate its space even in the face of serious challenges to its authority (cf. Mustapha 2002, 2006).

Within the African context, Nigeria is not a case of a weak and corrupt state with a patrimonial political culture (needing state-building), but one of a relatively strong, but corrupt state, confronted by a militantly assertive population (needing democratisation). Despite years of military dominance of the state, the military has never been able to establish a hegemonic justification of its continued stay in power; military rule always remained contingent on a promise of return to democracy. Writing in 1995 at the height of the terror unleashed by the Abacha junta, a prominent Kenyan political scientist noted that 'the independence of mind of Nigerians continues to be resilient'.[1] In a similar vein, Bratton et al. (2005: 326) note the assertiveness of the Nigerian public when they state that 'Demand for democracy in Nigeria (65 per cent) greatly exceeds perceived supply (46 per cent), suggesting that competition continues between elites and masses over the form of the political regime.'

The social struggles that framed the return to civilian rule in 1999 put the demand for accountability well before the demand for stability; democratisation is more prominent than 'state-building' in the political imagination of most Nigerians. Much of what outside observers characterise as ungovernability, most Nigerians will consider as legitimate contestation. Some of the chaos accompanying democratisation has revolved around competing notions of interest representation within a non-military vision of the country. The struggles leading to the return to democratic rule in 1999 suggest the types of governance challenges which many Nigerians expected the democratic government to address: that politics will be demilitarised; that many interests hitherto inadequately represented in the contested federal system will find better representation through the return to 'true federalism'; that there should be fiscal federalism and greater recognition of the rights of the minority nationalities, particularly in the Niger Delta; that improved accountability will stem the tide of corruption and arbitrariness associated with military rule; and that ordinary citizens will enjoy greater freedoms and an improvement in their economic circumstances – the oft-mentioned 'dividend of democracy'. Democratisation in 1999 was therefore not about stability, but about establishing a more legitimate state in tune with the aspirations of the majority of the citizenry. The key issue for Nigerians is whether democratisation has met these expectations.

In this chapter, I argue that Nigeria's experience of democracy has been contradictory. On the one hand, the burning desire to remove the military from politics in 1999 has largely been achieved. On the other, expectations of increased state accountability, legitimacy, and improved popular livelihoods have not materialised. While many important reforms have taken place since 1999, fundamental constitutional and governance problems have festered and even become worse in some instances. The frontiers of individual and group freedoms have both expanded and contracted during the same period. Since 1999, Nigeria seems to be stranded between authoritarianism and democratisation. Two reasons may be suggested for this contradictory experience: the hugeness of the challenges faced, and the specific failure of leadership under President Obasanjo.

Democratisation and the Challenge of Diversity

Democratisation in 1999 occurred against the background of a number of serious handicaps. The constitution imposed by the military just days before the handover of power did not have legitimacy. Many ethnic and regional interests did not feel adequately represented in the new democratic system and fundamental questions about the nature of Nigerian federalism were not resolved; in particular, questions such as the division of powers between the centre and the constitutive units, the number of the constitutive units, fiscal federalism which is often referred to in popular discourse as 'resource control', and the decentralisation of the police force. Secondly, the constitution did not establish a sufficiently robust mechanism for the reconciliation of conflicting interests. It was itself the immediate object of contestation as many interests continued to agitate for the convocation of a Sovereign National Conference. The new democratic system faced spirited challenges from a range of interests. These were made worse by economic, ethnic and religious tensions that had built up in the authoritarian military period still bubbling under the surface. Consequently, the magnitude of the challenge of managing the complex political situation is an important context for understanding the trajectory of Nigerian democratisation. Instead of democratisation providing a platform for the peaceful and constructive resolution of conflicts in society, it provided a 'vent for violence' by allowing long repressed frustrations to rush to the fore. The three most important conflicts that have defined the process of democratisation are the rash of ethnic violence that erupted after 1999, the declaration of full *Sharia* law in some northern states, and the escalating violence in the Niger Delta.

Ethnic Conflicts

The democratic opening gave vent to pent-up ethno-regional frustrations. New sectarian fears were also unleashed. The frequency of ethnic and communal clashes increased alarmingly from 1999; between May 1999 and February 2002, over 10,000 people are estimated to have lost their lives in 33 reported ethnic, religious and regional conflicts across Nigeria (Mustapha 2004). Illustrative of these conflicts is the conflict around the Jos Plateau, which claimed thousands of lives from 2001 to May 2004, and left 200,000 homeless (OCHA-IRIN, n.d). By 2003 there were 750,000 Internally Displaced Persons in the country as a result of post-1999 sectarian violence.[2] These events not only highlighted the fragile foundations for democratisation, they also influenced the style of managing power and contributed to a drift away from democratic ideals. Faced with non-democratic challenges, the Obasanjo administration was quick to adopt equally undemocratic responses.

Another destabilising aspect of ethnicity in the post-1999 period was the allegation of ethnic favouritism levelled against President Obasanjo. While many accused him of discrimination in favour of his ethnic Yoruba kin, others, particularly the Igbo and Hausa-Fulani elites, accused him of discrimination against them. According to the late northern activist, Wada Nas, at one point key figures in the financial management of the state were all ethnic Yoruba. Many northern elites, long favoured in bureaucratic appointments by the military regimes of Babangida and Abacha, were quick to point out that vital parastatals like Nigerian Telecommunications, the Nigerian Deposit Insurance Corporation and the Nigerian National Petroleum Company were all headed at one time under Obasanjo by ethnic Yoruba.

Similar allegations of ethnic favouritism were made with respect to the security apparatuses of the state. Prior to the creation of the positions of Deputy Inspector General of the Police, three out of the six Assistant Inspectors General (AIG) based at Police Headquarters were alleged to be ethnic Yoruba. And of the eight AIGs in charge of zonal commands, six were said to belong to the same ethnic group. Of the six strategic services, the Army, Navy, Air Force, Police, State Security and External Intelligence, only one, the Air Force, was said to be headed by a northerner. At the divisional command level within the Army, it was claimed that only one of the five divisions was headed by a northerner. Of the three most senior posts within the Air Force, only one was said to be held by a northerner. Igbos and northerners, particularly Hausa-Fulani, are said to be disadvantaged; even a highly respected politician like Shettima Ali Monguno accused Obasanjo of the 'Yorubanisation' of the Nigerian state (Nas 2002).[3]

Democratisation took place in the context of ethnic imbalances within some institutions of the state caused in part by the arbitrariness of previous military regimes (Mustapha 2004). Correcting these imbalances posed political challenges which the Obasanjo presidency failed to manage adequately. Since democratisation, the influence of 'moderate' ethnic organisations like Afenifere, Ohaneze and Arewa Consultative Forums has waned, some claim, due to their undermining by Obasanjo. Their places have been taken by more 'extremist' ethnic organisations such as the O'odua People's Congress (OPC), the Movement for the Actualisation of the Sovereign State of Biafra (MASSOB), and the Movement for the Emancipation of the Niger Delta (MEND). Under Obasanjo there was the increasing militarisation of ethnic demands by these latter organisations and continued demand for an ethnic federation like Ethiopia's through the Pro National Conference group (PRONACO).

Sharia

Closely associated with the challenge of ethno-regional conflict is the factor of Islamic radicalisation, which found expression in the declaration of full *Sharia* law in twelve states in the far north of the country. Shortly after May 1999, Zamfara State led the way in declaring 100 per cent *Sharia*. This was a unilateral repudiation of the complex compromise ironed out by northern regional leaders – Muslims and Christians alike – in 1958 which formed the basis of the regional Penal Code. Since 1977, there had been the increasing politicisation of religion, as northern politicians, now split up into many states, sought to use Islam as an alternative rallying platform to defunct regional institutions. While the 1958 Penal Code restricted *Sharia* to civil matters and abolished *hudud* punishments, such as the cutting of limbs and the stoning to death of adulterers, the new *Sharia* move unleashed by Zamfara sought to extend *Sharia* to criminal matters and re-introduced some *hudud* punishments (Sanusi 2002).

This move was as controversial as it was unilateral. There is no doubt that the declaration of *Sharia* had massive popular support within the Islamic populations of the northern states. Many were disappointed by the corruption and lack of moral rectitude that blighted the country under the military and saw a return to the simple, tried and tested judicial norms of Islam as the best way forward. There were also long-run historical, millenarian and psychological impulses which propelled this hankering for a return to Islamic norms (Last 2002, 2007, 2008). Drawing on this popular backing, many northern politicians saw *Sharia* as an opportunity for generating electoral support and, in some cases, mobilising a huge personal following. Collectively, northern political, military and bureaucratic elites which had been dominant in the governance of Nigeria could use the political heat generated by *Sharia* to shield their poor record of achievement from popular scrutiny (Karmanje 2003).

In the post-11 September 2001 world, many Western analysts completely misread the *Sharia* crisis and the associated Islamic radicalisation taking place in Nigeria. For example, former US ambassador to Nigeria, Princeton Lyman, stated that, after Al-Qaeda was chased out of Afghanistan, it shifted base to Nigeria where its influence was growing by the day. Lyman reportedly claims that Al-Qaeda is surreptitiously training young Muslims and building bases in Nigeria. The justification for Al-Qaeda targeting Nigeria is said to be Nigeria's closeness to Washington and the increasing dependence of the US on Nigerian oil.[4] Though two tiny Islamist fringe groups, generically tagged as the 'Taliban' in the media, took up arms against the Nigerian state in northeastern Nigeria in 2003 and in Kano in 2007, and were crushed by the army, the real motives and focus for Islamic radicalisation and the resurgence of *Sharia* are largely local and national. These disturbances fall squarely within the centuries-old psychological and millenarian traditions of Islam in northern Nigeria, and have little, if any, links with international terrorism (cf. Colonial Office 1904; Lubeck 1985; Hiskett 1987; Loimeier 2005). While some foreign funding and inspiration have come from Saudi Arabia, Iran, Egypt, and Pakistan – all part of the global Muslim *Umma* or community with which many in Nigeria identified – the immediate post-1999 Islamist events fed on more embedded societal trends relating to the moral panic caused by change, restive youth, and the intra-Islamic sectarian/ideological conflicts between the fundamentalist *Izala* and the more traditional *sufi* orders of the Tijjaniyya and Quadiriyya.[5] The focus of Islamic radicalism in northern Nigeria is largely the distribution of political and economic power within the country and within the Muslim communities, feeding on mass alienation from the state and its institutions.

The management of the *Sharia* crisis highlights some of the embedded strengths of the Nigerian state alluded to in the introduction. The federalist Constitution was used effectively by both sides to defend their positions. The states cited the Constitution – not the Koran – to defend their rights to adopt full *Sharia*. This very act meant that the rights of citizens seeking to protect themselves against the *Sharia* legal system could be pursued through the secular courts; sentences passed by state *Sharia* courts could be challenged on appeal to federal courts. Similarly, while rulings by the Supreme Court have legitimised the rights of states to have Islamic *hisbah* vigilante groups, the same rulings have specified the status of *hisbah* vis-à-vis the police, making it difficult for the groups to be used more aggressively as enforcement mechanisms for *Sharia* (cf. Suberu forthcoming).

In the end, the introduction of 100 per cent *Sharia* has addressed neither the moral panic in society nor the crisis of legitimacy facing northern political leaders. In many *Sharia* states, the rich have resisted paying the *zakat* that is supposed to go to the needy. In some instances, over-zealous *hisbah* groups came to blows with ordinary Muslims. In 2003, rampant drunkenness and prostitution were reported in Gusau, the capital of the first state to declare full *Sharia*, right under the noses of the *hisbah* (Suleiman 2003). Indeed, the real victims of the new *Sharia* legal system are the poor, particularly rural women. Rather than addressing the concerns of northern Muslims, what this new round of the politicisation of religion has done is to make Nigeria one of the most religiously polarised countries in the world, creating an inauspicious context for the process of democratisation.[6]

Niger Delta and the Distribution of Oil Rents

The primacy of oil rents in Nigerian public finance after 1970 has had negative consequences for productivity and wellbeing, the quality of governance, and the nature of interest representation. There is widespread poverty and squalor amidst increasing oil revenue, particularly in the oil-producing Niger Delta, which is populated by minority ethnic groups. Increasing rents from oil from 1970 freed the Nigerian state from the burden of extracting resources from its population. This had important implications for interest representation and the accountability of state institutions. Jane Guyer (1992) poignantly pointed out that oil-boom Nigeria could best be described as a situation of 'Representation without Taxation'. While people continued to have electoral rights, they paid no taxes. This meant that the level of scrutiny of what the government did with the national coffers was low. It also made the government less willing to listen to the citizenry and more voluntaristic in its conduct of public affairs. Corruption assumed elephantine proportions as the military elite and their supporters scrambled for the spoils of office. Finally, it reduced citizens and communities to seeking alternative ways of articulating their interests, due to the failure of the formal institutional linkages between the government and the governed. This corrosion of the links between governance, representation and accountability led to increasing sectarian politics of place, ethnicity or religion, as these are seen as the only way to gain the attention and patronage of powerful individuals and political blocs within the state. Politically disadvantaged minorities in the Niger Delta increasingly adopted desperate measures to make their voices heard. While democratisation directed more oil rents to the Niger Delta, it has so far failed to contain the increasingly militarised conflict in the region.

From the promulgation of Decree No. 13 of 1970, revenue became concentrated in the federal government at the expense of the Niger Delta states from which the revenue was derived. Prior to this change, pride of place was given to the principle of derivation in the distribution of revenue, with source states obtaining close to 50 per cent of the revenue derived from their territories. By 1982, the share of central government revenue going to the oil-producing states had dropped to 1.5 per cent of all government revenue. Agitation by the communities of the Niger Delta led to the creation of the Oil Mineral Producing Areas Development Commission (OMPADEC) which was allocated 3 per cent of federal revenue. The oil-producing states therefore obtained a total of 4.5 per cent of federal resources, only 1.5 per cent of which went through their own budgets. A significant proportion of the resources concentrated on the federal centre was further distributed to the states. By 1997, the federal government's share of its resource pool was 48.5 per cent, with 24 per cent and 20 per cent going to the states and local governments respectively, with 7.5 per cent devoted to special funds also under the control of the federal government (Frynas 1999: 44). With the recent democratisation, further changes took place in the principles for sharing the resources, both between the federal centre and the states, on the one hand, and within the various states, on the other. Prior to democratisation in 1999, there were severe vertical and horizontal imbalances in the sharing of oil rents between different levels of government (Ahmad & Singh 2003: 15).

With democratisation, the pattern of resource flows was re-shaped; from 1999 more revenue went to states and local governments, particularly those in the Niger Delta. Actual transfers during the eight-year period of Obasanjo's presidency to 2007 indicate that the federal share of the Federation Account went down to 45 per cent, while the share of the states went up to 34 per cent. The share of local governments remained constant at 20 per cent. This shift of revenue towards state governments was especially advantageous to states in the Niger Delta. Prior to 1999, only 1.5 per cent of federal revenue was allocated to these states under the principle of derivation. After 1999, the share of federal revenue going to these states under the same principle increased first to 7.8 per cent and finally to 13 per cent.

The rise in the international price of crude oil from around US$12 a barrel in May 1999 to US$67 in January 2008 – and hovering around $100 thereafter – further bolstered the resources going to all levels of government. The average monthly allocation to the 774 local government councils went up from N11 bn to N60 bn (Human Rights Watch 2007: 14). However, while the vertical imbalances in resource allocation between the states and the federal centre have been ameliorated under democratisation, there has been the exacerbation of horizontal imbalances between states. As Table 5.2 illustrates, the Niger Delta states of the South-South zone are the main beneficiaries; resources to most states have increased ten-fold between 1998 and 2007, while the states in the Niger Delta have seen a forty-fold increase. Some Niger Delta states now control revenues larger than those of some neighbouring countries.

Table 5.2 Trends in Shares of Federation Account 1998-2007

Zone	Share of total Federation Account, May 1999 to Oct. 2007 (%)	Average monthly per capita allocation, 1998 (N)	Average monthly per capita allocation, May-Oct 2007 (N)
Northwest	10.5	43	459.10
Northeast	7.3	78	639.70
Northcentral	6.8	72	587.00
Southwest	8.5	53	556.87
Southsouth	15.2	55	1,923.13
Southeast	5.6	59	633.20

Sources: 1998 figures computed from Ahmad & Singh, 2003: 20; 1999-2007 figures from data from Federal Ministry of Finance in 'GovernanceWatch', Nov. 2007, People & Passion Consult, Abuja (www.peoplen passion.com), p. 12 and Dailytrust.com, June 18 2007.

Throwing more money at the Niger Delta without addressing the political and governance problems has not had the desired calming effect. More money may be going into the region, but poor governance structures mean that these monies are not translated into improved social and economic conditions for the majority in those states. The combination of lack of effective accountability at the state and local government levels and greater resource flows has led to rampant corruption. Despite democratisation, the military-era culture of governance centred on arbitrariness, lack of accountability, corruption, and disregard for public welfare has continued in most states and local governments, especially in the Niger Delta (cf. Human Rights Watch 2007). A second strategy of addressing the Niger Delta problem under Obasanjo was the establishment of the Niger Delta Development Commission (NDDC) with funds contributed by both federal and state governments and the multinational oil companies. This top-down developmentalist approach has not adequately addressed the political issues raised by the different groups in the Niger Delta. Furthermore, the macroeconomic strategy of fighting inflation through restricted money supply also resulted in the federal government withholding about N224 bn which it was legally required to contribute to the NDDC.[7] Given these inadequacies, agitation for 'resource control' continues, with many militant groups veering towards criminality. In 2005 an effort was made to break this logjam at the National Political Reforms Conference called by President Obasanjo. While the South-South delegates from the Niger Delta demanded a share of 50 per cent of oil rents based on the principle of derivation, the Conference was only able to offer 18 per cent and no compromise was reached.

Obasanjo's Presidency and Institutional Change

With respect to these three structural tensions within Nigerian state and society – ethnicity, religion, and the special situation in the Niger Delta – democratisation has largely failed to provide a peaceful avenue for conflict resolution. Force was the method of choice of the Obasanjo administration, with little attempt made to address the underlying political and security issues.[8] Ethnic militias, some tied to particular politicians, continue to be a feature of politics in various parts of the country, including the pro-*Sharia hisbah* groups in the north and the MEND, OPC, MASSOB, and Bakassi Boys in the south. While none of the militias can seriously threaten the integrity of the state, they nevertheless contribute to a climate of insecurity which undermines the legitimacy of the state and erodes confidence in the alleged benefits of democratisation.

In a complicated and weakly institutionalised democratisation process, the role of the individual actor might assume special significance. The challenges faced by Obasanjo and the quality of his leadership have therefore had a significant bearing on the trajectory of the democratisation process. The emergence of Obasanjo as President in 1999 was unexpected. Efforts to assuage Yoruba feelings hurt by the annulment of the 1993 presidential election worked in his favour. He was seen by many northern military and political figures as a safe pair of Yoruba hands that could be trusted with running the country. In a game of high political choreography, he was drafted into the People's Democratic Party (PDP), won the presidential primaries and subsequently the actual elections. The Obasanjo administration was inaugurated in May 1999 with 84 per cent approval rating for the President and 81 per cent support for democracy (Lewis & Bratton 2000: 8). However, this groundswell of goodwill was subsequently squandered by Obasanjo; the rapidly declining quality of his leadership has been one of the defining characteristics of Nigerian democratisation.

Obasanjo frequently compared the Nigeria he left as a departing military Head of State in 1979 with the Nigeria of the late 1990s. He drew attention to economic decline, societal degeneration, and the collapse of the political class after 1979 (Obasanjo 1998). He cast himself as a purposeful leader who left a healthy legacy after his stint in office as military Head of State. His high standing in the international community for handing over power to a civilian successor in 1979 added to this sense of special importance. But when he took office in 1999, Obasanjo had no power base within the PDP; there was therefore a contradiction between his self-perception and the reality of his political position. I argue that Obasanjo resolved this contradiction by using presidential power to build a personal power base at the expense of consolidating the democratisation process.

At the inception of the democratisation process, Obasanjo relied on a faction of the PDP, the People's Democratic Movement (PDM), founded by his late subordinate General Shehu Yar' Adua. The PDM was then led by Atiku Abubakar whom Obasanjo chose as his running mate. However, fearing 'encirclement', he would not allow Atiku supporters in the PDM to take control of the National Assembly. When the newly elected PDP/PDM senators sought to choose an Atiku ally, the late Chuba Okadigbo, as Senate President, Obasanjo would have none of it. The power and purse of the presidency was used to break the ranks of the PDP majority in the Senate and Obasanjo imposed his choice of candidate, Evans Ewerem. Discord was thereby sown between the executive and the legislature.

Given these beginnings, Obasanjo's first civilian term (1999-2003) was marked more by institutional continuities with the military past. Lacking an independent political base, he manoeuvred between different political personalities and groupings that had come together under the PDP. He sought to secure his power by maintaining and manipulating the basic framework of institutions and rules left over from military rule – including the powerful Presidency, a non-existent or weakened legislature, the use of force to contain political challenges, and the use of bribery and clientage to buy support. In this early stage therefore, democratisation coincided with institutional continuity. Keenly aware of his weakness within the party, Obasanjo did not shy away from using the concentrated powers of the presidency to his personal advantage as previous military tyrants had done. According to erstwhile Vice President, Atiku Abubakar, Obasanjo confided in him that 'I am going to be the President, I am going to be the petroleum minister, I am going to be the defence minister, I am going to be the foreign affairs minister. I said ah, all these for you? He said yes, anybody I put there will be a robot.'[9] Obasanjo later admitted that his first term in office was a failure because of his insecure political position.[10]

Continuation of Presidential Authoritarianism

The major changes that took place under Obasanjo's first term were an improvement on the abysmal human rights record of the military era and the relative re-professionalisation of the military. However, many important issues like the disputed constitution, the dilapidated national infrastructure, and the comatose economy were not given the attention they deserved. For much of the period between 1999 and 2003, Obasanjo struggled to construct alliances to prop up his personal power. An important development during this first term was the gradual consolidation of his personal power base through the maintenance of the centralised, authoritarian presidency. Anxious to get the support of powerful political players from across the country, Obasanjo constituted a bloated Cabinet of almost sixty people, representing most shades of opinion within the PDP. The full complement of ministers and ministers of state were augmented by presidential aides with bewildering titles: 'Special Advisers', 'Senior Special Advisers', 'Special Assistants', and 'Personal Assistants'.

For the first time in Nigerian politics, we began to see the systematic promotion of the sons and daughters of prominent political personages into junior positions within the government as a strategy for tying-in their parents and their political networks. Some of the families involved were the prominent Awolowo, Adesanya, Wole Soyinka, Saraki, Shagari, Lar, Nweke, and Murtala Mohammed families. But apart from their function of including different political currents under the presidency, the many aides also served as the extension of the President's personal powers as they shadowed and monitored the ministers and enforced the President's personal wishes. Under Abacha, it is said that the Cabinet hardly met. Though Obasanjo promised to re-institute collective Cabinet action and went ahead to institute the weekly Wednesday Cabinet meetings followed by a press briefing, the unwieldy numbers of ministers, assistant ministers, and presidential aides created a climate of institutional confusion which placed the person of Obasanjo himself squarely at the heart of all governmental action.

As the new regime settled down, political postures which had been thought to be 'defensive' in nature because of Obasanjo's tenuous position, soon assumed 'offensive' attributes as he sought to stamp his authority on the administration, party, and the political system as a whole. The 2003 elections marked a shift in Obasanjo's political circumstances. He managed to beguile the mainstream Yoruba elite organisations into supporting his re-election and to seize control of five of the six Yoruba states in the South-West for the PDP. He was no longer a

President without a home base. In 2003 he also launched an effort to re-make the PDP in his own image, through the weeding out of the original founders of the party, and began an ambitious economic reform programme. From 2003 therefore we begin to see major institutional changes fuelled by visions of Obasanjo as a god-sent messiah for the salvation of the country. One minister declared him 'an instrument in the hand of God' for Nigeria's transformation.[11] Personal political insecurity had matured into hubris, with implications for the democratisation process.

Gone was Obasanjo the elder statesman and campaigner for good governance; gone also was Obasanjo the born-again Christian. Increasingly, Obasanjo was presented as the most patriotic, knowledgeable, and acceptable Nigerian for the job of president. He was frequently referred to as 'Baba', emphasising his paternalistic style. The command culture of politics inherited from years of military rule was increasingly re-asserted with a vengeance as Obasanjo virtually restored the military 'Imperial Presidency' created by Babangida. The relentless consolidation of presidential authoritarianism has undermined constitutional checks and balances particularly between the executive and legislature at the federal level, and between the federal executive and the state governments. Under Obasanjo, the basic democratic tenet of division of powers – horizontally within the federal government and vertically between the federal government and the states – came under severe strain.

Obasanjo's interests became even more overbearing in the election of the President of the Senate; a succession of three Senate Presidents within four years helped to undermine the legitimacy of the National Assembly as a whole. Charges of executive interference and offers of bribes were rife in the election or removal of particular Senate Presidents. As a consequence, the legislature has been extremely unstable since 1999, and its 'cash and carry' image among the public has seriously eroded its effectiveness. This weakness of the legislative arm is a marked departure from previous efforts at democratisation in Nigeria. The judiciary was also undermined under the Obasanjo presidency as court orders, including Supreme Court rulings, were sometimes ignored or selectively implemented.

Obasanjo has also used his control of federal finances, as well as the regulatory institutions of the federal government including the police, to bring elected state governors under his personal control, thereby weakening Nigerian federalism. The anti-corruption crusade of the Obasanjo regime has been conveniently used to beat recalcitrant governors into line as the anti-corruption agencies have been used to fight *both* corruption and the President's political enemies. Meanwhile, state-level political 'godfathers' vital to the President's personal political machine were given free rein to operate as they chose, including the instigation of the illegal impeachment of state governors in Oyo and Anambra and the unhindered perpetration of political violence in these states. Despite democratisation, Nigerian politics continued to be dominated by the undemocratic use of presidential powers, clientelism, and corruption. There was scant regard for the rule of law, respect for due process, and the doctrine of the separation of powers. Instead, the personalisation of powers characteristic of the military era continued.

Collapse of the Party System

Obasanjo's quest for control also undermined an already weak party system. Unlike Ghana where the party traditions established in the 1940s have largely persisted, in Nigeria General Babangida destroyed the old political system as he sought to entrench himself in power. The loss of political direction suffered by the political class under Babangida was compounded by Abacha's heavy-handed 'transition' between 1994 and 1997. By the time Abacha died, the military had been exhausted by mounting civil resistance and internal dissention, and its political will to govern was at an all-time low. The hurried nature of the Abdusalami transition between 1998 and 1999 gave very little time for the political class to organise political parties properly; the parties formed were often an opportunistic assemblage of odd bedfellows tied together by little more than shifting personal interests. The initial weaknesses of the political parties were then compounded by the exigencies of presidential power politics. Compared with the situation under previous transitions to civilian rule, the party system was particularly fragile in the current transition.

In 1999 there were three major political parties: the People's Democratic Party (PDP); the All Peoples' Party (APP), which later became the All Nigerian Peoples' Party (ANPP); and the Alliance for Democracy (AD). The PDP was the party of the Establishment, supported by large sections of the Hausa-Fulani north, the Igbo east, and the ethnic minorities. It also had a large contingent of the retired military. The ANPP was of a more conservative bent, and based largely in the northwest and northeast of the country. It was initially filled by Abacha apologists, earning the party the nickname of 'Abacha Peoples' Party'. The Alliance for Democracy was the grouping of the mainstream of the Yoruba ethnic elite, based largely in the southwest. The AD did not meet the criteria for registration but was registered to placate the Yoruba elite in the wake of the annulment of the 12 June 1993 election which a Yoruba politician, Abiola, was poised to win.[12]

From this unpromising beginning, the party system has disintegrated along three broad lines. Firstly, each of the three major parties has been seriously factionalised under internal and external pressure. The PDP has been deeply factionalised as Obasanjo and his supporters strengthened their hold over the party machinery. Perceived opponents were systematically sidelined, culminating in 2005 in a re-registration exercise which was allegedly for the purpose of membership revalidation, but which in reality threw out all Obasanjo opponents from the party. Power and patronage continue to glue bits of the PDP together, though intra-party violence, including assassinations, is common within it. Similarly, the AD split down the middle with two warring factions. By 2007, the mainstream Yoruba political elite had factionalised into the rump of the AD and two new parties, the Action Congress (AC) and the Democratic Peoples' Alliance (DPA). A similar process of factionalisation has taken place within the ANPP. Both the AD and ANPP have also suffered defections to the PDP.

The second trend in the collapse of the party system is observable in the mushrooming of political parties that have no discernible social base. As a consequence of a Supreme Court ruling relaxing the criteria for the registration of political parties, the number of parties has ballooned from 3 to over 50. However, most of the new parties are no more than one-man affairs set up by political entrepreneurs with the aim of jockeying for political relevance. They have nevertheless added to the confused political system since 1999.

The third strand is in the increasing prominence of personal political networks and organisations operating within the formal party structures. Prominent personal organisations like the Buhari Organisation within the ANPP and the *Ebeano* Organisation within the Enugu state PDP have ingrained a culture of factionalism and indiscipline within the party system. Many state branches of parties are personal fiefdoms of political godfathers and warlords. The parties are little more than collections of ambitious individuals, all intent on using legal and illegal means to capture political power, or failing that, at least to get a share of the spoils. The collapse of the party system compounded the problem of lack of accountability caused by presidential authoritarianism by removing an important institutional restraint on office-holders throughout the political system.

Other Dimensions of Institutional Continuity

The lack of democratic temperament and an overbearing executive were not limited to the federal level. Taking their cue from the Obasanjo presidency, the same military commandist impulse was dominant in the 36 state governments and 774 local governments across the country. State Houses of Assembly were often incapable of restraining Governors who also used bribery, patronage, and outright interference to cage their respective legislatures. Most elected Governors behaved just like the previous Military Governors; only the Presidency or the institutions it controlled could call them to order. Despite democratisation, accountability at state and local government levels continued to flow upwards, and not in the direction of the electorate. Many of the dysfunctions and lack of accountability at the state level were replicated at the local government level. Local government chairmen were often not accountable to their councillors and handled council funds in a corrupt and arbitrary manner.

Dividends of Democracy

Democratisation did have some positive consequences, particularly with respect to the formal disengagement of the military from politics, the institution of certain macroeconomic reforms, and the revitalisation of the judiciary. Nigeria had experienced two main phases of military rule: from 1966 to 1979, and from 1984 to 1999. By 1999, most Nigerians had come to detest military rule and its economic and political consequences (Mustapha 1999). Democratisation held out the promise of removing the military from politics and possibly ending the revolving door syndrome which saw the return of the military to power after each previous attempt at democratisation. One of the first things the Obasanjo administration did in 1999 was to retire all serving military officers who had held political office, particularly since 1983. Relatively non-political and more professional officers are now in charge of the armed forces and many of them are from ethnic minority groups in the north and south. This change in the composition of the officer corps is one factor in explaining why Nigeria is enjoying its longest spell of civilian rule.

Economic and Institutional Reforms

The main change associated with democratisation has been in the sphere of economic and social policy. With his re-election in 2003, Obasanjo unleashed a series of economic and social reforms, including macroeconomic reforms; institutional reforms of the pension system, the banking industry, and the civil service; and regulatory and policing reforms such as the creation and empowering of the Economic and Financial Crimes Commission (EFCC); and the institutionalisation of the monitoring of oil receipts through the Nigerian Extractive Industries Transparency Initiative (NEITI). The stated goal of these reforms is to turn Nigeria into one of the twenty largest economies by 2020. It is this convergence of authoritarian politics and socio-economic reforms which lies at the heart of the confusion about Nigeria's real trajectory since 1999.

Macroeconomic reforms have led to significant improvements in some sectors of the national economy. In telecommunications, the number of telephones in the country increased from 500,000 in 1999 to 20 million by 2005. Long queues at petrol stations which were prevalent before 1999 have largely disappeared. The electricity supply remains erratic, but generation and supply problems have been put on the agenda. Other economic gains are increased foreign direct investment, massive capital growth on the Nigerian Stock Exchange, decline in the rate of inflation, economic diversification and increased earnings from the non-oil sector, and the achievement of a relatively stable currency. However, President Umaru Yar' Adua has pointed out that US$10 bn was spent on the energy sector between 2000 and 2007 without any significant improvement. Critics also point to about N300 bn spent on roads in the same period with little effect.

The macroeconomic strategy has combined the usual neo-liberal prescriptions of privatisation and restricted money supply with some measure of state intervention in key sectors. There has also been an attempt to elaborate an overarching strategy called the National Economic Empowerment and Development Strategy (NEEDS), with state-level programmes called SEEDS. This is an attempt to develop a market-led, production-oriented, economic strategy with an emphasis on civil service reform, reform of the financial sector, infrastructural investment, improved regulatory powers, and some measure of state protection. Significantly, the launch by Obasanjo in 2004 of the Transnational Corporation of Nigeria, otherwise known as Transcorp Nigeria, was intended to mark a major realignment of the private sector and an attempt to copy the South Korean *chaebol* model of state-supported capitalist entrepreneurs. Organised around Obasanjo, the thirty-odd young and stupendously rich Nigerians in Transcorp have used their corporate and state connections to corner choice enterprises under Obasanjo's privatisation programme.[13] Allegations of corruption in the privatisation programme include the concessioning of the Ajaokuta Steel Company, valued at US$6 bn, for only US$525 million.[14]

Institutional reforms include the overhaul of the pension system; the rationalisation of the banking sector; and the reform of the core civil service. The pension system, which had collapsed by 1999, has undergone a root and branch reform and a contributory pension scheme has been introduced, along with efforts at clearing a backlog of debts owed to pensioners. The banking system has been rationalised from about 90 banks, some of questionable repute, to 25 stronger banks with their capital base strengthened and new corporate governance instruments put in place. The core civil service is being down-sized from 160,000 to 130,000 and examinations introduced for promotions to generate improvements in efficiency and monitoring. The Federal Inland Revenue Service (FIRS) has been reorganised, with taxes realised rising from N171 bn in 1999 to N2 trillion in 2006.

Regulatory reforms such as the NEITI have finally succeeded in shedding some light on the murky financial dealings in the oil industry. The National Administration for Food and Drugs Administration and Control (NAFDAC) has also been strengthened and empowered to tackle the menace of sub-standard and expired drugs. It has since emerged as the most important consumer protection agency in the country. Other important regulatory reforms have been the strengthening of the policing of corruption and drug smuggling through the Economic and Financial Crimes Commission (EFCC), the Independent Corrupt Practices Commission (ICPC), and the National Drugs Law Enforcement Agency (NDLEA). The contract-awarding system has also been reformed through the introduction of the Due Process Office which is reported to have saved hundreds of millions of US dollars. A National Procurement Act was passed, along with a Fiscal Responsibility Act. The EFCC has been involved in many high-profile investigations leading to 82 convictions. So far, the government has recovered vast sums of money, including about N160 bn (US$ 1.23 bn) from the money stashed abroad by the late General Sani Abacha. The total funds recovered by the EFCC is said to be around US$ 3.7 bn.[15] The EFCC has also indicted about 31 Governors whose term of office expired in 2007; seven are already before the courts on corruption charges. The Commission is also fighting the internet fraud letters popularly called '419'; many fraudsters have been jailed and their loot recovered and returned to their greedy victims. The United Nations Commission for Narcotic Drugs has praised efforts by the NDLEA to curb drugs smuggling and use.

These socio-economic reforms have injected a new sense of dynamism into the Nigerian economy. Privatisation and deregulation, as in the telecoms industry, have brought services to millions. Many small investors are now active on the Stock Exchange. The cost of running the government has been reduced through the policy of monetisation of fringe benefits. The regulatory institutions have been made more efficient, but these macroeconomic gains have not been translated into improvements in the lives of most citizens. The majority of Nigerians continue to wallow in poverty, unemployment, and the lack of basic services. There is also a mis-match between the dynamism and improvements on the social and economic front, and the continuing corruption, authoritarianism, and lack of accountability on the political front. For these two reasons, the Obasanjo administration faced a rising tide of opposition from a revived civil society after 2003.

Milestones in Nigerian Democratisation

There is a connection between the socio-economic reforms and the tendency towards authoritarianism; the success of the reforms was used to justify authoritarian practices. The need to 'continue' the reforms was cited as the justification for changing the constitutional limitation of two terms at the end of Obasanjo's second and final term in 2007. This became known as the campaign for a 'third term'. Democracy was to be sacrificed on the altar of economic reform.

Third Term Campaign
The first attack on the democratic process came at the National Political Reforms Conference (NPRC) called by the government in 2005. Many parts of the 1999 Constitution are either contentious or contradictory. The Constitution clearly failed to address the ferment unleashed by years of military dictatorship. Worse still, the provisions for changing the Constitution are cumbersome and politically

difficult. Opponents of the military and the PDP government largely from southern ethnic groups campaigned for a Sovereign National Conference (SNC) to re-examine the foundations of the Nigerian state. While some had separatist intent, most want 'true federalism' and fiscal federalism or 'resource control'.

For most of his first term in office, Obasanjo dismissed the calls for a SNC. Then in 2005, he made an about-turn, and initiated the NPRC, even after the National Assembly had refused to vote money for it. While his motives were hotly debated in the media, some of his aides sought, and failed, to introduce into the Conference a 'draft constitution' with contentious provisions capable of delivering the 'third term'. Loud protestations by civil society groups and in the media halted this surreptitious effort. After months of haggling along ethno-regional lines, the Conference collapsed without concluding its task. The main stumbling block was the demand by Niger Delta ethnic minority groups from the South-South zone for 'resource control'.

After the collapse of the NPRC, the constitutional review process shifted back to the National Assembly, where known friends of Obasanjo manoeuvred to revive the idea of the extension of the presidential term. An omnibus Constitution Amendment Bill with over a hundred clauses was introduced into the National Assembly, with the third term provision cleverly sandwiched amongst other items for which some interest groups had been agitating. Though Obasanjo was deafeningly silent throughout the months in which the argument over the third term raged, no one was in doubt about his support for the move. His behaviour spoke volumes about his real intentions; it was obvious that hubris had become a major obstacle to democratisation.

The campaign for a third term took the undemocratic aspects of the Obasanjo presidency to new heights. As a prelude to the campaign proper, the bizarre exercise to 'revalidate' members of the ruling PDP had weeded out all Obasanjo opponents within the party. That task completed, Obasanjo and his supporters turned their attention to the National Assembly and the thirty-six States. Under the terms of the 1999 Constitution, two-thirds of the National Assembly and 27 out of the 36 State legislatures must approve amendments to sections 137 (1)(b) and 182 (1)(b) which limit the term of office of the Executive arm to two terms of four years. State Governors were leaned on to deliver their assemblies, while the National Assembly was put under considerable pressure. All too conscious of the threat confronting them, thirty State Governors and large sections of the business community supported the extension of tenure. But delivering the votes at the National Assembly proved more difficult than anticipated, as public, civil-society and media opposition mounted. To win over members of the National Assembly, bribes were allegedly offered for votes: a mind-boggling N100 million (US$769,000) for the vote of each of the 109 Senators, N70 million for members of the House of Representatives and N50 million for each member of at least twenty-four States Houses of Assembly.[16]

From all available indicators, it was clear that the majority of Nigerians were deeply against the third term campaign. Eighty-one per cent of nation-wide respondents sampled by the respected *Nigerian Guardian* Opinion Poll expressed their opposition to the proposal. The poll results indicated that 69 per cent believed that President Obasanjo had the personal ambition of running for the third term. Eighty per cent of the respondents wanted him to leave office in 2007 as stipulated in the 1999 Constitution. An *Afrobarometer* nation-wide poll on the same subject reported that 84 per cent wanted the President to respect the

Constitution and stick to the two terms allowed, with 74 per cent rejecting 'one man' rule.[17]

The third term bid also exposed the questionable commitment to African democratisation on the part of important Western players. While the conflict over the constitutional changes raged within the Nigerian media and society, the British government adopted the dubious stance that the Constitution must be respected, without stating which constitution it was referring to – the 1999 Constitution or the new one advocated by Obasanjo's supporters. On a visit to Abuja, then Foreign Secretary Jack Straw declared that the third term '... is simply an internal matter. We do not go to other people's countries and advise them on how to treat their constitution.'[18] It was not until the very end, when more overt coercive measures were being contemplated against the National Assembly, that the British High Commissioner in Abuja came out with an oblique warning to the presidency.[19] Taking the British lead, EU ambassadors in Abuja bluntly said of the third term: 'It is none of our business.'[20] The US government was in the lone position of consistent condemnation of the third term project. Amidst repeated warnings, it observed that '... Nigeria may collapse if President Obasanjo stays beyond next year.'[21]

Sensing the depth of public anger – some legislators were physically assaulted by irate mobs in their home constituencies as the debate raged in the National Assembly – the full Senate voted down the Constitution Amendment Bill in March 2006. This defeat of tenure extension came about as a result of the convergence of a number of factors. Civil society groups were vociferous in their condemnation, mobilising both local and international opinion against it. The commercialisation of broadcasting and the decision of the National Assembly leadership to allow the African Independent Television to broadcast live debates on the Amendment Bill meant that legislators were open to an unprecedented level of public scrutiny. Opposition from civil society and sections of the media was further bolstered by the support of important political actors and organisations. Presidential threats and inducements proved incapable of swinging the legislators in the face of concerted public opposition. Presidential authoritarianism had hit an important limit; a groundswell of public opprobrium and hostility. Attention then turned to the April 2007 elections.

The Electoral Farce of 2007

Despite the excessive emphasis on electoralism that has characterised African democratisation, Lindberg (2006) argues that these elections still matter as they facilitate the gradual entrenchment of democratic values. Nigeria's experience since 1999 suggests that this conclusion is open to question. Unlike Ghana where the electoral institution has gained in legitimacy and prestige with time, the Nigerian electoral institution seems to be going from bad to worse. What is unique about Nigeria's elections since 1998-9 is the movement from competitive to coercive rigging, characterised by increasing coercion and diminishing legitimacy. Under competitive rigging, it was generally understood that there was a vague, but real, relationship between the declared votes and the popular will of the constituency. Where such a relationship was lacking, as in the Western Region in 1965 and Ondo State in 1983, violence often resulted. Under democratisation since 1998-9, Nigeria has moved steadily from competitive to coercive rigging, in which results bear no resemblance to any understood sociological realities.

A comparison of the three sets of elections held between 1998 and 2007 shows the continued deterioration of the electoral system since democratisation. In their observers' report on the 1998-9 elections, the Carter Center and the National Democratic Institute (1999) pointed out that the elections were 'conducted generally without violence', but noted problems with the process of voters' registration, electoral irregularities on voting days, 'and sometimes outright fraud'. Abuses of the electoral process included ballot stuffing, inflation of results, altered results, voter intimidation and disenfranchisement. The observers noted significant disparities between the voter turn-out they observed in many polling stations and the official results reported for those stations: 'In at least nine states, particularly in the South-South zone, NDI/Carter Center delegates observed voters turn out that were significantly lower than the official tally.' (Ibid: 28-9). Still, no one doubted that Obasanjo of the PDP won the election, even if his margin of victory – 18 million to Chief Falae of the AD/APP alliance's 11 million – was grossly inflated. Equally important was the relative lack of violence in the election and the concentration of the electoral skulduggery to the minority states of the South-South zone (Human Rights Watch 1999).

In the 2003 elections, violence became a major additional factor in undermining the electoral process and it spread beyond the South-South states where politicians and multinational oil companies colluded to promote armed vigilantes who perpetrated wanton violence at the various stages of the elections (Okonta 2007). Some states in the South-East zone witnessed substantial violence. There were also problems with voters' registration which was so bungled that many were disenfranchised. Other deficiencies in the 2003 polls included instances of the fraudulent use of the ballot box, the deliberate disenfranchisement of voters by electoral officials, lack of ballot secrecy, and the alteration of results. In one instance, a winning candidate with 14,405 votes found out four days later that his votes had reduced to 5,065, while his opponent who originally had 13,076 votes was declared winner with 67,857 votes (National Democratic Institute 2003)! Though clearly less transparent and free and fair than the 1998-9 elections, the 2003 elections still had some redeeming features. The International Republican Institute report broke the twelve states it observed into three groups: the category of 'relatively good' had six states,'improved with irregularities' three states, and 'significantly flawed' three states, all of them in the South-South and South-East zones (International Republican Institute 2003).

In the 2007 elections, brazen electoral manipulation and reckless violence hitherto limited to these zones were extended right across the country as the Obasanjo PDP sought to entrench itself in power. According to the Carter Center observer mission, the elections in all 36 states did not reflect the hopes and aspirations of the people 'except in Lagos and Kano states, where the will of the people prevailed'.[22] The elections were met by a chorus of national and international disapproval. As the observers noted, unparalleled illegalities were brazenly carried out before and during the elections. Weeks before the presidential election on 21 April 2007, local and international pollsters predicted a tight race, all putting the opposition ANPP candidate Mohamaddu Buhari slightly ahead.[23] In the end, the elections body, INEC, announced the victory of the Obasanjo protégé and PDP candidate Umaru Yar' Adua with 24.3 million votes, with Buhari garnering only 6.6 million votes and the Action Congress candidate and Obasanjo antagonist, Vice-President Atiku Abubakar, trailing with 2.6 million votes. By February 2009, election tribunals set up in the wake of the elections had overturned 7 of the gubernatorial results, all from the PDP, and issued a highly criticised ruling endorsing President Yar' Adua's election. The Supreme Court subsequently upheld Yar' Adua's election by a slim majority of 4 judges for and 3 against.

Umaru Yar' Adua Presidency
While Obasanjo failed to extend his own rule, he was able to impose a successor after a stage-managed PDP primary, followed by an equally questionable presidential election. Since assuming office in May 2007, Yar' Adua has sought to legitimise his shaky rule by reversing many of the unpopular and high-handed decisions taken by Obasanjo. For example, last-minute disposals of public assets to Obasanjo allies have been cancelled, along with custom duties waivers bestowed by Obasanjo on his favourites. Nigerian National Petroleum Corporation contracts worth N752 bn which Obasanjo gave out in his last week in office are being investigated. Yar' Adua is distancing himself from the Obasanjo legacy as much as he can without causing an open breach. Yar' Adua has also stressed respect for the rule of law, another departure from the Obasanjo days. He described himself as a 'servant-leader', a change in leadership tone from the abrasive messianic style of Obasanjo. While retaining some of the features and personnel of the Obasanjo administration, Yar' Adua has sought to undermine notions that he is an Obasanjo creation, rigged into office for ulterior motives. On the political front, he set up an Electoral Reform Committee to overhaul the discredited electoral system. He has also opened up discussions with militant groups in the Niger Delta. Beyond reversing Obasanjo's policies, Yar' Adua unfolded a 7-point programme including improving the energy supply, the revitalisation of agriculture, wealth creation and poverty alleviation, land reforms, improvements in transportation and human capital development. But very little had been achieved in any of these fields by early 2009. To start with, it took all of 33 days to draw up the Cabinet and almost 6 months to reshuffle it! There is an increasing feeling in the media that the new administration is bereft of fresh and critical ideas. Some analysts complain that it is colourless and lacks drive; Yar' Adua has been referred to as 'President do-nothing. Baba Go-Slow' (Abati 2008). The professed commitment to the rule of law is now derided as the 'rule of lull'. Even some elements within the PDP are claiming that, after eight months in office, the Yar' Adua administration is showing no sign of 'direction, vision, or vigour'.[24] Others complain about the populism that permeates the reversal of Obasanjo's policies, claiming that the 'administration has been adept at taking liberty with truth' (Eni-B 2007). Serious questions have also been raised about the administration's commitment to anti-corruption, especially in the handling of the personnel of the EFCC who are responsible for the prosecution of former Governors facing allegations of corruption. Many of these former Governors are rumoured to be close to the seat of power. Yoruba elites have accused Yar' Adua of discriminating against them by appointing a disproportionate number of northerners into key positions.[25] While most Nigerians initially warmed to Yar' Adua for distancing his administration from Obasanjo, doubts still remain about his ability to wrest control of the PDP from Obasanjo's allies, or rise to the enormous challenges confronting the country. He has also been undermined by ill health and related rumours of his death or imminent retirement.

Conclusion

Elections in Nigeria have not promoted voters' choice, accountability, or a credible means of deciding which group of elites will rule. While Nigerians continue to support democracy as a system of government, their general experience since 1999 has sorely tested their will and patience. This combination of high support for, and declining satisfaction with, democracy is clearly indicated in the results of *Afrobarometer* surveys conducted between 2000 and 2005 summarised in Table 5.3.

Table 5.3 Trend Indicators for Nigerian Democracy 1999-2005 (%)

	2000	2001	2003	2005
Support for democracy	81	71	68	65
Satisfaction with democracy	84	57	35	25
Approval of the President (Obasanjo)	84	72	39	32
Approval of National Assembly	58	46	32	23
Approval of local govt. representative	67	47	39	28

Source: For December 1999 figure, Lewis and Bratton (2000: 8). The rest of the data is from 'Performance and Legitimacy in Nigeria's New Democracy', *Afrobarometer Briefing* Paper No. 46, July 2006.

The problems associated with the April 2007 election suggest that Nigeria's democracy is still very fragile: the defective 1999 Constitution has yet to be reformed; elite factionalisation and lack of consensus on core issues remain extremely high; and the political party and electoral systems are in shambles and incapable of adequately regulating political competition. In the long run, the country faces three possible options: entrenching presidential authoritarianism, the return to some form of democratisation, or the return to military rule. The Yar' Adua administration is at a crossroads: it can either engage in fundamental political and economic reforms which begin to address the expectations Nigerians had of democratisation, or can gradually slide back into the authoritarian presidency of past rulers. It is far from clear which road he will choose but by 2009, the slide towards business as usual seemed more palpable.

Despite some rumours to the contrary, the military have so far stayed publicly clear of the political process since 1999. However, the circumstances restraining them may change. Indeed, some cynics have asked if the military ever left power in the first place. They point to the fact that all of the four main contenders for the presidency in 2003 had military backgrounds: Obasanjo of the PDP, his main opponent Muhammadu Buhari of the ANPP, Ike Nwachukwu of the National Democratic Party, and Chukwuemeka Ojukwu of the All People's Grand Alliance are all retired generals. According to one wary commentator, 'We seem set to give power back to the military through the ballot box.' The line-up of those who jockeyed for the presidency in 2007 contained a similar military presence: Generals Babangida, Buhari and Gusau, and Brigadier Buba Marwa. David Mark, a soldier turned politician, even publicly argued that only someone with a military background could have become president in 2007.

Meanwhile, the threat of the old-style military coup remains in the background, despite Obasanjo's assertion in May 2007 that 'military coups are no longer a word in the political lexicon of Nigeria and have disappeared forever'.[26] In June 2002, retired General Victor Malu, former Chief of Army Staff, said a coup was still possible. He followed this up in January 2006 by saying that he regretted not overthrowing President Obasanjo when he had command of the army.[27] It is indicative of the continuing threat of military intervention that the then Chairman of the ruling PDP, Ahmadu Ali, warned in early 2008 that by engaging in rampant political violence and fraud, politicians 'might just be playing into the hands of the military who often seize ... opportunities [of such violence] to sack civilian governments'.[28] Despite nearly a decade of democratisation, Nigeria remains precariously poised between authoritarianism and democratisation.

Notes

1. Annual Mazrui Newsletter No. 19, 1995. http://64.233.169.104/search?q=cache:mdfQZ8vTv VIJ:igcs.binghamton.edu/igcs_site/mltrs/Newsletter19.pdf+Mazrui,+Kenya,+ethnic+group&hl=e n&ct=clnk&cd=6&gl=us

2. 'Communal Clashes Displace 750,000 Nigerians – Atiku', statement by then Vice President Atiku, www.thisdayonline.com, 18 February 2003.

3. 'Yorubanisation of Federal appointments real – Monguno', www.sunnewsonline.com, April 15 2005.

4. US expert: Nigeria May be Al-Qaeda's New Haven', www.thisdayonline.com, 3 May 2005.

5. In 2006, a certain Mohammed Ashafa was taken before the courts in Abuja, charged with being the head of the 'Al-Qaeda Network in Nigeria'. He had been arrested in Pakistan and then deported, not to Guantanamo, as one would expect, but to Abuja. He claimed in court that his confessions were obtained after two years of torture. www.thisdayonline.com, 24 Jan. 2008.

6. Though many of those surveyed by the BBC World Service in Nigeria subscribed to the 'clash of civilisation' thesis (BBC World Service 2007), Last (2007) is right in arguing that this is not an appropriate prism for understanding the dynamics of religious conflict in Nigeria.

7. 'Withheld N224bn NDDC fund has expired – Yar' Adua', www.vanguardngr.com, 20 Jan. 2008.

8. The nomination of Jonathan Goodluck as Vice-Presidential candidate of the PDP in the 2007 election was the main political concession to the Niger Delta.

9. 'Atiku accuses Obasanjo of hijacking three ministries', www.ngrguardiannews.com, 7 March 2007. Obasanjo retained the Petroleum portfolio between 1999 and 2007; he fell out with his first Minister of Defence, and his first Foreign Minister was generally regarded as an international relations lightweight.

10. 'Obasanjo admits unsuccessful first term', www.ngrguardiannews.com, 13 February 2007.

11. 'A Daughter of Zion', www.ngrguardiannews.com, 5 January 2006.

12. The 12 June 1993 Presidential election was supposed to mark the final stage of the transition to civil rule programme under the Babangida regime. Its annulment led to widespread civil unrest and the subsequent regime of General Sani Abacha.

13. Some acquisitions, such as the Port-Harcourt Refinery, have been reversed by President Yar' Adua.

14. 'Senate probes sale of Ajaokuta Steel firm', www.ngrguardiannews.com, 7 March 2008.

15. 'War Against Corruption's Yielding Results – Ribadu', www.thisdayonline.com, 10 September 2006.

16. 'MDD: FG Corrupting Democratic Process', www.thisdayonline, 23 November 2005. Based on an earlier Supreme Court ruling on a related matter, Obasanjo could also have used the amendment to stay on for a further twelve years.

17. 'Nigerians Oppose Third Term Agenda', www.ngrguardiannews.com, 18 December 2005; 'Term Limits, the Presidency, and the Quality of Elections: What Do Nigerians Think?' *Afrobarometer*, March 2006.

18. 'Britain to return loot, list challenges of Nigeria', www.ngrguardiannews.com, 15 February 2006.

19. 'UK warns against flawed amendment', www.thisdayonline.com, 12 May 2006.

20. 'European Union Undecided on Third Term', www.ngrguardiannews.com, 19 February 2006.
21. 'Dangers of tenure extention in Nigeria, by US', www.ngrguardiannews.com, 2 March 2006; 'Bush writes Obasanjo, Kicks against third term', www.sunnewsonline.com, 3 May 2006.
22. 'Carter Center Rates Lagos, Kano Polls Best in Nigeria' www.ngrguardiannews.com, 21 April 2007.
23. 'Buhari leads presidential preference rating', www.ngrguardiannews.com, 2 April 2007.
24. 'Anxiety in Abuja Over Fresh Presidential Poll', www.ngrguardiannews.com, 20 January 2008.
25. 'Afenifere Alleges Marginalisation of Yoruba By Yar'Adua', www.ngrguardiannews.com, 5 Jan. 2008.
26. 'Era of Coups Over, Says Obasanjo', www.ngrguardiannews.com, 6 May 2007.
27. 'Interview', *Newswatch*, 17 June 2002; 'I Regret Not Overthrowing Obasanjo – Malu', www.thisdayonline.com, 30 January 2006.
28. 'Don't invite Military, Ali warns politicians', www.thisdayonline.com, 6 March 2008.

References

Abati, Reuben. 2008. 'The President's Missing Ears', www.ngrguardiannews.com, 4 January.

Ahmad, Ehtisham and Raju Singh. 2003. *Political Economy of Oil-Revenue Sharing in a Developing Country: Illustrations from Nigeria*, IMF Working Paper, WP/03/16, Washington, DC: Fiscal Affairs Department, January.

BBC World Service Poll. 2007. 'Global Poll Finds that Religion and Culture are Not to Blame for Tension between Islam and the West'.

Bratton, Michael, Robert Mattes and Emmanuel Gyimah-Boadi. 2005. *Public Opinion, Democracy and Market Reforms in Africa*, Cambridge: Cambridge University Press.

Carter Center and National Democratic Institute for International Affairs. 1999. *Observing the 1998-99 Nigeria Elections, Final Report*. Atlanta, GA: Carter Center, Emory University and Washington, DC: NDIIR.

Chabal, Patrick and Jean-Pascal Daloz. 2006. *Cultural Troubles: Politics and the Interpretation of Meaning*. London: Hurst & Co.

Colonial Office, 1904, correspondence from Wallace to Chamberlain, Northern Nigeria, Further Correspondence relating to Kano Africa (West), No. 718. pp. 71-2.

Eni-B. 2007. 'After the Reversals ...', www.thisdayonline.com, 23 December.

Frynas, Jedrzej G. 1999. *Oil in Nigeria: Conflict and Litigation between Oil Companies and Village Communities*. Hamburg: LIT Verlag.

Guyer, Jane. 1992. Representation without Taxation: An Essay on Democracy in Rural Nigeria, 1952-1990. *African Studies Review* 35(1): 41-79.

Hiskett, Mervyn. 1987, The Maitatsine Riots in Kano, 1980: An Assessment, *Journal of Religion in Africa*, Vol. 17 Fasc. 3 Oct.: 209-23.

Human Rights Watch. 1999. Nigeria: Crackdown in the Niger Delta, *Human Rights Watch* Vol. 2, No. 2 (A).

Human Rights Watch. 2007. Chop Fine: The Human Rights Impact of Local Government Corruption and Mismanagement in Rivers State, Nigeria, *Human Rights Watch* Vol. 19, No. 2 (A).

International Republican Institute. 2003. International Republican Institute Report on the April 19, 2003 Elections. Washington DC: IRI.

Karmanje, Lawal. 2003. '2003 Events: Is Political Sharia Prematurely Dead?', website archive, www.gamji.com.

Last, Murray. 2002. Notes on the implementation of shari'a in northern Nigeria, *FAIS Journal of Humanities* (Bayero University, Kano) 2(2): 1-17.

——. 2007. Muslims and Christians in Nigeria: An Economy of Political Panic. *The Round Table* 96(392): 605-16.

——. 2008. The Search for Security in Muslim Northern Nigeria. *Africa* 78(1).

Lewis, Peter. 1994. Endgame in Nigeria? The Politics of a Failed Democratic Transition. *African Affairs* 93 (372): 323-40.

Lewis, Peter and Michael Bratton. 2000. Attitudes to Democracy and Markets in Nigeria. *Afrobarometer Paper*, No. 3.

Lindberg, Staffan. 2006. The Surprising Significance of African Elections. *Journal of Democracy* 17(1): 139-51.

Loimeier, Roman, 2005, Playing with Affiliations: Muslims in Northern Nigeria in the 20th Century. In *Entreprises religieuses transnationales en Afrique de l'Ouest*, eds Laurent Fourchard, Mary Andre and

René Otayek. Ibadan: IFRA and Paris: Karthala.

Lubeck, Paul. 1985. Islamic Protest Under Semi-Industrial Capitalism: 'Yan Tatsine Explained'. *Africa* 55(4): 369-89.

Mustapha, Abdul Raufu. 1999. The Nigerian Transition: Third Time Lucky or More of the Same? *Review of African Political Economy* 26(80): 277-91.

——. 2002. Coping With Diversity: The Nigerian State in Historical Perspective. In *The African State: Reconsiderations*, eds AI Samatar and AI Samatar. Portsmouth, NH: Heinemann.

——. 2004. Ethnicity and the Politics of Democratization in Nigeria. In *Ethnicity and Democracy in Africa*, eds Bruce Berman, Dickson Eyoh and Will Kymlicka. Oxford: James Currey.

——. 2006. Ethnic Structure, Inequality and Governance of the Public Sector in Nigeria. In *Ethnic Inequalities and Public Sector Governance*. ed. Yusuf Bangura. Basingstoke: Palgrave Macmillan.

Nas, Wada. 2002. More Positive Action, *Weekly Trust*, 29 March, web archive, www.gamji.com.

National Democratic Institute. 2003. Preliminary Statement of the National Democratic Institute. Washington, DC: NDI.

Obasanjo, Olusegun. 1998. The Country of Anything Goes. *New York Review of Books* 45(14): 55-7.

OCHA-IRIN, n.d. 'Nigeria: Plateau State IDPs face daunting obstacles to return to "home of peace and tourism"', www.irinnews.org.

Okonta, Ike. 2007. When does the 'Indigene' become a Citizen? Thoughts on the April 2007 Elections in Nigeria's Niger Delta. University of Oxford, Department of Politics and International Relations, mimeo.

Sanusi, Lamido. 2002. 'The Hudood Punishments in the Northern Nigeroa: A Muslim Criticism', paper for *ISIM NEWS*, Institute for the Study of Islam in Modernity, Leiden, Holland, website archive, www.gamji.com.

Suberu, Rotimi. Forthcoming 2009, Federalism and the Management of Conflicts Over Sharia in Nigeria, *Journal of International Development*, Special Issue on Diversity and Discord: Ethnicity and Conflict in West Africa.

Suleiman, Abdul-Azeez. 2003. 'Sharia', *Weekly Trust*, www.gamji.com, 26 July.

6

Kenya Since 2002
The More Things Change the More They Stay the Same
NIC CHEESEMAN*

In 2002 the victory of Mwai Kibaki and his National Rainbow Coalition (NaRC) over the incumbent Kenya African National Union was widely expected to usher in a period of political reform and economic prosperity (Wolf *et al.* 2004). Both international and domestic actors expected the Kibaki regime to curb corruption, show greater respect for political rights and civil liberties, and reform Kenya's over-centralised political institutions. According to opinion polls, in early 2003 Kenyans were the most optimistic people on earth (Gallup International 2002). Just fifteen months later, optimism about the future had plummeted, as a direct result of the failure of Kibaki and NaRC to break away from what David Bartlett (2000) has called 'older political logics'. As in Zambia and elsewhere in Africa, the removal of the dominant party of the post-independence period has not yet resulted in a radical change in the way politics is conducted.

The continued reproduction of the dominant institutions of the one-party era explains the limited nature of Kenya's democratic transition. The most significant formal institution has been the 'bureaucratic-executive' state, in which power is concentrated in the President and exercised through a prefectural structure of provincial administration. The strength of this executive-administrative axis has conferred great coercive capacity on the executive and limited the political space available to opposition leaders and movements. Despite this, some formal 'civil society' organisations, most notably the National Christian Council of Kenya and the Law Society of Kenya, proved able to mobilise their resources to protect targets of government aggression and promote democratic reform.

The central informal institution in Kenyan politics has been the network of patron-client relationships consolidated via the distribution of patronage at *harambee* (self-help) drives, which serve to cement the relationship between diverse Kenyan communities and their leaders. In doing so, Kenya's network of patron-client relations structures political mobilisation along ethnic lines. Together, these formal and informal institutions have worked to confer great power on the incumbent executive, to exaggerate the salience of ethnic cleavages, and to reduce the possibility of independent political mobilisation 'from below'.

Although they are perhaps more contested now than they have ever been, these institutions have not yet relinquished their hold over Kenyan politics. The heated debate surrounding the constitutional review process demonstrated that Kenyan political actors are well aware of the impact of the over-centralised state structure. However, like the late President Mwanawasa in Zambia, Kibaki proved unwilling to preside over a decentralisation of authority that would ultimately empower his opponents. With the defeat of the draft constitution in 2005, the executive-administrative axis remains in place, and continues to confer great resources on the incumbent. The NaRC government has done more to reform the patron-client nature of Kenyan politics, prohibiting the involvement of MPs in *harambee* activity and creating a centrally regulated Constituency Development Fund with the aim of rendering the process of community development more transparent and accountable. However, the impact of the Constituency Development Fund has been undermined as MPs have employed corrupt procurement contracts to divert development funds to their supporters, maintaining their patron-client relations in the process. Consequently, the form and structure of political competition in 2006 looked much like it has done throughout the post-independence period: the more things change, the more they stay the same.

Recent commentaries on Kenyan politics have generally argued that democratic consolidation requires the triumph of popular morality and commonly shared values over the divisive ethnic patriotisms which are fostered by elite actors (see Lonsdale 1992a; Orvis 2001; Klopp 2002). Rather than focus on the areas of conflict between mass and elite values, this chapter demonstrates that Kenya's dominant informal political institutions are maintained as a result of pressure *both* from 'above' and from 'below'. From above, the government has resisted calls to decentralise power, and political leaders of all persuasions have sought to consolidate their positions by maintaining patronage networks through alternative pathways, effectively undermining the impact of the restrictions placed on *harambee* activity. From below, Kenyan voters have continued to understand the primary role of their elected representatives as being one of 'linking' the community to sources of influence and patronage (Barkan 1984). The combined effect of these two trends has been to enable MPs to perpetuate existing political practices and to restrict the growth of cross-ethnic political movements. In this case, 'older political logics' have survived not because elite and mass values differ, but because they are mutually reinforcing.

A Brief Overview of Kenyan Political History

Since independence Kenya has been characterised by a relatively competitive and stable political landscape. In large part, this is due to the strength of elite actors, the security of tenure of Kenya's first President Jomo Kenyatta, and the durability of its coercive institutions (Gertzel 1970: 12; Tamarkin 1978). The significance of elite actors derived from the strength of a tier of high-profile ethnic patrons, whose political power was rooted in the salience of ethnic cleavages and the development of a localised 'boss politics' during the late colonial period. Following independence in 1964, the role of ethnic patrons was consciously enhanced by Kenyatta, who opted to channel patronage funds through local leaders and *harambee* projects. Kenyatta's creation of 'a federation of tribal baronies' ensured that his Kenya African National Union (KANU) party would become a classic 'patron party' (Lonsdale 1992a: 12), reliant not on a formal party infrastructure, but on the ability of a tier of local leaders to deliver the support of their constituents, as depicted in Figure 6.1 (Barkan 1984: 73). Significantly, by

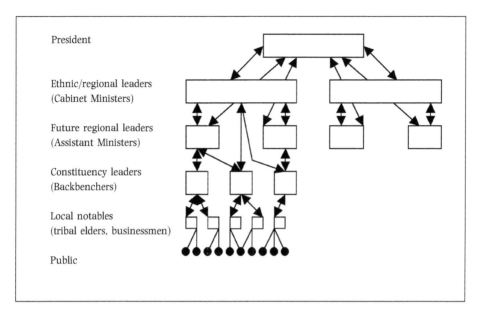

Figure 6.1 The structure of patron-client networks in Kenya

creating a system in which local communities were able to select their favoured patron via one-party elections, Kenyatta established a structure in which there was a considerable decentralisation of political power, making Kenya one of Africa's more competitive civil-authoritarian regimes.[1]

Kenyatta's personal popularity and the ability of KANU's predominantly Luo and Kikuyu leaders to effectively mobilise their communities *en masse* underpinned the party's electoral strength. KANU's dominance was further secured through the assimilation of all political opposition, which rendered Kenya a *de facto* one-party state soon after independence.[2] As in Zambia, the one-party structure empowered the executive (here understood to be the President and his closest allies and advisers) by facilitating the central regulation of competition over political office, and by extension, competition over access to state resources (Allen 1995). However, Kenyan politics remained relatively open, with a vibrant 'semi-competitive' electoral system and an occasionally vociferous legislature (Barkan 1984; Gertzel 1970: 39).

Despite these fragments of democracy, both the Kenyatta and Moi regimes resorted to violence and coercion to contain challenges to their hegemony. Most significantly, the inherited colonial bureaucracy of the provincial administration provided a direct line of command from the executive, through provincial commissioners, to district commissioners and local administrative officers on the ground. From its inception the provincial administration acted as the agent of the executive, playing a central role in the regulation of political space. This 'bureaucratic-executive' form of rule conferred great power on incumbent Presidents by enabling them to exert central control independently of the legislature and the conventional legal system (Branch & Cheeseman 2006). In the rare event that the administration proved to be an unsuitable tool for containing opposition, Kenyan rulers have proved willing to resort to political violence. Most notably, prominent political actors have been assassinated because of the very different threats they posed to vested interests within the government: Pio Pinto (1965), Tom Mboya (1969), J.M. Kariuki (1975) and Robert Ouko (1990).

There appears to be a general consensus that Kenyan politics became progressively more violent, arbitrary and authoritarian under the leadership of Kenya's second President, Daniel arap Moi, who succeeded Kenyatta on his death in 1978 (Throup & Hornsby 1998: 26). Certainly, Moi became an increasingly paranoid president following a failed coup attempt in 1982, and presided over a decline in the political rights and civil liberties enjoyed by Kenyan citizens. However, it is misleading to represent the Moi era as a radical break from past practice; three of the four assassinations listed above occurred during Kenyatta's time. In part, Moi's greater willingness to centralise authority, repress dissent violently, and manipulate ethnic cleavages to play divide-and-rule politics, was a response to the greater challenges he faced. As John Lonsdale (1992a) has argued, Moi was a considerably less lucky president than Kenyatta. The oil price shocks of 1973 and 1979 ensured that Moi faced a far more challenging economic context than his predecessor. At the same time, Moi lacked Kenyatta's strong ethnic base, personal wealth, and national appeal, and inherited a set of political institutions staffed with officers loyal to his predecessor.

Transition from Authoritarian Rule

From the mid-1980s onwards the stability of the Moi state was undermined from all sides. Firstly, low levels of economic growth combined with a rapidly expanding population weakened the ability of the Moi regime to fund the patronage networks on which its support base depended. Secondly, the collapse of the Soviet Union in 1989 transformed the international environment and reduced the ability of authoritarian leaders to access international funds. Thirdly, Kenyan civil society groups, strengthened by growing numbers of disaffected university graduates, and emboldened by the changing international context, worked to increase the constraints on the Moi regime. KANU struggled to respond to the more challenging political-economic situation, and while the repressive tactics utilised by Moi forced political opposition underground, they also discredited the Moi state (Haugerud 1995). In 1988 the explicit rigging of parliamentary and party elections proved to be an important catalyst for transition from authoritarian rule, alienating Kenyans of all classes. At the mass level, the implementation of a corrupt 'queue voting' system effectively under-mined the parliamentary elections which had previously been a key source of legitimacy for the regime (Throup 1993). At the elite level, many of those who lost their seats in 1988 responded by adopting prominent positions in the campaign for multiparty politics.

From 1990 onwards Moi began to lose control of political developments. In February 1990 the assassination of Foreign Minister Robert Ouko galvanised opponents of the Moi regime (Throup & Hornsby 1998: 59). Shortly after, prominent Kikuyu leaders Charles Rubia and Kenneth Matiba called publicly for the introduction of multiparty politics. In doing so they provided the necessary leadership to galvanise Kenya's 'diffuse' opposition (Widner 1992: 177). In July 1990 both men were detained, but KANU repression failed to contain the out-pouring of popular criticism. Civil society bodies such as the National Christian Council of Kenya and the Law Society of Kenya mobilised to use their organisa-tional capacity to protect pro-democracy activists, expanding both the physical and intellectual space within which the opposition could operate, and offering practical and legal support to its leading lights. On the first anniversary of Matiba and Rubia's detention the Luo leader Oginga Odinga announced the formation of a multi-ethnic pro-democracy movement called the Forum for the Restoration of Democracy (FORD). The great support for FORD, along with Kenya's fall from international grace, left KANU increasingly isolated both at home and abroad. Most significantly, the decision of donors at the Paris Group Meeting of November 1992 to withhold vital funds pending 'good governance' reforms, prompted Moi to abandon the one-party state (Throup & Hornsby 1998: 84).

Multiparty Politics Kenyan Style

Despite FORD's initial momentum, KANU retained power in the 'founding elections' of 1992 due to four main factors. Firstly, the opposition rapidly fragmented. FORD divided into two rival parties, one mainly Luo group led by Oginga Odinga (FORD-Kenya) and one mainly Kikuyu group headed by Kenneth Matiba (FORD-Asili). The opposition vote was further divided by Mwai Kibaki's decision to establish his own Democratic Party. Opposition fragmentation enabled Moi to secure re-election with just 36 per cent of the vote. Secondly, the provincial administration manipulated the voter registration process and employed widespread ballot box stuffing to deny the opposition a level playing field. Throup and Hornsby (1998) have estimated that KANU would have won 8 per cent fewer seats in the absence of electoral malpractice. Thirdly, the government sponsored a process of 'ethnic cleansing' in which more than 1,500 people lost their lives and over 300,000 were displaced, ensuring that the election was conducted in an atmosphere of fear. Finally, KANU effectively distributed patronage through its well established patron-client networks to recruit a broad multi-ethnic support base from well beyond its traditional heartlands, securing the election of 100 MPs from 21 ethnic groups (Throup 1993: 393).

KANU's victory ensured that the dominant formal and informal institutions of the one-party era survived the initial process of political liberalisation. Consequently, political competition continued in a similar vein. KANU's ability to retain power remained dependent on the ability of the administration to regulate political space and on the effectiveness of the party's patronage network. In turn, the distribution of patronage was made possible by the willingness of foreign donors to release funds despite Moi's refusal to implement anything other than minimal political reforms (Brown 2001). The elections of 1997 demonstrated strong parallels to those of 1992, as Moi retained the presidency, defeating a divided opposition.

Ultimately, it was not multiparty politics but internal divisions that undermined KANU rule (Anderson 2003). In the run-up to the 2002 elections, KANU fragmented around the issue of the Moi succession. Moi had served two terms as President of multiparty Kenya and was therefore constitutionally prevented from running again. However, no obvious successor stood out and Moi's choice of Uhuru Kenyatta (son of Jomo Kenyatta) as KANU's presidential candidate proved extremely controversial. In response, Raila Odinga (son of Oginga Odinga), who had been persuaded to join KANU just months earlier, left the party along with a number of hard-line KANU leaders to establish the rival Liberal Democratic Party (LDP).

While KANU was breaking up, opposition to it was becoming increasingly co-ordinated (see Oyugi *et al.* 2003). During 2000 and 2001 the Kikuyu leader

Mwai Kibaki had been carefully developing his own coalition, which ultimately brought together the Democratic Party, FORD-Kenya, the National Party of Kenya, and a number of smaller parties under the banner of the National Alliance Party of Kenya. Recognising the dangers of once again dividing the opposition vote, the Liberal Democratic Party and the National Alliance Party signed a memorandum of understanding in October 2002 to form a 'super alliance', the National Rainbow Coalition (NaRC). The agreement contained details of the power-sharing arrangements that would govern the distribution of posts and responsibilities should NaRC gain power (Anderson 2003: 3). Despite fears that KANU would be able to divide and rule once again, the campaign proved that the party had run out of ideas and lacked a credible presidential candidate. Kibaki won a landslide victory in the presidential poll with 62 per cent of the vote. In the parliamentary poll, KANU was finally removed from power, as NaRC won 125 (of 210) seats to KANU's 64.

Conceptualising Democratic Consolidation in Kenya

NaRC's victory promised the radical political change which many Kenyans had expected multiparty politics to deliver. The party's manifesto committed it to 'comprehensive political and economic changes in Kenya', and these reforms were expected to include a less aggressive use of patronage structures and the rapid 'completion of the current constitutional review process' (NaRC 2002: 7). In evaluating the impact of NaRC, this chapter focuses on the fate of the 'bureaucratic-executive' state and the network of patron-client relations. In doing so, it points to the role of forces both 'from above' and 'from below' in maintaining the dominant institutions of the one-party period. This argument differs from much of the recent literature on Kenya which has tended to focus on the role of elite actors in manipulating the process of political liberalisation, and which views local communities and 'local morality' as a positive democratic force (Lonsdale 1992a; Brown 2001). In order to demonstrate the limitations of this dominant understanding of Kenyan political culture, it is important to begin by interrogating the conceptual roots of the idea that popular morality represents a suitable foundation for a more democratic political landscape.

Democracy and Elites
The idea that the control of elites is integral to the process of democratisation is a natural extension of the neo-patrimonial model through which most commentators view African politics (Good 2003). After all, neo-patrimonialism, especially in its more extreme forms, emphasises the role of political elites in shaping and controlling political outcomes. In the literature on Kenya, the tension between elite and mass values and actions is often discussed in the context of John Lonsdale's influential distinction between moral ethnicity and political tribalism. Lonsdale argues that it is important to separate 'the moral ethnicity of the small working community which springs from below, and the political tribalism of invented nationality which may be manipulated from above' (1992a: 2). Put simply, moral ethnicity refers to what it means to belong and fulfil one's role within the local community – it is therefore organic and rises from the bottom up. In contrast, political tribalism is a device used by elite actors to mobilise support based on the manipulation of a community's fear of exclusion

from power and access to resources. Consequently, political tribalism generates a 'necessarily corrupt' relationship: 'however personally honest a patron may be, small society has no way of knowing' (ibid.: 3).

Following Lonsdale, analysts of Kenyan politics have tended to view the successful consolidation of Kenyan democracy as being synonymous with the triumph of moral ethnicity over political tribalism (Orvis 2001; Klopp 2002). This argument is best summarised by Lonsdale himself, who claims that 'Kenya's (and Africa's) real struggles are not between one-party autocracy and multi-party democracy but between the moral ethnicity of individual self-mastery and the political tribalism of group competition, between individual human rights and the patronage of wealth, and between the sorcerous unknowability of state power and new forms of public accountability' (1992a: 19). For Lonsdale, Klopp, and Orvis, moral ethnicity should be encouraged because it has 'distinct democ-ratising effects' (Orvis 2001: 12). Klopp, for example, sees an 'emancipatory potential' in the 'projection of moral ethnicity, the moral debate within local politics, onto the national public arena' (2002: 271).

Moral Ethnicity and Political Tribalism
The argument in favour of moral ethnicity is premised on two main claims that it is important to separate: the claim that political tribalism is a danger to the process of democratisation, and the claim that moral ethnicity represents a suitable foundation on which to build a democratic polity. The former claim is unproblematic. From the ethnic clashes of the early 1990s to the strong patterns of 'ethnic voting' surrounding the constitutional referendum of 2006, it is clear that elite actors remain able to manipulate ethnic loyalties for their own benefit (Throup & Hornsby 1998; Lynch 2006). However, the latter claim that moral ethnicity can provide an alternative ethical foundation for a democratic Kenya needs to be more rigorously examined. This claim is dependent on the assump-tion that 'moral ethnicity' can be used as shorthand for a political culture which promotes transparency, accountability, inclusivity and civic responsibility. However, Lonsdale himself recognises that moral ethnicity is a far more complex and problematic phenomenon than this assumption allows. Indeed, he is generally more cautious about the democratic potential of moral ethnicity than many of those who have subsequently adopted the term. His central thesis is not that moral ethnicity *as it is currently manifested* represents a strong foundation for a democratic Kenya. Rather, his point is that moral ethnicity is the only plausible source from which a more unifying and powerful critique of neo-patrimonial politics can emerge (2004: 75).

Despite this, those who have followed in Lonsdale's footsteps have tended to concentrate solely on those aspects of moral ethnicity which are compatible with democratic norms; commentators such as Klopp and Orvis pay far less attention to the 'dark side' of moral ethnicity. This is only natural, given their focus on identi-fying recent democratic gains, but it risks exaggerating the democratic virtue of politics 'from below'. Consequently, there is a pressing need to re-evaluate moral ethnicity in light of Lonsdale's reservations. Such an analysis reveals both the symbiotic relationship between moral ethnicity and political tribalism, and the extent to which moral ethnicity needs to evolve if it is to provide a cultural foundation for a democratic Kenya. These findings are significant because they call into question Lonsdale's hope that the routine failings of Kenya's patrons will transform moral ethnicity into a more radical and progressive democratic force (2004: 81, 93).

The democratic limitations of Kenyan moral ethnicity are best brought out by a focus on how merit, virtue, legitimacy, and appropriate governance are conceptualised in local debates. According to Lonsdale, the 'most lasting part of Kenya's political culture' is the idea that wealth is meritorious and poverty delinquent, that 'fatness was fertile, poverty a life-sucking parasite' (1992a: 4). Consequently, moral ethnicity is not underpinned by any egalitarian notion but by an explicitly elitist understanding of political obligation in which the rich are responsible not to the poor in general, but to the 'poor to whom one is related or whose service one needs' (ibid.: 8). In other words, the moral relationship between the poor and the rich is not based on an understanding of *civic* responsibility, but on ties of kinship and a calculating instrumentality. It is unclear how this key component of Kenyan moral ethnicity can be made compatible with the notion that democratic leaders should govern in the interests of all.

This is not to say that moral ethnicity does not promote a form of accountability. There are many examples of Kenyans acting *en masse* to ensure that patrons fulfil their duties and create wealth and opportunities for the community (Barkan 1984). As a result, there are real constraints on political leaders, who know that they must attend to the desires of their constituencies or risk rejection. In this way, moral ethnicity serves as an important check on the worst excesses of political tribalism, as Lonsdale, Klopp and Orvis have shown. But the patron-client nature of this relationship ensures that it is not equal, and that the accountability implied by moral ethnicity is limited. As Lonsdale notes, 'Wealth ineluctably incurred obligations; the poor, if they were to survive, inevitably owed obedience' (1992a: 5). The notion that well treated clients owe obedience to their patrons is an unsuitable norm on which to develop a more transparent and accountable system of government.

The moral connection between wealth and virtue, and between patronage and legitimacy, is also problematic. Lonsdale suggests that patrons are evaluated on their ability to use their wealth and access to power to the benefit of the community. This understanding of the duties and obligations of a community patron would seem to support, rather than challenge, a political system based on patronage networks in which criticism of abuse of public office is minimal so long as the bounty is shared. It is this very moral economy which grounds the idea that MPs are personally responsible for funding local development and all manner of other local needs. In turn, the pressure to deliver patronage encourages political leaders to seek new forms of income, and in doing so provides an additional incentive for the abuse of state funds. In this way, elements of moral ethnicity are complicit in the creation and maintenance of the informal patronage networks that dominate Kenyan political life. It is therefore imperative that we take a more critical attitude towards the relationship between moral ethnicity and democracy. We must recognise that when Kenyans protest against their patron they are not necessarily seeking to challenge the existing moral or political order. Rather, their actions may be premised on local understandings of the appropriate role of a 'good' patron, which themselves presuppose the existence of a patron-client contract and a moral economy premised upon patronage politics.

Of course, it is possible that disgruntled 'clients' from different ethnic groups will come to recognise their mutual exploitation at the hands of a group of failing 'patrons'. Moral ethnicity refers to a historically constituted and constantly evolving set of ideas, which raises the question of what the next transformation might bring. Lonsdale argues that in the pre-colonial period moral ethnicity had a 'multi-ethnic' nature because trade and inter-marriage offered a form of insurance against the unpredictability of the 'pre-state' world; it is possible that the failure of Kenya's patrons to deliver might just create the conditions under which a broader conception of citizenship will re-emerge (2004: 78). Perhaps inspired by this insight, Klopp and Orvis focus on specific instances in which the currents of accountability embedded within moral ethnicity have threatened to spill over into cross-ethnic coalitions that offer a more general critique of the status quo, raising the possibility of a 'politics from below' that is ordered along lines of status and wealth, rather than ethnicity.

However, the moments of solidarity identified by Klopp remain the exception rather than the rule because Kenyan moral ethnicity is far from completing a 'democratic transformation'. Significantly, this transformation remains unlikely because the barriers to it are not simply the result of the practice of political tribalism; rather, they are built into the very fabric of moral ethnicity itself. There are two important points to be made here. Firstly, it is far from clear that the notion of accountability, which gives moral ethnicity its critical standpoint, would be as coherent or powerful outside of the patron-client contract in which it is founded. If the norm of accountability cannot be separated from the patron-client contract that gave rise to it, it seems unlikely that the more democratic elements of moral ethnicity can be preserved while the more problematic elements are simultaneously discarded. Consequently, the relationship between moral ethnicity and democracy, and the idea that the former can support the latter, is highly problematic. Secondly, moral ethnicity (in its current manifestation) is part of the reason why Kenyans do not unite against their leaders. Moral ethnicity promotes both the significance of kinship, and the notion that clients should only expect favours from *their* patrons and that patrons should only be held accountable by *their* clients. Both of these notions embody norms that undermine the possibility of a unified challenge by a diverse group of clients against a diverse set of patrons.

Assessing the Impact of NaRC (1):
Patronage Politics in Kenya

The ambiguous relationship between moral ethnicity and democratic consolidation is best illustrated by the case of *harambee* self-help projects. The principle of *harambee* development was that if local communities established the start-up costs for local development projects such as schools and hospitals, the state would take over the running cost.[3] It was the job of MPs to facilitate community development by helping to organise and fund *harambee* projects. Large *harambee* fundraisers involved sizeable public gatherings at which MPs and other local notables were expected to make large contributions (TI Kenya 2001). The *harambee* system was therefore perfectly compatible with two key strands of moral ethnicity, namely, that patrons have a duty to use their positions to benefit the community and that this patronage should be extended to those who have worked hard to help themselves.

Harambee and moral ethnicity became mutually reinforcing: the cultural relevance of *harambee* ensured its success, and the success of *harambee* reinforced local understandings of the appropriate roles of the rich and the poor, the patron and the client. Most significantly, *harambee* encouraged Kenyans to evaluate their

MP on the basis of the resources that the MP could personally provide, or could divert to the local community from the political centre (Barkan & Holmquist 1989). As a result, 'With each successive national election in Kenya the key local issue has been one of determining which candidate has done the most for self-help' (Holmquist 1984: 185). In the short run, the demand for patronage encouraged MPs to borrow money and align themselves with wealthy patrons in order to satisfy their supporters (Widner 1992: 64-6). In the long run, the interaction of *harambee* and moral ethnicity cemented the connection between wealth, virtue, and legitimacy, within local moral discourse. In doing so, it created a legacy of norms and expectations that sustained a political system in which support is exchanged for patronage and state funds are distributed as personal largesse.

The Significance of Harambee

Harambee is a classic example of an informal institution that is manipulated by elite actors for their own benefit but sustained by its widespread popular legitimacy. While no panacea, Kenyatta's practice of *harambee* encouraged grass-roots participation and forced MPs to be attentive to the needs of their constituents. Under Moi, the function of *harambee* changed rapidly as the executive manipulated the provision of *harambee* funds to reward loyal MPs and punish dissidents. While Kenyatta used *harambee* to compensate ethnic groups which lost out in the overall distribution of government expenditure, Moi used it to play divide-and-rule politics (Widner 1992: 142-3). Under Moi, the unequal distribution of resources through centrally sponsored ethnic patrons significantly increased the salience of ethnic cleavages. During the 1980s, grass-roots *harambee* efforts quickly became crowded out by large-scale 'prestige projects' that could enhance the image of senior figures within the Moi coalition and boost the legitimacy of a vulnerable executive. As illustrated in Figure 6.2, in the immediate period surrounding times of crises (including the elections of 1983, 1988, 1992, and 1997), the executive consistently resorted to increasing the flow of *harambee* funds (TI Kenya 2001: 10). The partisan distribution of patronage via *harambee* has significant implications for the consolidation of democracy because it perpetuates the structure of indirect rule in which local communities are mobilised 'from above' by ethnic patrons. This 'top heavy' political system creates the conditions within which appeals to political tribalism are most effective. Furthermore, the centrality of the patron-client contract combined with the salience of ethno-political cleavages crowds out the emergence of alternative forms of political legitimacy and mobilisation.

Evidence of the central role played by MPs in Kenyan political life, the 'local focus' of Kenyan voters, and the ambiguous relationship between local moral discourse and patronage politics is provided by the *Afrobarometer* survey of political and economic attitudes in Kenya in 2005. According to the survey, an impressive 86 per cent of Kenyans could correctly name their MP compared with 63 per cent of Zambians and 67 per cent of Ghanaians, indicating the central role played by MPs in the Kenyan political landscape (*Afrobarometer* 2005). While 18 per cent of Ghanaians and 21 per cent of South Africans responded that an MP should spend no time in their home constituency or visit only once a year, only 10 per cent of Kenyans thought this was appropriate. Perhaps more significantly, Kenyan attitudes to corruption and the appropriate distribution of resources appear to reflect a set of norms entrenched in moral ethnicity and institutionalised through the *harambee* system. Put simply, many Kenyans do not

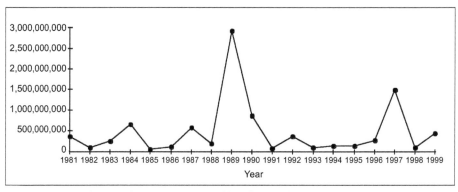

Figure 6.2 *Harambee* contributions per year (KSh), inflation adjusted

see the distribution of patronage through the manipulation of development expenditure as corrupt. This is well illustrated by the responses given by Kenyans to a series of questions about whether certain acts by government officials were 'not wrong at all', 'wrong but understandable', or 'wrong and punishable'. In Africa's more democratic nations such as Ghana and South Africa,[4] 80 to 90 per cent of respondents typically answer that all of the actions described – an official giving a job to a family member who is unqualified, an official demanding a bribe, and an official situating development projects in their home area – are 'wrong and punishable'. However, Kenyans seem to make a distinction between bribery and patronage. The vast majority of Kenyans (84 per cent) responded that it was 'wrong and punishable' for an official to demand an additional payment for 'some service that is part of his job'. But only 55 per cent thought that it was 'wrong and punishable' for an official to 'locate a development project in an area where his friends and supporters live'. In other words, while Kenyans are extremely hostile to corruption, they do not necessarily see the use of development projects to reward family and supporters as corrupt. This ambiguity perfectly illustrates the point that, although Kenyan moral ethnicity includes norms of accountability, the democratic potential of these norms is limited. The 'bottom-up' pressure on MPs to divert funds from their legitimate target towards maintaining patron-client relations remains. Combined with the desire of political leaders for personal enrichment, these pressures sustain a political system in which patronage is the main political currency.

Patronage Politics under NaRC
The significance of *harambee* was well understood by NaRC leaders, many of whom had used *harambee* donations to develop their own support base. In the period 1980-89, Kibaki and Vice-President Moody Awori were the fourth and fifth largest *harambee* donors, respectively (TI Kenya 2001: 19). In 2003 NaRC established a task force to investigate *harambee* which provided concrete evidence of the relationship between *harambee*, the distribution of patronage, and the corruption of the Moi regime (Republic of Kenya 2003a). In response, NaRC adopted two policies. The first prohibited MPs from donating to *harambee* projects, theoretically breaking the chain that connected the constituency to State House. The second established a Constituency Development Fund (CDF) intended to replace *harambee* as the focus of local development and to ensure that develop-

ment funds are spent in a transparent and accountable manner (Republic of Kenya 2004). Although the 'de-politicisation' of *harambee* and the creation of the CDF have modified the structure of patronage in Kenya, they have not altered its basic logic. In fact, the CDF is best interpreted as further institutionalising the norm that MPs are primarily local patrons, important because of their access to development funds.

The regulation of *harambee* activity and the introduction of the CDF benefited the NaRC leadership in a number of ways. Most obviously, the policy could be sold to donors as evidence that NaRC was taking corruption seriously. Perhaps more significantly, the prohibition of MPs taking part in *harambee* activity restricted the ability of the regime's key opponents (most obviously Moi and Uhuru Kenyatta) to use their vast personal wealth to mobilise support. The CDF also strengthens the position of incumbent MPs and hence the government. The Fund is distributed through Constituency Development Committees that are appointed by the constituency MP (see Figure 6.3), who also sits on the Committee (Republic of Kenya 2003b, 2004). Consequently, although MPs do not chair the committees, they are the 'power behind the throne' and can effectively control the local distribution of CDF funds.

Many commentators have interpreted the CDF as a positive development. The designer of the Fund, Muriuki Karue, was awarded a UN-Habitat award in recognition of his work. Certainly, there are many positive aspects to the CDF. The Fund has the potential to enable a more equitable distribution of resources, as 75 per cent of the total fund is allocated equally among all 210 constituencies, with the remaining 25 per cent allocated according to constituency poverty levels. Furthermore, by regularising the flow of resources for development and removing them from presidential control, the Fund has weakened the link between local patrons and the executive. This is a significant development, and one that promises to reduce the ability of the executive to manage political events through the control of the patronage structure. The Fund has also made it easier for ordinary Kenyans to track development expenditure through the creation of a website which provides constituency level data on the composition and activities of each Constituency Development Committee.

However, the positive elements of the CDF have been compromised as a result of pressures arising both 'from above' and 'from below'. From above, the Kibaki administration has proved willing to extend patronage through alternative mechanisms when the need arises. During the constitutional referendum campaign in 2006, the President announced a number of measures designed to boost the regime's support in key areas. One strategy was to declare the creation of 27 new Districts, providing greater representation and hence potential benefits for the relevant constituencies. Another tactic was to distribute land by decreeing that part of the Mau Forest be opened up to selected squatters.[5] The manipulation of government policy to secure votes undermines the impact of the ban on *harambee* activity and retards the development of a political system in which policies, rather than patronage, are the primary focus of voters.

From below, MPs and local communities appear to have interpreted the CDF through the lens of their *harambee* experience. To appreciate this point it is important to recognise that the CDF has actually institutionalised some of the key elements of *harambee* practice. Indeed, Martin Shikuku, a former MP and leading critic of *harambee*, argues that the CDF will be successful precisely because it recognises that Kenyan communities place impossible financial demands on their

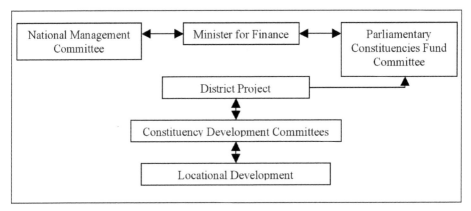

Figure 6.3 Constitutional Development Fund project submission flow-chart

MPs; it provides MPs with 'their own funds' to meet their 'local responsibilities'. In other words, the CDF is designed to reduce the need for political leaders to enter into corrupt practices in order to meet local expectations. However, by providing MPs with easier access to development funds the CDF is likely to further entrench the relationship between local communities, MPs, development funds, and political legitimacy. This is a crucial point, because the ability of the CDF to deliver a more transparent and accountable politics depends on the willingness of constituencies to scrutinise the actions of their MPs. Yet the norm of accountability embedded in Londsale's moral ethnicity supports evaluations of patrons on the basis of the quantity and quality of 'development' they provide and is blind to the question of how that development was funded (Holmquist 1984; Throup 1993). As the *Afrobarometer* findings quoted above suggest, popular morality cannot be relied upon to challenge patronage politics, especially where local electorates feel included in the distribution of largesse.

As the CDF is only four years old at the time of writing, it is far too early to test these hypotheses and to fully gauge its long-term impact. However, the story so far is far from promising. A recent audit report by the CDF National Committee criticised managers 'in most of the 210 constituency development committees, saying they influenced the use of the KSh7.2 billion fund for their selfish and personal interests'.[6] Much of the questionable use of CDF funds is rooted in the abuse of procurement procedures – a classic Kenyan corruption scam. Reviewing 11,128 projects undertaken nationwide, the Commission found that many Constituency Development Committees were awarding lucrative contracts to companies with links to Committee members without competitive tendering and had paid for goods which were never delivered. The report also suggests a widespread bias in the awarding of educational bursaries, which can make up 10 per cent of the Constituency Development Committee's budget under the Constituency Development Fund Act of 2003. The findings of the report only serve to confirm a growing sense of disquiet that the CDF has been used by MPs to reward their supporters, with funds trickling down from the CDF through businesses associated with the MP, via local elites, to local communities.[7] In this way the CDF has replicated the vertical flow of patronage funds under *harambee*, albeit on a more limited scale and without the direct involvement of the executive.

The parallels between the CDF and *harambee* are likely to grow as the size of the Fund increases. MPs are responsible for setting the CDF budget in Parliament and have a clear incentive to increase the resources at their disposal. Originally, the Fund was set at 2.5 per cent of 'ordinary government revenue' in any given year. However, in May 2006 MPs voted to treble the Fund's allocation to 7.5 per cent. The vote brought instant criticism from Colin Bruce, head of the World Bank's Nairobi Office, who argued that the implementation of the CDF had betrayed its early promise.[8] Significantly, the CDF is now worth only slightly less as a proportion of government spending than *harambee* projects were during the 1980s. While the expansion and manipulation of the CDF have clearly been led by a self-interested tier of political leaders, it is a mistake to focus exclusively on the negative role played by elite actors and to see the promotion of local moral discourses as an unproblematic solution. Rather, we must recognise that Kenya's patron-client networks have proved durable precisely because they are rooted in local norms and values; they will only be undermined by the triumph of moral ethnicity if it first undergoes a radical – and unlikely - transformation.

Assessing the Impact of NaRC (2): The Kenyan State

The argument that moral ethnicity does not yet represent a suitable foundation for a democratic Kenya is not intended to downplay the role of elite actors in restricting democratic reform. Clearly, the strong continuities in the structure of the Kenyan state result from the advantages it confers on the executive and the willingness of the government to manipulate the constitutional review process to serve its own interests. NaRC's failure to introduce the constitutional reforms the party promised in its manifesto is the best possible evidence of the negative impact of elite actors on the process of democratisation, and illustrates the growing recognition of the potential impact of formal political institutions on the continent.

The Kenyan state is widely recognised as being one of the more capable and significant formal political institutions in sub-Saharan Africa (see Jackson & Rosberg 1982).[9] As previewed above, the dominant feature of the Kenyan state since the colonial period has been the concentration of power in the hands of the executive (whether colonial governor or post-colonial president), and the ability of the executive to exert control through the prefectural structure of the provincial administration. This 'bureaucratic-executive' formation has survived every major political transition including the onset of independence and the transition to multiparty politics (Branch & Cheeseman 2006). The structure of the Kenyan state has been maintained because it confers considerable benefits on incumbent leaders. Despite the liveliness of the Kenyan legislature, Kenyan presidents have suffered few restraints on their ability to formulate policy. Most obviously, the lack of constitutional constraints on presidential authority, coupled with the ability to determine appointments to the cabinet, the military, and parastatals, has enabled the executive to effectively develop a loyal support base through its control over access to patronage (Gertzel *et al.* 1969: 312-4). Both Kenyatta and Moi ruled via a closed 'inner circle' staffed with their closest allies. However, while Kenyatta presided over a relatively small and stable Cabinet in which senior leaders were allowed to construct their own mini-empires within a given ministry, under Moi the composition and size of the Cabinet proved remarkably unstable. By rotating MPs through ministries, and by continually increasing the number of ministers, Moi sought to prevent the emergence of independent sources of authority within his government, while enhancing the scope of patronage available to the executive. The lack of checks and balances confers awesome power on the executive and minimises the ability of the opposition to scrutinise government policy and performance.

The Significance of the Kenyan State
Since the colonial period, responsibility for maintaining political order has fallen on the administration, not the police.[10] Given this, the strength of the executive-administrative axis has empowered the President to regulate political space and control competition over spoils. The reach of the provincial administration to the most distant rural areas allowed the executive to monitor political developments and control the distribution of patronage down to the local level (Mueller 1984: 407). Although there are considerable geographical variations in the scope and coercive capacity of the administration, to date it has been strong in those areas in which the authority of the regime has been most threatened. Consequently, the degree of penetration of the provincial administration has enabled the executive to contain 'peripheral' unrest: the centre-periphery divide which characterises many African countries does not apply in the Kenyan case (see Jackson & Rosberg 1982; Mueller 1984). Significantly, the administration has continually been used to defeat political movements 'from below' that have sought to promote a more egalitarian politics and increase political space. In the late 1960s the administration was at the forefront of KANU's campaign against the Kenya People's Union and played a similar role in KANU's attempts to hold on to power following the re-introduction of multiparty politics (Mueller 1984: 413; Throup & Hornsby 1998: 372).

It is precisely the advantages which the executive-administrative axis confers on incumbent leaders which explain the longevity of this institutional configuration. Although the internal structure of the administration has been subject to significant variation since independence, every Kenyan President has sought to maintain the basic structure of the 'bureaucratic-executive' state (Barkan & Chege 1989). This point is well illustrated by the flawed process of constitutional review under the Kibaki regime.

Constitutional Review and the Bureaucratic-executive State under NaRC
During the 2002 election campaign NaRC had promised to reform the 'KANU state', and these changes were expected to include greater checks on the power of the President, the creation of the post of Prime Minister, and the destruction of the provincial administration. Following the election, NaRC quickly established a National Constitutional Conference to revise the constitutional proposals that had already been drawn up in the last years of KANU rule. In March 2002 the Conference produced a new draft Constitution, popularly known as the Bomas Draft. This draft 'boasted broad participation and extended debate' and contained clauses to limit the powers of the President, including the creation of the post of Prime Minister (Lynch 2006: 7). The Bomas Draft also included plans for a multi-tiered structure of regional government that appeared to be both unwieldy and costly. There were therefore good reasons to question the feasibility of the Bomas Draft. This, however, was not the main concern of the Kibaki camp within NaRC, who sought to resist the implementation of constitutional reforms that would significantly reduce the control of central government and the powers of the

President. By the time the new constitution was finally presented to Parliament for debate and amendment, the executive had already taken steps to ensure that the Bomas Draft could be undermined. In December 2004 the government forced through an amendment to the Constitution of Kenya Review Bill that reduced the majority required to change the Bomas Draft from two-thirds to a simple majority. This ensured that the Kibaki faction within NaRC could amend the Bomas Draft against the wishes of both the KANU opposition and the Liberal Democratic Party, itself a member of the NaRC government.

Following the amendment to the Constitutional Review Bill, Attorney General Amos Wako was given the responsibility of generating a 'final text' that was supposed to be based on the Bomas Draft and the amendments suggested within the Parliament. Unsurprisingly, the draft that Parliament ultimately put forward for public approval by referendum was very different to that agreed at the National Constitutional Conference (Andreassen *et al.* 2006: 3). Most contentiously, the redrafted Constitution retained the powers of the President and the central government and reduced the responsibilities of the proposed office of Prime Minister (Republic of Kenya 2005). In doing so it reflected the growing tension between Kibaki and Raila Odinga, who had played a crucial role in leading NaRC's campaign for the 2002 general elections during Kibaki's period of ill health.

Less attention was paid to the proposed fate of the bureaucracy, but there were significant changes to the Bomas Draft here also. In the original text the provincial administration was effectively dismantled in favour of a form of devolved government in which greater powers would be given to the provinces. The Bomas Draft also provided for a decentralisation of the administrative system that would have empowered 'divisions' and 'locations' at the sub-district level. While the government acceded to the demise of the provincial administration, the 'final draft' proposed an elected district administration that would remain answerable to the central government. Furthermore, all forms of devolution of power below the district level were resisted, effectively protecting the influence of the district administration that has for so long underpinned the strength of the bureaucratic-executive state.

Disagreement over the draft Constitution split the already fractious NaRC coalition. Ahead of the referendum held in November 2005, Cabinet members openly campaigned against one another. During the campaign two broad camps emerged based around the symbols used in the referenda: banana for yes and orange for no. The Banana camp was led by the President, who, along with 115 other MPs, declared his support for the Wako Draft (Lynch 2006: 12). At the parliamentary level the Orange camp was composed of 80 MPs from the major opposition parties plus disgruntled members of NaRC led by Raila Odinga's LDP. Crucially, although the Orange camp had the support of fewer MPs, their ethnic appeal was far wider. While the main source of 'Banana' support was Kibaki's Kikuyu base in Central Province, the 'Orange' campaign combined the Luo, Kalenjin, and to a lesser extent Kamba and Luhya communities. Although the elections were far from an 'ethnic census', Kenyan leaders once again proved able to mobilise their ethnic communities (Lynch 2006). Ultimately, the broader support base of the leaders of the Orange campaign provided the foundation of the government's defeat, with 57 per cent of voters rejecting the new Constitution.

The comparative absence of electoral manipulation combined with the government's willingness to accept defeat was interpreted by some commentators as evidence that Kenyan democracy is consolidating and that the pernicious influence of the administration is on the wane. For example, Andreassen *et al.* argue that the relatively low level of tension on polling day 'suggests that democratic rule and behaviour is taking root and gradually maturing, which augurs well for the future' (2006: 5). This interpretation is lent some credibility by Kibaki's 'hands-off' leadership style, in which the executive has governed in a manner reminiscent of the Kenyatta period and has not attempted to control all aspects of public policy. However, like Kenyatta, Kibaki has also been prepared to assert the dominance of the presidency during periods of crisis, for example by sacking the entire Cabinet following the defeat of the draft Constitution.[11] What Andreassen *et al.*'s optimistic interpretation of the referendum misses is that the government had already rigged the entire review process to protect the bureaucratic-executive state. By ensuring that the draft to be voted on preserved the key structures of the executive-administrative axis, the Kibaki camp placed itself in a no-lose situation. Had the draft Constitution been accepted there would have been no great devolution or decentralisation of power, and the issue of constitutional review could have been put to rest. With the defeat of the proposed Constitution, Kenya's existing 'top-heavy' Constitution remains in place and continues to be a great resource for the President.

This is not to say that the executive has not been damaged by the controversy surrounding the review process. Kibaki's intransigence effectively ended any pretence of unity within NaRC and resulted in a more fragmented political system that the President subsequently struggled to control. Furthermore, the ability of the Orange Democratic Movement (ODM) to outmanoeuvre the government during the election campaign revealed Kibaki's vulnerability and encouraged greater unity among the Kenyan opposition. The victory of the ODM has also enhanced the image of Raila Odinga as a 'Kingmaker' in the Kenyan political scene, which represented an important step in his bid to demonstrate his 'electability' to the country at large. All four developments proved detrimental to the executive in the run-up to the 2007 elections. However, given the executive's careful manipulation of the review process, Kibaki had more to lose than to gain in the referendum campaign of 2005 by unleashing the coercive capacity of the provincial administration and drastically running down the regime's patronage reserves. It is therefore unsurprising that Andreassen *et al.* found that the referendum was conducted in a more open and relaxed atmosphere than previous elections. However, the constitutional referendum of 2005 was a poor test of the willingness of the government to manipulate the institutions under its control in order to preserve its hold on power.

Postscript

This chapter was written in late 2006, over a year before the disputed December 2007 general elections which inspired ethnic clashes that left more than 1,000 dead and more than 250,000 displaced, according to the official figures alone. The flawed electoral process, in which Mwai Kibaki was controversially declared to have secured 225,174 more votes than ODM leader Raila Odinga amid widespread accusations of electoral malpractice, revealed the real significance of the failed constitutional review process. Kenya's unbalanced institutional landscape underpinned the events which resulted in the 'Kenya crisis' at every stage. Before the polls, the continued existence of the bureaucratic-executive state meant that Kibaki could deploy considerable government resources, including the provincial administration, to support his campaign (European Union EOM 2008: 9). During the election attention turned to the Electoral Commission of Kenya. The appointment of 19 of the 22 Electoral Commissioners in the year leading up to the polls, in the absence of cross-party consultation, undermined confidence in the electoral process. Election observers allege that the government used its influence over the Commission to manipulate the vote-counting and tallying process (ibid.: 15).

Following the polls, the refusal of ODM leaders to call off mass protests, take up their seats in Parliament, and pursue their complaints in the courts was motivated in part by their appreciation of the chronic weakness of these institutions. The opposition was well aware that petitions relating to electoral malpractice in the 2002 parliamentary elections were only resolved in the months immediately before the 2007 polls, and that Kibaki had moved to consolidate his control over the judiciary by appointing six new judges to the Court of Appeal and High Court just three days before election-day. Of course, Kibaki's ability to prevent the ODM from holding a protest rally in Uhuru Park in the immediate aftermath of the election also demonstrates the coercive capacity of the Kenyan state. As in the past, the executive relied on the police, the General Service Unit, and the provincial administration, to maintain control of the centre of Nairobi.

While the elections clearly demonstrated the continued centrality of the Kenyan state to political outcomes, they also confirmed the importance of the control of elites for the process of democratic consolidation. The eruption of violence revealed the hidden legacy of the instrumental use of violence in the 1990s and represented the ultimate victory of political tribalism. As a result, the events of early 2008 will no doubt inspire students of Kenyan politics to devote greater energies to the search for moral ethnicity. This is a noble project; despite the importance of the bureaucratic-executive state to Kenyan politics, it is clear that institutional reform alone will be insufficient to secure democratic consolidation. So long as 'older political logics' are ingrained in sufficient communities at both the mass and the elite level, institutional engineering will be undermined by the everyday practice of politics. Lonsdale, Klopp, and Orvis are therefore right to look for alternative political cultures that might ground a more accountable and transparent set of institutions.

However, there are good reasons to doubt that the triumph of moral ethnicity over political tribalism will be enough to effect this transformation. This chapter has argued that the informal institutions which dominate Kenyan politics, most notably the patron-client relations that constituted the *harambee* patronage system, have proved durable precisely because they enjoy great popular legitimacy. The case of *harambee* demonstrates that not only is moral ethnicity compatible with Kenya's dominant informal institutions, in some cases the two are mutually reinforcing. The norms of accountability and sense of duty which Lonsdale identifies within moral ethnicity are certainly there, but they are intimately bound up in local understandings of the very patron–client relations that serve to undermine democratic reform. It is unclear how moral ethnicity can evolve so that its more 'democratic' components are isolated and preserved, while the patron–client contract on which they are founded is simultaneously discarded and forgotten, especially in the current political context. There can be no doubt that successful democratic consolidation in Kenya requires the defeat of political tribalism, but moral ethnicity is no panacea.

Notes

* The author would like to thank David Anderson, Daniel Branch, Miles Larmer, John Lonsdale, Steve Orvis, and the editors for their thoughtful advice.
1. At its most basic level, the term 'civil-authoritarian' refers to non-democratic rule by domestic non-military (i.e. civilian) forces.
2. Splits within KANU resulted in the emergence of the Kenya People's Union (KPU) and a return to multiparty politics in 1966-69. The KPU was prohibited in 1969 following disturbances at a political rally in Kisumu, leaving Kenya a *de facto* one-party state until Moi moved to establish a *de jure* one-party state in 1982.
3. For an in-depth discussion of *harambee* projects, see Mbithi and Rasmusson (1977).
4. These are the two most democratic countries in the *Afrobarometer* sample, according to Freedom House, see www.freedomhouse.org.
5. See the *East African Standard*, Joseph Murimi, 'Accusing Kibaki', 5/10/2005.
6. *Daily Nation*, Odhiambo Orlale, 'Report Reveals Misuse of CDF Cash', 20/10/2006.
7. *Daily Nation* Editorial, 'Tighten Loose Ends on CDF', 21/10/2006.
8. *Daily Nation* David Mugonyi, 'World Bank Boss and MPs Clash Over CDF, 5/5/2006.
9. Here I follow Lonsdale and Berman (1979: 489) in understanding the state to be 'the historically conditioned set of institutions in any class society which, more or less adequately, secures the social conditions for the reproduction of the dominant mode of production'.
10. Under colonial rule the administration was granted its own police force, the Tribal Police (later the Administrative Police). This force was separate from the Kenya Police, and formally had more limited powers, although in practice these boundaries were hazy and restrictions on the force's jurisdiction were often transgressed, see Anderson (1994).
11. *Daily Nation*, Eric Shimoli, 'Tough Rules for the Cabinet', 12/6/2005.

References

Afrobarometer. 2005. Summary of Results Kenya. www.afrobarometer.org.
Allen, Chris. 1995. Understanding African Politics. *Review of African Political Economy* 22 (65):301-320.
Anderson, David M. 1994. Policing the settler state: Kenya, 1900-52. In *Contesting Colonial Hegemony: state and society in Africa and India*, ed. Dagmar Engels and Shula Marks. London: British Academic Press.
——. 2003. Kenya's Elections 2002: The dawning of a new era? *African Affairs* 102 (407): 331-42.
Andreassen, Bêard-Anders, Gisela Geisler and Arne Tostensen. 2006. *Of Oranges and Bananas: The 2005 Kenya referendum on the constitution*. Bergen: Chr. Michelson Institute.
Barkan, Joel. 1984. Legislators, Elections, Political Linkage. In *Politics and Public Policy in Kenya and Tanzania*, eds Joel D. Barkan and John Okumu. Nairobi: Heinemann Kenya.
Barkan, Joel and Michael Chege. 1989. Decentralising the State: District focus and the politics of reallocation in Kenya. *Journal of Modern African Studies* 27 (3):431-53.
Barkan, Joel and Frank Holmquist. 1989. Peasant-State Relations and the Social Base of Self-Help in Kenya. *World Politics* 41 (3): 359-80.
Bartlett, David. 2000. Civil Society and Democracy: A Zambian case study. *Journal of Southern African Studies* 26 (3):429-46.
Berman, Bruce. 1998. Ethnicity, Patronage and the African State: The politics of uncivil nationalism. *African Affairs* 97 (388):305-41.
Branch, Daniel and Nic Cheeseman. 2005. Using Opinion Polls to Evaluate Kenyan Politics, March 2004-January 2005. *African Affairs* 104 (415):325-36.
——. 2006. The Politics of Control in Kenya: Understanding the bureaucratic-executive state, 1954-73. *Review of African Political Economy* 33 (107):11-31.
Brown, Stephen. 2001. Authoritarian Leaders and Multiparty Elections in Africa: How foreign donors help to keep Kenya's Daniel arap Moi in power. *Third World Quarterly* 22 (5): 725-39.
European Union Electoral Observers Mission (EU EOM). 2008. Preliminary Statement: Doubts about the credibility of the presidential results hamper Kenya's democratic progress. http://ec.europa.eu/external_relations/human_rights/eu_election_ass_observ/kenya07/prelim_stat.pdf.
Gallup International. 2002. *End of Year Survey*, www.gallup.com.
Gertzel, Cherry. 1970. *The Politics of Independent Kenya, 1963-8*. Nairobi: East African Publishing House.

Gertzel, Cherry, Maure Leonard Goldschmidt and Donald S. Rothchild. 1969. *Government and Politics in Kenya: A nation building text.* Nairobi: East African Publishing House.
Good, Kenneth. 2003. Democracy and the Control of Elites. *Journal of Contemporary African Studies* 21 (2):155-72.
Haugerud, Angelique. 1995. *The Culture of Politics in Modern Kenya.* Cambridge: Cambridge University Press.
Holmquist, Frank. 1984. Self-Help: The state and peasant leverage in Kenya. *Africa: Journal of the International African Institute* 54 (3):72-91.
Jackson, Robert and Carl Rosberg. 1982. Why Africa's Weak States Persist: The empirical and the juridical in statehood. *World Politics* 35 (1):1-24.
Kenya, Republic of. 2003a. *Report of the Task Force on Public Collections or "Harambees".* Nairobi: Government Printer.
——. 2003b. *The Constituency Development Fund Act.* Nairobi: Government Printer.
——. 2004. *Constituency Development Fund Information,* http://www.cdf.go.ke/.
——. 2005. *Kenya Gazette Supplement, 2005: The proposed new constitution of Kenya.* Nairobi: Government Printer.
Klopp, Jacqueline. 2002. Can Moral Ethnicity Trump Political Tribalism? The Struggle for Land and Nation in Kenya. *African Studies* 61 (2):269-94.
Lonsdale, John and Bruce Berman. 1979. Coping With the Contradictions: The development of the colonial state in Kenya, 1895-1914. *Journal of African History* 20 (4):487-505.
Lonsdale, John. 1992a. *The Political Culture of Kenya.* Occasional Paper 37, Edinburgh: Centre of African Studies, Edinburgh University.
——. 1992b. The Moral Economy of Mau Mau: Wealth, Poverty and Civic Virtue in Kikuyu Political Thought. In *Unhappy valley: conflict in Kenya & Africa book I,* ed. Bruce Berman and John Lonsdale. London: James Currey. 315-504.
——. 2004. Moral and Political Arguments in Kenya. In *Ethnicity and Democracy in Africa,* eds Bruce Berman, Dickson Eyoh and Will Kymlicka. Oxford: James Currey.
Lynch, Gabrielle. 2006. The Fruits of Perception: 'Ethnic politics' and the case of Kenya's constitutional referendum. *African Studies* 65 (2):233-70.
Mbithi, Philip and Rasmus Rasmusson. 1977. *Self Reliance in Kenya: The case of harambee.* Uppsala: Scandinavian Instutute of African Studies.
Mueller, Suzanne. 1984. Government and Opposition in Kenya, 1966-69. *Journal of Modern African Studies* 22 (3):399-427.
National Rainbow Coalition (NaRC). 2002. *Democracy and Empowerment; Manifesto for the National Rainbow Coalition.* Nairobi: NaRC.
Orvis, Stephen. 2001. Moral Ethnicity and Political Tribalism in Kenya's 'Virtual Democracy'. *African Issues* 29 (1/2):8-13.
Oyugi, Walter O., Peter Wanyande and C. Odhiambo Mbai. 2003. *The Politics of Transition in Kenya: from KANU to NARC.* Nairobi: Heinrich Boll Foundation.
Tamarkin, Mordechai. 1978. The Roots of Political Stability in Kenya. *African Affairs* 77 (308):297-320.
Throup, David. 1993. Elections and Political Legitimacy in Kenya. *Africa* 63 (3):371-96.
Throup, David and Charles Hornsby. 1998. *Multi-Party Politics in Kenya: The Kenyatta and Moi states and the triumph of the system in the 1992 election.* Oxford: James Currey.
(TI Kenya) Transparency International Kenya. 2001. *Harambee: Pulling together or pulling apart?.* Nairobi: Transparency International Kenya.
Widner, Jennifer. 1992. *The Rise of a Party-State in Kenya: From 'Harambee!' to 'Nyayo!'* San Francisco, CA and Oxford: University of California Press.
Wolf, Tom, Carolyn Logan and Paul Kiage. 2004. A New Dawn? Popular optimism in Kenya after the transition. *Afrobarometer Working Paper No: 33,* www.afrobarometer.net.

Interviews

Shikiku, Martin. Interviewed 08/09/2005. Former Member of Parliament for Butere, KANU & Founding Member, FORD. Nairobi, Kenya.
wa Mwachofi, Mashengu. Interviewed 9/09/2005. Former Member of Parliament for Wundanyi constituency, KANU & National Chairman, Shirikisho Party of Kenya. Nairobi, Kenya.
wa Wamwere, Koigi. Interviewed 12/09/2005. Member of Parliament for Subukia constituency and Assistant Minister for Information, NaRC. Nairobi, Kenya.

7

Zambia since 1990
Paradoxes of Democratic Transition

MILES LARMER

In September 2006, the Movement for Multiparty Democracy (MMD) and its presidential candidate, the late Levy Mwanawasa, were re-elected as the government of Zambia. The MMD's fourth successive election victory since Zambia's return to multiparty democracy in 1990-91 suggests that effective pluralism has yet to be entrenched in Zambian political life.[1] Certainly, the optimism that surrounded that transition regarding the potential of democratisation to address the country's profound social, economic and political problems proved unfounded. By the late 1990s, amidst economic collapse and a renewed authoritarianism that echoed aspects of the Zambian one-party state of the 1970s and 1980s, it appeared that formal democratisation had made little impact either on political culture or the lives of ordinary Zambians (Bratton & Posner 1999). In this sense, Zambia bore a strong resemblance to many other sub-Saharan African countries that experienced similar transitions in the early 1990s, only to see the 'capture' of new democratic structures by what Bartlett calls 'older political logics' (Bartlett 2000: 445).

This chapter finds that, if the initial optimism surrounding the transition was overstated, then the subsequent pessimism was equally unwarranted. It will show how the pro-democracy movement that swept aside the apparently hegemonic one-party state was itself a complex alliance of popular and elite forces, in which supposedly popular civil society movements played a limited and problematic role. In an unconscious echo of Nkrumah's directive to nationalist movements to 'Seek ye first the political kingdom', the MMD, first as popular movement and subsequently as political party, achieved a relatively smooth transition to power only by postponing the underlying questions that it faced regarding the nature of post-colonial governance and Zambia's peripheral position in the global economy. The limited nature of formal democratisation was exemplified in the incomplete process of constitutional reform, denying the vast majority of Zambians effective mechanisms through which to channel their democratic demands. Such outcomes throw doubts on the relevance of formal democratisation processes that do not enable genuine political competition which reflects the aspirations of ordinary Africans.

To what extent can Zambia be said to have undergone a genuine democratic transition since 1990? This chapter argues that Zambia's formal political system remains, despite a plethora of political parties and a system of competitive elections, severely constrained as a vehicle for the reflection and representation of the aspirations of the Zambian people. Nevertheless, it equally finds that Zambia, perhaps more than most African countries (and certainly more than Kenya), has undergone a practical deepening of democratic culture in which these aspirations find partial expression in civil society and the media in ways that impact indirectly on the formal structures of power. Until recently, a growing demand for effective democratic accountability co-existed uneasily alongside Zambia's limited formal democracy, expressed in parallel discourses of civil society participation, constitutional reform and neo-nationalist developmentalism. Whilst these are unlikely in themselves to provide a coherent challenge to the dominance of neo-liberal economic policies, they appear to be helping Zambian citizens to ask relevant questions about their position in their country and their country's position in the world. In the long run, the capacity of Zambia's democracy to address such issues will determine whether it founders on the rocks of enduring external dependence or finds ways of becoming truly receptive to popular demands.

Political Liberalisation in Zambia:
A Review of the Debate

Zambia, alongside Benin and Senegal, was initially identified as having had one of the easiest and most complete processes of democratic transition in the early 1990s (Joseph 1992: 199-201). Baylies and Szeftel (1997) were amongst the first to argue that formal democratisation had not solved problems of political accountability. As disillusionment with the limited extent of genuine democratisation became evident, Bartlett (2000) identified the ways in which older political elites and practices had not only survived the process of democratisation, but also found ways of replicating themselves in Zambia's Third Republic. Burnell's work on political institutions demonstrates the profoundly constrained nature of Presidential accountability to Zambia's weak Parliament (Burnell 2003). Likewise, Simon (2005) points to both institutional and non-institutional constraints on the health of Zambia's democratic practice. Both Rakner (2003) and Abrahamsen (2000) demonstrate ways in which economic liberalisation constrained the development of an effective democracy. They disagree, however, on its causes: Rakner argues that Zambia's 'partial (economic) reform' arises from incumbent politicians resisting (implicitly) necessary liberalisation, whilst Abrahamsen blames the external imposition of economic liberalisation by the international financial institutions for Zambia's 'disciplined democracy'.

The existing literature certainly demonstrates the limited reform of Zambia's political institutions since formal democratisation, and their consequently limited capacity to genuinely reflect the concerns and aspirations of Zambian people. This chapter will revisit and enlarge on the reasons for this. In addition, Zambia's external dependence is rightly acknowledged to have had a significant constraining effect on effective political accountability and policy-making. However, the tendency of much of the existing political science literature to define democratic transition in largely *institutional* terms (the independence of electoral commissions, the formal powers of Parliament, the laws governing free speech and assembly) frequently neglects the equally important *cultural* aspects of achieving and entrenching democracy (see Williams 2003). Whilst celebrating the notion of liberal democracy, many writers conceive of political participation primarily in electoral terms, regarding appeals to mass action as worrying evidence of populist politics, to be avoided in the hoped-for process to a stable democracy that is defined largely in institutional terms (Simon 2005: 215).

As this chapter will show, popular political mobilisations were important in securing the transition to multiparty democracy in 1990-91 and in preventing Chiluba's attempt to secure a third term in office in 2001. More recently, such mobilisations have expressed popular feeling against privatisation and in favour of constitutional reform. The relative success of the opposition Patriotic Front in the 2006 elections (see below) is a demonstration that politicians who tap into such discontent can achieve considerable electoral success. Historical evidence, from Zambia and elsewhere, suggests that instability is a necessary (although by no means sufficient) criterion for the deepening of democratic practice. This study, whilst analysing the weaknesses of Zambia's democratic institutions, suggests that the country is in the process of establishing an increasingly robust political culture which demands that politicians address the concerns of ordinary Zambians ahead of those of donors and international investors.

From Independence to the End of the One-Party State

Zambia's independence was constrained by two factors. First, its uneasy and periodically conflicting relationship with its racist settler and hostile Portuguese colonial neighbours limited democratic self-expression and economic self-sufficiency. Secondly, its profound and enduring dependence on copper (and subsequently cobalt) exports, whilst providing the funding for significant social investment in the decade after independence in 1964, effectively prevented more balanced and sustainable development. President Kaunda's claims to be moving Zambia 'towards economic independence' were belied by a consistent practical reliance on foreign advisers, investment and (later) aid. In one of Africa's wealthiest and most urbanised countries, the inability of Kaunda's United National Independence Party (UNIP) to influence the value of copper limited its capacity to achieve economic development. In the long run, UNIP's primary task was the increasingly coercive management of the expectations of the Zambian people for post-colonial social and economic advancement.

The initial post-Independence copper boom provided some funds for ethno-regionally-based patronage. Agricultural loans were treated as non-refundable rewards for political support and were utilised by government ministers to maintain rural bases of support (Szeftel 1983). Initial inter-regional competition over the allocation of development funds created ethnically-based conflict within UNIP and was characteristically addressed by President Kenneth Kaunda through centralisation of power around his person and position. Local government accountability was fatally undermined by the appointment of District Governors directly accountable to Kaunda.

Zambia's failure to attract international investment led UNIP to see the state as the driving force of economic development. The nationalisation of the copper mining industry created the basis for a state-dominated economy. Whilst such investments helped secure UNIP's initial legitimacy, it did not provide a basis for self-sustaining economic growth. Most parastatals struggled to achieve profitability. The considerable overlap between state and parastatal appointments enabled considerable opportunities for patronage, but the flow of meaningful resources to clients outside the urbanised 'line of rail' was limited.

For Kaunda, the external threat posed by Zambia's neighbours and the potential for ethnically-based political mobilisation provided compelling reasons for the centralisation of power in the Presidency. Parliament, particularly during the one-party Second Republic of 1973-90, failed to check Presidential authority. Members of Parliament, notwithstanding their electoral claims, lacked significant capacity to direct resources to their constituents, in sharp contrast to Kenya's one-party state (Posner 2005). Local UNIP structures atrophied in rural areas, whilst in the Copperbelt, disillusionment following the breakaway and suppression of former Vice-President Simon Kapwepwe's United Progressive Party in 1971 (the event which presaged the one-party state) led some of UNIP's strongest branches to wither under the glare of suspicion that fell on leaders of Bemba origin (Larmer 2006: 59-60).

The sudden and sustained collapse in the international copper price in 1974-5 and the related negative shift in Zambia's terms of trade destroyed the assumptions of UNIP's developmental model. Whilst most sub-Saharan African countries suffered significant reversals during this period, Zambia's overwhelming dependence on copper led to a decline in livelihoods with virtually no parallel anywhere in the world. Regional conflict substantially added to the cost of exporting copper. Zambia substituted for lost revenue by international borrowing. When these debts could not be repaid, Zambia became dependent on Western donors and the IMF, with which an agreement was first signed in 1973.

Patronage opportunities were reduced by economic decline and real-terms reductions in state expenditure. The Second Republican Constitution legally entrenched UNIP supremacy and shifted power from the Cabinet to the Central Committee and its sub-committees. Real power, however, lay with the President and his State House advisers. UNIP's political dominance was, like its control of the economy, more official than effective. The weak local party structures described by Bratton (1980) were probably replicated in much of the rest of Zambia.

UNIP's response to economic decline fluctuated between increased state control and limited market reforms, reflecting tension between older nationalist leaders, who sought to centralise economic power, and a younger business-oriented group, many of whom acquired substantial wealth through state positions and who sought to realise its value in a liberalised environment. In the 1970s, Zambia's small business-oriented elite, many of whom occupied state or parastatal positions, were increasingly critical of UNIP's inability to arrest economic decline. This critique was most visibly expressed by the 1977 report of the Parliamentary Select Committee on the Economy, which recommended cuts in public spending and the removal of subsidies on basic foodstuffs. Its main findings were rejected and UNIP's strongest pro-market advocates were marginalised. Access to essential goods became increasingly dependent on one's economic position and links to UNIP, contributing to a sense of inequality and class discontent amongst urban Zambians.

Politics in the 1980s was dominated by efforts to manage economic decline. Per capita income fell from $630 in 1981 to $200 in 1987 and fell increasingly thereafter. Shortages of foreign exchange contributed to low industrial productivity. Charges were introduced for health and education services. Public awareness of economic mismanagement and corruption in the government and parastatals grew. The loss-making copper industry functioned as a source of credit for politically prestigious projects and luxury consumption by senior politicians (Aron 1992). By 1984, debt servicing consumed 65 per cent of foreign-exchange earnings, making Zambia the most heavily indebted country in sub-Saharan Africa and increasing the influence of the World Bank and IMF. In 1986, the removal of food subsidies as a condition of the IMF agreement led to a doubling in the mealie meal price and to widespread rioting on the Copperbelt. The riots forced UNIP to reverse the price rises, to which donors responded by reducing financial support. Ultimately, popular discontent proved more influential than the IMF. In May 1987, Kaunda broke with the Bank and Fund. Despite the popularity of this decision, donors' refusal to fund alternative economic programmes brought the government back to the negotiating table. In the late 1980s, UNIP sought to introduce further liberalisation, devaluing the national currency, signing management contracts for foreign firms to run parastatals and attempting to decontrol the price of basic goods, which led to renewed protests on the Copperbelt. In 1989, the IMF and World Bank agreed a new economic policy framework, and a new austerity programme further reduced public spending in 1990.

Throughout the Second Republic, UNIP organised one-party elections that appeared to demonstrate significant popular support. UNIP, however, continued to struggle with recruitment and organisation. Despite the centralisation of Parliamentary candidate selection to weed out dissidents, backbench MPs were increasingly critical. At a local level, labour activists met secretly with leaders such as Chairman General of the Zambian Congress of Trade Unions Frederick Chiluba to plot UNIP's downfall (Larmer 2007: 151-4). The national labour movement developed ties with business representatives, with whom it shared a negative perception of structural adjustment policies that appeared advantageous to multinational capital and the parastatal-dominated Zambian economy with which it collaborated (Woldring 1984: 205). UNIP's ultimate inability to over-come donor dependence led leftist intellectuals to seek common cause with both groupings. The legal community, the Catholic Church and student organisations all helped to undermine UNIP hegemony through their criticisms of government policies.

The Pro-Democracy Movement

Zambia become a multiparty democracy in 1990-91 after nearly twenty years of a one-party state that, for most of its existence, had appeared largely hegemonic over political and economic life. How did the MMD construct such a united and effective electoral coalition in such a short time and in unpropitious circum-stances?

The MMD of 1990-91 is best understood as an uneasy coalition of social forces that opposed UNIP for a variety of reasons and made temporary common cause to oust the ruling party. As detailed above, these forces had increasingly collabo-rated in the 1980s in response to increasing economic crisis and its impact on their constituencies (Mbikusita-Lewanika 2003). The capacity of former politicians such as Arthur Wina and Humphrey Mulemba to lead emerging opposition was circumscribed by the perception that they were tainted by their history in UNIP. Chiluba, in contrast, was widely viewed as a fearless critic of the ruling party. He was the first leading public figure to respond to the fall of Eastern European regimes in December 1989 and to call for African countries to consider a return to multiparty rule. In May 1990, Kaunda conceded to hold a referendum on multipartyism, but argued that such a system would re-ignite tribalism. He failed, however, to resist donor pressure to remove food subsidies. In June, mealie meal prices more than doubled, leading to major riots in Lusaka and a subsequent unsuccessful coup attempt. By publicly revealing popular opposition to UNIP, these events provided a 'moment of transparency' and a significant spur to the emergent pro-democracy campaign (Nordlund 1996: 101).

In July 1990, multiparty advocates representing all these constituencies met in Lusaka to launch a campaign for multiparty democracy. In August, the unregistered multiparty democracy movement held its first rallies in Copperbelt towns. Such events helped prevent the suppression of the multiparty campaign during its period of ambiguous legal status (Nordlund 1996). Kaunda initially postponed the planned referendum and then declared that Zambia would hold multiparty elections the following year. UNIP initially sought to prevent multi-party advocates from holding meetings. In practice, the overwhelming public support for the multiparty movement deterred UNIP from any systematic attempt at its repression. Kaunda subsequently confirmed that he had abandoned plans to detain Chiluba for fear of the consequent unrest (Nordlund 1996: 106).

In December, the multiparty movement re-launched itself as a political party, the MMD. In March 1991, Chiluba was elected as its presidential candidate. Whilst the unity demonstrated by multiparty advocates enabled a coherent challenge to UNIP, there was little public discussion of its policies. MMD interim chairman Arthur Wina privately argued in 1991 that Chiluba was elected party President because, with his trade union background, he was the only leader who could implement economic adjustment policies without the opposition of organised labour. Wina had already assured World Bank officials that an MMD government would honour Zambia's debt obligations. The MMD manifesto proposed a 'social market economy', with government as a facilitator rather than a participant in the economy (Rakner 2003: 68). In May, radically reversing his previous position in the Zambian Congress of Trade Unions, Chiluba declared that privatisation would play a major role in its economic policy. UNIP initially attacked these policies as a copy of their own privatisation plans. The market reforms promised by both parties reflected popular discontent with the deteriorating economic situation. Prices more than doubled during 1991, amidst continuing food shortages. Support for economic liberalisation was, it should be noted, not limited to business-oriented elites. The negative experience of the domination of economic activity by the UNIP state, and the ways in which it led to increased economic inequality, meant that many ordinary Zambians were receptive to the MMD's arguments that privatisation and other market-oriented reforms would stimulate economic activity and ensure that its gains flowed to a larger proportion of the population than hitherto (Larmer 2007: 168-70).

The October 1991 election was generally peaceful, with Kaunda quickly conceding defeat. Chiluba received 75 per cent of the vote for the Presidency and the MMD won 125 Parliamentary seats to UNIP's 25. Bartlett (2000) emphasises that the MMD, celebrated as representative of a new wave of civil society influence over political change, was dominated by many of the same elites that had dominated UNIP. Thirteen of Chiluba's first 24-member Cabinet were business figures; only one was a former trade unionist. More significantly, the limited development of civil society enabled little practical influence over government policy through the party's embryonic structures. The labour movement lacked both a coherent ideological position and institutionalised representation to shape its relationship with the ruling party (Larmer 2007: 172).

It has also been suggested that the democratisation process was driven more by external actors than by internal dissent. Certainly, the decision by donors to withhold financial support in 1990 played an important part in undermining Kaunda's hold on political power. The suspension of all foreign aid in September 1991, in contrast, occurred too late to influence the outcome of the imminent election significantly. The sources of the MMD's financial support – for example, Chiluba's personal links to Taiwanese donors and the flow of funds via their South African Embassy, coupled with the predominance of white funders to the new party – raised questions regarding the influence of these supporters on subsequent policy that have yet to be satisfactorily addressed (Mbikusita-Lewanika 2003: 202-5). Outside pressure undoubtedly reinforced domestic pressure for democratic change, and the timing of events was shaped in large part by the precedent set in Eastern Europe. The substance of the transformation was, however, internal. A flow of discontent, previously dammed by state repression, co-option and divisions amongst UNIP's opponents, was unstoppable, except through a level of violence that Kaunda was unwilling, or unable, to unleash. Whilst elites dominated the MMD leadership, the party was perceived by the majority of poor Zambians as the product of their own demands, not simply for democracy *per se*, but rather as a means of realising material aspirations for themselves and their communities (Abrahamsen 2000: 99).

Economics in the Third Republic

When it came to power in October 1991, the MMD inherited an economy in near collapse. Zambia's dependence on international donors left it with little choice but to carry out further economic liberalisation. Its programme was, however, one of the most radical structural adjustment programmes ever implemented in sub-Saharan Africa. All consumer subsidies were removed by 1992. Tariffs and other barriers to imports were removed. A decade-long programme to privatise 250 state-owned companies was implemented. State support to agricultural production was substantially reduced. User fees were introduced for health and education services. The result has been a dramatic increase in poverty and little obvious improvement to the Zambian economy (Rakner 2003: 78-9).

From 1992 to 1998, Gross Domestic Product (GDP) declined by an average of 0.2 per cent per annum. Formal sector employment fell from 544,200 in 1991 to 436,066 in 2004 and now accounts for just 11 per cent of the labour force.[2] Social indicators drastically declined under the MMD. Primary school attendance fell to 68 per cent by 2001. Education spending as a percentage of Gross National Product fell from 4.5 per cent in 1991 to 2.9 per cent in 1994 (although it has subsequently increased). Twenty per cent of rural adults have never attended school. In 2002, 33 per cent of children were not attending primary school, whilst only 22 per cent were receiving secondary education.[3] Health expenditure fell in proportion with overall cuts in government spending at a time when HIV/AIDS was emerging as a devastating pandemic. Infant and child mortality increased with the introduction of user fees; access to clean water and sanitation services declined. By 1997, Zambia had the distinction of being the only country in the world with a lower Human Development Index in 1997 than it had in 1975. The percentage of Zambians living in poverty rose from 70 per cent in 1991 to 74 per cent in 1993; the figure was still 73 per cent in 1998.[4]

Winners and Losers

The closure of uncompetitive state-owned industries was not matched, as was forecast, by a revitalisation of the agricultural sector. Indeed, the removal of agricultural subsidies led to a drastic decline in maize production, which was only reversed by their limited reintroduction. Farmers' organisations complained that agricultural reforms had harmed local production, whilst business associations (that had originally supported liberalisation) claimed structural adjustment had butchered Zambian industry (Rakner 2003: 85). Structural factors continued to deter productive investment. These included high inflation and interest rates, Zambia's geographical isolation from major international markets and the poor transport infrastructure. Most Zambians were simply too poor to support a functioning market in basic goods that would attract potential investors. Whilst some commercial farmers benefited from the open market in maize and tobacco, the MMD's liberal policy on profit repatriation prevented the benefits of these investments from spreading to the wider economy.

By February 1998, 128 of the 188 privatised companies had been sold to Zambian businessmen, with many being asset-stripped and closed. However, the 70 companies sold to foreigners were worth eight times as much as those sold to Zambians (Inter-African Network for Human Rights and Development *et al.* 2000). Overseas investors were the primary winners from economic liberalisation. Whilst a few wealthy Zambians got wealthier through their links to the MMD leadership, the wider indigenous business community was marginalised by policies that favoured foreign-owned corporations. By the late 1990s, accusations of corrupt links between such companies and the Chiluba administration were rife, particularly in relation to the privatisation of the country's strategic copper mining industry (ibid.). Whilst this generated increasing popular discontent, opposition parties failed to offer policy alternatives.

Rakner (2003) convincingly argues that the dominance of external donors in policy-making prevented domestic politicians from effectively presenting alternative policies. Today, 53 per cent of government expenditure is funded by foreign aid. Despite the evident failure of economic liberalisation and privatisation, donor pressure has ensured their continued implementation. Their negative impact has, in recent years, stimulated a popular movement against the privatisation of the few remaining state-owned companies (Larmer 2005).

Diversification and Dependence

Since 2003, significant pockets of agricultural export production, for example in sugar, have taken advantage of Zambia's liberalised economy. Tourism has also grown in recent years, boosted in part by the collapse of the Zimbabwean economy. However, no significant replacement has been found for the mining sector in terms of generating income, employment and higher living standards. Agriculture, fisheries and forestry contributed only 14-15 per cent of GDP in 2004-5.[5] Since independence, Zambia's dependence on the revenue generated by copper, and more recently cobalt, exports has been identified by policy-makers as a major problem to overcome. The 1964 Seers report that provided the basis for Zambia's first post-colonial development plans reflected the paradox that has afflicted policy-makers ever since: in the absence of significant private investment, diversification could only be funded by revenue generated by the expansion of copper production (UN/ECA/FAO 1964).

One of the consequences of the skewed nature of the economy is the marginalisation of indigenous business interests in Zambian society and political decision-making. Indeed, their lack of policy influence was highlighted by the return to profitability of the mining sector between 2004 and 2008, during which the international copper price quadrupled. Political rhetoric regarding diversification was shelved as the political class gratefully embraced the renewed flow of mining investment as the solution to Zambia's problems. The recent rise of the copper price has once again demonstrated that, notwithstanding decades of 'diversification' efforts, Zambia's political economy remains rooted in the internationally-determined value of its mineral exports. Whilst Chinese investment in Zambia's mining sector and the wider economy has been welcomed by the MMD, the poor labour and environmental standards of Chinese-owned mines has generated substantial discontent amongst the urban population, emerging as a major issue in the 2006 national election (Fraser & Lungu 2007; Larmer & Fraser 2007).

Zambia's recently published Fifth National Development Plan, discussed below, again outlines a course to economic diversification, but in practice Zambia remains for all practical purposes a mono-economy, of international relevance only insofar as mineral production remains profitable. Its landlocked location, lack of agricultural and communications infrastructure, and comparatively exorbitant interest rates and wider business costs make it a perennially unattractive place to do business. The need to diversify the economy away from dependence on copper is as pressing as ever. Zambia's ability to do so is, as ever, in doubt.

Politics in the Third Republic

Whilst the MMD's election victory enabled the pro-business elite to secure the liberalisation policies they desired, their expectation that they would be the political power behind Chiluba's throne proved mistaken. Chiluba demonstrated considerable political acumen in utilising centralised state structures largely unreformed from the one-party state era to gain control of the MMD, which was transformed from a broad political alliance to a personalised patrimonial machine. Even before the 1991 transition, Chiluba's new lieutenants, many with a history in UNIP, replicated the ruling party's methods (for example, the paid mobilisation of youths to harass political opponents) to ensure his election as MMD leader (Mbikusita-Lewanika 2003: 201). The party subsequently utilised the official media, as UNIP had, as propaganda vehicles. In addition, its overwhelming victory initially undermined the potential for competitive multiparty democracy. However, its uneasy coalition of interests, vital to ending UNIP rule, rapidly fractured. Four Cabinet ministers were dismissed in April 1993, strengthening the position of Chiluba and his allies and leading to the breakaway of the National Party. As with the NaRC in Kenya, the MMD in Zambia reneged on its electoral promise to reduce presidential powers. Chiluba's appointment of District Administrators replicated Kaunda's system of District Governors in enabling the central control and distribution of power. Such officials have significant powers and play an important role in directing the flow of central resources to districts. The loyalty of MMD Members of Parliament was assured by their appointment to an increased number of ministerial positions. The MMD's weak organisational structures entirely failed to operate as a check on presidential power, never mind acting as a channel for the expression of popular mobilisation. In this sense, Zambia resembles other countries such as Kenya where presidential incumbents are able to mobilise state resources to prevent the emergence of competition, even from within their own party.

Whilst the negative impact of liberalisation contributed substantially to the unpopularity of the MMD, Chiluba again utilised the state machine to marginalise and intimidate his political opponents, including former President Kaunda, now a reinvented advocate of political and civil liberties. The MMD won the 1996 elections in a poll boycotted by UNIP and marked by vote buying and the intimidation of opposition candidates. In 1997, in the wake of the election, the discovery of the so-called 'zero option' plan for the overthrow of the government led Chiluba to declare a state of emergency, briefly detaining Kaunda and other political opponents.

By the late 1990s, the widespread hopes of ordinary Zambians for a transition to an effective and accountable democracy and an economic recovery were largely dashed. However, whilst donors, external observers and many Zambians were at their most pessimistic regarding the prospects for reform, internal social forces were emerging that were able to offer a successful challenge to the worst aspects of MMD authoritarianism. Under pressure from both a repressive government and suffering a loss of external funding from a disillusioned donor community, Zambia's most progressive civil society organisations, in an alliance with the independent press, developed an advocacy-based critique of Chiluba's approach to governance. This approach saw fruition in the successful 2001 campaign to prevent the President seeking a third term in office, as illustrated shortly.

This success did little to limit the MMD's utilisation of state resources to remain in office. In the run-up to the 2001 elections, 150 vehicles purchased by the government were handed to the MMD for use in its campaign. The ruling party's capacity to mobilise state resources in its favour, the patronage powers of the Presidency and a proliferation of presidential candidates enabled Levy Mwanawasa to be elected with just 28.7 per cent of the vote. The results stood despite significant protests and a petition to the Supreme Court, which heard evidence of organised bribery coordinated from State House. Mwanawasa, however, surprised local and international observers by reinventing himself as an anti-corruption crusader. He persuaded Parliament and the Supreme Court to remove Chiluba's immunity from prosecution in 2002, an unprecedented event in sub-Saharan Africa. Chiluba's trial on corruption charges initially became mired in bureaucratic delay and complex political machinations. After numerous delays, in 2007 a London court found Chiluba guilty of stealing $46 million of public funds, although he refused to recognise the verdict of a foreign court.

More generally, Zambia's state institutions, whilst somewhat stronger than in the late 1980s and early 1990s, remain weak and susceptible to political manipulation. The precedent of recent corruption trials, the independent media and stronger civil society organisations act as limited checks on the ruling party's capacity to utilise state institutions for its own benefit. Nevertheless, economic liberalisation has left many government departments unable to fulfil their role.

Effective constitutional change (see below) will be required to strengthen the weak National Assembly and rein in the bloated Presidency.

Centre-Local Relations

President Kaunda's warning that the return of multipartyism would lead to a renewal of tribalism in political life has been partly fulfilled. However, this is a reflection of the fact that the one-party system had itself failed to overcome such divisions. Kaunda's tribal balancing in appointments to UNIP's Central Committee, for example, in practice legitimised appointment on the basis of ethnicity, rather than ability, a practice which persisted after 1991. Posner (2003) shows the extent to which ethnicity, whilst explicitly outlawed as a form of political mobilisation, was central to the practical politics of the one-party system. A widespread perception of bias in favour of Eastern Province, linked to Kaunda's Malawian ancestry, informed the oppositional stance of many Zambians from Bemba-speaking areas (Larmer 2006). Although the initial post-election fracturing of the MMD was ostensibly based on issues of economic management and style of government, the breakaway National Party was led primarily by businessmen and intellectuals from Western and North-Western Provinces. In their absence, Chiluba was able to strengthen his power base by directing patronage towards Bemba speakers, to the extent that the MMD came to be perceived by its critics as a Bemba or Northern party. Most significant political parties are regarded as regionally or ethnically based, drawing their leaders and supporters from one or more provinces and generating electoral support almost exclusively from those areas.[6]

Nevertheless, *overt* ethnic politicking remains largely illegitimate in Zambia, in striking contrast to much of Africa, for example Kenya. Kaunda's sustained anti-tribal 'One Zambia, One Nation' directives may have played some role in this, but almost certainly more important was Zambia's early and sustained urbanisation, leading to significant inter-ethnic interaction and intermarriage. Whilst miscegenation is not itself a recipe for ethnic harmonisation, urban Zambians' close relationships with members of other ethnic groups are widely believed to have contributed to a realisation that to unleash a more exclusivist ethnic politics would be to attack one's friends and family. Rather, ethno-regional political discourse is carefully blended with arguments regarding the need to address the particular economic and social grievances of a particular area of Zambia. Indeed, such arguments often, though not always, do reflect the decidedly uneven development of the country. Southern Province politics has, since at least the 1950s, been marked by an economic conservatism that reflected its relative agricultural prosperity, finding its most recent expression in the United Party for National Development (Momba 1989). Western Province politics continues to be shaped by the continued hostility of the Lozi aristocracy to the form of its integration into the post-colonial state, whilst politicians seeking office in North-Western Province gain electoral mileage by expressing popular anger at the area's historic marginalisation in the allocation of central resources. Ethnic and economic forms of political mobilisation are intertwined and, in the minds of those involved, often indistinguishable. The utilitarian nature of Zambia's ethnic politics is evidenced in the coalitions of convenience hastily constructed in advance of the 2006 elections, reinforcing the widely held view that electoral success in a country of numerous minorities requires the successful construction of a broad cross-ethnic alliance.

Regional patrimonialism, at least in the Kenyan sense of channelling large-scale resources to rural areas via Members of Parliament, has never been part of the Zambian political scene. Parliament's limited control over state finances and the comparatively low level of resources available for patronage purposes have limited local expectations of what constituents can expect from their elected politicians. Ethno-regional politics is rather played out in Lusaka by metropolitan elites and acted out in rural areas only during election campaigns. Zambia's political elite, happy to utilise ethnic mobilisation, itself forms a highly homogenous grouping that mingles happily across these divisions in the wealthier suburbs of Lusaka and has in many cases perpetuated itself into a second generation of politically influential families.

The New Developmentalism

Notwithstanding the MMD's dramatic opening to international investment and influences from 1991 onwards, President Chiluba was not averse to resorting to populist attacks on international interference, for example in rejecting international criticism of the 1996 election (Van Donge 1998). More recently, disillusionment with the results of economic liberalisation led the Mwanawasa administration to utilise neo-nationalist arguments to shift the blame for such failures onto external parties, particularly donors and foreign governments. In 2002, Zambia was the only African country to reject Western genetically modified food aid, reflecting popular anger about Zambia's dependence on foreign powers.

Mwanawasa also responded to popular pressure in continually postponing and revising the terms of the unpopular privatisation of the Zambia National Commercial Bank, despite the fact that its sale was a condition of Zambia's Poverty Reduction Strategy Paper (PRSP). More generally, his administration sought to blame external agencies for severe financial controls on, for example, public sector wages. In the midst of public sector strikes in 2004, prompted by pay restrictions arising from the PRSP, Finance Minister Ng'andu Magande publicly explained, 'We are running the country but the budget is controlled by donors'. Internationally classified as a Highly Indebted Poor Country, Zambia became one of the first countries to complete its PRSP as required to access debt relief in 2005. The resulting reduction of its international debt from US$6.7 billion to $502 million has the potential to reduce the domination of its economic policy-making by the World Bank and IMF and should remove the excuse of impotence from domestic policy-makers. The PRSP also provided a new opportunity for civil society to increase its influence on decision-making.

Zambia's partial return to nationalist developmentalism is symbolised by the publication of the Fifth National Development Plan in 2006.[7] In the two decades after Independence in 1964, state-dominated development planning formed the basis for post-colonial economic policy. In the mid-1980s, development plans were abandoned in favour of reform-oriented agreements with the World Bank and IMF. Since then, 'national development' has been superseded by supply-side market economic policies. Although the Fifth National Development Plan is still constructed in a neo-liberal macroeconomic framework, the reversion to the language of planning and state intervention is a partial response to popular disillusionment with economic liberalisation. Notably, it has the support of both external donors and civil society, which participated in the drawing up of the new Plan.

In 2006, the Finance Minister first announced his intention to increase the mineral royalties paid by mining companies. The companies, however, resisted a voluntary increase in taxation. In his annual address to the nation in January 2008, President Mwanawasa announced a new tax on mining profits that will effectively increase taxation of mining profits from 31.7 to 47 per cent, bringing the country into line with international norms.[8] It does, however, reflect widespread discontent with the perceived profiteering of the foreign-owned companies and a continued belief, undiluted by decades of neo-liberalism, that investors have social responsibilities to their workforce and to wider Zambian society. It is projected that this will increase government revenue by US$400 million in 2008. The mining companies can be expected to use negotiations to resist the new tax levels.

Political Participation and a New Democratic Transition

The significant role of civil society in Zambia's transition to democracy demonstrated that, notwithstanding UNIP's dominance of official public space during the Second Republic, popular organisations, particularly churches and the labour movement, were able to maintain a degree of effective autonomy. Trade unions were a vital part of the MMD coalition, providing not only its leader but also significant financial and logistical support. In the transition to the Third Republic, a host of new non-governmental organisations were established. Some had roots in the democracy movement, such as the Foundation for Democratic Process, whose activists monitored the 1991 elections and which, like many of the new organisations, had roots in the church. In contrast, the labour movement was increasingly marginalised by the fall in formal employment, the exclusion of unions from decision-making and the mistaken loyalty of labour leaders to their former colleagues now in politics.

Despite the initial optimism regarding the potential of civil society to entrench democratic change, the establishment of many new organisations was motivated more by the sudden availability of donor funding than by any significant roots in popular movements. In the mid-1990s, as disillusionment with the failure of the MMD to address Zambia's acute social and economic problems set in, rising civil society criticism of the government led to state repression of activists and organisations, accused of acting as fronts for opposition parties and foreign interests. Civil society activists were threatened and detained in 1996-7 alongside opposition leaders. Whilst civil society actively defended itself against such attacks, it was acknowledged that the proliferation of donor-dependent organisations limited democratic accountability, which made the accusation of outside manipulation difficult to disprove. It was necessary to show that civil society was not simply a liberal metropolitan elite. Organisations worked to strengthen their grassroots linkages and consultation processes, particularly in the rural areas. Under pressure, disparate organisations strove to improve their coordination, working closely with the independent media that had developed since 1991, in particular *The Post* newspaper.

By 2000, civil society was increasingly criticising the Chiluba administration's evident corruption, as well as the negative impact of economic liberalisation in general and the disastrous privatisation of the mining industry in particular. It was, however, Chiluba's bid for an unconstitutional third term in office that focused civil society on what it saw as a threat to the peace of the nation. Improved coordination amongst a core group of advocacy-oriented activists led to the establishment of the Oasis Forum in 2001 by Zambia's three main church bodies, and of the Non-Governmental Organisation Coordinating Committee and the Law Association of Zambia. Despite intimidation, the Oasis Forum and the wider civil society led a coordinated and successful campaign that ultimately prevented Chiluba from standing for a third term as president.

Since 2001, Zambian civil society has sought to build upon the confidence and coordination it gained through the Third Term campaign in its relationships with the Mwanawasa government and with the World Bank and IMF. Zambia's PRSP, implemented from 2002-4 under the Highly Indebted Poor Countries Initiative, presented the possibility of civil society participation in its preparation, monitoring and implementation. Whilst it was recognised that the PRSP was in essence a repackaged economic liberalisation programme, the vast majority of Zambian civil society saw participation in drawing it up as an opportunity rather than a threat and rejected calls by a minority of activists to boycott the process.

Admittedly, the extent of genuine participation was severely limited. As noted, it also required the privatisation of key remaining state assets, although this has in practice been limited by a combination of popular opposition and drawn-out negotiations (Larmer 2005). Tight controls on public sector pay prompted a major public sector strike in 2004.[9] Today, however, the successful completion of the PRSP, and the consequent reduction in the country's debt burden, provides for many civil society activists the vindication of their decision to participate. Jubilee Zambia suggests that 80 per cent of the Fifth National Development Plan was significantly influenced by civil society inputs. However, the macroeconomic framework that remains outside civil society purview continues to follow the contours of the neo-liberal Washington consensus. The capacity of Zambian civil society to influence the allocation of government expenditure, but not the amount of money in the overall budget nor where it comes from, places it in the invidious position of tacitly approving policies that, at best, make Zambia a more efficiently administered place for poor people to live. Alive to this dilemma, organisations like Jubilee Zambia are seeking to extend their influence into this still protected area of policy-making, ensuring that all aspects of governmental activity are subject not to the strictures of the World Bank and IMF, but rather to 'conditionality from below'.

Constitutionalism and Deepening Democracy

For all its undoubted flaws, the PRSP provided a precedent for civil society participation in other areas of governance and decision-making in Zambia. Buoyed by the success of the Third Term campaign, the reform of the Constitution, an important issue since the return of multiparty democracy, was placed firmly on the agenda by civil society activists.

Can the reform of Zambia's Constitution deepen democratic practice and strengthen the relationship between popular aspirations and political decision-making? Presidential manipulation of constitution-making has a long history in Zambia. The Chona Commission that oversaw the introduction of the new one-party state Constitution in 1972 recommended limiting the powers of the Presidency, but was overruled by Kaunda. In 1991, formal multiparty democracy was welded onto an otherwise authoritarian and centralised one-party state Constitution. In the heady days of the multiparty transition, the 1990 Mvunga Commission's review of the Constitution recommended reforms such as freedom of the press, but these were not introduced in the interim reforms put in place for the 1991 election (Bartlett 2000: 62). Wholesale reforms were not in UNIP's interest, whilst the MMD, confident of electoral success, promised to implement a far-reaching process of constitutional reform (Simon 2005: 202).

The MMD was slow to initiate such reforms once in office. However, the appointment of the Mwanakatwe Commission in 1994 raised hopes for sweeping democratic reform. The Commission's 1996 report recommended a reduction of Presidential powers, the strengthening of Parliamentary accountability and significant improvements in freedoms of speech and assembly. Many of Mwanakatwe's recommendations were, however, ignored by the MMD, whose Constitutional Amendment Bill, passed by a Parliament it dominated, only furthered its own interests. For example, it disqualified presidential candidates whose parents were born outside Zambia, a measure designed to exclude Kaunda (Simon 2005: 202). Civil society demands for the adoption of the new Constitution via a Constituent Assembly and a referendum were refused by the MMD and rejected by the courts (Van Donge 1998).

A new Constitutional Review Commission, chaired by Wila Mung'omba, sat from 2003 to 2005, making similar recommendations. Despite initial civil society scepticism about this process, it stimulated significant popular participation, hearing 12,647 submissions from ordinary Zambians across the country. The Mung'omba Constitution, *inter alia*, strengthens Parliamentary oversight powers (for example, Parliamentary approval of new international loans and ratification of a State of Emergency), removes the Presidential power to set the date for elections and provides for freedoms of speech and assembly in a new Bill of Rights. It also institutes a '50 per cent plus one' hurdle for successful presidential candidates to clear.[10] When it appeared that the Mwanawasa government would block acceptance of the Commission's recommendations, a series of demonstrations and conferences throughout 2005 demanded that it be implemented in full. These culminated in November in a 'procession' of 12,000 Zambians to Parliament. Simultaneous marches took place across the country, including in small rural centres. The endorsement and organisation of mass demonstrations indicate an increasing willingness amongst civil society to embrace the tactics of popular mobilisation.

In 2007, a new National Constitutional Conference (NCC) was established by President Mwanawasa to re-examine the findings of the Mung'omba Constitution and put a revised constitution to a national referendum in 2008. Opposition leader Michael Sata and some civil society leaders boycotted the NCC, condemning it as an attempt by Mwanawasa to manipulate the findings of the original Commission. However, other civil society representatives and many political leaders are participating in the NCC.

Constitutional reform could, argue some people in civil society, provide ordinary Zambians with a framework of rights within which they could pursue their social and economic rights.[11] Although formal democratisation since 1991 did not lead ordinary Zambians to realise their economic aspirations, this has not led to disillusionment with the principles of democracy. The *Afrobarometer* survey finds that 75 per cent of Zambians prefer democracy to other political systems. However, only 60 per cent are satisfied with the democracy they have and only 25 per cent believe they have a 'full democracy'. Strikingly, ordinary Zambians do not closely associate political and economic liberalisation: only 18 per cent are satisfied with economic reform programmes, whilst 72 per cent believe that structural adjustment policies have hurt most people, associating them with rising inequality. A majority support state involvement in market pricing and oppose privatisation (Bratton *et al.* 2005: 6-95). Rather, they believe that a deeper, more effective form of democracy can enable them to begin to bring about a society that enables the realisation of their hopes for themselves and their communities.

However, the tendency to see constitutional reform as the answer to Zambia's problems obscures the deeper problems with the country's political institutions. The failure of Parliament, for example, to hold the executive to account is only partly the result of legally weak oversight powers (Burnell 2003). It is also a reflection of MPs' unwillingness to use the limited powers they do possess to influence the national budget, for example (Simon 2005: 209). Chiluba was able to abuse his significant presidential powers because of the general acceptance by the political class of neo-patrimonial approaches, not because they were legally prevented from challenging his behaviour. President Mwanawasa turned the hung Parliament elected in 2001 into one with a MMD majority, notwithstanding the laws preventing 'floor crossing'. This was possible because opposition MPs were willing to be bought by the ruling party and to use state resources in by-elections to retain their seats under a MMD banner. A new Constitution should make it easier to hold the government to account, but this will only occur if politicians begin to reflect more directly the wishes of the electorate.

The 2006 election – a new turning point?

An institutional analysis of the re-election of the MMD would suggest that it represents an endorsement of Mwanawasa's policies of 'good governance' that, in recent years, have secured both steady economic growth and the relief of 92.5 per cent of Zambia's previously crippling external debt. The MMD's retention of power was not, however, the election's most significant outcome. Rather, the rapid and largely unexpected emergence of the Patriotic Front, led by Michael Sata, as the leading opposition party, represents a significant break in institutional politics. Since 2001, Sata has built the PF into a significant political force on the Copperbelt and in parts of northern Zambia, sometimes by taking wholesale control of MMD branch structures. This support was built via the still significant network of mineworkers (both retired and still employed) and the local structures of the Mineworkers' Union of Zambia (MUZ), reinforced in some cases by influential Catholic church leaders. These were precisely the networks through which the MMD had been built in these areas in 1990-91. The PF was able to gain from the widespread sense of disillusionment in the MMD's failure to meet the expectations of the pro-democracy period (Larmer & Fraser 2007: 24-5). Sata won 29 per cent of the Presidential vote (while Mwanawasa claimed victory with 42 per cent), and Patriotic Front MPs won every urban parliamentary seat. The party also gained control of most urban municipal councils.[12] Sata's preparedness to reflect the urban electorate's concerns in populist language and symbols, particularly in attacking the poor record of foreign (particularly Chinese) investors, enabled him to win the allegiance of the urban populace.

The Patriotic Front did not achieve its limited success because of institutional changes since the largely 'choiceless' 1996 and 2001 elections. Rather, Sata articulated an increasingly assertive critique of a political system that has been more responsive to the demands of donors and international investors than of the Zambian people. In a context of limited economic recovery, high international mineral prices and the removal of debt-based donor dependence, a deepening of Zambia's democracy appears to be occurring. Whilst such undisciplined 'populist' politics may not reflect the type of 'stable' democracy that many outside observers would wish to see, a democratic praxis rooted in the aspirations of ordinary Zambians will surely provide the basis for a deeper and more sustainable system of accountable democracy.

Conclusion

Fifteen years of formal democracy has not led to the development of a political system that provides the Zambian people with a policy choice that genuinely reflects their aspirations. Government programmes have been significantly more responsive to donor conditionality than to popular will. Rather than demonstrating any inter-linkage of economic and political liberalisation, the imposition of the former has in practice curtailed the development of the latter. Underlying Zambia's transition to democracy (and indeed its entire post-colonial history) is a debate about the nature of accountable governance that, in raising questions regarding the potential for effective national sovereignty in a country acutely dependent on the vagaries of the global economy, prefigured recent wider debates regarding the nature of democracy in an era of neo-liberal globalisation.

This debate is rooted in Zambia's long-standing and, in African terms, highly unusual experience of urban mass organisation independent of the nationalist project. UNIP's failure to fully incorporate the labour movement after independence enabled Zambia's trade unions to play a leading role in the pro-democracy movement. The existence of a semi-autonomous urban political space initially created by the labour movement was subsequently utilised by other social movements, including church-based organisations with a significant presence in rural areas, to highlight the grievances of poorer Zambians. The limited reach of the Zambian post-colonial state and its ruling party, in terms of both its systems of repression and its capacity to deliver politically effective patronage, was further reduced with the country's radical economic decline from the mid-1970s on. This weakening provided gaps in which progressive social forces could organise a growing challenge to the one-party state.

Whilst these forces were damaged by the failure of the MMD to significantly address their demands once in power, democratic space has enabled popular movements to develop and articulate an understanding of the complementary relationship between the Zambian state, the World Bank and IMF, and multinational capitalism, rooted in Zambia's own negative experience of the neo-liberal economic policies. At the same time as increasing their own legitimacy by strengthening communication with their constituencies, some Zambian civil society activists have broken out of a historically isolated national analysis to learn from the experiences of those facing similar issues elsewhere in Africa. Limited concessions have been wrung from the state reflecting the wishes of many ordinary Zambians for a return to state economic intervention and the provision of social welfare.

Nevertheless, Mwanawasa's 2006 re-election highlighted the limited capacity of the Zambian political system to reflect the electoral wishes of its people. The granting of debt relief and the return to mining profitability created the possibility for the Zambian state to better reflect popular aspirations in, for example, increasing taxes on the private mine companies. Without effective democratic reform and increased political accountability, however, there is the danger that increased revenues, for example from the mining taxes announced in January 2008, will accrue to elites and not benefit the wider population, as they did during the era of the one-party state. Constitutional reform creates the potential for this, but this reform remains an uncertain process and one subject, as ever, to Presidential interference. Whether the enduring realities of economic dependence, a still authoritarian political system and the policy-free politics of ethno-regional neo-patrimonialism are undermined by, or will themselves undermine, Zambia's ongoing democratic transition is a question that the next few years are likely to address.

Notes

1. Zambia has so far failed Samuel Huntington's 'alternation' test, requiring two changes of government to demonstrate effective democratic consolidation (Huntington 1991).
2. 'Formal Sector Employment Trends in Zambia, 1985-2005': www.zamstats.gov.zm/qtr/labour.asp
3. Zambia Demographic and Health Survey (DHS) EdData Survey, Central Statistical Office, Lusaka (2002): www.zamstats.gov.zm/dload/zdes/zdes.pdf
4. Zambia Central Statistics Office, 'National Trends in Poverty, 1991 – 2004': www.zamstats.gov.zm/qtr/lcms.asp
5. www.zamstats.gov.zm/qtr/gdp.asp.
6. Apart from the MMD, Zambia's main political parties are the United Party for National Development (UPND), which draws most of its support from Western and Southern Provinces; and the Patriotic Front (PF), which is supported by Bemba-speaking Zambians in Northern, Luapula and Copperbelt Provinces. In 2006, PF extended its support to non-Bemba-speaking areas of Lusaka.
7. The Fifth National Development Plan can be accessed at: http://www.cspr.org.zm/Reports&Updates/FNDP.pdf
8. Reuters, 'Zambia sees $400 mln revenue from new mining tax', 11 January 2008: http://africa.reuters.com/business/news/usnBAN144464.html, accessed 12 January 2008.
9. BBC World Service, Network Africa, 18 February 2004.
10. The full CRC report is available at: http://www.crc.org.zm
11. Fr Peter Henriot of the influential Jesuit Centre for Theological Reform has specifically argued that the new Bill of Rights offers the potential for Zambians to realise their social and economic rights through legal process.
12. The Electoral Commission of Zambia, 'General Elections 2006, Presidential - National Result by Candidate, 2 October 2006'; The Electoral Commission Of Zambia, 'Parliamentary Results Summary 2 October 2006'.

References

Abrahamsen, Rita. 2000. *Disciplining Democracy: Development discourse and good government in Africa.* London: Zed Books.

Aron, Janine. 1992. Economic Policy in a Mineral-Dependent Economy: The case of Zambia. DPhil thesis, University of Oxford.

Bartlett, David M.C. 2000. Civil Society and Democracy: a Zambian case study. *Journal of Southern African Studies* 26 (3):429–46.

Baylies, Carolyn and Morris Szeftel. 1997. The 1996 Zambian Elections: Still awaiting democratic consolidation. *Review of African Political Economy* 24 (71): 113-28.

Bratton, Michael. 1980. *The Local Politics of Rural Development: Peasant and party-state in Zambia.* Hanover, NH: University Press of New England.

——. 1994. Economic Crisis and Political Realignment in Zambia. In *Economic Change and Political Liberalization in sub-Saharan Africa,* ed. Jennifer Widner. Baltimore: John Hopkins Press. 101-128.

Bratton, Michael and Daniel Posner. 1999. A First Look at Second Elections in Africa, with Illustrations from Zambia. In *State, Conflict & Democracy in Africa,* ed. Richard Joseph. Boulder, CO: Lynne Rienner Publishers.

Bratton, Michael, Robert Mattes and Emmanuel Gyimah-Boadi (eds) 2005. *Public Opinion, Democracy, and Market Reform in Africa.* Cambridge: Cambridge University Press.

Burnell, Peter. 2002. Zambia's 2001 Elections: The tyranny of small decisions, 'non-decisions', and 'not decisions'. *Third World Quarterly* 23 (6):1103-20.

——. 2003. Legislative-Executive Relations in Zambia: Parliamentary reform on the agenda. *Journal of Contemporary African Studies* 21 (1):47-68.

Ferguson, James. 1999. *Expectations of Modernity: Myths and meanings of modern life on the Zambian Copperbelt.* Berkeley CA: University of California Press.

Fraser, Alastair and John Lungu. 2007. *For Whom the Windfalls: Winners and losers in the privatisation of Zambia's copper mines.* Lusaka: Civil Society Trade Network of Zambia and Catholic Commission for Justice Development and Peace. www.minewatchzambia.com.

Gertzel, Cherry, Carolyn Baylies and Morris Szeftel (eds.). 1984. *The Dynamics of the One-Party State in Zambia.* Manchester: Manchester University Press.

Huntington, Samuel. 1991. *The Third Wave: Democratisation in the late Twentieth Century.* Norman, OK: University of Oklahoma Press.

Inter-African Network for Human Rights and Development (Afronet), Citizens for a Better Environment (CBE) and Rights and Accountability in Development (RAID). 2000. *Zambia: Deregulation and the denial of human rights.* Lusaka, Kitwe, Oxford: Submission to the OECD Committee on Economic, Social and Cultural Rights.

Joseph, Richard. 1992. Zambia: a model for democratic change. *Current History* 91 (565):199-201.

Larmer, Miles. 2005. Reaction and Resistance to Neo-liberalism in Zambia. *Review of African Political Economy* 103:29-45.

——. 2006. "A little bit like a volcano" – The United Progressive Party and resistance to one-party rule in Zambia, 1964–1980. *International Journal of African Historical Studies* 39 (1): 49-83.

——. 2007. *Mineworkers in Zambia: Labour and political change in post-colonial Africa.* London and New York: I.B. Tauris.

Larmer, Miles and Alastair Fraser. 2007. Of Cabbages and Kings: populist politics and Zambia's 2006 election. *African Affairs* 106 (425): 611-37.

Mbikusita-Lewanika, Akashambwita. 2003. *Hour for Reunion, Movement for Multi-Party Democracy: Conception, dissension and reconciliation.* Mongu-Lealui: African Lineki Courier.

Momba, Jonathan. 1989. The State, Rural Class Formation and Peasant Political Participation in Zambia: the case of Southern Province, *African Affairs* 88: 331-57.

Nordlund, Per. 1996. *Organising the Political Agora: Domination and democratisation in Zambia and Zimbabwe,* Uppsala: Uppsala University Press.

Posner, Daniel. 2005. *Institutions and Ethnic Politics in Africa.* Cambridge: Cambridge University Press.

Rakner, Lise. 2003. *Political and Economic Liberalisation in Zambia, 1991-2001.* Uppsala: Nordic Africa Institute.

Simon, David. 2005. Democracy Unrealized: Zambia's Third Republic under Chiluba. In *The Fate of Africa's Democratic Experiments: Elites and institutions,* eds Leonardo Villalon and Peter VonDoepp. Bloomington, IN: Indiana University Press.

Szeftel, Morris. 1983. Political Graft and the Spoils System in Zambia - the state as a resource in itself. *Review of African Political Economy* 24:4-21.
United Nations/Economic Commission for Africa/Food and Agriculture Organization. 1964. *Economic Survey Mission on the Economic Development of Zambia*, Ndola.
Van Donge, Jan Kees. 1998. Reflections on Donors, Opposition and Popular Will in the 1996 Zambian Elections, *Journal of Modern African Studies* 36 (1):71-99.
Williams, Gavin. 2003. Democracy as Idea and Democracy as Process. *Journal of African American History* 88 (4):339-360.
Woldring, Klaas. 1984. Survey of Recent Inquiries and their Results. In *Political Independence: Zambia's Development Predicament in the 1980s*, ed. Klaas Woldring. Berlin: Mouton Publishers.
Zambia Demographic and Health Survey (DHS) EdData Survey. 2002. Lusaka: Central Statistical Office: www.zamstats.gov.zm/dload/zdes/zdes.pdf.

Interviews

Henriot, Fr Peter. Interviewed 10 April 2006. Director, Zambia/Jesuit Centre for Theological Reflection. Lusaka, Zambia.
Kasonde, Emmanuel. Interviewed 10 August 2006. First Minister of Finance, Zambia/MMD. Lusaka, Zambia.
Lombanya, Villie. Interviewed 6 April 2006. Secretary, Zambia/Constitutional Review Commission. Lusaka, Zambia.
Muyoyeta, Lucy. Interviewed 6 April 2006. Chief Executive, Zambia/NGO Coordinating Committee, Lusaka, Zambia.
Muyoyeta, Lucy. Interviewed 10 December 2004. Chief Executive, Zambia/NGO Coordinating Committee. Lusaka, Zambia.
Ndhlovu, Rev. Japhet. Interviewed 7 April 2006. Executive Director, Zambia/Oasis Forum. Lusaka, Zambia.
Wina, Arthur. Interviewed 12 July 1991. Former National Chairman, Zambia/MMD. Lusaka, Zambia.
Zulu, Jack Jones. Interviewed 6 April 2006. Coordinator, Jubilee Zambia. Lusaka, Zambia.

Newspapers
The Post, 2002-06
Times of Zambia, 1989-1991
Sunday Times of Zambia, 1990-91

8

South Africa since 1994
Who Holds Power after Apartheid?

JEREMY SEEKINGS

The transition from apartheid to democracy in South Africa, marked above all by the election in 1994 of a government led by the African National Congress (ANC) and headed by President Nelson Mandela, represented a milestone not only for South Africa but for Africa generally. The transition meant the end of formal colonial or settler rule in Africa. On one level, the new South African democracy appears robust and substantive. Whilst there has been no turnover in office at the national level, free and fair legislative elections have been held regularly with universal franchise and multiparty competition, and there is an independent judiciary, a critical press, and a vigorous civil society. But there are at least two grounds for questioning the quality of the new democracy. First, the strength of the ANC undermines the constitutional separation of powers and the accountability of the executive to the electorate. Secondly, the ANC is widely accused of having 'betrayed' the working class and poor by adopting neo-liberal policies that serve the interests of capital and therefore represent continuity from the apartheid era. Whilst there is some merit in each critique, the formal procedures of representative democracy are not inconsequential, and more importantly a range of classes and interest groups besides 'capital' wield power, albeit in different ways.

The struggle for a non-racial democracy in South Africa dates back to the very formation of the Union of South Africa – comprising two defeated Boer Republics and two British colonies – in 1910. The former colony of the Cape had, and retained until the 1930s, a franchise defined primarily by property, with a significant minority of African and coloured voters. The Cape franchise was not, however, extended to the other provinces of the new Union. Indeed, racial discrimination and exclusion intensified in the 1930s and then again after the election of the National Party and the enactment of apartheid after 1948. Demands for an end to racial discrimination and exclusion were raised through legal and institutional processes during the first half of the century, before the turn to direct action in the 1950s and armed struggle in the 1960s. By the end of the 1960s, with the ANC and other 'liberation movements' defeated, internal dissent quelled, and the economy growing rapidly, it appeared that white minority rule was secure.

The very economic growth and change that seemed to sustain apartheid also served to undermine it. The demand for semi-skilled and skilled labour drove the rapid expansion of public education, albeit of racially unequal quality. Despite restrictions on urbanisation, the settled urban African population grew steadily. The result was, by the 1980s, an organised African working class and an aspirant African middle class, both of which resented the remaining and severe restrictions on their standard of living and opportunities for upward mobility as well as the denial of political rights. At the same time, rapidly growing numbers of unemployed and landless poor provided a ready constituency for direct action. Militant trade unions combined with resistance in the townships (and some rural areas) to push the apartheid state to limited concessions and, later, negotiations. The ban on the ANC was lifted, and Nelson Mandela released in early 1990. Formal negotiations led to agreement over an interim constitution and transitional power-sharing, and then to the elections of 1994.

The Institutional Architecture of South African Democracy

The legislature elected in 1994 also served as a constitutional assembly to complete the process of drafting a new constitution. The result, in 1996, was a liberal democratic Constitution that rejected consociational power-sharing but set real constraints on executive power. In contrast to the apartheid era, it is the Constitution and not Parliament that is sovereign. The Constitution provides for a separation of powers between the branches of government: the executive, legislature, judiciary, and a set of independent statutory bodies such as the Auditor-General and the Electoral Commission. The Reserve Bank is independent, but by Act of Parliament, not under the Constitution. The Constitution also provides for a separation of powers between different tiers of government: national, provincial and local government. The third constraint on executive power stems from the inclusion of a Bill of Rights that stipulates not only civil and political freedoms but also socio-economic rights.

But many of the checks and balances have proved ineffective in the face of a generally centralised governing party with overwhelming electoral support. The Constitution provides for a parliamentary system, with a Parliament that is elected by the citizenry (the National Assembly by direct election, the National Council of Provinces by the provincial legislatures) and a President who is elected by and is accountable to Parliament. Local, provincial and national legislatures are elected separately, and each tier of government enjoys considerable autonomy from the others. There is even an independent Fiscal and Financial Commission to guide the division of government revenues 'vertically', between the different tiers, and 'horizontally', between the different provinces (and municipalities). In practice, however, the system is more like a hybrid presidential-parliamentary system and more unitary than federal. The national executive has come to predominate, and the national legislature and sub-national tiers of government have been reduced to minor roles.

The legislature has proved to be the weakest institution of state. It has done little more than pass legislation prepared by the executive and has rarely even tried to hold the executive to account. With very occasional exceptions, primarily during 1996–7, parliamentary portfolio committees play only passive roles. This is largely due to the heavy hand of the ANC, which 'redeployed' Members of Parliament and was quick to suppress independent action. For example, when the Finance Committee dared to examine the government's policy of inflation-targeting in 2000, the entire ANC membership of the committee was summoned to a personal dressing-down by the President. And when the Standing Committee on Public Accounts began to flex its muscles, the chairman (from the Inkatha Freedom Party) was ousted and the senior ANC member sidelined, ensuring that the committee resumed a quiescent role. Parliament has not been diligent in overseeing executive action. Nor has it been diligent in punishing misconduct among its own members, most notably in the 'travelgate' scandal when Members of Parliament, almost all from the governing party (and probably including very senior members), defrauded Parliament with bogus travel claims (Murray & Nijzink 2002; Nijzink & Piombo 2005; February 2006; Calland 2006; Feinstein 2007).

Provincial governments have also failed to use the power accorded to them by the Constitution. Whilst the national government and party leaderships might not be able to impose their will on the provinces in all respects, there is no doubt as to where real power lies in terms of policy-making and the allocation of resources.

'All around the world, critics lament the extent of executive dominance and the tyranny of party discipline in parliament', note Murray and Nijzink (2002: 133); 'complaints about the lack of a truly deliberative style of decision-making and weak links between members and the people are equally common.' But there are specific features of the South African political landscape that accentuate these problems. The passivity of the South African Parliament is due in large part to the combination of the electoral system and the dominance of one party. A system of closed-list proportional representation, with provincial and national lists, serves to concentrate considerable power in the party leaders who control or influence whether someone's name appears high or low on the list. This is true of all parties, but for MPs from the governing ANC it means that they are deferential to the executive. In 2003, the majority on a multiparty 'Electoral Task Team' recommended the division of the existing 9 provincial constituencies into 69 smaller, but still multi-member, constituencies. Three-quarters of the MPs would be elected in these constituencies, and the remaining one-quarter proportionally to the parties' total national votes. The governing party rejected the majority recommendation, preferring instead the minority recommendation to retain the status quo (Nijzink & Piombo 2005). At the same time, the fact that the governing party has controlled the national government as well as almost all provinces (and after 2004 all provinces) also allows party discipline to trump the supposed national-provincial separation of powers.

Given the passivity of the legislature and provincial governments and the inclusion of rights in the Constitution, it is unsurprising that the Constitutional Court has become a prospective player in policy-making. Not all cases coming before the Constitutional Court entail challenges to executive power. The legislature and executive happily hand over to the courts issues such as the abolition of capital punishment and the legalisation of abortion, because it is decidedly convenient for the courts to take responsibility for unpopular 'policies'. Other cases have been more inconvenient to the government. The most notable was the case brought by the Treatment Action Campaign (TAC), demanding that the Department of Health treat pregnant women who are HIV-positive so as to reduce the likelihood of the transmission of HIV from mother to child. In general, however, the Constitutional Court has been reluctant to trespass on the policy-making roles of the legislature and executive. In two other cases dealing with socio-economic rights, the Court required little of the executive. In *Soobramooney*, the Court decided that the government was not obliged to provide kidney dialysis, which is very expensive, to a patient with multiple medical problems. In

Grootboom, it decided that the government was not obliged to provide housing for some homeless people, but it was obliged to have a plan under which it would realise progressively the right to shelter. When a non-governmental organisation challenged in court the political parties' refusal to disclose the sources of their funds, the High Court decided that it was the role of the legislature, not the courts, to make policy on such matters.

The Constitutional Court is itself far from monolithic. There have been important split decisions. Such splits seem to be based in differing commitments to an executive-led model of social and economic transformation. In perhaps the most important of these cases, the *New Clicks* case concerning state regulation of pharmaceutical prices, the Constitutional Court decided by the narrowest possible majority to overturn the regulations. The dissenting minority were, in contrast, deferential to the executive. The Court's vote had racial overtones, given that all but one of the majority were white and all of the minority were black (Dyzenhaus 2006).

What the Court has achieved is the partial establishment of a culture of justification. The Court may be reluctant to engage in policy-making, but it has required repeatedly that the executive justify its actions, demonstrate their reasonableness, and show that its policies entail progress towards the realisation of socio-economic rights. This has partially filled the void left by Parliament's passivity, but the courts have not stopped the government dragging its heels on the provision of treatment to the AIDS-sick, with the result that the death toll of a largely treatable disease has moved toward one million.

At the same time as power has become concentrated in the executive branch of government, there has been a centralisation of power within the executive itself. The executive comprises the range of departments shaped by the Westminster model: a powerful National Treasury (which includes the former Department of Finance); a set of spending departments (especially Education, Health, Social Development – which is responsible for welfare programmes – and Housing); and the departments concerned with criminal justice, Foreign Affairs, Labour, and so on. In 1994, a separate Ministry of Reconstruction and Development was established, with powers to top-slice the budgets of other departments and allocate these funds to promote development. In the face of considerable and unsurprising opposition from the spending departments, the ministry was abolished in 1996 (Blumenfeld 1997; Nattrass & Seekings 1998). The National Treasury is a 'sort of government within a government', with the Minister of Finance (Trevor Manuel) enjoying an 'almost first-among-equals status in the cabinet' (Calland 2006: 2). The National Treasury's power derives from both its control of multi-year financial planning and Trevor Manuel's personal authority within the ANC.

The greatest concentration of power, however, is in the Presidency itself, after Thabo Mbeki succeeded Nelson Mandela as President in 1999 (Clothia & Jacobs 2002). With ever-growing budget and staff, the Policy Co-ordination and Advisory Services within the Presidency promotes 'better co-ordination and implementation' of policy. It comprises five units, each working with one of the five 'clusters' of ministers in the Cabinet concerned with economics, social services, criminal justice, international relations and intergovernmental relations. There are also five presidential 'working groups' (for big business, black business, agriculture, education, and religion) and two international advisory groups providing for regular communication between presidential officials and players outside of the state. The President also appoints Director-

Generals in all government departments. The power of the presidency means that key advisers or officials within it – especially Mbeki's legal adviser and the head of the Policy Co-ordination and Advisory Services – wield considerable influence (Calland 2006).

Technocratic officials clearly wield considerable power in many government departments. Critics of the government's macroeconomic policy often point to shadowy officials in the National Treasury who 'wrote' the Growth, Employment and Redistribution (GEAR) macroeconomic strategy in 1996. But technocrats wield power only insofar as Ministers and the President allow them to do so. Several Director-Generals have resigned, retired or been fired after serious disagreements with their Ministers. In some cases, for example the Department of Land Affairs, whole cohorts of officials have been ousted when a new Minister decides to change the direction of policy. In Health, reformist officials are unable to effect a progressive AIDS policy in the face of a reactionary Minister. If technocrats within the National Treasury have power, it is because the Minister of Finance (and, ultimately, the President) chooses to give it to them.

The reasons for the centralisation of power within the executive, and within the Presidency more specifically, remain unclear. The fact that this has gone along with a centralisation of power within the ANC and President Mbeki's intolerance of opposition inside or outside the party suggests that the President's personality is part of the story. Calland (2006: 41) describes Mbeki as 'a man with a devotion to long-term strategy and an egocentric view of his own epic place in history' and who 'knows his own mind, stubbornly so at times (as on HIV/AIDS)'. Mbeki's passion for centralised power is rooted in a lifetime spent in exile in an ANC that was wedded to a vanguard role. A vanguard conception of armed struggle easily led to a vanguard conception of political and economic management.

Elections, Voters and Parties

Since 1994, the South African government has been formed by the ANC, albeit in the form of a 'government of national unity' in which the ANC has chosen to give a handful of cabinet or deputy-ministerial posts to other parties. The ANC has secured about two-thirds of the total vote in each election, although the relative strength of opposition parties has shifted considerably. The ANC also won control of seven of the nine provinces in the 1994 elections, gained partial control of an eighth in the 1999 elections, and won control of the ninth in 2002 when it lured legislators from other parties to defect to the ANC. The ANC retained control of all nine provinces after the 2004 elections. Overall, South Africa is a 'dominant-party democracy', in which the governing party is largely immune from effective challenge, there is little or no uncertainty about election results, and the electoral system provides for only weak accountability.

In the founding elections of April 1994, the ANC won 63 per cent of the votes. It increased its share to 66 per cent in the second general election in 1999, and to almost 70 per cent in the third general election in 2004. But it won fewer votes in both 1999 and 2004 than it had in 1994. Despite the fact that the voting-age population had risen by about one-fifth between 1994 and 2004, the total number of votes cast for all parties declined by about one-fifth over the same decade. Elections have been conducted professionally and with little sign of intimidation. Declining turnout is rather due to rising apathy. Despite extra activities to boost voter registration, only 75 per cent of the voting-age population were registered for the 2004 elections. Only 75 per cent of the registered voters cast their votes. This meant that only 58 per cent of the voting-age population actually voted. This was way down from the 86 per cent estimated for the 1994 elections, but in line with the turnout in other dominant-party democracies (Piombo 2005).

Part of the decline in voting was due to declining satisfaction with the performance of the government. Thabo Mbeki (President 1999-2008) had lower performance ratings than his predecessor, Nelson Mandela (President 1994-9), although Mbeki's ratings edged up somewhat during the 2004 general election campaign. The proportion of survey respondents that approved of the performance of the national government dipped below 50 per cent in 2000-01, but rose somewhat thereafter (Mattes 2005). The ANC government was probably unique in the world in that a majority of its own declared supporters assessed that the government's performance on the most important problem facing the country – unemployment and job creation – had been poor.

Alongside the decline in voting was a decline in partisan identification, i.e. in the proportion of voters who have a deep-rooted psychological attachment to one or other party. In 1994, in the midst of liberation, levels of partisan identification were very high, but they declined rapidly thereafter. By late 1995, fewer than 6 out of 10 adults said that they identified with or felt 'especially close' to one or other party, and this proportion has changed little since then (Mattes 2005). It is certainly possible that the exceptionally high levels of partisan identification found in 1993-4, almost all with the ANC, reflected a short-lived rush of enthusiasm and endorsement rather than a deep-rooted loyalty (Seekings 1997).

Of course, the electorate in 2004 did not comprise the same individuals as the electorate ten years earlier. One in three potential voters in 2004 had been too young to vote in 1994. The emergence of a post-apartheid generation of voters will surely bring some changes in attitudes, but it cannot explain sharp drops in measured identification, such as that between 1994 and 1995. Migration also reshapes the electorate at the provincial and local levels. This is especially important in the Western Cape, where immigration from the ANC-supporting Eastern Cape has swollen the numbers of ANC supporters even faster than the immigration of white middle-class voters from other parts of the country has swollen the numbers of supporters for the rival Democratic Alliance. The ANC's rising share of the vote in the Western Cape (until 2004) seems to have been due more to the changing demographics than to any success by the ANC in converting voters from other parties (Seekings 2006).

The results of the 1994 elections were generally interpreted in racial terms. In its extreme form, elections were dismissed as racial censuses. Some (white) scholars, shocked at the high votes for the ANC, concluded that African voters were not capable of reasoned voting, but were simply voting on the basis of racialised identities and loyalties. Whilst it was not difficult to rebut extreme forms of this argument (Mattes 1995; Seekings 1997) and Mattes *et al.* (1999) demonstrated that almost all voting behaviour could be explained in terms of partisan identification and issue-voting without any reference to race, it is clear that racialised identities and cultures do play some part in voting behaviour. Among African voters, discontent with the performance of the ANC government does not lead to support for opposition parties. Among white voters, even positive assessments of ANC government will rarely convert into actual votes for the ANC (Friedman 2005). Race is an especially important prism through which some issues and interests are perceived and understood in the multi-cultural Western Cape (Eldridge & Seekings 1996; Seekings 2006).

Identities are not immutable. Whilst race remains important in many aspects of life (Seekings 2008), consciousness of class has grown in importance. When asked in 2003 to identify the biggest division in contemporary South Africa, 1 in 5 survey respondents pointed to racial divisions, and a similar proportion said divisions between political parties. However, almost 1 in 3 respondents pointed to the division between rich and poor. If there is a shift in popular attitudes, it surely reflects in part the readily visible reality of a large African elite and middle class and hence of deep inequalities within the African population. It is no longer true that all rich people are white or that all African people are disadvantaged (Seekings & Nattrass 2005).

The continuing dominance of the ANC does not mean that there have been no changes in the party political landscape. On the contrary, there has been dramatic change among the opposition political parties, as the National Party (NP) – the party of apartheid – collapsed and died. In the early 1990s, NP leaders fondly entertained the hope of being able to achieve a majority in a democratic election, through a combination of the party's own strong support and alliances with conservative parties with support in African areas, such as the Zulu-nationalist Inkatha Freedom Party based in KwaZulu-Natal. The NP won only 20 per cent of the vote and became the very junior partner to the ANC in the Government of National Unity. In 1996, worried that its participation in government was costing it support, the NP went into opposition. Its support continued to decline, however, and in 1999, the NP – born again as the New National Party (NNP) – was trounced by the resurgent, 'liberal' Democratic Party (DP). Desperate, the NNP first joined with the DP as the Democratic Alliance (DA), then in 2001 one part of it split away and entered into an alternative coalition with the ANC. In 2004, the NNP won less than 2 per cent of the vote (Schulz-Hertzenberg 2005). Finally, in 2005, the NNP resolved to disband, with most of its remaining leaders being absorbed into the ANC.

The collapse of the NNP was mirrored by the rise of the DP/DA. From less than 2 per cent of the vote in 1994, the DP won almost 10 per cent in 1999 and the DA won more than 12 per cent in 2004. In 2004, the newly-formed Independent Democrats (ID) won some support among Coloured, former NNP supporters in Cape Town and elsewhere. However dramatic, the rise of the DP/DA and ID reflected shifts between opposition parties, not success in eroding the ANC's support. Although the DA espouses a combination of free market economics and pro-poor social policies, it has failed to attract either rich or poor African supporters and remains the party of South Africa's racial minorities: white (English- and Afrikaans-speaking), Coloured and Indian voters. It also retains the public support of 'white' capital, although it seems that many prudent 'white' companies also contribute financially to the ANC.

The demise of the NNP was hastened by 'floor-crossing'. In order to absorb part of the rump of the NNP, the ANC introduced legislation allowing for MPs to 'cross the floor' and join other parties during specified and infrequent windows. In early 2003, floor-crossing gave the ANC the two-thirds majority in Parliament that the electorate had twice denied it. Floor-crossing also brought the ANC shared power in the Western Cape and KwaZulu-Natal, the only two provinces hitherto run by opposition parties (Nijzink & Piombo 2005: 79-82).

The Political Economy of Neo-Liberalism

A narrow analysis of the new institutions of democracy suggests that power lies with the ANC leadership. The predominant interpretation of the political economy of South Africa, however, views the ANC leadership as the mere handmaidens of international and (to a lesser extent) domestic capital. In this view, key ANC leaders in the Mandela government – including Thabo Mbeki (deputy president), Trevor Manuel (Minister of Trade and Industry from 1994-5 and then Minister of Finance) and Alec Erwin (Manuel's successor at Trade and Industry) – used their powerful positions to ram through business-friendly policies, shifting the ANC from a pro-poor to a pro-business, 'neo-liberal' position, symbolised by the adoption of the Growth, Employment and Redistribution (GEAR) macroeconomic strategy in 1996.

This interpretation rests on the disappointment that some on the political left felt when capitalism survived the end of apartheid. For Patrick Bond the challenge was to understand how a 'popular-nationalist anti-apartheid project' had given way to 'official neoliberalism, by which is meant adherence to free market economic principles, bolstered by the narrowest practical definition of democracy' (2000: 1). Hein Marais (1998) emphasised the 'limits to change', to quote the subtitle of his book. John Saul writes that 'South Africa's dramatic transition to a democratic dispensation ("one person, one vote in a united South Africa") has been twinned with a simultaneous transition towards an ever more sweeping neo-liberal socio-economic dispensation that has negated in practice a great deal of the country's democratic advance' (2002: 28). 'Apartheid did not die' declares the ubiquitous journalist John Pilger (2006), in the title of a chapter on South Africa in his book *Freedom Next Time*.

Foreign and domestic business elites certainly wield influence, mostly behind closed doors or on the golf course away from prying eyes. In office, as both Deputy President and President, Mbeki allegedly gave 'business leaders unprecedented scope to shape government policies' and drew 'heavily on business advice'. Mbeki 'has gathered around him a select group of prominent people, mostly business leaders, divided into five working groups and three councils which he consults on key economic and social issues'. The international investment council includes, *inter alia*, the chief executive officers of Unilever, Ashanti Goldfields, Petronas and DaimlerChrysler as well as the international financier George Soros (Gumede 2002: 201-3). Senior ministers meet regularly with senior South African and foreign businessmen, as is the case in any capitalist economy, but there is a big gap between acknowledging that Mbeki and senior ministers consult with businessmen and claiming that businessmen determine policy-making.

Businessmen, as well as international agencies such as the World Bank and IMF, exerted some influence in the early and mid-1990s, shaping a concern over economic stability within the ANC. A series of 'scenario-planning' exercises in the early 1990s alerted the ANC leadership to the perils of economic crisis (Bond 2000: ch. 2). But the fears that led to the adoption of GEAR in 1996 were not unreasonable. President Mandela, when forming his government in 1994, had retained as Finance Minister the incumbent, who was a former businessman,

When the minister resigned later in 1994, Mandela appointed a banker as his successor. These choices reflected the ANC's anxiety about jitters among both local and international businessmen. Only in 1996 did Mandela feel confident enough to appoint a black ANC member, Trevor Manuel, as Minister of Finance.

As a former academic economist who ended up working in the presidency under Mbeki explains, the economy was not only already shrinking (at least in terms of per capita incomes), but it could all too easily shrink yet further (Hirsch 2005). GEAR was 'the result of a number of vectors: unfounded rumours about President Mandela's health; unfounded concerns about the appointment of the first ANC Finance Minister; noisy criticisms of the ANC's economic policies by labour and big business; international uncertainties leading to a teetering rand; the high interest rate policy of the South African Reserve Bank; and what the government belatedly realized was an excessively generous public sector wage settlement'. Above all, the combination of fiscal crisis and a weakening currency required decisive signals about the government's fiscal conservatism and other policies. The ANC, confident that the 'liberation political dividend' would ensure continuing electoral success, felt no need to introduce populist but short-sighted economic policies, and could instead look to growth in the medium term (Hirsch 2005: 4-6, 66-9).

By the late 1990s, the ANC appeared not so much pro-business as pro-*black* business. ANC political and black business elites are intertwined in the 'new establishment' (Calland 2006: 265). Under Mbeki, the ANC government has promoted energetically 'black economic empowerment' (BEE). The origins of BEE can be traced back to a meeting in 1993 at Mopane Lodge in the Kruger National Park, where ANC and black business leaders agreed to work together. More importantly, a Black Economic Empowerment Commission was appointed in 1999, headed by ANC heavyweight Cyril Ramaphosa. In a series of speeches, Mbeki defended the government's investment in building a black business elite on the basis that it was part of its commitment to deracialisation. The first major legislation effecting BEE was the Preferential Procurement Framework Act of 2000, which required that government favour tenders from black-owned companies. The 2001 report of the BEE Commission led to further BEE legislation in 2003 and an explicit government strategy. Central to the new strategy was the requirement that existing companies in each sector of the economy commit themselves to 'charters' specifying targets in terms of BEE deals. A BEE Council would be established in the President's office to monitor compliance (Gumede 2002; Hirsch 2005; Gqubule 2006).

'The ANC has firmly established itself as the party of black business, the black middle class and professionals,' wrote Gumede (2002: 252). The ANC 'will instinctively place the needs of these groups before those of the slum dwellers, unemployed, rural constituents and the youth'. Many members of the new super-rich black elite are ANC insiders: Tokyo Sexwale was premier[1] of Gauteng Province; Cyril Ramaphosa was Mbeki's main rival to succeed Mandela; Patrice Motsepe has never been active in the ANC, but he is linked by marriage to ANC leaders; Mathews Phosa was premier of Mpumalanga Province; Popo Molefe was premier of North-West Province; Saki Macozoma was a prominent ANC spokesperson; Moss Ngoasheng was Mbeki's economic adviser; Wendy Luhabe is the wife of the current ANC premier of Gauteng. Past and present ANC leaders have business interests; senior state officials know that they can build business careers quickly on leaving state employment; and ANC leaders and state officials live in the same social world as the new black economic elite. The result is an unabashed ideology that the promotion of a black business elite is just (on the grounds of deracialising opportunities) *and* what is good for black business is good for South Africa (on a range of grounds, including the social democratic argument that wealth creation provides the resources that can be redistributed to the poor through the government's social expenditure).

The ANC's own ally, the South African Communist Party (SACP), provides a more political interpretation of the political elite's sponsorship of black business. In a May 2006 discussion document, the SACP identified the construction of an 'alliance between emerging black capital and ... state-related technical/ managerial strata' as 'a key part of the 1996 GEAR offensive ... against the left'. Because of the highly-developed character of South African capitalism, 'emerging black capital ... is excessively compradorist and parasitic', dependent on state power to compel 'established capital to cut this emerging faction a slice of the action in order to remain in favour' with the new political elite. But the relationship between black capital and the ANC leadership is symbiotic: the latter need the former against more progressive opponents (SACP 2006). It certainly suits the ANC leadership to be able to play off their allies in the trade unions and SACP against their (black) allies in business, weakening both and thereby strengthening the ANC political elite itself. Whether or not this was the intention, it is certainly the outcome.

Working-class Power and the Limits of 'Neo-Liberalism'

The power of business notwithstanding, arguments about the triumph of neo-liberalism in South Africa misunderstand the nature, and thus seriously under-estimate the importance, of working-class power. The power of the organised labour movement is the primary reason why large parts of the GEAR strategy were never implemented. GEAR consisted of four major components: fiscal conservatism, trade liberalisation, flexible labour market policies, and privatisation of state assets. The budget deficit *was* controlled and trade *was* liberalised, or more precisely was further liberalised, given that most liberalisation preceded 1996. However, labour market policies were *not* reformed, and the promised programme of privatisation barely started. These proposed policy reforms were vehemently opposed by the trade unions. The much vaunted failure of GEAR to achieve its targets in terms of rising investment and job creation might be attributed to the failure to implement key parts of the strategy as much as to the parts that were in fact implemented.

Gold-mining is one of the sectors of the economy to experience massive job losses since the early 1990s. Declining employment is routinely attributed by the unions to GEAR, but as Tshitereke (2006) shows, the decline in mining employment has been part of a series of structural changes which predated or were independent of GEAR. These changes included technological change, the changing price of gold, the growing difficulties of mining gold, and the rising cost of labour (especially unskilled labour) due to union militancy and pro-union labour policy. GEAR served in part as a convenient scapegoat for these other factors. Tshitereke suggests further that the real threat that GEAR posed to the mineworkers' union was the prospect of outsourcing that would undermine the union's organisational basis. The implication is that the macroeconomic aspects of GEAR were symbolic, whilst the promised labour market policy reforms were of direct and immediate concern to the union as an organisation.

South Africa has a very strong trade union movement, built on the basis of delivering improved wages and employment conditions to workers. In 2000, the 460 registered trade unions had a total membership of about 3.5 million. Just over one half of these members belong to one or other of the nineteen unions affiliated with the largest and most important trade union federation, the Congress of South African Trade Unions (COSATU). COSATU's affiliates have over 1,800 full-time officials, and the federation has a dedicated parliamentary office and research wing (Webster & Buhlungu 2004). Only 38 per cent of trade union members are unskilled or semi-skilled workers, in sharp contrast to the position in the 1970s when the independent trade union movement emerged. The median wage of a unionised worker is more than double the median of non-unionised workers. One in three COSATU members is in the public sector. Its largest affiliate is still the National Union of Mineworkers, but the next four biggest affiliated unions are all in the public sector. Almost no union member is in the poorest half of the South African population, which comprises instead households with workers in non-unionised sectors (such as domestic work and agriculture) and marginal forms of employment, or who are unemployed. South Africa's unemployment rate stands at about 30 to 40 per cent depending on how it is measured. In the South African context, trade unions are a powerful movement of the non-poor.

The power of the trade unions lies not in their use of industrial protest, but rather in the threat of such action, their entrenched position in union-friendly labour institutions, and particularly their influence within the ANC. There has been little strike action in post-apartheid South Africa, because there has been little need for it. The high point of union power was in the mid-1990s, when COSATU secured desired reforms of labour legislation. Institutions and policies designed in the 1920s to protect the interests of skilled white workers were extended and strengthened in the 1990s to protect the interests of the skilled black workers who (then) comprised the backbone of COSATU. The 1995 Labour Relations Act provided for centralised bargaining between employers and unions within sectoral 'bargaining councils', procedures for the arbitration and settlement of disputes, and strong restrictions on dismissal by employers. Wages negotiated in bargaining councils can be extended across entire sectors, including to non-participants in the negotiations, by ministerial fiat. The 1997 Basic Conditions of Employment Act provided, *inter alia*, for statutory minimum wages in sectors where workers are not organised, helping further to contain any downward pressure on union members' wages, given the scale of unemployment. At much the same time, unions secured favourable industrial policies that emphasised skills, rising productivity and hence rising wages (Nattrass 2001), and public sector workers secured large pay increases (which contributed to the fiscal crisis and GEAR). Unions were central players in the corporatist National Economic, Development and Labour Council. The unions were also able to veto most of the privatisation agenda associated with GEAR.

Employers probably felt too weak to bargain more forcefully. Big business was, in any case, not altogether unhappy with high wages as long as they were accompanied by high productivity and low levels of strike action. Employers responded to this high-wage environment by shedding unskilled labour and investing in more capital- and skill-intensive technologies. Employers are unhappy with provisions for dismissing workers. By one estimate, three times the number of work-days is lost through dismissal procedures than through work stoppages. Many employers adjust to such costs by reducing employment further, especially of unskilled workers. The consequence of these policies was that average real wages rose, in part because the demand for unskilled labour declined, whilst the profit share rose. The post-apartheid growth path was good for employers and for those workers who kept their jobs. The losers were workers who lost their jobs and did not find new employment and the chronically unemployed (Seekings & Nattrass 2005).

GEAR had envisaged reforms to labour-market policies to render them more flexible and employer-friendly. In 1999, the government initiated a review of labour legislation, but only very minor reforms were implemented. In the same year, the Minister of Labour introduced very minor changes to the regulations affecting small businesses employing fewer than ten workers. Most recently, in mid-2005, ANC leaders finally declared their intention of tackling the 'holy cow' of labour-market policy. A discussion document, tabled at a major ANC conference in 2005, proposed excluding small employers from some regulatory requirements and from the sectoral wage deals negotiated between large employers and unions. This was opposed strongly by COSATU and the South African Communist Party, who secured a conference resolution that left labour-market reform off the immediate agenda. The only major reverse to the labour movement has been the government's sidelining of the National Economic, Development and Labour Council.

Critics charge that the continued participation of COSATU in an alliance with the ANC is bad for workers. The COSATU leadership is accused of selling out union members and buying into 'neo-liberal corporatism' in order to secure marginal influence on economic and social policy-making (see Bramble & Barchiesi 2003). But participation in the alliance has led to substantial gains for unionised workers. Webster and Adler (1999) understated the case when they wrote that there were moves 'towards' a class compromise between capital and labour in South Africa. In important respects, workers achieved a class compromise: they accepted the capitalist economy in return for real wage increases, constraints on dismissal, and improved conditions at work. In addition, many workers have benefited from changes outside of the workplace since 1994. Many working people live in better housing, with better services, than they did before 1994. Their children have better opportunities to complete high school or even study further. Many are very aware that their lives are much better than they were under apartheid and much better than their parents' lives. For this relatively privileged section of the 'working class', labour-market reforms, deracialisation and improved service delivery represent good reasons to support the ANC, and to continue to support COSATU's alliance with the ANC. If COSATU were to leave the alliance with the ANC, it would not take all (or perhaps even most) of its members with it, would probably prompt the establishment of a rival pro-ANC federation and would risk losing the capacity to veto reforms of labour-market policy or privatisation.

In post-apartheid South Africa, the power of capital and labour cannot be measured in terms of strikes or lock-outs or their consequences. Nor should power simply be measured in terms of trends in wages and profits, although these are important indicators. Rather, power should be understood primarily in terms of the working of the institutions and procedures within or through which wages are determined and employment is regulated. The power of the organised working-class in the mid-1990s resulted in the reform of institutions and procedures that favoured high wages and favourable conditions of employment for union members. Even when the apparent power of the unions and organised working-class diminished in the late 1990s and early 2000s, the class remained capable of vetoing explicit policy shifts. In contrast, capital had to learn to live with a second-best labour policy environment in the 1990s and to accept BEE in the 2000s. The power of capital lies not in any direct veto over such policies, but in its capacity to adapt to the new environment by withholding investment.

Having remained within the ANC alliance, COSATU's influence rose again in the mid-2000s amidst struggles within the ANC over who should succeed Mbeki as President. The organisational power of the Left, within both COSATU and the South African Communist Party, means that the Left punches above its weight. Few candidates for the succession are going to risk alienating important and organised constituencies. Most candidates are likely, instead, to court these constituencies through fresh promises.

The State

Critics of neo-liberalism portray the post-apartheid state as a neo-liberal state committed to rolling back its own reach and extending markets wherever possible. The energetic embrace of trade liberalisation in the early 1990s provided some evidence for this, and the GEAR wish-list provided more. The sidelining of the Economic, Development and Labour Council suggests that the state should not be seen as a corporatist state, and the presence of (black) businessmen and women in the 'new establishment' certainly indicates that this is not a worker's state. However, there is too much evidence of active state intervention in the economy, and more specifically of the subversion of markets, to suggest that the state can be viewed as neo-liberal.

The government itself denies that it has abandoned interventions in the market. Since 2004, it refers to its attempts to build a 'developmental' state. The government was at pains to emphasise that growth and development would not simply be left to market forces. The state would play an active and interventionist role, as states have in parts of East and South-east Asia. Throughout the late 1990s, the Department of Trade and Industry tried to develop pro-active industrial policies, and in the 2000s this developmental role extended to state investments in infrastructure (Southall 2006). The rhetoric of a 'developmental' state probably appealed to some ANC leaders because of their vanguardist approach to the armed struggle in the 1970s and 1980s, and to others who were grappling with the meaning of communism or socialism in a post-Soviet world. But the reality of the South African state was very different from the models of the 'developmental' states of East and South-east Asia. The post-apartheid state has weak links with existing 'white' capital, quite unlike the links that characterised the developmental states of East Asia. The relationship between state and capital has many adversarial features, including the imposition on capital of the state's agenda of racial transformation. New 'black' capital is too dependent on both the state and established capital for it to develop a meaningful economic partnership with the state. The state might be vanguardist, imposing racial transformation on capital, but it is not yet a developmental state pushing and pulling capital in developmental directions.

'Development' was a key component of the ANC's 'Reconstruction and Development Programme', which began life as the party's manifesto in the 1994 elections.

The other ingredient in the manifesto was 'reconstruction' and, implicitly, redistribution. The ANC has consistently trumpeted its concern with redistribution as well as growth, although little thought was put into the redistributive side of the picture. *Redistribution* really meant distribution that was more *just*. For example, the working poor should be paid more through minimum wage legislation, and public schools and clinics should be improved. But the state inherited a functional and highly effective set of redistributive social welfare programmes that effectively meant the South African state was a welfare state. Between 1993-94 and the mid-2000s, the share of GDP being redistributed to the poor through non-contributory social assistance programmes rose from about 2 per cent to about 3.6 per cent. Old-age pensions remained the largest single programme, but child support grants cost about 1 per cent of GDP and disability grants (many paid to AIDS-sick people) cost almost as much. In total, more than 10 million grants were paid monthly, in a country with just 45 million people (Seekings 2007).

Key ANC leaders were for a long time deeply ambivalent about the welfare state that they inherited. The first phase of proposed welfare reforms in the late 1990s entailed a shift from grants to 'developmental' welfare. These reforms were not implemented, but ANC leaders continued to denounce 'hand-outs' to the poor. The government was said to be spending 'too much' on social assistance, and any movement towards a 'welfare state' should be resisted. In this way, the post-apartheid state has adopted the discourse of the late-apartheid state. Poverty reduction should focus on employment creation – including, in the short term, public works programmes – rather than welfare programmes. However, the failure to deliver job creation or even significant numbers of job 'opportunities' in public works programmes resulted in the government reluctantly embracing welfare. Government ministers now take pride in what Mbeki has called the 'third pillar' of the government's strategy. The first pillar is the promotion of 'the growth and development of the First Economy'; the second is addressing 'the challenges of the Second Economy' (i.e. unemployment and the informal economy); and the third comprises 'building a social security net to meet the objective of poverty alleviation'. It is important to note the absence of any serious mention of land reform. In South Africa, the safety-net for the poor comprises cash transfers, not access to land.

The South African state is a modern state in other respects also. It includes an unusually efficient tax office (the South African Revenue Service). It also regulates employment relationships, as we have seen already, through legislation such as the Labour Relations Act. This combination of pro-union employment regulation, welfare programmes, and moderate, pro-business developmentalism invites comparison with social democratic states of the global North. Indeed, Hirsch (2005: 3) argues that 'the ANC government followed a consistent economic philosophy':

> At the centre is a social democratic approach to social reform – it is the state's job to underwrite the improvement in the quality of life of the poor and to reduce inequalities, but with a firmly entrenched fear of the risks of personal dependency on the state and of the emergence of entitlement attitudes. The state exists within a market economy that depends on private investment, and therefore a successful state creates an environment that supports high levels of private investment. This does not require the state simply to step aside for business, but rather that it should work with business and labour to develop growth-oriented strategies.

Whilst broadly persuasive, this interpretation requires a number of qualifications. First, the state is, in some important respects, distinctly non-modern. In the early

2000s, the ANC-led government legislated the transfer of powers to unelected chiefs, including over the allocation of land. It did so without regard for regional differences, as if all chiefs enjoyed equal legitimacy. In some areas, including Xhalanga in the Eastern Cape, chiefs did not control the land and did not enjoy either power or legitimacy prior to apartheid; the apartheid state sought to impose chiefs, but this was thwarted by popular resistance. The democratic state's policies of reviving chieftainship and 're-tribalisation', driven by the ANC's bid for the support of chiefs and traditionalists, have compromised democracy (Ntsebeza 2005), and are clearly antithetical to a meaningfully social democratic worldview.

Secondly, what does social democracy mean in a developing country context like South Africa, especially one in which there is a massive surplus of labour? Unemployment drives poverty, and the welfare state provides no direct protection against unemployment. In this context, a social democratic approach would surely require either massive efforts in terms of low-wage job creation or the extension of the welfare state to cover those who are unable to work because there are no jobs for them. The South African state has not tackled either of these challenges (Seekings & Nattrass 2005). Nor has it tackled the land question, abandoning a commitment to pro-poor land reform (peasantisation) in favour of fostering a class of black large-scale farmers (Ntsebeza & Hall 2006).

Thirdly, the state is not homogeneous and monolithic. The Department of Labour, headed by a former trade union leader and staffed primarily by former unionists, is an active advocate of the interests of trade unions, and cannot be viewed as a pro-business institution. The Department of Education was, during the first decade of democracy, largely unwilling to challenge the South African Democratic Teachers' Union. Only in 2005-6 did the Minister and senior officials begin to confront the challenge of bringing teachers – many of whom are incompetent – to account. The National Treasury is obviously concerned with macroeconomic stability, but is not nearly so hostile to redistributive programmes as left-wing critics imagine, as long as redistribution is efficient in terms of reaching the poor and is not hijacked by special interests (such as public sector workers). Whilst the Department of Labour is broadly hostile to labour-market policy reform, the National Treasury is broadly in favour.

Finally, events in 2007-8 revealed other respects in which the state arguably fell short of the neo-liberal ideal. Accumulating evidence of pervasive corruption indicated that the rule of law did not apply to a wide and growing range of economic transactions. And the crisis over power supplies dispelled the state's claim to steady economic management. Even the neo-liberal state is required to ensure an economic environment that is conducive to production and hence profit. The post-apartheid state – and the ANC at its helm – readily boasted of economic success, as South Africa presided over its longest sustained period of economic growth for decades. But the failure to invest in power stations and the resulting blackouts – and shutting down of mines and other businesses – both revealed extraordinary mismanagement and dispelled any hopes of continuing rapid growth over the following three to five years.

A Pluralist Analysis of the State and Ruling Party

The complexity of the state mirrors, and is in part rooted in, the diverse and heterogeneous character of the ANC. Lodge (2003) compares the ANC to the

Congress Party of India. Both parties are essentially coalitions, and different factions are linked to or influenced by groups in the broader society. Old 'white' businesses, new 'black' businesses and organised labour all exert influence through different factions and mechanisms. Overall, Lodge concluded that no single movement is dominant.

The power of different social groups has changed over time, however, and can take different forms. The early 2000s appear to have seen the growing influence of black businessmen and women within the ANC, and the decline in trade union influence. Black Economic Empowerment moved to the centre of state policy. Corruption, especially over the award of state contracts in the name of BEE, was pervasive (Camerer 2006; Feinstein 2007). Much of the ANC leadership is preoccupied with sharing in the opportunities for rapid financial enrichment through BEE. It is not surprising that critics wonder whether their enthusiasm for sharing in these opportunities might have led political elites to enact the policies that create these very opportunities. No other social group has the pervasive influence of the aspiring black bourgeoisie. It might be unclear how important was financial self-interest in the original adoption of BEE policies, relative to other objectives such as general Africanisation or the stabilisation of capitalism in a racially-charged environment. But it is clear that the political elite is now too entangled in capitalism either to allow too much power to anti-capitalist critics on its left or to go too far down the Zimbabwean route of under-mining capitalist production itself.

Trade unions retain power, but in specific forms. In terms of policy-making, their power lies primarily in inhibiting undesirable changes to the status quo. Trade unions have mobilised effectively against labour-market policy reform and against reforms of the public sector, especially in education (see Seekings 2004). Their mobilisation is within the ANC alliance rather than in the street or workplace. The competition over who would succeed Thabo Mbeki as President of South Africa after the 2009 elections reveals the great investment that unions are making in ANC politics.

The politics of the succession in 2007 and 2008 revealed much about the ANC and the nature of power in South Africa. At the end of 2007 the ANC elected its president, other office-bearers and National Executive Committee for the following three years. For the first time in a generation, the ANC presidency was contested, with the incumbent (Thabo Mbeki) standing for re-election against Jacob Zuma, the deputy-president of the party and the former deputy-president of South Africa (until he faced charges of corruption and Mbeki replaced him). What was at stake was not just the presidency of the party, and the powers of patronage that the position entailed, but also the ANC's nomination for the national Presidency in the next, 2009 general election. If Zuma became ANC president, he would become the presumptive ANC nominee for 2009; if Mbeki secured re-election, Zuma's chances would be slim. At its conference, the ANC resoundingly rejected Mbeki and elected Zuma (and a slate of ANC leaders critical of Mbeki). This was a classic populist revolt against incumbent leadership. It exposed, firstly, the limits of executive power: the party leadership and national presidency retain power only as long as they are expected to remain in office; as soon as their departure seems imminent they lose power to their prospective successors and become 'lame ducks'. As soon as it became clear that Mbeki no longer commanded *complete* support and power, he lost *almost all* power and support; he was forced to resign from the Presidency itself in September 2008 by the ANC National Executive Committee. The splits within the ANC also exposed the absence of programmatic intra-party politics. Observers were hard-pressed to distinguish any clear difference between the policy preferences of the Zuma and Mbeki factions. Both sides enjoyed the support of groups of black businessmen. The unions did support Zuma, but without securing clear promises of more pro-union policy. The struggle over leadership was a struggle between personalised factions rather than ones defined by policy or even ideology.

Some social groups enjoy little power, outside or within the ANC. The rural and urban poor lack organisational muscle, and the electoral system effectively denies them the power to hold elected representatives to account. Life expectancy has fallen drastically, because of AIDS and the government's foot-dragging response; inequality has worsened; unemployment has risen; and poverty worsened in the late 1990s before (probably) declining somewhat in the early 2000s. The poor have not got land, jobs, good health, or good education for their children. They have received more redistribution through welfare programmes and improved (and subsidised) services such as water and electricity (especially in urban areas). Rising expenditure on welfare is the major reason why poverty probably declined slightly in the early 2000s, but even this needs to be put into perspective. The ANC has not introduced any major new welfare programmes, but rather has introduced minor (but important) reforms to a system of welfare programmes that was substantially in place not only prior to democracy, but prior to apartheid. And the real value of the old-age pension, the primary pillar of the welfare state, had in 2007 still not reached its level of mid-1993, prior to the transition to democracy (Seekings 2007).

The emergence of 'new social movements' might be seen as the demand by the poor and excluded for a place at the table (see Ballard *et al.* 2006). Whilst some of the most important movements such as the trade unions and the Treatment Action Campaign have assiduously maintained their loyalty to the ANC whilst criticising specific policies, others have united in a coalition that is explicitly hostile to the ANC government (and has therefore been dubbed by the ANC as 'ultra-left'). Their demands focus on access to urban land, housing and services. Recurrent episodes of direct action in townships around the country give the impression of breadth and depth to the movement. Yet, when movement leaders have contested local elections, they have almost always performed poorly. Their support base seems to be fickle and shallow, and the ANC is likely to be able to contain dissent through judicious concessions on access to and the affordability of urban land, housing and services.

In the late 1990s, Webster and Adler (1999) suggested that South Africa was moving 'towards' a class compromise, between capital and labour. The capitalist system remained, and capitalists even secured some neo-liberal policies, but with powerful safeguards of workers' rights and higher wages. This formulation neglected the role of the welfare state in redistributing to the poor. A more appropriate formulation seemed to be that of a double class compromise, with the poor benefiting from redistribution through the budget and the prospect of job creation. This might have reflected the electoral power of the poor (Nattrass & Seekings 2001). A closer inspection of some of the gains for the poor revealed that they were driven, in part, by the self-interest of public sector unions, suggesting that the class compromise was less inclusive (Seekings 2004). Developments in the early 2000s demand further modifications to the class-compromise story. Unions, specifically

COSATU, continue to exert influence within the ANC alliance, but the rising social group is clearly black business. Insofar as the South African policy regime has social democratic characteristics, these are combined with distinctly reactionary concessions to chiefs in rural areas, Africanist elements in terms of both chiefs and BEE, and a neglect of the interests of the unemployed. In struggles between established business, new black business, and trade unions, and with chiefs demanding benefits too, the poor are likely to continue to be trampled underfoot.

Note

1. Premier is the prime minister of the provincial government.

References

Ballard, Richard, Adam Habib and Imraan Valodia. eds. 2006. *Voices of Protest: Social Movements in Post-Apartheid South Africa.* Pietermaritzburg: University of KwaZulu-Natal Press.
Blumenfeld, Jesmond. 1997. From Icon to Scapegoat? The Experience of South Africa's Reconstruction and Development Programme. *Development Policy Review* 15 (1): 65-91.
Bond, Patrick. 2000. *Elite Transition: From Apartheid to Neoliberalism in South Africa.* Pietermaritzburg: University of Natal Press and London: Pluto Press.
Bramble, Tom, and Franco Barchiesi, eds. 2003. *Rethinking the Labour Movement in the 'New South Africa'.* Aldershot: Ashgate.
Buhlungu, Sakhela, ed. 2006. *Trade Unions and Democracy: COSATU Workers' Political Attitudes in South Africa.* Pretoria: HSRC Press.
Calland, Richard. 2006. *Anatomy of South Africa: Who Holds the Power?* Cape Town: Zebra.
Camerer, Marianne. 2006. 'Corruption'. Paper presented at conference on South Africa After Apartheid, Cape Town.
Chothia, Farouk, and Sean Jacobs. 2002. Remaking the Presidency; The Tension between Co-ordination and Centralization. In *Thabo Mbeki's World: The Politics and Ideology of the South African President,* eds Sean Jacobs and Richard Calland. Pietermaritzburg: University of KwaZulu-Natal Press.
Dyzenhaus, David. 2006. 'The Pasts of Law: The Politics of the Rule of Law in South Africa', Paper presented at the conference on South Africa After Apartheid, Cape Town.
Eldridge, Matthew, and Jeremy Seekings. 1996. Mandela's Lost Province: The African National Congress and the Western Cape Electorate in the 1994 South African Elections. *Journal of Southern African Studies* 22(4): 517-40.
February, Judith. 2006. More than a Law-making Production Line? Parliament and its Oversight Role. In *State of the Nation: South Africa, 2005-2006,* eds Sakhela Buhlungu, John Daniel, Roger Southall and Jessica Lutchman. Pretoria: HSRC Press.
Feinstein, Andrew. 2007. *After the Party: A Personal and Political Journey Inside the ANC.* Johannesburg: Jonathan Ball.
Friedman, Steven. 2005. A Vote for Some: South Africa's Decade of Democracy. In *Electoral Politics in South Africa: Assessing the First Democratic Decade,* eds Jessica Piombo and Lia Nijzink. Basingstoke: Palgrave Macmillan.
Gqubule, Duma, ed. 2006. *Making Mistakes, Righting Wrongs: Insights into Black Economic Empowerment.* Johannesburg: Jonathan Ball.
Gumede, William Mervin. 2002. Down to Business, but Nothing to Show. In *Thabo Mbeki's World: The Politics and Ideology of the South African President,* eds Sean Jacobs and Richard Calland. Pietermaritzburg: University of KwaZulu-Natal Press.
———. 2005. *Thabo Mbeki and the Battle for the Soul of the ANC.* Cape Town: Zebra Books.
Hirsch, Alan. 2005. *Season of Hope: Economic Reform under Mandela and Mbeki.* Pietermaritzburg: University of KwaZulu-Natal Press.
Johnson, R.W. and Lawrence Schlemmer, eds. 1996. *Launching Democracy in South Africa: The First Open Election, April 1994.* New Haven, CT: Yale University Press.
Lodge, Tom. 2003. *Politics in South Africa: From Mandela to Mbeki.* Oxford: James Currey.
Marais, Hein. 2002. *South Africa: Limits to Change; the Political Economy of Transformation.* Cape Town:

University of Cape Town Press.

Mattes, Robert. 1995. *The Election Book: Judgement and Choice in South Africa's 1994 Election.* Cape Town: Institute for a Democratic South Africa.

———. 2005. Voter Information, Government Evaluations, and Party Images in the First Democratic Decade. In *Electoral Politics in South Africa: Assessing the First Democratic Decade,* eds Jessica Piombo and Lia Nijzink. Basingstoke: Palgrave Macmillan.

Mattes, Robert, Helen Taylor and Cherrel Africa. 1999. Judgement and Choice in the 1999 South African Election. *Politikon* 26(2): 235-47.

Murray, Christina and Lia Nijzink. 2002. *Building Representative Democracy: South Africa's Legislatures and the Constitution.* Cape Town: Parliamentary Support Programme.

Nattrass, Nicoli. 2001. High Productivity Now: A Critical Review of South Africa's Growth Strategy. *Transformation* 45:1-24.

Nattrass, Nicoli and Jeremy Seekings. 1998. Democratic Institutions and Development in Post-apartheid South Africa. In *The Democratic Developmental State: Political and Institutional Design,* eds Mark Robinson and Gordon White. Oxford: Oxford University Press.

———. 2001. Democracy and Distribution in Highly Unequal Economies: The Case of South Africa. *Journal of Modern African Studies* 39(3): 471-98.

Nijzink, Lia and Jessica Piombo. 2005. Parliament and the Electoral System: How are South Africans being Represented?. In *Electoral Politics in South Africa: Assessing the First Democratic Decade,* eds Jessica Piombo and Lia Nijzink. Basingstoke: Palgrave Macmillan.

Ntsebeza, Lungisile. 2005. *Democracy Compromised: Chiefs and the Politics of the Land in South Africa.* Leiden and Boston, MA: Brill.

Ntsebeza, Lungisile and Ruth Hall, eds. 2006. *The Land Question in South Africa: The Challenge of Transformation and Redistribution.* Pretoria: HSRC Press.

Pilger, John. 2006. *Freedom Next Time.* London: Bantam.

Piombo, Jessica. 2005. The Results of Election 2004. In *Electoral Politics in South Africa: Assessing the First Democratic Decade,* eds Jessica Piombo and Lia Nijzink. Basingstoke: Palgrave Macmillan.

Piombo, Jessica and Lia Nijzink, eds. 2005. *Electoral Politics in South Africa: Assessing the First Democratic Decade.* Basingstoke: Palgrave Macmillan.

SACP. 2006. Class Struggles and the Post-1994 State in South Africa, Part 2 of South African Communist Party (SACP) Central Committee Discussion Document, published in *Bua Komanisi* 5(1) (May 2006).

Saul, John. 2002. Cry for the Beloved Country: The Post-Apartheid Denouement. In *Thabo Mbeki's World: The Politics and Ideology of the South African President,* eds Sean Jacobs and Richard Calland. Pietermaritzburg: University of KwaZulu-Natal Press.

Schulz-Hertzenberg, Collette. 2005. The New National Party: The End of the Road. In *Electoral Politics in South Africa: Assessing the First Democratic Decade,* eds Jessica Piombo and Lia Nijzink. Basingstoke: Palgrave Macmillan.

Seekings, Jeremy. 1997. From the Ballot Box to the Bookshelf: Studies of the 1994 South African General Election. *Journal of Contemporary African Studies* 115(2): 287309.

———. 2004. Trade Unions, Social Policy and Class Compromise in Post-Apartheid South Africa. *Review of African Political Economy* 100: 299-312.

——— 2006. Partisan Realignment in Cape Town, 1994-2004. *Journal of African Elections* 5(1): 176-203.

———. 2007. 'The Expansion of Social Assistance Programmes in South Africa', unpublished paper.

———. 2008. The Continuing Salience of Race: Discrimination and Diversity in South Africa. *Journal of Contemporary African Studies* 26(1):1-26.

Seekings, Jeremy and Nicoli Nattrass. 2005. *Class, Race and Inequality in South Africa.* New Haven, CT: Yale University Press.

Southall, Roger. 2006. Black Empowerment and Present Limits to a More Democratic Capitalism in South Africa. In *State of the Nation: South Africa 2005/06,* eds Sakhela Buhlungu *et al.* Pretoria: HSRC Press.

Tshitereke, Clarence. 2006. *The Experience of Economic Redistribution: The Growth, Employment and Redistribution Strategy in South Africa.* New York and London: Routledge.

Webster, Edward and Glenn Adler. 1999. Towards a Class Compromise in South Africa's Double Transition. *Politics and Society* 27(3): 347-85.

Webster, Edward and Sakhela Buhlungu. 2004. Between Marginalisation and Revitalisation? The State of Trade Unionism in South Africa. *Review of African Political Economy* 100: 229-45.

9

Mozambique since 1989
Shaping Democracy after Socialism

ERIC MORIER-GENOUD

Mozambique has undergone radical changes since 1989. After Frelimo's fifth Congress in 1989, the country abandoned Socialism and moved to a liberal democratic political and economic system. After negotiations in Rome in 1990-92 in which Frelimo and Renamo came to agreement over their differences, the civil war ended and peace returned. Mozambique has thereafter seen peace and a blossoming of liberalism in social, economic and political affairs. Almost everything changed in Mozambique in the 1990s. In matters political, elections have been held every three years, at the national and municipal level. Although Frelimo has won all the elections and thus remained in power, the political sphere has become competitive.

The literature on Mozambique has tended to interpret the transformation of the late 1980s-90s in two ways. To some, the historical changes constitute the return to a normal state of affairs and the question is how to consolidate economic growth and political democracy. Authors have accordingly investigated issues of 'elite habituation' or the development of political parties (Manning 2002; Carbone 2005; Ostheimer 2001). To others in contrast, the historical shift of the late 1980s is a return to an abnormal state of affairs. Mozambique is being 're-colonised' by the very capitalist forces which were behind the civil war. Analyses have accordingly focused on imperialism, the development of a local 'comprador class' and popular resistance (Saul 1993; Hanlon 1996).

One way or another, the literature has tended to naturalise the changes in Mozambique in the late 1980s-early 1990s. These changes have often been under-studied or dismissed as external impositions, with little attention being paid to the precise chronology of events, their forms and the struggles around them. The literature has failed to address key questions such as: why did Frelimo decide to adopt liberal democracy? When and how did it do so? Considering Frelimo is still in power today, the literature has also not asked whether the party in power is still the same one as before and whether its exercise of power has changed. To put the question differently, the literature has not looked at how Frelimo might have shaped events and how, in turn, it might have been affected by the transition from war to peace and from Socialism to liberal democracy. Answering such questions is necessary to better understand the transition from Socialism to liberalism as well as the political situation in Mozambique today.

To analyse the coming and unfolding of liberalism in Mozambique, this chapter adopts an opportunity structure or historical sociology of action approach. This means it will look at how political actors have chosen to act within structural constraints that are historically driven. The chapter proceeds in three sections. The first section investigates when and how Frelimo dropped Socialism and what kind of liberal democracy it decided to adopt in its stead. The second section investigates the impact political and economic liberalism has had on the country and the challenges this has brought to Frelimo as the party in power. The last section looks at how the party in power has been transformed by its abandonment of Socialism and the way it is adapting in order to continue to rule. The argument advanced is that Frelimo shaped the social, economic and political system which was to follow Socialism in such a way that it has remained in power. This was not without cost, however. The post-Socialist system has changed the nature and social basis of the party, and has brought new challenges to Frelimo's domination. Up to 2000, the liberal democratic system permitted Frelimo to remain in power, but from then on, the changes have tended to undermine its rule. We shall see how Frelimo is trying to address that challenge to its hegemony.

Establishing and Shaping Democracy

By the mid-1980s, the Socialist revolution in Mozambique which had begun with independence from Portugal in 1975 (and followed on a ten-year liberation war) was undermined on three fronts. On the international front, Frelimo faced outright opposition from Western and Arab countries and a refusal on the part of the Soviet Union to secure the Socialist regime in the face of Western opposition. Indeed, although Mozambique declared itself officially Socialist, the Soviet Union only recognised it as 'a country of Socialist orientation' and refused to provide the substantial material or military support necessary in the face of international hostility. On the regional front, Mozambique was suffering from a war of destabilisation initiated in 1977 by the Rhodesian regime and then waged by the apartheid regime of South Africa. By 1986, the war had crossed the Zambezi River southwards and extended to the whole country. Finally, on the internal front, the implementation of the Socialist revolution had generated much resistance and opposition, in particular from the social groups and regions which had been marginalised if not attacked by the new regime, e.g. traditional authorities, religious organisations, traders, the province of Zambezia, etc. By the mid-1980s, all three dynamics, internal, regional and international, had coalesced to turn the war of aggression into a civil war and undermine the Socialist revolution irremediably. The situation was such that by 1987 some scholars were talking of an 'implosion of the Revolution' (Cahen 1987).

From 1981 the Frelimo regime tried to correct some of its 'mistakes' by reversing elements of its Revolution which generated resistance. It authorised the operation of small traders once again, abandoned its attack on religion, and in 1984 even negotiated a peace treaty with the apartheid South African regime under which Frelimo stopped supporting the ANC in exchange for South Africa putting an end to its assistance to Renamo, the proxy guerrilla movement. But this did not have the expected results. The war continued to expand and the economy continued to collapse, so that more fundamental changes were soon being considered. This is something which Samora Machel, the first President of Mozambique, began to do in 1985-6 when he started to shift the regime away from Socialist countries towards the West. After the death of Machel in a puzzling plane crash in late 1986, Joaquim Chissano succeeded to the Presidency and continued the reorientation of the regime, even signing a comprehensive accord with the IMF and World Bank in 1987 (Hall & Young 1997). But again these changes did not have the expected outcome of restoring peace or revitalising the economy. In fact, the social and political crisis even deepened as a result of the structural adjustment measures taken. The crisis was eventually such that the regime decided in 1988-9 to embrace what it could no longer oppose: political and economic liberalism. Frelimo decided to drop Socialism immediately and shift its regime towards liberal democratic and free-market forces. This was a strategic choice to remain in power. Anne Pitcher (2002) appropriately calls it a strategy of 'preservation through transformation'.

It is difficult to know exactly when, where and how the decision to drop Socialism and adopt liberalism was taken by Frelimo – probably by the Political Bureau sometime in 1988. But, broadly speaking, we can say that the shift happened between 1989 and 1990 when two decisive events took place. First, in July 1989 Frelimo held its fifth Congress, the third since independence. At the Congress, it was decided to abandon all references to Marxism-Leninism, to adopt liberal values and to open the party to all social categories. Party members were now allowed, if not encouraged, to engage in capitalist enterprise, and previously excluded groups such as religious people and traders were welcomed into the party. The second event which shows Frelimo's definitive strategic shift is the revision of the Constitution which took place between 1989 and 1990. There had been previous constitutional revisions in Mozambique since independence in 1975. But this particular revision amounted to a complete overhaul of the Constitution, almost the drafting of a new document. The decision to revise the Constitution was taken by the Assembly of the Popular Republic in September 1989 (just after the fifth Congress) and the new document was adopted later in the year and published in January 1990. The new text made no reference to Socialist principles; instead it adopted a resolutely liberal understanding of the state and politics, with a separation of powers and an opening of the way for multiparty democracy (Hall & Young 1991).

To secure its strategy of preservation through transformation, Frelimo took four specific measures for the transition to liberalism. First, the new Constitution was liberal, hence undermining Renamo's claim to be fighting for democracy, but it was also an 'open text' which left room for manoeuvre should Frelimo decide not to adopt full multipartyism but only a pluralist dominant party state (Cahen 1990: 49-50). Second, Frelimo took its time in opening direct negotiations with Renamo, thus ensuring that it was in an optimal position at the negotiating table and giving itself time to define the details of the political system as events unfolded. Moreover, just like the MPLA in Angola a year earlier, Frelimo made sure that it negotiated a peace accord favourable to itself. The accord, signed in 1992 and implemented under the aegis of the United Nations, eventually recognised Frelimo as the legitimate holder of state power, something which gave the party a definite edge over the opposition. It provided Frelimo with the 'arms of sovereignty' which allowed it to contest any foreign attempt to influence national politics. It also allowed Frelimo to avoid demobilising some of its best troops by transferring them discreetly into the police force, with which the peace accord did not deal. Needless to say, this was a crucial element in the run-up to the elections as well as in the years to come, as there would be no army to speak of any more, but a police force boosted by the most loyal and capable of Frelimo troops (Messiant 1997).

Third, the new political system chosen was strongly presidential. As in many other African countries, democratisation and presidentialism went hand in hand. The President of the Republic was to nominate the Prime Minister, all the Ministers and vice-ministers, the head of the judiciary, the heads of universities, the heads of the provinces, including the provinces where the opposition would win, and he was to have significant legislative powers as well (Cahen 1990; Lala & Ostheimer 2003). The ability of the Mozambican President to project his powers over the provinces is similar to the role of the Ghanaian President in the Districts, but different from the situation in Nigeria and South Africa, where states/ provinces have some constitutional and political independence from the centre.

Fourthly, Frelimo established a particular political framework for the liberal regime to come. Notably, presidential candidates and political parties were only to be allowed if they had a basis in each and every province of the country, thus ensuring that they could not be regionally, ethnically or religiously based: Frelimo feared that regionalism, ethnicity and religion could undermine national unity and threaten its own domination. Elections were also to be decided by a simple majority for the Presidency and by proportional representation on the basis of provincial lists with a threshold of 5 per cent for Parliament, something which again was aimed at ironing out regional differences as well as polarising the political game and thus ensuring a clear-cut domination for the party which won a majority of the votes. In short, Frelimo set up and shaped a liberal democratic political system which was rather well fitted for it to continue dominating the state and society should it manage to win the promised multiparty elections.

The first multiparty elections were held in October 1994, two years after Frelimo signed a peace accord in Rome with the Renamo rebel movement (Vines 1994; Rocca 1994).[1] The elections were relatively peaceful and engaged a high rate of participation (88 per cent of the registered voters). Indeed, many people saw the elections as a way of ending the hostilities. In fact some Catholic clerics even asked people to spread their vote to ensure that everyone would be represented in Parliament and thus have an interest in maintaining the peace.[2] This first free-and-fair election saw the victory of Frelimo, but with a much smaller majority than many observers had expected.

Table 9.1 Election Results 1994 (%)

Parliament	Frelimo	Renamo
	44.33	37.78
Presidential	J.Chissano	A.Dhlakama
	53.30	33.73

There was at the time some debate about the size of the 'useful vote' (i.e. people voting for Renamo in order to bring them into the system), but the size of the vote (and in subsequent elections) shows that Renamo did have a significant social base. It should be noted that the Frelimo Presidential candidate did much better than his party – an important fact in view of the concentration of powers on the Presidency. Finally, many small parties took part in the elections, but eventually only a coalition (of three tiny parties) passed the parliamentarian threshold of 5 per cent, and it seems they did so only because of their prime position on the ballot papers (Mazula 1995). The upshot was that Frelimo and Joaquim Chissano won the elections, which meant that they succeeded in their strategy of preservation through transformation. This demonstrates that, rather than being a logical progression in policy, and even if it was externally driven, the shift to liberalism was effectively worked on by Frelimo to ensure that the change met the party's own objectives.

Successes and Pitfalls of Democracy

After the first multiparty elections of 1994 which brought about peace, the changes in the Constitution and the legal, political and economic system began to bear fruit. As a result of the disappearance of a series of Socialist controls, there was a new freedom of movement and association. Ethnic and regional associations began to crop up, new religious organisations were launched (or moved into the country), and several development and human rights NGOs were set up locally or came in from abroad. In the same vein, the press blossomed and the tone of public discussion changed. While the official media were given more freedom, a new law permitted the launching of independent publications (by print, fax, email) and of independent radio stations and websites (Jone 2005; Fauvet & Mosse 2003). As a consequence, the number of actors in public debates increased and the nature of the debates altered. Though Frelimo continued to control the state administration and managed to win all subsequent elections (municipal in 1998, second national in 1999 and second municipal in 2003), there was a new sense of freedom and democracy in the land. In 2001, a national poll indicated that 70 per cent of the population felt free to say what they wanted, free to join any organisations they desired and free to vote as they wished. Although their rating of the government's performance was negative, 74 per cent felt that Mozambique was now a democracy, with or without problems (Pereira *et al.* 2003).[3]

Economically, the changes were just as profound and positive for Frelimo. After 1989, the economy was liberalised, enterprises were privatised and foreign investments wooed back to the country. After peace returned, most factories reopened and many economic activities started up again. Many new investments were made, and some important projects and mega-projects were launched, such as an aluminium smelter in Maputo and gas production in Inhambane. By 1997, the country's GDP began to creep towards double-digit growth figures, peaking at a 12 per cent growth rate in 1998 (Ardeni 1999). With a growing economy and regular elections, Mozambique gained an excellent reputation abroad. The IMF and the World Bank regarded the country as a showcase for structural adjustment, an African success story combining peace-building, democracy and economic growth (de Renzio & Hanlon 2007). In sum, after 1994 Frelimo gained a renewed, and possibly unprecedented, legitimacy from both the international community and the Mozambican population.

But a liberal economy and polity also entailed problems. First, most of the economic development taking place after 1994 was export-oriented and not geared towards industrialisation, hence creating little local sustainable development and few jobs (Castel-Branco 2003). Secondly, the growth of the economy was regionally unbalanced. Most investments went to the south of the country, while the centre and north lagged behind. While no major investments were made in the north, the two most southern provinces saw two mega-projects, one of which soon produced half of the country's exports. According to a UNDP report, by 2002-4 47 per cent of all real production was concentrated in the south (UNDP 2006). This showed in differences in regional and provincial rates of growth and in the composition of economic activities in each region – industrial development in the south as against agricultural growth in the centre and north. Thirdly, capitalist development also exacerbated inequalities within the population. While the elite became very rich, the poorer social strata saw little of the two-digit national growth. This was particularly true in the countryside, especially in the north and centre. Research conducted by the Ministry of Agriculture in the early 2000s found that economic development in the rural areas was limited (mostly the result of price increases) and experienced very unevenly. The income of the top 20 per cent of households was 15 times higher than that of the poorest 20 per cent (Boughton *et al.* 2006: 57). Such patterns of regional and individual inequality invariably created dissatisfaction among the poorest sections of the population, and this could not but have a political cost for Frelimo.

A second set of problems resulting from the passage to liberalism was the explosion in the level of crime. At one end of the spectrum, violent crime escalated. Hijacks, robberies, thefts affected all sections of society. In part, this was an inheritance of the war period, not least in relation to the ready availability of small arms. In part, however, it was also the result of a poorly regulated process of liberalisation which allowed a few people to become very rich while the majority remained poor with unfulfilled expectations. The crises of unmet expectations, ready access to arms, no army left to absorb the unemployed workforce, and weak policing all contributed to the ballooning of violent crime. At the other end of the spectrum, rising crime levels were reflected in white-collar crime, i.e. an explosion in corruption and dubious enrichment of a good part of the national elite. This elite get-rich-quick culture is in stark contrast with the previous Socialist period when the *nomenklatura* was famously ethical, if not almost puritan. While not all the elite engage in illegal activities, some had a predatory view of accumulation and engaged in an active looting of public or state assets. As in South Africa, democratisation and privatisation led to the enrichment of the elite power. The most infamous case of elite corruption in Mozambique was the looting of millions of US dollars at one of the two state banks – Bank Austral – during its privatisation (Hanlon 2002). With time, violence and corruption undermined Frelimo's legitimacy, inside the country as well as outside. Worse still, the internal cohesion of the party was threatened. After the Bank Austral affair, there emerged new factions within Frelimo precisely over issues of corruption and ethics. By the year 2000, commentators and academics alike talked openly about three factions: a predatory faction; a black-nationalist, developmentalist faction; and an old Socialist, ethical faction (*Africa Confidential* 2001, 2003; Pitcher 2002).

These problems came to a head in 1999. In that year, Mozambique held its second multiparty elections and, to everyone's surprise, Frelimo almost lost the Presidency (and therefore control of the country) to the leader of the opposition, Alfonso Dhlakama. In spite of being the incumbent and having the support of the state apparatus, Joaquim Chissano won by a margin of less than 5 per cent – 52.29 per cent to Dhlakama's 47.71 per cent. Unsurprisingly, Frelimo's and Chissano's worst results were in the rural areas and the centre and north of the country where the economy was weakest. While Frelimo was still in shock, Renamo accused the party-in-power of having rigged the elections, and threatened to take control of the provinces where it had won. There followed months of tension, oscillating between negotiation and escalation.[4]

During the second half of 2000, the situation span out of control. After some local demonstrations and even a riot against the electoral results, the opposition decided to organise a countrywide mass protest to mark its rejection of the results and demand their annulment. This took place in November 2000 and was met by violent repression on the part of the Frelimo-controlled state. The police shot into the crowd in several places and killed at least 41 individuals. In Montepuez, the police also jailed tens of Renamo protesters in a cell so small that at least 80 of them died of suffocation (Amnesty International 2001). Then, just as these events began to be reported in the press, one of the country's top journalists, Carlos Cardoso (a long-time Frelimo supporter), was assassinated because he was investigating too thoroughly the theft at the Austral Bank. It is no exaggeration to say that by the end of November 2000, Mozambique was a democracy in crisis and Frelimo's project of preservation through transformation had exhausted itself (Cahen 2000).

A word is needed here about the opposition, Renamo. For good reasons, the party has a reputation for ideological and organisational weakness. But we have also seen that Frelimo designed democratic institutions in Mozambique with the aim of undermining the opposition. Renamo's interests were threatened by Presidential control of the Provinces where it was dominant and the exclusion of all losing presidential candidates from Parliament. This effectively excluded Dhlakama from any institutional political role and prevented him from directly controlling Renamo members in Parliament, thus creating tensions and leadership problems. Nevertheless, against all odds, Renamo did almost win the 1999 elections; it possibly even won them if the rigging was as severe as some claim. The dominant explanation for this state of affairs was that a vote in favour of Renamo was 'merely' an expression of protest against Frelimo. While there is doubtless an element of truth in this, we still need to understand why such protest was not expressed in abstentions, spoilt ballots, or blank voting. And the most sensible explanation is that Renamo ran a successful election campaign, something which was shown to have been the case already in the 1994 elections (Cahen 2004). A second reason for Renamo's success has to do with another element of campaigning, namely, its decision to enter into an electoral alliance. Rebranding itself Renamo-Electoral Union, the party managed to bring together 10 small parties which together probably brought an additional 10 per cent of the popular vote. In sum, for all its weaknesses, and in spite of a system designed to undermine it, Renamo has developed a quite effective campaigning strategy.

Re-shaping Democracy

The shift to liberal democracy transformed Frelimo as much as it did the country. Because Frelimo initiated the changes of the 1990s, it could partly shape and control the direction of social, economic and political transformation thereafter. To start with, Frelimo managed to hold on to power, and it retained certain aspects of the party's organisation and ideology. Among other things, the same elite managed to keep control of the party machine – an elite originating from an alliance during the liberation war between elements of the nationalist colonial petit-bourgeoisie of the south (mostly *mestiços* and *assimilados* working in the state apparatus) and military leaders drawn from the Makonde ethnic group in the extreme north of the country. Moreover, Frelimo managed to retain its organisational structure and principles which remain today, as in the past, those of 'democratic centralism'. It simply adjusted the names and titles of party organs, renaming, for example, the Political Bureau (where all matters are decided) the Political Commission. Finally, and this is not an exhaustive list, Frelimo retained several key ideological tenets in spite of its shift to liberal democracy and liberalisation of the economy. It certainly abandoned Socialism, but it continues today to promote the same form of nationalism (state-fostered, focused on unity, and opposed to ethnicity); it continues to hold a strong belief in grand projects to develop the country, such as the Cabora Bassa dam, the Mozal multi-billion smelter factory and two heavy-sands mines; and it continues to believe that Frelimo represents the whole nation, if it does not actually believe that *it is* the nation!

Nevertheless, Frelimo could not avoid being seriously transformed by the shift to liberalism in the 1990s. We saw earlier that corruption developed among party cadres and that the elite were greatly enriched – some legally and morally, others not so. More importantly and more profoundly, it was the very nature and social base of Frelimo which changed after the fifth Congress. Opening up to new social groups and undergoing a process of liberalisation, Frelimo's social composition experienced a profound transformation. At the top, the opening up of the party did not alter the composition of the elite, but this group became fabulously rich and its *habitus*, its social and political objectives, changed (Sumich 2005). At the bottom (the regular membership), no data are available but we can presume that a great change took place, namely, that people from a much wider spectrum of social backgrounds joined the party. For the middle strata of the party, we know in some detail that the party has greatly changed. The social composition of the delegates at the last party Congress in 2006 shows this quite clearly. While previously Frelimo was officially a party of workers and peasants and most of its delegates were from corresponding social backgrounds (57 per cent of the delegates at the fifth Congress were farmers or workers), delegates to the ninth Congress held in 2006 were mostly from the state and the party's administration (70 per cent of the delegates were from the state administration, the party administration or state employees, such as teachers and nurses). Farmers were down to a mere 6.7 per cent and industrial workers were below 1 per cent. This is quite a radical change, and it has led commentators to say that Frelimo was now the party of the 'bureaucracy' and/or the party of the 'medium and high bourgeoisie' (Hanlon 2006; Graça 2006).

Becoming a full blown bourgeois party may seem a logical development in the face of a liberalised economy and polity. But this did not prevent a serious political crisis by the year 2000; in fact, it probably precipitated it. We have seen the causes of this crisis – uneven and unbalanced economic development, corruption, criminal violence, and political factionalism. Among these factors, one needs to be discussed further, namely, the crisis within Frelimo. Indeed, the 2000 crisis deepened divisions in the party and started a power struggle within it for the leadership. Wishing to redress the political situation, Armando Guebuza, from the so-called black-nationalist, developmentalist faction, decided to take control of the party from President Joaquim Chissano who was seen as personally responsible for the crisis and the poor election result.[5]

Armando Guebuza had always been a powerful element in Frelimo since the time of the liberation struggle. But he is also seen as responsible for the most violent episodes of the Socialist regime, and this had been preventing him from running for the Presidency for which he always had obvious ambitions.[6] Yet, in the unstable context of the early 2000s, Guebuza's reputation for forceful conduct, his 'Stalinist hand', turned into a political advantage. Allied with the so-called ethical faction led by Samora Machel's widow, Graça Machel, who desired a clean-up of politics, he began a campaign to oust Joaquim Chissano from party and state office. Guebuza's campaign presented him as the strong man necessary to restore order, rein in corruption, and root out criminality in the country – all the ills he captured in the handy formula of *deixa-andar* laxity.[7] His discourse appealed to many sectors of Frelimo and, just as importantly, to large sections of society and the international community. Among other things, the new bourgeoisie longed for stability after its rapid enrichment, and the international community wanted to secure its investments in the country. The common people wanted security and stability. By June 2002, Guebuza managed to get himself elected Secretary-General of Frelimo in place of Chissano, and in early 2005 he was elected Mozambique's new President after the third general elections in December 2004 which Frelimo won with a solid majority. In short, if Frelimo managed to remain in power after 2001, it was through an adjustment within the party which saw the coming to power of a new faction.

Once in power, Guebuza began to implement some of the changes he had promised in his political programme. First, he nominated a new Cabinet which saw many new figures, among whom were younger professionals and a slightly changed dominant ethnic composition. Whereas the party leadership had traditionally been dominated by (southern) Shangaan and (northern) Makonde individuals, the Cabinet was now dominated by (southern) Rongas and (northern) Makuas.[8] Secondly, Guebuza launched a new style of politics which revived elements of the Socialist times under the late President Samora Machel. There were *Machelian* tones to Guebuza's discourse. Though he no longer spoke of equality or Socialism, he referred to 'Liberation', to the 'fight against absolute poverty', to the need for 'national unity' and to the dangers of tribalism and its divisions.[9] He talked of self-esteem and patriotism, and he used a highly combative vocabulary to talk of bureaucracy, corruption, and organised crime – all now re-labelled as the 'sentinels of underdevelopment'. Guebuza and his ministers also launched a new style of political action. This also drew on the Socialist period: Ministers engaged in surprise visits to the administration, ministries and hospitals, for example, while Guebuza engaged in an 'open presidency' for which he made regular visits to the provinces where he met with the population. Lastly, and more substantially, Guebuza and his government changed the leadership of the army, the police and the secret services, and launched a new police force aimed at tackling street crime – the Anti-Crime Brigade. Economically, Guebuza accelerated the development plans set out by his party; his programme was, and remains, to fight 'absolute poverty' in line with World Bank and IMF recommendations. To this end, he accelerated decentralisation and announced an engagement of the state in agriculture along the lines of a 'green revolution'.

Two and a half years after Guebuza's coming to power, there is increasing scepticism within the population about the new President. First, the Guebuza government has not changed the economic dynamics in the country. It continues to privilege a neo-liberal model, focused on grand projects and exports. The patterns of inequality have not changed, and some have even worsened. To give but one example, investments continue to be made mostly in the south of the country. In 2006, 89 per cent of all investments in Mozambique were located in the sole province of Maputo.[10] Worse, it seems that various development programmes launched by the government are not really concerned with development, but are politically motivated. Various policies and projects seem to have the prime aim of helping the central state to increase its presence locally and the extension of a patrimonial system of politics. The official policy of decentralisation is in reality one of deconcentration, and the allocation of a budget of 7 billion Meticais per year for each district in the country has turned out to be little more than an avenue through which the state tries to gain control of the activities of local administrations.

Secondly, for all the nice talk, few concrete or effective measures have been taken against crime, corruption or the excessively bureaucratic nature of the administration. The expected rupture with Chissano's rule in this respect is not materialising. Worse, by the second half of 2006, crime actually rose to a level not seen since the end of the war; break-ins and thefts were reported in ministerial properties, in the house of the former President, and even in the offices of the secret services! As a consequence, mobs resorted to taking the law into their own hands in dealing with suspected criminals, while the police resorted to old quick-fix measures such as the summary execution of known gang leaders.[11] Regarding corruption, there were great expectations in 2005 and 2006 as a series of reports by foreign and independent national organisations were published, and the government presented and adopted an official anti-corruption strategy. But the strategy proved of little consequence. During Guebuza's first two years in government, not a single important case of corruption was brought to justice, and the Corruption Forum launched officially by the government in early 2007 saw at its head figures who were themselves accused of corruption (Mosse 2006).[12]

Third and lastly, Frelimo's attitude towards democracy has become problematic, and its relationship with the opposition has grown increasingly conflictual. Since Guebuza took power, Frelimo and the Mozambican government have shown less openness towards the opposition and have adopted a heavier hand in dealing with Renamo. This came out clearly, first, during the elections of 2004 where fraud and violence were used at levels unseen before. As Secretary-general, Guebuza was in charge of Frelimo's electoral campaign. While fraud is said not to have been substantive enough to tip the balance (Hanlon & Fox 2004), the combination of the manipulation of the registration procedures and outright electoral violence may have done just that.[13] Indeed, Frelimo won the 2004 election not by winning more votes than it had previously, but by ensuring that Renamo lost more votes than Frelimo. In other words, Frelimo neutralised Renamo's electorate more than it mobilised its own. While the Renamo presidential candidate lost 53 per cent of the 1999 vote in 2004, the Frelimo candidate lost only 14 per cent. This electoral catastrophe led Renamo into a severe crisis. It is difficult to say exactly how much of the crisis was due to Frelimo's aggressive stance and how much to Renamo's own incapacity. The point, however, is that Frelimo began to play hard ball with the opposition and with democracy.

Since the 2004 elections, President Guebuza has also stopped consulting the opposition leader (as his predecessor used to do), and he has begun to use all the governmental structures to neutralise the opposition. At one level, it is a matter of the party, state and secret services conducting surveillance on Renamo and harassing its members and structures all over the country. At another level, it is a matter of opposing everything constructive which Renamo does, in particular its running of municipalities. The case of the municipality of Beira, which is particularly well run, is exemplary in this respect. Frelimo has gone to great lengths to undermine the rule of Daviz Simango, attempting to remove the ownership of the municipality's buildings by arguing that they belonged to Frelimo, nominating an administrator to shadow the Mayor, and even engaging in gerrymandering by trying to split the municipality in two along party lines.[14]

Needless to say, such undemocratic behaviour has not helped Frelimo's legitimacy. While Guebuza was given the benefit of the doubt in 2005 and early 2006, disappointment and dissatisfaction increased dramatically in the second half of 2006. Popular discontent reached new heights, and criticism from international donors became scathing as the government seemed unable to tackle crime, unwilling to deal with corruption and uncompromising in its relations with the opposition. In several reports, international donors argued that Frelimo was moving towards an authoritarian model or had returned to a one-party state, and this was seen as being dangerous for 'governance' (Vaux *et al.* 2006: 31).[15] Internally, discussions developed in Frelimo circles about a need to change the political model, possibly towards a Botswana model where the economic sphere is open but the political system is closed, and tightly controlled by the party in power.

In some darker reaches of the corridors of power, some went further and gave some thought to the idea of bringing down Guebuza through a *coup d'état* – something unheard of since 1994. The crisis has been such that conspiracy discourses have returned in force within society and even within government and Frelimo circles. It was commonly argued in 2007, for example, that criminality and instability were fostered by disgruntled Frelimo elements, possibly linked to Chissano, with the aim of undermining Guebuza. Whether this is true or not is irrelevant; the fact is that such rumours suggest that Mozambique had returned to a state of political crisis in 2007. Interestingly, Guebuza remained steady in the face of criticism and eventually rode the storm in this way. The problem with this approach is that Guebuza does not seem to have addressed any of the core problems at the root of the crisis and, unless he manages to continually suppress discontentment and opposition by force, we may expect crisis to return to Mozambique before long.

Conclusion

This chapter analysed the shift from Socialism in Mozambique after 1989. It aimed to understand why the shift happened, when and how it did so, and what kind of liberal democratic political system Frelimo chose in its stead. The chapter also tried to explain the consequences of the transformations which were launched for both the country and Frelimo. The adoption of liberal democracy is best understood as a purposive historical act and not simply as an external imposition or a natural teleological transformation. In spite of external coercion and pressure, Frelimo managed to shape democracy to meet its own ends. Using the concept of preservation through transformation, the chapter has shown how Frelimo adopted a liberal model of the economy, society and politics which permitted it to remain in power and even enhance its legitimacy. This strategy worked particularly well in the late 1980s and the 1990s, as Frelimo won the first multiparty elections in 1994 and gained unprecedented legitimacy at home and abroad. But contradictions within the economy and society were growing, due to an unequal, unbalanced and unregulated capitalist development of the country. By 1999 crime and corruption were at record levels and regional inequalities profound, and, partly as a result, Joaquim Chissano almost lost the second multiparty general elections. This led to a serious crisis in Frelimo and to a shift in the balance of force within it, resulting in the gradual retirement of President Chissano after 2000 and the rise of Armando Guebuza and his supporters to power. After the 2004 elections, Guebuza and his men took control of the government with an agenda to deal with the contradictions in Mozambican society and politics, in particular corruption, crime and *deixa-andar*. But, as of 2007, the promise behind the agenda was not fulfilled, although, as has been shown, other changes did take place. Guebuza failed to clean up politics in Mozambique, he did not change the model of democracy, but he changed the practice of the party and state to become more patriotic, more authoritarian and much less tolerant of the opposition.

What does this analysis mean for our understanding of liberalism and democracy in Mozambique and Africa more generally? First, it shows that, though emphasis on the theme of re-colonisation as an approach to understanding contemporary politics might help to explain the inequalities inherent in the international system, it does not help to understand the specific dynamics in a particular country, the choices made, and the internal changes which might result in the economy, society or polity. Similarly, the analysis shows that discussions about the institutionalisation or consolidation of democracy may be useful, but they often fail to explain the lived trajectory of democracy, its functionality and above all the agenda and motivation of the actors in relation to the system. The future of democracy in Mozambique, as elsewhere, has as much to do with the agenda and motivations of actors within the party-in-power as with issues about consolidation, institutionalisation and elite habituation.

A second contribution of this chapter relates to Mozambique as a case study. The chapter has shown that the development of the capitalist economy and society created, and continues to create, contradictions in the country, inequalities and regional imbalances in particular, which Frelimo is at pains to resolve even though it has itself turned into a fully pro-capitalist party and manages to shape the system to meet its own ends. Until 2000, Frelimo and Joaquim Chissano seemed to have ridden most of the contradictions. Subsequently, there was a hope that Guebuza would somehow find a solution to these contradictions. But hopes of Guebuza making any significant changes while keeping to the liberal democracy model have now collapsed. There is instead talk of his maintaining the formal system while changing the praxis; in other words, moving towards a more illiberal model of democracy.

Notes

1. An exhaustive non-teleological analysis of the peace process is still missing.
2. *MediaFAX* (Maputo), 02/11/94 and *Demos* (Maputo), 02/11/94.
3. The year 2000 was a particularly bad year for the government as we shall see later.
4. Part of the reason why months elapsed before an outcome to the crisis was seen was the massive floods which put the country in a state of emergency during the first half of 2000. On the floods, see Christie and Hanlon (2001).
5. The accuracy of the qualification of these factions is debatable. There are indeed issues over which the party divides itself differently and there are factors at play other than just ethics and corruption – notably leadership styles, racial views, ethnicity, etc. But this description gives an

idea of the new internal organisation (or divisions) and it was used in the media and for the power struggle within Frelimo at the time.

6. Guebuza is seen as responsible, among other things, for the deportation of thousands of Jehovah's Witnesses in 1975 to camps in Zambezia and for Operation Production, which saw the forced removal in 1983 of thousands of 'non-productive individuals' to the isolated rural Niassa province. For an authorised biography of Guebuza, see Matusse (2004). For something more critical, see Mosse (2004).

7. See, for example, Armando Guebuza, Moçambicanidade e unidade nacional. Os desafios do futuro. Comunicação apresentada no quadro das celebrações do 3 de Fevereiro. Maputo, 2 February, p.12; and also his Presidential inauguration speech, 'Our mission: the fight against poverty', 2 February, 2005. An edited version of the discourse can be found in *LATITUDES* (Paris) no. 25, December 2005, pp. 3-6.

8. This new alliance had been in the making since 1995 at least when Guebuza and his allies launched an association called *Ngiyana*, the aim of which was to unite the Rongas who are in historical contention with the Shangaan. At the time, commentators debated whether Guebuza was making a move within the party or whether he was about to create a new party outside Frelimo. See *Savana* (Maputo), 28 July 1995, p.4; *Savana*, 11 August 1995, pp.11 and 16; *Domingo* (Maputo), 11 August 1995, p.18; and *Imparcial* (Maputo), 21 August 1995, p.2.

9. See Note 7. Also Matusse (2004: 211ff).

10. *South Africa Monthly Regional Bulletin*, 'Year ends with yet more promising economic prospects', vol.15, no.12, December 2006, p.5.

11. Among others, see *Savana*, 14 July 2006, 1 September and 6 October 2006; *Notícias* (Maputo), 10 January, 24 May and 8 August 2006, and 20 January and 14 November 2007.

12. See also USAID, *Corruption Assessment: Mozambique*, 16 December 2005; "Editorial", *Savana*, 16 March 2007; and Edwin Hounnou, 'Gente duvidosa assalta Fórum Anti-Corrupção!', *Tribuna Fax* (Maputo), 19 March 2007.

13. I personally witnessed orchestrated violence during the pre-electoral campaign at Ilha de Moçambique.

14. *Canal de Moçambique* (Maputo), no.269, 2 March 2007. For gerrymandering, see, for example, *Notícias*, 16 December 2006.

15. Swisspeace, *FAST Update Mozambique. Semi-annual risk assessment*, July to December 2006, p.10.

References

Africa Confidential. 2001. Murder again. 42(25): 8.
——. 2003. Guebuza blues. 44(12): 6-7.
Amnesty International. 2001. *Report 2001 – Mozambique*. London: Amnesty International, 1 June.
Ardeni, Pier Giorgio. 1999. Economic Growth in Mozambique? An Assessment Working Paper No.381. Bologna (Italy); University of Bologna, Department of Economic Sciences.
Boughton, Duncan *et al.* 2006. *Changes in Rural Household Income Patterns in Mozambique, 1996-2002 and Implications for Agriculture's Contribution to Poverty Reduction*, Research Report No. 61. Maputo: Ministry of Agriculture.
Cahen, Michel, 1987. *Mozambique, La révolution implosée. Etudes sur 12 ans d'indépendance (1975-1987)*, Paris: L'Harmattan.
——. 1990. *Mozambique: analyse politique de conjoncture*. Paris: Indigo Publication.
——. 2000. Mozambique: l'instabilité comme gouvernance?, *Politique africaine* 80: 111-35.
——. 2004. *Os Outros. Um historiador em Moçambique, 1994*. Basel (Switzerland): P. Schlettwein Publishing.
Carbone, Giovanni. 2005. Continuidade na renovação? Ten years of multiparty politics in Mozambique: roots, evolution and stabilisation of the Frelimo-Renamo party system. *Journal of Modern African Studies* 43(3): 417-42.
Castel-Branco, Carlos Nunes. 2003. Indústria e Industrialização em Moçambique: Análise da Situação Actual e Linhas Estratégicas de Desenvolvimento. Southern African Regional Poverty Network (www.sarpn.org.za).
Christie, Frances and Joesph Hanlon. 2001. *Mozambique and the Great Flood of 2000*. Oxford: James Currey.
Fauvet, Paul and Marcello Mosse. 2003. *Carlos Cardoso. Telling the Truth in Mozambique*, Cape Town: Juta Double Storey.
Graça, Machado da. 2006. O Congresso dos chefes. *Savana* (Maputo), 24 November.

Hall, Margret and Tom Young. 1991. Recent Constitutional Developments in Mozambique. *Journal of African Law* 35(1/2): 102-15.
——. 1997. *Confronting Leviathan. Mozambique since Independence.* London: Hurst & Co.
Hanlon, Joseph. 1996. *Peace Without Profit: How the IMF Blocks Rebuilding in Mozambique.* Oxford: James Currey.
——. 2002. Bank Corruption Becomes Site of Struggle in Mozambique. *Review of African Political Economy* 29(91): 53-72.
——. 2006. Frelimo is now the party of the bureaucracy. *News Reports & clippings,* No. 102.
Hanlon, Joseph and Sean Fox. 2006. *Identifying Fraud in Democratic Elections. A case study of the 2004 presidential elections in Mozambique.* LSE Crisis State Working Papers No.8. London: London School of Economics.
Jone, Claudio 2005. *Press and Democratic Transition in Mozambique, 1990-2000.* Working Paper Series No.7, Johannesburg: IFAS.
Lalá, Anícia and Andrea Ostheimer. 2003. *How to Remove the Stains on Mozambique's Democratic Track Record. Challenges for the democratisation process between 1990 and 2003,* KAS Occasional Paper, Maputo: Konrad Adenauer-Stiftung.
Manning, Carrie. 2002. *The Politics of Peace in Mozambique. Post-conflict democratization, 1992-2000.* Westport, CT: Praeger.
Matusse, Renato. 2004. *Guebuza. A Paixão pela Terra.* Maputo: Macmillan.
Mazula, Brazão. ed. 1995. *Moçambique: Eleições, Democracia e Desenvolvimento.* Maputo: Inter-Africa Group.
Messiant, Christine. 1997. La paix au Mozambique: un succès de l'ONU. In R. Marchal and C. Messiant eds, *Les chemins de la guerre et de la paix. Fins de conflits en Afrique orientale et australe.* Paris: Karthala.
Mosse, Marcelo. 2004. Armando Guebuza. The new Frelimo candidate. *African Security Review* 13(1): 79-82
——. 2006. *Breve análise à Estratégia Anti-Corrupção. Do dilema salarial, dos códicos de conduta e da urgência de planos de acçção sectoriais.* Maputo: Centro de Integridade Pública.
Ostheimer, Andrea E. 2001. Mozambique. The permanent entrenchment of democratic minimalism?. *African Security Review* 10(1), [online at http://www.iss.co.za].
Pereira, João, et al. 2003. Mozambicans' Views of Democracy and Political Reform: A Comparative Perspective. *Afrobarometer Working Papers* No.22.
Pitcher, Anne. 2002. *Transforming Mozambique. The politics of privatization, 1975-2000.* Cambridge: Cambridge University Press.
Renzio, Paolo de and Joseph Hanlon. 2007. Contested Sovereignty in Mozambique: The Dilemmas of Aid Dependence. Global Economic Governance Programme Working Paper No.25. www.globaleconomicgovernance.org.
Rocca, Roberto Morozzo Hella. 1994. *Mozambico: della guerra alla pace: storia di una mediazione insolita.* Milan: San Paolo.
Saul, John S. 1993. *Recolonization and Resistance in Southern Africa in the 1990s.* Trenton, NJ: Africa World Press.
Sumich, Jason. 2005. Elites and Modernity in Mozambique. PhD thesis, Department of Anthropology, London School of Economics.
United Nations Development Programme (UNDP). 2006. *Mozambique. National Human Development Report 2005. Human Development to 2015. Reaching for the Millennium Development Goals,* Maputo: UNDP.
Vaux, Tony *et al.* 2006. *Mozambique: Strategic Assessment.* London: Department for International Development, April.
Vines, Alex. 1994. *'No Democracy Without Money': The Road to Peace in Mozambique.* London: Catholic Institute for International Relations.

10

Rwanda & Burundi since 1994
An End to the Discriminatory State?

PATRICIA DALEY

In line with the continent-wide political changes, Rwanda and Burundi embarked on democratic transitions in the 1990s. Both states have recently emerged from genocidal violence, protracted warfare and unrepresentative political regimes. Many comparisons have been drawn between the two nations because of their similarities in ethnic composition and the political instability and genocide that have clouded their post-colonial history.[1] Both countries experienced colonialism, German (1897-1916) and Belgian (1916-62), that transformed their pre-colonial socio-political structures. Since gaining independence on the same date, 1 July 1962, both states have been dominated by mono-ethnic single-party regimes that practised discrimination and subscribed to genocidal ideologies. Changes in political leadership took place via coup d'états, whereby one faction of the elite would replace another. As a consequence, both states have had a turbulent political history, attributed largely to the capture of the state by one ethnic group (Hutus in Rwanda and Tutsis in Burundi) whose leaders have systematically prevented the other from accessing state institutions and resources, using discrimination and repression that resulted in violent uprisings and protracted warfare.

Popular interpretation of political violence in Rwanda and Burundi focuses on ethnicity as the primary factor. Indeed, a substantial amount of violence is manifested along ethnic lines. However, any analysis that dwells purely on ethnicity as the root cause of the violence and instability would be seriously flawed. While ethnicity might form a fault line along which the groups separate, a substantial part of the political competition and violence in both countries can be attributed to regional and personal differences between intra-ethnic elites.

The degree to which ethnicity or political violence has deep pre-colonial roots is dependent on one's interpretation of the contested histories of the exact power relations between the ethnic groups – Hutu, Tutsi and Twa – prior to colonialism. The discourse of ethnicity that emerged in the colonial world drew on European racial ideology and Christian theology, but was also dependent on the production of a local history that justified the social advancement and the retention of power by the Tutsi minority in the new dispensation. De Forges (1995: 44) notes that the Europeans ascribed stereotypical intellectual and moral qualities to the people of each category. With little hesitation, they decided that the Tutsi were more intelligent – and perhaps more devious – and so born to rule, while the Hutu, dumb but good-natured, could never be other than productive, loyal subjects. Tutsi intellectuals, often under the supervision of European missionaries, scholars and administrators, perpetuated and embellished the myths of Tutsi power and elitism. Both high-status Tutsi and '*petit*-Tutsi' (groups known as Tutsi-Hima and low-status Tutsis) benefited from what Mamdani (2001) terms 'legally-inscribed identities'. For Mamdani, genocidal tendencies manifested themselves when the post-colonial state failed to transcend these identities and the discriminatory practices that they supported. He argues that Rwanda's 'Hutu revolution' of 1959 promoted majoritarian democracy and at the same time articulated sectarian politics. Hutu elites framed their claims to political power in terms of liberation from Tutsi domination. This is in contrast to Tutsi politicians who campaigned under a nationalist, anti-colonial platform in their quest for independence. Mamdani fails to give emphasis to the role of the departing Belgian colonial administration in stoking anti-Tutsi sentiments and their failure to intervene during the first genocide of Tutsis in 1959 and later in 1961, abrogating the responsibilities that came with their UN trusteeship role. The lack of security led to the flight of some 50,000 Tutsis into exile and the emergence of guerrilla groups (e.g. the *Inyenzi* – 1960-66) among the refugees, precursors of the Rwandese Patriotic Front of the 1980s and 1990s.

The post-colonial history of exclusionary politics in majority-dominated Rwanda and minority-dominated Burundi, coupled with the imbalance in the size of their ethnic groups, has shown that a winner-takes-all democracy would not resolve the issues of representation. The democratisation process at the beginning of the 1990s was highly contested and had violent repercussions. In Rwanda it was halted before the multiparty elections by the genocide of 1994. In Burundi, while the transition seemed to have gone more smoothly, the democratically elected President was assassinated in October 1993, just a hundred days after taking office. His governing party was forced to share power for almost two years before being overthrown in a coup d'état in July 1996, as the military retook the reins of power.

In both countries, regionally brokered peace agreements have determined the parameters for democratic governance. Power-sharing transitional governments were established, paving the way for new constitutions and multiparty elections. The post-genocide regime in Rwanda sought to implement the peace agreement and, between 1999 and 2003, held local, district, presidential and parliamentary elections. In Burundi, despite the state-sponsored and insurgent violence that accompanied the peace negotiations, the democratic process outlined in the agreement was allowed to run its course, if somewhat tardily. In both countries, there has been both change and continuity. While the ethnic and political complexion of the dominant parties has altered, the discriminatory and violent character of the state remained. Essentially, power has become concentrated in the hands of an elected clique from the ruling party that has strong ethnic affiliations, and the abuses by the security forces, the *Documentation Nationale* in particular, were condemned by human rights organisations (HRW 2006).

The Post-Colonial State and Ethnicity

The position of the post-colonial state regarding ethnicity is often quite instructive. In post-colonial Rwanda, Hutus justified their claim to power by drawing on the mythical history of Tutsi oppression and Hutu subjection as a rallying point in nationalist and democratic struggles and by using the democratic majority thesis to justify their hold on power. Tutsis, in turn, denied that rigid social demarcation existed in the pre-colonial period, and blamed the colonial construction of ethnicity for the origin of ethnic hatred and genocidal ideology. According to Prunier (1995: 80), Rwandan ideology demonised the Tutsis as foreigners and positioned the Hutus as the only 'legitimate rulers'. He refers to a common understanding between the ethnic groups which was 'do not mess with politics, this is a Hutu preserve' (Prunier 1995: 76). The Hutu-dominated military republics of Gregorie Kayibanda (1961-73) and his Parmehutu (All Hutu) party and of Juvenal Habyarimana (1973-94) and his *Révolutionnaire National pour le Développement* (MRND) party, formed in 1974, practised systematic ethnic discrimination and exclusion of Tutsis from political power. For most of Habyarimana's rule, Tutsi participation in government was minimal: 2 out of 70 parliamentarians and 1 Cabinet member out of a maximum of 30 (ibid.: 75). Furthermore, a 9 per cent ethnic quota was used to limit Tutsi acquisition of education and civil service positions.

State-sponsored violence was used to counter demands for greater representation. This included the massacre of Tutsi by government troops in 1988. The family of Habyarimana's wife belonged to the ruling elite from the Ruhengeri area of northern Rwanda that held on to a historical hatred of the Tutsi aristocracy who, with the help of the Germans, annexed their territory in the early part of the twentieth century. Mrs Habyarimana's family and their *coterie* formed the powerful *Akazu* (ruling elite), whose struggle to retain control of the state encouraged the emergence of genocidal politics.

In the 1990s, in response to the rebel incursions of the Tutsi-dominated Rwandese Patriotic Front (RPF), extremist Hutu parties, in particular the Coalition for the Defence of the Republic, were formed and used the modern state bureaucracy and the media to plan and execute genocide. Following the shooting down of Habyarimana's jet over the capital city Kigali, almost a million people – Tutsi and moderate Hutu – were killed in a hundred days between April and July 1994. The military victory of the RPF ended the genocide, overthrew the Hutu-dominated regime and transformed the ethnic make-up of the ruling elite. The Tutsi minority, who formed the bulk of the rebel army, captured the state in a power-sharing government with Hutu moderates.

Pottier (2002) argues that the post-genocide Tutsi-dominated regime has skilfully managed the media with the help of international NGOs and post-genocide sympathisers, to construct a history of the genocide that victimises all Tutsis and prevents criticism of the regime. The regime has promoted an idealised, socially harmonious vision of pre-colonial Rwanda and has refused to acknowledge the presence of ethnic groups in contemporary society, preferring to use the term 'cultural communities'. However, it does commit itself in the Constitution of 23 May 2003 to fight genocidal ideology and to eradicate ethnic and regional divisions (Article 9). In pursuit of national reconciliation and unity, the regime established the National Unity and Reconciliation Commission (NURC) in 1999. The NURC was created with the aim of 'eradicating the devastating consequences of the policies of discrimination and exclusion which had characterised the successive repressive regimes of Rwanda' (RoR 1999). It uses the term 'communities' instead of ethnic groups, emphasising the cultural commonalities between the groups. Anecdotal evidence suggests that Hutus do not subscribe to this vision of society, and there has been no national debate on the genocide. Consequently, revisionist interpretations of the genocide have emerged, coming especially from exiled remnants of the genocidal army and the political class (ICG 2003).

In neighbouring Burundi, where Tutsi-dominated regimes had held on to power since independence through the use of the military as a repressive apparatus, successive regimes denied the existence of ethnicity while simultaneously legitimising inequality and discrimination by using the Hutu threat to exclude the population from playing prominent roles in the political and economic spheres of the state. The fear of genocide against the Tutsi was used to demonise the Hutu and to counter their claims for greater representation. From 1966, the Tutsi military elite consolidated its grip on the state through the establishment of a single-party dictatorship and the use of genocidal violence to deal with challenges from Hutus or progressive Tutsis. In 1972, the state used the pretext of a peasant uprising to massacre some 250,000 people, mainly Hutu and Tutsis on the ideological 'left', and forced an equal number into exile in neighbouring countries. In August 1988, a minor skirmish between local Hutus and Tutsis in Kirundo Province resulted in a full-scale military operation against the Hutu, killing some 20,000 people. International criticism following this massacre forced the state to acknowledge ethnicity as a problem in the country when it set up a National Commission to Study the Question of National Unity, the outcome of which was the incorporation of Hutu representatives into the regime. This did not prevent further incidences of state-sponsored genocide, as in November 1991 when the security forces retaliated against the Hutu population following an insurgency by the Hutu rebel group Palipehutu in two northern provinces. Some 1,000 Hutus were killed by the military in reprisal. As we shall see later, while ethnicity was critical to the power-sharing agreement of the peace accords and to divisions within the post-genocide army, it was a taboo term in the political discourse. The Tutsi elites tended to use euphemisms to distinguish themselves from the Hutus; 'the educated' was a term used to refer to the Tutsi.

In summary, warfare in Rwanda and Burundi was true to the dictum of 'politics by other means'. In Rwanda, the reluctance of the state to acknowledge the rights of the Tutsi minority, particularly those of refugee origin seeking to return, and their demands for more inclusive politics led to the outbreak of hostilities. In Burundi, rebel movements saw violent insurrection as the only way of dealing with a discriminatory minority regime that controlled the state's security apparatus. State repression and persistent discrimination ruled out non-violent means of political participation.

Intra-Ethnic and Intra-Elite Rivalries

Rwanda and Burundi's population is much more heterogeneous than is implied by the ethnic classification of Hutu, Tutsi and Twa. Acknowledging the presence of internal diversity leads us to a more nuanced explanation for the persistence of conflict and the struggles over the state. Social cleavages exist around pre-colonial social status and around clans, families, communes and regions that permeate and cut across ethnic boundaries.

In pre-genocide Rwanda, regional differences and extremist genocidal ideology divided the ruling Hutu party and the Hutu elite. Prunier (1995) notes the divisions within the Hutu elite between those clansmen from central Rwanda, around the town of Gitarama, and those from the northern regions of Ruhengeri. Political infighting between these groups was intense during the transition to democratic politics in the early 1990s: numerous opponents were assassinated and moderate Hutus even sought early alliance with the RPF. In post-genocide Rwanda, according to the International Crisis Group (2002: 17), 'the legacy of the genocide includes not only severing regional ties (among the Hutu political class) and the dominance of ethnic-based identifiers, but also the claiming of victim status by all the communities.' Divisions among the Tutsi reflect their recent exile histories; that is, between the Francophone stayers and the returnee Anglophones (coming from Uganda and Tanzania). Many observers of the post-2003 government point to the existence of a new clan – *Akazu*, composed of family members closest to President Paul Kagame – and the power struggles and divisions that have emerged among the Tutsi elite on policy matters, especially the 1998 military expedition into the Democratic Republic of Congo.

In Burundi, the main cleavage within the Tutsi population was between the Tutsis and the lower-status Tutsi-Hima; members of the latter who were early recruits to the army originated from the province of Bururi. Clan and personal rivalries amongst members of the military from Bururi have manifested themselves on the national stage through coups and counter-coups. During almost forty years of its post-colonial history, the country has had four military regimes headed by Tutsi-Himas originating from southern Burundi: Michel Michombero (1966-76), Jean-Baptiste Bagaza (1976-87) and Pierre Buyoya (1987-93 and 1996-2003). The *raison d'étre* for the coups appears to be intra-Tutsi rivalry between regional elites (Lemarchand 1994).

Tutsis from the southern provinces came to dominate Burundi's political life. Regionalism determined access to the senior ranks of the army and civil service and the chairmanships of parastatals. Political contests occurred between those from Bururi and those from the central regions and between southerners and northerners (Ngaruko & Nkurunziza 2000). In the post-colonial Burundi state, one can identify five distinct cleavages around which conflict occurred: (i) intra-aristocracy, between the old guard and the young modernised elite; (ii) between Hutu and Tutsi; (iii) intra-Tutsi, between supporters of the various coup leaders and regional alliances; (iv) between the military and the political elite; (v) and recently intra-Hutu. Some of these differences have an ideological basis, others economic and social, but it is the ethnic difference that is easiest to articulate and manipulate, and which fits the popular discourse on conflict in African societies.

Given the above differences among the elite, opposition voices were never mono-ethnic. In both countries, nationalist political parties emerged alongside ethnic sectarian parties. In Rwanda, these were primarily the pro-independence party, National Union of Rwanda (UNAR), and the sectarian Hutu party, Parmehutu. The latter sought independence from Tutsi domination rather than from colonial rule. In contrast, Burundi's two prominent parties were both Tutsi-dominated: UPRONA (*Union Pour le Progrès National*), the nationalist party headed by Prince Louis Rwagasore, and PDC (*Parti Démocrate Chrétien*), the conservative party that was close to the Belgian rulers. UPRONA had a mass following among Hutus, which gradually disappeared after the assassination of Rwagasore in October 1961 and subsequent purges in the party.

Despite the presence of genocidal ideology amongst the elite in both countries, there was scope for cross-ethnic alliances, even between those considered to be extremists. Prior to the 1990 war in Rwanda, Hutu politicians and Tutsi businessmen sought alliances with the RPF in the hope that it would help them to remove the Habyarimana regime. Similarly, in Burundi during the peace negotiations, the Tutsi military regime sought to divide the dominant Hutu party by seeking a settlement with those members remaining in the country. Elite consensus seems to work where there is a general threat from the incumbent regime that may have implications for the operations of the elite on the regional and, especially, international stage. The deposing of Michel Michombero (1973) and Jean-Baptiste Bagaza (1986) occurred after international unease about the policies of the Burundi government: Michombero's government had conducted the genocide of 1972, while Bagaza's had started to persecute members of the Catholic Church. Elite consensus was also achieved at the time of the peace agreement. Despite the presence of 'spoilers', many among the political elite saw peace as a possible option – some observers remarked cynically, in order to capture rents from the aid for reconstruction.

Peace Agreements: The Foundations for Democratisation

Externally mediated peace agreements have played a major role in shaping the democratic outcomes in both countries. Peace negotiations took place in Arusha, Tanzania. For Rwanda they occurred between October 1992 and August 1993 and for Burundi between April 1996 and August 2000. The negotiations culminated in the signing of peace agreements that were flawed. The Rwanda agreement excluded the extremist party and did not have the full commitment of the participants, whilst that of Burundi was not accompanied by a ceasefire, as the main rebel movements were incorporated into the talks only in the final stages and refused to accept the draft agreement (Jones 2001; Clapham 1998).

These agreements tended to be formulaic, focusing on the establishment of a power-sharing transitional government and the rewriting of the Constitution, followed by democratic elections and the installation of a democratically-elected government. The trajectory is one that fits the concept of the 'liberal peace' – a restructuring of the state to make it more representative, while reforming the security sector and liberalising the economy to reduce the degree of state intervention and to minimise the neo-patrimonial relations associated with access to state-run enterprises. Conceptually, power-sharing means dividing the institutions of governance between political parties and rebel movements, in the context of a new constitution and democratic elections. Spears (2000: 105) contends that power-sharing provides 'a reasonable alternative to ... high stakes winner-takes-all elections, without the abandonment of democratic principles and procedures', making it 'compatible with democracy while diminishing its most destabilising side effects'.

The Rwandan protagonists signed an agreement on 9 January 1993 indicating that they would participate initially in a power-sharing broad-based transitional government to include parties of different political persuasion operating in the country. According to the accord, the ruling party, the MNRD(D) and the rebel Tutsi-dominated RPF, were each to be allocated five Cabinet posts. The smaller parties, PSD (Social Democratic) and PL (Liberal Party), were given three each and the PDC one. The army rank and file were also to be divided equally between the existing military and the RPF, with Hutus occupying 60 per cent of the upper ranks.

The task of the transitional government would involve putting in place the modalities for multiparty elections as the basis for democratic governance. However, not all parties were included in the talks. The Hutu extremist party, the Coalition for the Defence of the Republic, was excluded and started to mobilise anti-Arusha and anti-Tutsi sentiments in the country. The peace agreement not only failed to tackle the festering disputes within the Hutu elite but could not resolve the anxieties, stirred up by extremists, that power-sharing with the Tutsi would lead to a return to Tutsi domination. Consequently, there was no elite consensus for peace, and the hardliners found sufficient political space in which to begin organising for a final solution to the Tutsi menace – genocide, which took shape after the shooting down of President Habyarimana's plane on 6 April 1994. The victory of the Rwandese Patriotic Front that ended the genocide was followed by the reintroduction of the power-sharing proposals contained in the peace agreement.

In Burundi, the power-sharing agreement that was negotiated as part of the Arusha Peace and Reconciliation Agreement in 2000 aimed to satisfy the ethnic elites. It sought to ensure ethnic parity between Hutus and Tutsis primarily, whilst giving a disproportionate number of seats to the Tutsi minority, and to establish a three-year transitional government, headed for the first eighteen months by a Tutsi and the second by a Hutu. It stipulated that legislative power would be exercised by a National Assembly of at least 100 members and a Senate comprising two delegates from each province (one Tutsi, one Hutu). The Cabinet would have 60/40 Hutu/Tutsi representation of which 30 per cent would be women. The transitional government would put in place the modalities that would produce the legislative bodies: the writing of a new Constitution and the setting up of an independent electoral commission to organise elections. As in Rwanda, ethnic parity was sought in the national army which should not contain more than 50 per cent of one ethnic group. It took over one year from the signing of the agreement for the transitional government to be put in place, but the peace trajectory was followed through under the supervisory presence of an implementation monitoring committee and an international peace-keeping force.

The Narrowing of the Political Community

Contemporary peace negotiations are riddled with contradictions. Whilst appearing to open up the political space with a shift to a more inclusive process, the absence of civil society or a broader conceptualisation of what constitutes the political community is quite stark. In both instances, participation at the peace negotiations was restricted to members of the political elite. For Rwanda, Clapham (1998: 205) claims that any protagonist 'who could muster evident support now had to be admitted too...on terms of broad equality with existing regimes' and was given a status 'that only very inadequately reflected their popular support or military strength'. In the case of Burundi, this took the form of the political parties that fought the elections in June 1993 (see below) and those formed thereafter, plus the government and the National Assembly. Some nineteen Burundian political groups were represented, seven of them Hutu-dominated and ten Tutsi-dominated. Most had not tested their legitimacy with the Burundi electorate. The main parties, *Union pour le Progrès National* (UPRONA) – Tutsi-dominated and the President's party – and *Front pour la Démocratie au Burundi* (FRODEBU) – Hutu-dominated and the victors of the 1993 election – were the key peace brokers. However, smaller parties, especially among the Tutsi group, sought to influence the process in a negative way.

In Burundi, the rebel movements, *Conseil National pour le Défense de la Démocratie /Forces pour le Défense de la Démocratie* (CNDD/FDD) and *Parti pour la Libération du Peuple Hutu /Forces National de Libération* (Palipehutu/FNL), were initially excluded from the talks. They sought to enter negotiations not with political parties but with the Burundi military, which they claimed was the true power in the country. The ceasefire negotiations that followed the peace agreements resulted in Pierre

Nkurunziza's CNDD/FDD faction gaining Cabinet posts and the national army being divided not just along ethnic lines, but also according to membership of the rebel groups (50/50 Hutu/Tutsi and 40 per cent of the senior ranks going to CNDD/FDD).

Tull and Mehler (2005) have expressed concern that power-sharing agreements that enable rebel leaders to gain state power can lead to the reproduction of 'insurgent violence', as leaders might take up arms in order to gain political leverage and international acceptance, thus making access to political power difficult for those who champion non-violence. In effect, power-sharing can legitimise and thus normalise violence as part of the political discourse. All the rebel groups targeted civilians to gain leverage in the negotiations. The largest branch of Palipehutu/ FNL asked to join the peace talks in April 2005, after regional Heads of State declared the FNL a 'terrorist organisation'. The FNL increasingly relied on terror tactics against civilians to strengthen its negotiating position. Though its leader, Agathon Rwasa, signed a peace agreement with the government in September 2006, a breakaway faction refused to accept the agreement and has continued hostilities. Furthermore, Rwasa's demands for guarantees regarding FNL's integration into the security forces and its leaders securing political positions, plus a $12 million advance, have not been met (ICG 2007).

Elite consensus on power-sharing was more evident in Burundi than in Rwanda. Why? Was it the result in Burundi of the over-representation of Tutsi parties, or to do with the fact that the long years of war, and the reduction in aid, and its impact on the economy, had led to a desire for peace among the belligerents. Or was it largely regional and donor-driven?

The failure of civil society organisations to play any meaningful role in the peace negotiations reflects not just the unwillingness of the political forces to acknowledge their possible role in peace-making, but also the nature of civil society in both countries. In Burundi under President Buyoya, civil society representatives were co-opted on to legislative bodies by the President, in order to demonstrate the inclusivity of the government. Even senior officials in the Catholic Church were keen supporters of the genocidal regimes in Rwanda and Burundi. Human rights groups, such as LIPRODHOR (League for the Promotion and Defence of Human Rights) in Rwanda and Ligue Iteka in Burundi, are externally funded and have presented the only consistent dissenting voices. Critical voices in the media were often silenced, and the experience of the Rwandan genocide has shown that the media can act equally as an organ of hate as well as of peace and unity. While women's groups have been active in campaigning for peace, they tended to be divided along ethnic lines, as well as being affiliated to political parties.

Constitutional Reform and Multiparty Elections

Constitutional reform has not been a panacea in either Rwanda or Burundi. Historically, each new coup leader has suspended the existing Constitution in order to give legality to his usurpation of power. Successive rewriting of the Constitution has not brought political stability and respect for the rule of law. With regard to constitutions, this chapter focuses on two issues: multiparty elections and ethnic parity.

In Rwanda, after taking power in 1973, Habyarimana banned the ruling Hutu-dominated political party MDR (*Mouvement Démocratique Républicain*) – Parmehutu, presumably because it was the party of the ousted Head of State and its regional support base differed from that of Habyarimana. Multiparty politics were banned by Habyaramina a year later, when he created the MRND (*Mouvement Révolutionaire National pour le Développment*) and enshrined single-party rule in Article 7 of the 1978 Constitution. Prunier (1995) describes the MRND as a totalitarian party that exercised considerable control over the populace, membership of which determined ability to access posts in the civil service. Identity cards and the need to obtain permission for a permanent change of residence facilitated administrative control. It was only in 1981 that Habyarimana sought to create a parliament, known as *Conseil National du Développement*, which according to Prunier (1995: 77) constituted a 'development dictatorship' – a situation in which politics became the personal business of the President, while the people were occupied with the task of 'development' through agriculture. Habyarimana, who stood as the sole candidate for the presidential elections of 1983 and 1988, was re-elected 'with 99.98% of the vote' (ibid.: 78).

Under pressure from France, Rwanda's dictatorship conceded to political reforms and announced the move to permit multiparty democracy on 5 July 1990, but it could not have anticipated the invasion by the Rwandese Patriotic Front (RPF) on 1 October 1990. The Hutu opposition, some of whom had courted the RPF, moved quickly to form political parties. In early 1991 the first to take shape was the resurrection of the old MDR, which, though having a populist appeal, contained members of the old MDR-Parmehutu – a party that still carried the stigma of being associated with the genocidal violence of the early 1960s. The *Parti Social Démocrate* (PSD) catered to the professional class, the *Parti Libéral* (PL) for businessmen, with Tutsi among its ranks, and the *Parti Démocrate-Chrétien* (PDC) was a Christian party that sought to break the hold that the MRND had on the Catholic Church (Prunier 1995). The MRND soon added *Démocrate* to its name, MRND(D), to reflect the new mood in the country. The new Constitution allowing multipartyism came into effect on 10 June 1991 and was quickly followed by the registering of ten more smaller parties, including the formation of the extremist party (Coalition for the Defence of the Republic) – a major participant in mobilising anti-Tutsi sentiment through the media and in the 1994 genocide.

According to Prunier (1995: 131), it was not that there were few among Rwanda's political opposition who supported genuine democracy but that the conjunction of a power structure that was resistant 'to any type of genuine democratisation and the selfish greed of a large part of the opposition leadership' marred the possibility of a peaceful democratic transition. The MRNDD capitulated to sharing power and the formation of a new Cabinet in April 1992 that included reforming moderates. However, hardliners in the MRNDD continued to hold on to power and, along with the numerous smaller ultra-rightwing Hutu-dominated political parties, were to frustrate the democratisation process by obstructing reforms and sponsoring violent protests by extremists. Corruption nurtured cross-party alliances, and those leaders excluded from senior positions in government used the military activities of the RPF and the concessions being made at the Arusha peace negotiations to rally popular support among Hutus. These moves hindered the transfer of power to the Broad-Based Transitional Government as agreed in the Arusha Peace Agreement of August 1993.

As a precursor to the genocide of 1994, the MRNDD and the extremist political parties were inciting ordinary people to violence. Systematic attacks on members of the opposition and on Tutsi, partly as a response to the RPF military advance in the north of the country, led to the massacre of Tutsi at Bagogwe in January 1991, in the Bugesera region in March 1992, and in various other geographical areas up to the genocide of April-June 1994 (Prunier 1995). These attacks were orchestrated by local administrators and carried out by local Hutu peasants called to carry out *umuganda* (communal) labour.

In spite of its discriminatory practices, the Rwandan regime failed to recognise officially the existence of ethnic groups within the country. It was not until 1989 that ethnic groups were mentioned in the Constitution, but with no genuine move for ethnic parity. Consequently, the dismantling of the ethnic quotas by the power-sharing government of 1992, along with the war, provided evidence for those who sought to stoke fears of the return to Tutsi domination.

If the genocide was the culmination of a democratisation process gone wrong, then one could anticipate that the post-genocide state would take measures to avert further tragedy through better representation. The RPF-dominated government that took power in July 1994 sought to implement the Arusha Accord and respect the 1991 multiparty Constitution. A Broad-Based Transitional Government (consisting of a National Assembly and a Chamber of Deputies, each with 30 per cent women) was established for five years. This Transitional Government was made up of representatives from the RPF and Hutu representatives of moderate parties, who were identified as not being complicit in the genocide. Two Hutus occupied the senior positions: Pasteur Bizimungu became President and Faustin Twagiramungu – head of the *Mouvement Démocratique Républicain* – Prime Minister, with the leader of the RPF, Paul Kagame, as Vice-President and Minister of Defence.

From the start, the transitional government was disunited; in August 1995, prominent Hutus resigned, including Prime Minister Twagiramungu and Interior Minister Seth Sendashonga. Between January and March 2000, political in-fighting between the RPF and other parties and within the RPF resulted in resignations from the government of the Speaker of the National Assembly, Joseph Kabuyu Sebarenzi, the Prime Minister Pierre-Celestin Rwigwema, and President Bizimungu. Critics focused on the consolidation of power around Paul Kagame. Opponents were imprisoned on trumped-up charges and many went into exile. New opposition parties were prevented from forming, including the *Parti Démocratie pour le Renouveau (PDR-UBuyanja)*, headed by Bizimungu, who was soon arrested and held in prison for two years before being tried and found guilty of embezzlement, inciting civil disobedience and forming a militia group. He was sentenced to fifteen years imprisonment in 2004, but released after a presidential pardon in April 2007 (Samset & Dalby 2003; Jordaan 2006).

The move towards multiparty elections was tightly controlled by the regime. It is argued that the communal (*cellule*) elections held in March 1999 were used to identify supporters at the local level in order to control the outcome of future parliamentary and presidential elections (ICG 2001). Numerous irregularities were noted, such as queuing behind candidates and the use of RPF Bourgomasters (centrally-appointed administrative heads of communes – the smallest adminis-trative areas) to direct the process. The International Crisis Group claims that the National Electoral Commission was too close to the ruling party. Observers noted a number of irregularities in the district elections held in March 2001. The main opposition party, Twagiramungu's MDR, was banned from participating in the elections and dissolved by the government. Voters were also said to have been intimidated. In the run–up to parliamentary and presidential elections in 2003, the state attempted to paralyse the opposition forces; again political parties, such as Twagiramungu's new party, the *Alliance pour la Démocratie, l'Equité et le Progrès* (ADEP-Mizero), were prohibited from contesting the elections, some presidential candidates were not approved and, without any formal rules on party financing, some parties, such as the ruling RPF had more financial resources at their disposal than the opposition parties (Samset & Dalby 2003; Jordaan 2006). Paul Kagame was elected President after obtaining 95 per cent of the votes cast.

It was not until May 2003 that a new democratic Constitution was put to a referendum. The Constitution recognised a multiparty system that reflected the ethnic composition of the country, and put in place a consultative forum for political parties. It gave considerable power to the President to appoint a significant proportion of members of the Senate (30 per cent) and the Chamber of Deputies (8 out of 27). While noting the progressive elements in the Constitution, Uvin (2003) is critical of the limitations on freedom of speech and on the functioning of political parties. Clearly, the RPF wanted to prevent the formation of extremist parties. Thus the Constitution reflected the concerns of the ruling Tutsi elite.

The current leadership has encountered considerable criticism for using Western guilt over not preventing the 1994 genocide to gain international support for its policies, and for returning to a late nineteenth-century version of the Tutsi-dominated state (Melvern & Williams 2004; Vansina 2004). Many observers have expressed concern about the gradual 'Tutsification' of the government, as moderate Hutus are forced to resign, and the continued presence of a mono-ethnic army. Meanwhile, the state has embarked on a process of administrative reform, which uses the language of decentralisation but is actually reinforcing centralisation. The reduction in the number of provinces from 12 to 5 in January 2006 could be interpreted as a strategy to gain more effective control of the country.

Burundi, in contrast to Rwanda, has not suffered from a constitutional deficit; a series of Constitutions in 1962, 1981, 1992 and 2005 represent contestation among the prevailing elites. Challenges to the Constitution tend to come from rival or new elites rather than from below. What we see in Burundi is the evolution of a Constitution that privileges the minority, but not at the expense of the majority.

With UPRONA designated as the single party until 1992, opposition parties had to be formed abroad – six in Tanzania, three in Rwanda and one in Belgium. Of these, the *Parti pour la Libération du Peuple Hutu* (Palipehutu) and *Parti pour la Libération National* (Frolina) were committed to using violence to overthrow Tutsi hegemony. However, it took pressure from the West for President Buyoya to introduce multiparty politics. Six parties fought the democratic elections of June 1993, when FRODEBU won and Melchior Ndadaye, a Hutu, was elected President. His assassination a hundred days later in an attempted coup by Tutsi officers led eventually to the overthrow of the elected government, the re-instatement in July 1996 of a military regime headed once again by Pierre Buyoya, and twelve years of war.

The Arusha peace agreement of 2000 laid the basis for the formulation of a new Constitution to be debated and approved by the transitional National Assembly before being put to a referendum. The governance structure, outlined in the peace agreement and enshrined in the Constitution, sought to ensure ethnic parity in the context of multiparty politics: parties had to be multi-ethnic in composition and the National Assembly was to be composed of about 60 per cent Hutu, 40 per cent Tutsi plus 3 individually co-opted Twa. It was also to have a minimum of 30 per cent women, even though this was hotly debated. As well as a President, there were to be two Vice-Presidents, one from each of the main ethnic groups. To forestall spoils tactics, former Presidents were given uncontested seats in the Senate, which would have 50/50 per cent ethnic parity. After a turbulent drafting phase, the new Constitution received overwhelming support from 92 per cent of registered voters on 28 February 2005. UPRONA's Central Committee and three other Tutsi parties had urged a 'no' vote and refused to sign a code of good conduct during the referendum.

Communal and parliamentary elections took place in June and July 2005. Approximately 34 parties contested the elections, including former rebel groups that had registered as political parties. The *Conseil National pour le Défense de la Démocratie/Forces pour le Défense de la Démocratie* (CNDD/FDD) was confirmed as the winner of municipal communal (senatorial) elections held on 3 June, with a voter turnout of 80.6 per cent of the registered voters. Of the 3,225 seats, CNDD/FDD won 1,781 (55.4 per cent), followed by FRODEBU with 822, UPRONA with 260 seats and the Movement for the Rehabilitation of Citizens (MRC) with 88 seats.

Elections for the National Assembly were held on 4 July 2005. CNDD-FDD won 58.55 per cent of the votes, FRODEBU 21.69 per cent, UPRONA 10 per cent, CNDD 4 per cent and MRC 2 per cent. At the end of August 2005, Pierre Nkurunziza, as the head of the largest elected party, was chosen as President by the National Assembly and Senate. Tutsis were co-opted into the National Assembly and the Senate in order to reflect the ethnic quota as stipulated in the peace agreement. The composition of the Cabinet, according to Reyntjens (2005: 130), remains 'unconstitutional', with representation from parties that did not gain 5 per cent or more of the vote (MSP-Inkinzo and PARENA have one seat each, plus two Ministers without party affiliations). Both UPRONA and FRODEBU are under-represented and CNDD-FDD has proportionately more seats in the Cabinet than it holds in the National Assembly (Reyntjens 2005). Women obtained 35 per cent of the Cabinet seats, achieving greater representation than envisaged in the peace agreement.

The elections were declared free and fair by UN observers, though there were reports of pre-election harassment by CNDD/FDD militants. A critical outcome of the elections was the marginalisation of the former democratically elected party, FRODEBU. It was argued that, as the main party at the Arusha peace negotiations, it made concessions to the Tutsi regime that were unacceptable to the Hutu electorate. FRODEBU lost out in a peace process that favoured military might.

Justice, Truth and Reconciliation

The recent history of genocide and crimes against humanity, plus the persistent culture of impunity, make justice and reconciliation sound prerequisites for political stability. The issue of justice has been a major preoccupation of the Rwandan state and of those in the international community who would like to prevent another genocide and see the 'never again' dictum of the Holocaust become a reality. One pertinent question has been: who should be punished when so many people participated in the genocide?

Almost one million people were killed in Rwanda; the majority of them were Tutsis, although some moderate Hutus who sought national unity and opposed the genocide were also killed. The issue of the genocide is still contentious. Despite overwhelming evidence, some Hutu intellectuals and government representatives still refuse to acknowledge that genocide took place and focus instead on the human rights abuses of the RPF and what they see as a return to Tutsi hegemony (ICG 2002).

There is, of course, a tendency to heap collective guilt on the whole Hutu population and ignore the revenge killings by the RPF as they swept to victory and put a stop to the genocide. Indeed, the focus has rightly fallen on those who masterminded the genocide and those in positions of leadership who coordinated the killings. In November 1994, the United Nations established the International Criminal Tribunal for Rwanda based in Arusha, Tanzania, which issued arrest warrants for masterminds. Since 1994, the Tribunal has tried 26 accused, issued 23 convictions and acquitted 3 people. A major landmark has been its successful prosecution of a perpetrator of rape, recognising rape as an act of genocide (Oomen 2005). The relationship between the International Criminal Tribunal for Rwanda and the Rwandan government has not always been good; the latter was opposed to the absence of the death penalty among the Tribunal's punishments.

The government and the donor community saw re-establishing an internal justice system that could deal with the perpetrators of genocide as essential to the process of reconciliation. At the end of 1998, there were some 140,000 genocide suspects in Rwandan jails, which were severely overcrowded. The formal court system was virtually destroyed during the genocide; most judges were killed or fled the country. The physical infrastructure was also destroyed. Consequently, only a thousand people were tried annually.

Between 1994 and 2000, some US$100 million was spent by the donor community on justice-related projects; 80 per cent of the Ministry of Justice budget came from donors (Uvin 2001). Donors pressed for the restitution of the traditional *Gacaca* courts – grassroots conflict resolution bodies – in order to speed up the trial of suspects. In 2001, the law was passed and the first pilot courts began operating in 2002. *Gacaca* courts reflected the state's commitment to decentralise power with respect to good governance. However, these new *Gacacas* were highly regulated by the state and, according to Oomen (2005: 905), the purpose of the *Gacaca* was not to bring 'true justice, but rather about entrenching the minority government'. The *Gacacas* have limited judicial powers; they cannot try acts of rape and do not allow evidentiary support (Corey & Joireman 2004; Oomen 2005).

Critics of the current justice system argue that it focuses purely on genocide, and not on the crimes committed by the RPF or the Rwandan government in its pursuit of the refugees and *génocidaires* in Zaire in 1998 (Oomen 2005; Umutesi 2000). Uvin (2001: 179) notes 'within the international human rights community, it is now common to state that Rwanda, like Israel, is skilfully using the genocide, and the general imagery of victimhood, to justify brutal policies and deflect international scrutiny'. There is no doubt that justice is a major challenge to national reconciliation. Justice in Rwanda remains only partial, and the state has banned any organisation or activity that may be interpreted as promoting divisions (ICG 2002). The conflict of interest, between the security and the self-preservation of a minority and the need for justice and reconciliation that gives space to the majority, will not be easily resolved.

In Burundi, a culture of impunity is embedded in the society as there had been no international attempt to deal with genocide, even those acts recognised by the United Nations. As part of the peace agreement, in August 2003 a temporary immunity law was passed covering crimes with a political aim committed after 1 July 1962 up to the date of promulgation (27 August 2003). This allowed the return of exiled politicians and rebels to participate in the transitional government and democratic elections, and to protect politicians and members of the state security forces, despite considerable opposition from human rights groups, Tutsi parties and extremist organisations.[2]

The Accord also called for the establishment of a Truth and Reconciliation Commission. On 1 September 2004, the National Assembly passed a law allowing the UN to set up a non-Judicial Truth Commission, with a substantial international component and the creation of a special chamber within the Burundi justice system to tackle crimes against humanity. Its effectiveness is likely to be undermined by its lack of independence from the government. Political leaders appear keen to protect themselves from any future criminal charges. As one key participant claimed, 'truth and reconciliation is no longer considered to be necessary ... realising that wrong things were done in the past, but the future does not involve exclusion'.[3] This viewpoint is in sharp contrast to that presented in post-election reports by human rights organisations, citing the continuation of summary execution and torture by Burundian soldiers, intelligence agents and Palipehutu/FNL rebels, and rape, thefts and murders by criminal elements, especially ex-paramilitary armed gangs (HRW 2005; Ligue Iteka 2005a, 2005b).

In August 2006, human rights abuses and political in-fighting within CNDD/FDD also threatened the stability of Nkurunziza's government. The arrest and alleged torture of several prominent political figures, including former President Domitien Ndayizeye, the former vice-president, Alphonse Kadege, and Alain Mugabarabona of FNL-Incanzo on a charge of coup-plotting, revealed the failure of the elections to settle the differences within the Hutu political elite (HRW 2006; ICG 2006). In January 2007, five of the seven accused, including Ndayizeye and Kadege, were acquitted due to insufficient evidence, and two, one of whom was Mugabarabona, were sentenced to up to twenty years imprisonment for allegedly confessing to the coup-plotting. Faced with considerable international criticism, CNDD/FDD reacted by removing its party chairman, Hussein Rajabu, who was seen as being the architect behind the drift towards authoritarian practices. Rajabu was later arrested and accused of fomenting instability. Opposition to Rajabu's removal within the ruling party and protests over the arrests by opposition political parties led to a boycott of Parliament, which was only able to function after a Cabinet reshuffle in November 2007 that brought more members of the opposition parties (Hutu and Tutsi-dominated) into government. External observers view this as a move towards a government of consensus, but it was clearly a more strategic form of power-sharing than that envisaged in the Arusha peace agreement and mandated by the electorate.[4] One may yet see the resurgence of the old political forces that were thought to have been crushed by electoral defeat in 2005.

Regional and National Security

Peace and reconciliation in Rwanda and in Burundi to some extent cannot be considered without reference to the militarisation of the region and its intersection with long-term questions of national and regional security. The integrity of the present Rwandan state is challenged by both external and internal security threats. Can a regime dominated by a minority, which experienced genocide at the hands of the majority, create any genuine and long-lasting reconciliation without compromising its own security? The presence of remnants of the routed genocidal army and militias still in exile in the region makes the political transition in Rwanda far from stable.

Members of the ex-Rwandan Army (FAR), the *interahamwe* militias and ex-government officials who 'subscribe[d] to genocidal ideology' 'found refuge in Congo-Brazzaville, Angola, Central African Republic, Zambia, Malawi, Namibia, Tanzania and Kenya', where they obtained military support from the Mobutu and later the Laurent Kabila Congolese regime (ICG 2003: 4-5). The 15,000-20,000 strong genocidal Hutu army and militias re-established themselves in the Democratic Republic of Congo, initially under the name of *Armée de Libération Rwanda* (ALR) and more recently in 2000 as FDLR (*Armées pour la Libération du Rwanda*), and launched attacks against post-genocide Rwanda in late 1996 and periodically since then (Terry 2002; OAU 2000).

These incursions led to Rwanda's military invasion of the DRC. From November 1996 to May 1997 the Rwandan army, under the umbrella of a Congolese liberation army, *Alliance des Forces Démocratiques pour la Libération du Congo* (AFDL), 'hunted down Hutus by the thousands, only some of whom were *génocidaires*'. An estimated 240,000 people were missing, allegedly massacred by RPA/AFDL forces (Emizet 2000; Umutesi 2000). Rwanda's support for the Congolese rebel faction, RCD-Goma, was seen as opportunistic, as it gave the Rwandan state access to the natural resources of the DRC. Both Rwanda and Burundi's economies have relied on legal and illegal access to the mineral-rich Eastern Congo (UNSC 2001). After the Pretoria peace agreement of 30 July 2002 that stipulated the withdrawal of foreign troops, including Rwandans, from Congolese soil in September 2002, the Rwandan rebels received less direct support from the Congolese state. Some joined Palipehutu/FNL in Burundi, others remained in the country receiving support from the Hutu populations of the Eastern Congo and local militia leaders.

Burundi's rebels also found support in the region. Palipehutu and Frolina started up in refugee camps in Tanzania during the 1980s. During the 1990s the Democratic Republic of Congo under Laurent Kabila, along with the Zimbabwean army, provided training and weapons for CNDD/FDD, which they used to fight against Rwandan and Ugandan-backed forces in Lubumbashi (OAU 2000). Palipehutu/FNL also launched attacks on Burundi from the DRC in the late 1990s and 2000s. The Burundi army also made excursions into the Congo to root out rebels.

Clearly, political stability in Rwanda and Burundi is bound up with regional politics, in terms of inter-state relations and the level of commitment to democratisation and an end to coups and wars as politics by other means.

Conclusion

Violence of a genocidal nature has framed the democratic transitions of Rwanda and Burundi since the late 1980s. Lack of political representation linked to ethnic discrimination has undermined the legitimacy of the state and been the source of instability. Despite recent elections, elite competition and an ideology of violence continue to challenge the salience of the democratic transition.

Issues of justice and reconciliation remain unresolved despite the enforcement of electoral democracy by the peace agreements. In Rwanda, the state lacked the capacity to deal effectively with the sheer number of those accused of genocide. Despite the return to traditional (communal) justice mechanisms and the opportunity for *génocidaires* to gain absolution by confession, there has been no reconciliation, as the Hutu population feels besieged by the assumptions of common guilt and the integrity of the state continues to be threatened by rebel incursions from the Democratic Republic of Congo. Furthermore, observers have pointed to the emergence of an authoritarian and militaristic Tutsi-dominated state and have accused the current government of using the genocide as political capital to avoid international criticism of its policies. In Burundi, the victorious Hutu-dominated party has shown no eagerness to institute effective judicial systems to deal with the past genocidal episodes that continue to throw a shadow over the country's political system, presumably for fear that many politicians would be implicated.

To what extent have these states overcome the dominance of ethnic identification? In essence, the Rwandan state seems adept at using the language of national unity and neo-liberalism, while implementing policies that reinforce the position of the minority. In contrast, in Burundi the significance of ethnicity on the political scene appears to have declined with the election of a Hutu-majority power-sharing government. By August 2005, there was the unlikely scenario of a Hutu rebel movement, Palipehutu/FNL, fighting a Hutu-dominated democratically elected government. Most of the political tensions seem to have shifted to the Hutu elites, while the Tutsi political class positions itself to capture some of the economic gains arising from economic liberalisation.

In the democratisation process of both states, the enduring nature of ethnicity is clearly visible. In the Rwanda case, it continues to be deployed by Hutu rebels, mostly *génocidaires*, to justify the rightfulness of their claim to power – even after committing genocide, whilst in Burundi, once power is acquired, previously disadvantaged Hutus use the history of ethnic marginalisation to justify the replacement of Tutsi civil servants with Hutus.

The peace agreements that shaped the democratic frameworks did not include civil society organisations in their formulations and were essentially agreements between armed groups and ethnic elites. This lack of civil society participation is reflected in the top-down approach to their implementation. In both states, continued intolerance of opposition voices and the persistence of violence by state security forces suggest that the democratic moment is quite tenuous. What we see in both countries is the advent of multipartyism but no democracy.

Notes

1. Since colonial categorisation of the population into ethnic groups, the people of Rwanda and Burundi have been defined as comprising 85 per cent Hutu, 14 per cent Tutsi and 1 per cent Twa.
2. Irinnews.org. Burundi: Approval of Temporary Immunity Law Sparks Heated Debate, 3 September 2003, Africa English Reports. Nairobi: United Nations, Integrated Regional Information Network.
3. Interview with a member of the facilitation team, Dar es Salaam, Tanzania, 2005.
4. Irinnews.org. Burundi: Government of Consensus formed, 28 January 2008.

References

Clapham, Christopher. 1998. Rwanda: The Perils of Peacemaking. *Journal of Peace Research*. 35(2):193-210.
Corey, A. and S. F. Joireman. 2004. Retributive Justice: The Gacaca courts in Rwanda. *African Affairs* 103(410): 73-89.
De Forges, A. 1995. The Ideology of Genocide. *Issue: a Journal of Opinion* 23(2): 44-7.

Emizet, Kisangani, N. F. 2000. The Massacre of Refugees in Congo: A case of UN peace-keeping failure and International Law. *Journal of Modern African Studies* 38(2): 163-202.

(HRW) Human Rights Watch. 2005. *Burundi: Missteps at a Crucial Moment.* New York and London: Human Rights Watch.

(HRW) Human Rights Watch. 2006. 'Burundi: Alleged coup plotters tortured'; http://hrw.org/english/docs/2006/08/04/burundi/13920.htm [accessed 28 January 2008].

(ICG) International Crisis Group. 1999. *Five Years after the Genocide in Rwanda: Justice in Question.* Brussels: ICG.

——. 2001. *Burundi: Breaking the Deadlock,* Nairobi/Brussels: ICG Africa Report No.29.

——. 2002. *Rwanda at the End of the Transition: A Necessary Political Liberalization.* Nairobi/Brussels: ICG, Africa Report No.53.

——. 2003. *Rwandan Rebels in the Congo: A New Approach to Disarmament and Reintegration.* Nairobi/Brussels: ICG Africa Report No. 63.

——. 2006. *Burundi: Democracy and Peace at Risk,* Nairobi/Brussels: Africa Report No. 120.

——. 2007. *Burundi: Conclure la Paix avec les FNL,* Nairobi/Brussels: Rapport Afrique No. 131.

Jefremovas, V. 2000. Treacherous Waters: The politics of history and the politics of genocide in Rwanda and Burundi. *Africa* 70(2): 298-308.

Jones, Bruce. 2001. *Peacemaking in Rwanda: the Dynamics of Failure.* Boulder, CO and London: Lynne Rienner Publishers.

Jordaan, Eduard. 2006. Inadequately Self-critical: Rwanda's Self-Assessment for the African Peer Review Mechanism. *African Affairs* 105(420): 333-51.

Lemarchand, René. 1994. *Burundi: Ethnocide as Discourse and Practice.* Cambridge: Woodrow Wilson Press and Cambridge University Press.

Ligue Iteka. 2005a. *De la Logique de Guerre aux Vicissitudes d' Application des Accords, Rapport Annuel sur la Situation des Droits d l'homme au Burundi, Edition 2004.* Bujumbura, Burundi: Ligue ITEKA, March.

Ligue Iteka. 2005b. Déclaration de la Ligue ITEKA: Violence Certaines Localités du Burundi I. Http://www.ligue-iteka.africa-web.org/ [accessed December 2005].

Mamdani, Mahmoud. 2001. *When Victims Become Killers: Colonialism, Nativism, and the Genocide in Rwanda.* Oxford: James Currey.

Melvern, Linda and Paul Williams. 2004. Britannia Waived the Rules: The Major government and the 1994 genocide. *African Affairs* 103:1-22.

Newbury, D. 1995. Rwanda: Genocide and After. *Journal of Opinion – ASA* xxxiii (2): 4-7.

Ngaruko, Floribert and D. Nkurunziza Janvier. 2000. An Economic Interpretation of Conflict in Burundi. *Journal of African Economies* 9(3): 370-409.

Oomen, B. 2005. Donor-driven Justice and its Discontents: The case of Rwanda. *Development and Change* 36(5): 887-910.

(OAU) Organization of African Unity. 2000. *International Panel of Eminent Personalities to Investigate the 1994 Genocide in Rwanda and the Surrounding Events, Special Report,* Addis Ababa: OAU.

Pottier, Johan. 2002. *Re-imagining Rwanda: Conflict, Survival and Disinformation in the Late Twentieth Century.* Cambridge: Cambridge University Press.

Prunier, Gerard. 1995. *The Rwandan Crisis: History of a Genocide.* London: Hurst & Co.

Reyntjens, Filip. 2004. Rwanda, Ten Years On: From Genocide to Dictatorship. *African Affairs* 103: 177-210.

——. 2005. Briefing: Burundi: A Peaceful Transition After a Decade of War? *African Affairs* 105(418): 117-35.

——. 2006. Post-1994 Politics in Rwanda: Problematising 'liberation' and 'democratisation'. *Third World Quarterly* 27(6): 1103-17.

(ROR) Republic of Rwanda, National Unity and Reconciliation Commission. 1999. Background to NURC at http://nurc.gov.rw/ [last accessed 28 May 2007]

Samset, Ingrid and Orrvar Dalby. 2003. *Rwanda: Presidential & Parliamentary Elections 2003,* NORDEM Report 12/2003, Oslo: Norwegian Centre for Human Rights, University of Oslo.

Spears, Ian. 2000. Understanding Inclusive Peace Agreements in Africa: The problems of sharing power. *Third World Quarterly* 21(1): 105-18.

Terry, Fiona. 2002. *Condemned to Repeat? The Paradox of Humanitarian Action.* Ithaca, NY and London: Cornell University Press.

Tull, Dennis M. and Andreas Mehler. 2005. The Hidden Cost of Power-Sharing: Reproducing insurgent violence in Africa. *African Affairs* 104(416): 375-98.

Umutesi, Beatrice. 2000. *Surviving the Slaughter: The Ordeal of a Rwandan Refugee in Zaire.* Madison, WI: University of Wisconsin Press.

(UNSC) United Nations Security Council. 2001. *Report of the Panel of Experts on the Illegal Exploitation of Natural Resources and Other Forms of Wealth of the DR Congo* (S/2001/357).

Uvin, Peter. 1998. *Aiding Violence: The Development Enterprise in Rwanda*. West Hartford, CT: Kumarian Press.

——. 2001. Difficult Choices in the New Post-conflict Agenda: The international community in Rwanda after the genocide. *Third World Quarterly* (22)2: 177-89.

——. 2003. Rwanda's draft constitution: Some reflections on democracy and conflict and the role of the international community. http://www.grandlacs.net/doc/2601.pdf [last accessed 28 January 2008]

Vansina, Jan. 2004. *Antecedents to Modern Rwanda: The Nyiginga Kingdom*. Oxford: James Currey.

11

Zimbabwe since 1997
Land & the Legacies of War

JOCELYN ALEXANDER

The combination of a new and vibrant political opposition, the violent 'invasion' of largely white-owned farms, and the first of a series of deeply flawed elections transformed Zimbabwean political life in 2000. These dramatic upheavals require careful explanation. They were rooted in both the complex legacies of nationalist struggle and the socio-economic pressures of the 1990s, while their specific – and unusual – form was a product of two events that had reshaped the possibilities of Zimbabwean politics in 1997. The first of these was the Zanu(PF) government's decision to accede to the demands for material compensation made by veterans of the 1970s liberation war. The second was the designation of over 1,400 mostly white-owned commercial farms for compulsory acquisition by the state. Amidst expanding protest, strikes and economic decline, land and the legacies of war moved centre stage, creating a new set of political alliances, a shift in public discourse, and asserting the party's direct control over land as a political and patronage resource. What critical voices have termed the 'crisis' of 2000 and what the government has termed the 'third chimurenga' or uprising followed. In the next years, hundreds of thousands of black Zimbabweans moved onto what had been 'white' land, often under the leadership of veterans of Zimbabwe's war of independence. At the same time, veterans, the ruling party, and a shifting range of other groups worked to transform Zimbabwe's political sphere and state institutions through the propagation of an intolerant 'patriotism' and a violent practice known as *jambanja*.

In explaining the extraordinary transformation of Zimbabwean politics in recent years, this chapter does not focus on elections as markers of change or measures of democracy, though the many well documented failings of electoral practice were certainly important to the story.[1] Rather, it focuses on the ways in which political agents set about reconfiguring institutions and political practices, and legitimising their actions with reference to history and political ideas. These processes had profound implications for democratic participation, the exercise of civic rights, and the social contract between state and society. In approaching Zimbabwean politics in this way, the chapter draws on a rich multi-disciplinary seam in the analysis of the 'crisis'. This literature builds on a long-standing and sophisticated political economy tradition in Zimbabwean historiography, but has added to it a focus on discursive practices, rights and the state itself.[2]

Histories of Land and War

Terence Ranger (2004: 217) has recently wondered whether Zimbabwe has 'too much history'. Prolific though they are, he did not mean that historians of Zimbabwe were at any risk of over-production. He referred instead to the dangers of a repetitive 'single, narrow historical narrative', as in the Rhodesia of the 1950s. This he identified anew in what he called the 'patriotic history' promoted after 2000 by Zanu(PF) and its allies in the media and academe. As others have pointed out, patriotic history is part of a broader process of polarisation, a production of 'discursive divides' that reinforced 'static and essentialised representations of difference' (Hammar & Raftopoulos 2003: 16-17). In particular, the history of nationalism, war and land became the terrain on which Zanu(PF)'s legitimacy was heatedly asserted and contested.

The narrative of patriotic history is teleological, and its purpose is to legitimise and glorify a particular political regime. This is not a new or unusual role for history; it is in keeping with a very long tradition of history-writing in the service of the nation state, and it has echoes in the post-colonial politics of many African countries (Triulzi 2006; Werbner 1998). The choices made in the construction of Zanu(PF)'s history are nonetheless revealing, as all such charters of legitimacy are. Patriotic history is not a grab-bag of unsophisticated fabrications, but rather a shifting, adaptable set of stories that address real grievance and popular memory as well as the specific needs of Zanu(PF)'s political project (Tendi 2008). Zimbabwe was, above all, portrayed as 'the product of bitter and protracted armed struggle' against colonialism (Ranger 2004: 219; see also Raftopoulos 2004). The two chimurengas of the past – the doomed risings against conquest of the 1890s and the liberation war of the 1970s – are central to the narrative, and both claim land as their defining cause and Britain as their enemy.

The energetic elaboration of patriotic history is new in its virulence and, to an extent, in its content, but it draws on a well established lineage of official nationalist history. This is a history which focuses on the dispossession and injustice of settler rule, from the rapacious looting of Cecil Rhodes' pioneer column to the humiliations of racial segregation and the cruel evictions consequent on the enforcement of land alienation. Against these outrages struggle the authentic sons of the soil, the constituents of a shifting but constant liberation movement. The villains are their antithesis, the colonisers and their traitorous African allies, men and women who have been bought off or lost touch with their culture and values. In the context of the third chimurenga, Zanu(PF) sought to remove any ambiguity as to who these villains might be by publishing a long list of historical sell-outs. For their part, heroes and patriots have been canonised with official pomp and ceremony since independence (Kriger 1995). While the membership of the two sides has not been fixed over the whole of the post-independence period, the construction of the divide and its central political role has been a constant.[3]

The omissions in patriotic history are important to an understanding of Zanu(PF)'s political project. Zimbabwe's first two chimurengas were not, of course, straightforward battles between Britain on the one side and sons of the soil on the other. The 1890s risings counter-posed a range of at times antagonistic African polities to Cecil Rhodes' British South Africa Company and its band of more or less unsavoury recruits and African allies. The 1970s war was waged between the illegal regime of Ian Smith's Rhodesian Front and not one but two liberation armies. Black Zimbabweans fought on all sides, while the liberation movements suffered repeated division and at times paralysing internal mutiny. As important, the goals of the liberation war and the means by which it should be pursued were heatedly debated among guerrillas and civilians on the battlefield and in exile (Alexander *et al.* 2000; Kriger 1992; Bhebe & Ranger 1996). These debates carried forward a long history of political contest within the nationalist movement. Land was not the only goal of this struggle, and war was not the only means by which struggle was effected. Nationalism encompassed demands for the redistribution of resources and an end to discrimination, as well as demands for an accountable state and civil rights. Nationalist struggle took place in the trade unions, townships and the domestic arena of the home, as well as in the rural bases of the guerrillas. It produced a rich political ferment defined by shifting divisions and alliances and social struggle, not single-minded purpose and Manichaean oppositions. It could not be reduced to a process of sifting sell-outs from patriots.[4]

The language of selling out has nonetheless been a crucial element of Zimbabwean political discourse and practice, precisely because it served to simplify and to legitimise violence. It had flourished in the 1960s when Zimbabwe's single nationalist party, Zapu, split into two, marking the birth of Zanu.[5] If the early 1960s marked a new high in violent intolerance within the nationalist movements, the liberation war that followed raised the stakes considerably. To be accused of disloyalty – of selling out – placed one in the enemy camp, and to be in the enemy camp made one a target of armed violence. These accusations were, however, very rarely straightforward. Defining, identifying, and authenticating a 'sell-out' was a murky process in which fear, disinformation, unfixed identities and witchcraft were mixed with personal and political agendas. In some areas, sell-out killings were cast as among the prime failings of nationalism, not as its righteous expression (Alexander *et al.* 2000); everywhere they left a legacy that defied easy resolution and preoccupied community leaders many years after the end of war.

Violence and intolerance were not, of course, the sole province of the nationalist camp, and nor were they in any way unique to Zimbabwean nationalism. Such tendencies were commonplace among other southern African – and many more – liberation movements. On its side, the Rhodesian state mobilised a vast and sophisticated military and was willing to use the dirtiest of tricks including chemical weapons to defend what it called civilisation. Nonetheless, the entrenchment of a violent intolerance of dissent and disloyalty within the nationalist movements was an important legacy of the liberation struggle, and one to which the ideologues of the third chimurenga knowingly referred. The focus on enemies and sell-outs in Zanu(PF) rhetoric has an all too real history, and when it is linked to the narrative of war and land – as in patriotic history – it promises an authoritarian and coercive politics that threatens both civic rights and democratic practice.

Zimbabwe's Inheritance

That Zimbabwe's politics and public debates over history at the turn of the twenty-first century would focus on land and war, sell-outs and heroes, race and imperialism was not predicted by analysts of Zimbabwe in its earlier years. The nation's inheritance in 1980 seemed to indicate other trajectories. The Rhodesian Front had bequeathed Zimbabwe a sophisticated, centralised and powerful bureaucratic state alongside a vastly unequal, racially based economy. The newly elected Zanu(PF) government promised to heal racial division through a policy of reconciliation, and to use the state to redress inequality. It accepted the institutions of parliamentary democracy, constitutional protection for property rights, and even the humiliating proviso of 20 guaranteed white seats in the 100-seat Parliament for seven years. At first Zanu(PF) talked of socialism, but it was a commitment to modernising development, powerfully shaped by Rhodesian practice, that formed the central plank of the new government's programme of change.

The inheritance of the bureaucratic state was used to great effect in the 1980s. Efficient and capable, if not accountable, this state was able to deliver. Most Zimbabweans gained access to education and health care as never before, and a resettlement programme had in a little over ten years redistributed some 3 million hectares of what had been mostly white-owned land to over 70,000 black households. It was one of the biggest land redistribution exercises of its kind in Africa. Zimbabwe could boast of a substantial middle class, an educated population, a diversified economy and enviable infrastructure. To an important extent the Zanu(PF) government was able to claim legitimacy as a result of its delivery of development; modernising development formed an indisputably central part of the ideology of Zanu(PF) elites.[6]

The legacy of wartime politics was, however, also felt almost immediately as the new Zanu(PF) government moved to assert its control over a wide range of independent organisations, from trade unions to local party branches, and from churches to women's groups. Its most dramatic expression came in the political conflict of the early 1980s known as *gukurahundi*. This conflict did not fall into the heroic sequence of the chimurengas. It was a war of repression fought against the only real political opposition the newly elected Zanu(PF) faced – the nationalist party Zapu. In keeping with the liberation-war practice of treating dissent or alternative loyalties as treason, Zapu members bore the brunt of a violent campaign that killed well over 10,000 and probably closer to 20,000 people, and eventually led to the absorption of Zapu by Zanu(PF) under the Unity Accord of 1987.[7] This period should have set alarm bells ringing, but it was largely brushed under the carpet nationally and internationally, not least because it was deemed crucial that Zimbabwe's new democracy succeed in the face of apartheid South Africa.

The peace, stability and apparent return to democratic politics of post-Unity Zimbabwe were superficial. In 1987, the Constitution was amended so as to create an executive Presidency, signalling the centralisation of power in the executive at the expense of the legislature and judiciary and sparking a widespread debate over the dangers of a one-party state (Mandaza & Sachikonye 1991). The adoption of a structural adjustment package shortly thereafter created other kinds of disaffection by undermining the state expansion and social advances of the 1980s and, as a result, the government's ability to pursue its programme of modernising development.[8] The changes of the 1990s struck a blow at the significant part of the black middle class that was rooted in the civil service. As in the case of the Zambian working class, it also severely undercut the living standards of formal sector workers, leading them and their umbrella union to move away from corporatist trade union politics towards a confrontational stance. In the mid-1990s, workers and civil servants struck repeatedly. Others were also unhappy with the shifts of the late 1980s and 1990s: the independent press blossomed and grew increasingly outspoken and critical, students protested time and again not least over corruption, intellectuals vocally expressed their disenchantment, and civic groups were formed to demand political rights, state accountability and constitutional change. Constitutional change steadily climbed the agenda as disillusionment with what was seen as an increasingly authoritarian politics grew (Saunders 2000; Kagoro 2004).

Some factions of the black elite at the same time engaged in a politics of what has been called 'economic nationalism' (Moyo 1994). This elite no longer suffered from racial and political discrimination, but it saw all too clearly that the lion's share of the nation's wealth still lay in white and foreign hands. Black business elites formed a series of organisations in the 1990s, such as the Indigenous Business Development Centre and the Affirmative Action Group, and pressed the state and party to level a playing-field that was still distinctly uneven. Vocal and visible, these groups met with some political sympathy, but did not succeed in gaining significant concessions from the state in the 1990s, in part due to the strictures of structural adjustment.

Much of this political activism was urban-based, but the rural areas were also far from steeped in a state of quiet contentment. Outside the cities, the local state and party came under pressure from a constituency angry over the failure of resettlement to meet demands for restitution or lessen land pressures in the communal areas (the significant scale of resettlement notwithstanding), declining state accountability, and the deterioration in service provision and market opportunities. New service user fees were prohibitive to many, while the quality of services declined. The contraction in formal sector jobs in conjunction with rising urban costs of living undercut the transfer of wealth to the rural areas by migrant workers. Workers moved into the informal sector, and they needed land as a safety-net more than ever before (Potts 2000). For the landless, unemployed and land-poor, gaining access to land was essential to survival, and they increasingly relied on the tactics of squatting and 'resource poaching', such as illegally cutting grass or wood, gold panning, driving livestock onto commercial farms and stock theft. These strategies brought them into conflict with other communal area farmers, the state, Zanu(PF) and private land owners (Alexander 2006; Yeros 1999; Moyo 2000). The costs to state and party legitimacy were high.

In the 1990s, land also preoccupied the ruling party's leaders. From the run-up to the 1990 elections, the Zanu(PF) leadership had deployed a heated rhetoric. Blaming whites, demanding that Britain pay for the land, and invoking colonial injustice were all commonplace. Despite the proposal of new policies and the passage of new legislation intended to ease the state's acquisition of land, little action was taken, however. Resettlement proceeded at a trickle while the most high-profile – though still small-scale – interventions focused on securing land for members of the 'indigenous' elite, a concession to the pressures of 'economic nationalism'. The effect was to buttress an image of Zanu(PF) as corrupt, unaccountable, and only concerned with the wealthy and the well-connected.

The Zanu(PF) government's strategies in the mid-1990s left it politically vulnerable. Structural adjustment, a stalled land reform programme, declining state capacity and accountability, and elite corruption combined to undermine the political capital derived from the delivery of development and the nationalist mantle. The resulting challenge to Zanu(PF)'s legitimacy required a response, but the nature of this response was by no means predetermined: Zanu(PF) and the Zimbabwean state were deeply divided in their views and interests. It was the assertiveness and symbolic utility of veterans of Zimbabwe's liberation war, along-side a renewed politicisation of the land, that would set the scene for the promulgation of patriotic history and the practice of an increasingly authoritarian politics, rooted once again in the divisive language of the sell-out.

The Turning Point: 1997

Workers, civil servants, students, smallholders and black elites were not the only ones who made their unhappiness known in the 1990s. The veterans of Zimbabwe's liberation war also found their collective voice. The government's acknowledgement of their demands, coupled with the increasingly heated politics of land, marked a turning point that would shape the strategies of Zanu(PF)'s third chimurenga.

Veterans of both liberation armies formed a single association in 1989. This was the first time it was possible to do so following the political divisions and conflict of the 1980s in which veterans on both sides had been centrally involved. In the 1990s, veterans came together to demand material compensation for their war-time sacrifices (see Kriger 2003). This process at first developed into something of a farce, and then into the makings of a tragedy. The farce was the 'looting' of the official war victims' fund by the Zanu(PF) elite. Payouts to veterans were based on the medically assessed percentage by which they were judged to be disabled. It turned out that some of Zimbabwe's senior serving ministers were almost totally disabled, either or both mentally and physically, thus making them eligible for massive payouts. Millions of dollars were siphoned off into the hands of the ruling elite.

Such behaviour enraged those rank-and-file veterans who had not prospered since the end of the war in 1979. Many were living in poverty and a state of social marginalisation. They were unable to acquire jobs due to their lack of educational qualifications, in part because they had spent their youth training and fighting and not in school. At times they proved unable to build and maintain stable relationships, living instead on the edges of society, unmarried and unable to create a home. It is difficult to exaggerate just how enraged such men were as they watched Mercedes-driving ministers – members of the 'Kompressor class' – claiming such massive payouts that they left the war victim's fund penniless.[9]

Many of these veterans reacted to the very public consumption of what they saw as their benefits with protest and riot. They heckled Mugabe at his heroes' day speech, they stormed the party headquarters, and they physically threatened and insulted senior party leaders and ministers, some of whom literally had to run for safety. In the end, Mugabe responded by acceding to the veterans' demands for pensions and payouts in 1997. The result was a dramatic repositioning of veterans that would prove central to the ruling party's strategies of subsequent years, and the political narratives used to justify those strategies. The veterans and their association had moved from an antagonistic and marginal role to the very heart of political change. They did so at a time when Zanu(PF)'s political base had been substantially narrowed, thus inflating and distorting their influence and importance.

The successful claims of veterans to compensation had immediate effects. Veterans were suddenly set apart materially and often also politically from the civilians amongst whom they lived, many of whom were at this point struggling with the hardships of a declining economy and thoroughly fed up with Zanu(PF). The payouts also occasioned a re-institutionalisation of veterans and a transformation of their relationship to state authority and to political leaders (Alexander & McGregor 2006). The veterans' association undertook intense vetting procedures before payouts were made. Former guerrillas had to reclaim their war names, recall their comrades, and rehearse the story of their training camps, operational areas, and battles. This process brought veterans into renewed contact with one another, as they went to meeting after meeting all over the country, formed local associations, and congregated in the barracks in Harare where their credentials were assessed. Rank-and-file guerrillas were reunited with their former commanders and interacted with the local and national leadership of the veterans' association, men whose authority often lay in their political connections and acumen. In this process, a new veteran identity was forged, and it was linked directly to an embattled ruling party in desperate need of allies and a fresh means of legitimising itself.

It is important to stress just how controversial and costly the payouts to veterans were (Alexander *et al.* 2000: 254-7). The economic price was high: the making of the unbudgeted payouts triggered the collapse of the Zimbabwe dollar, a symbolic moment that can arguably be taken as the start of a period of dramatic economic decline from which Zimbabwe has yet to recover. It was also politically divisive and destabilising. A host of protests in the streets and in the media followed the singling out of veterans as a special class to whom the nation owed a debt. Those who had been detained in the nationalist era, or who had aided guerrillas on the battlefield but had not received formal training, struggled to gain access to the suddenly privileged category of 'veteran' and threatened Zanu(PF)'s leaders with revelations about illegitimate uses of violence in the 1970s. Some veterans proper refused the payouts, and the alliance with Zanu(PF) that they implied; they formed their own organisation and denounced Zanu(PF) as a traitor to the ideals of the liberation war. Trade unionists meanwhile angrily attacked the special status accorded veterans, stressing that everyone – civilians and fighting men alike – had paid a heavy price in the war. This was an argument that appealed to a good many communal area farmers too: they recalled the food and goods they had provided without compensation to guerrillas and the devastating losses they had suffered at the hands of the Rhodesian security forces. For people born after independence, the so-called 'born frees', the constant invocation of the liberation war and the notion of heroic sacrifice for the nation were often meaningless if not alienating.

The Zanu(PF) government's alliance with veterans – and in effect its decision not to try to build alliances with other disaffected social groups – was a potentially costly gamble. It was, however, to prove extraordinarily effective when linked to a new politics of land. As noted above, the rhetoric around land had been extremely heated in the 1990s, but little action had followed. In 1997, however, in the aftermath of the payouts to the veterans, the Zanu(PF) government used powers it had long possessed but never exercised effectively to designate over 1,400 large-scale farms for compulsory acquisition. Zanu(PF) needed to offer something tangible to its key rural constituency: land was one of its few options. The farm designations were accompanied by a heightened rhetoric in which the British government played the role of unreconstructed imperialist, and 'Rhodesians' – white Zimbabweans – were cast as colonialists unwilling to give up their ill-gotten gains. Though the majority of white farmers had purchased their land after independence, they were glossed as the direct descendants of the pioneers by right of their race. White farmers – yet another constituency in a state of disaffection with Zanu(PF) – proved to be dispensable, their own belief in their essential place in Zimbabwe's economy (if not its society) notwithstanding (Selby 2006).

The 1997 designations signalled a key shift in the struggle within the state and ruling party over land policy. From the early 1990s, party leaders had sought to wrest control from technocratic state bureaucracies of the process by which land was designated for acquisition. The designations of 1993, which came to little, had led to the creation of the Zanu(PF)-dominated National Land Task Force. In 1997, party-run land committees were central in the identification of land to be listed for acquisition. This made the lists vulnerable to technocratic and legal objection, but it also marked a significant shift in the decision-making locus of land policy: politicians appeared to have successfully sidelined ministerial bureaucracies and their expertise-based claims to authority over the land (Selby 2006; Alexander 2006). Zanu-PF elites were working to move land into the realm of partisan patronage politics.

The immediate effect of the land designations was not, however, massive land redistribution to the party faithful but a flurry of legal contestation, 'de-listing', 'squatter' occupations, concerned intervention on the part of Zimbabwean officials and politicians, and attempts to come to some form of agreement with aid agencies and bilateral donors on the part of technocrats in the ministries of lands and agriculture. Attempts to reach a compromise were repeatedly – and eventually fatally – undermined by incompatible agendas on all sides. Instead, the alliance with veterans and the new politics of land were about to come together in a dramatic conflagration.

The Third Chimurenga

The troubled negotiations over land of the late 1990s were overtaken by the constitutional referendum of early 2000, another key moment in recent Zimbabwean politics. The referendum marked a watershed. The campaign itself occasioned widespread popular mobilisation around an agenda that focused not just on anger over economic hardship but on civil rights, state accountability and specifically the curtailment of the autonomy of an executive that had gathered power over the preceding decade, not least through legal and constitutional amendment (see Rich Dorman 2003). Many of the groups mobilised in this process – and they were disparate groups with disparate interests, including white farmers, black smallholders, businessmen, professionals, workers, and students – came together to form the Movement for Democratic Change (MDC) in late 1999. The movement's backbone was the increasingly confrontational Zimbabwe Congress of Trade Unions, led by Morgan Tsvangirai.

The work of civics, churches, unions and voter education campaigns alongside the MDC meant that debates over Zimbabwe's political future took place all over the country – in the remotest rural areas, on white farms, and in the corners of every township. The result was defeat for the Zanu(PF) government in February 2000. This was the first national-level defeat Zanu(PF) had suffered, and it stunned the party's leaders. They were now painfully aware that they had only a brief period in which to rebuild their hold on the electorate and on power. This is the moment when land and veterans took on dramatically new roles. It was time to take the land, and taking it required a chimurenga. In this context, veterans were thrust forward as the long-denied liberators of the land, as the agents of 'real' decolonisation. They were central in instigating the land 'invasions' – the movement of black Zimbabweans of a wide variety of descriptions onto largely white-owned land – just weeks after the referendum defeat.

In order to make the third chimurenga a convincing vehicle by which to buttress its authority, Zanu(PF) invested in sustained intellectual labour (Tendi 2008). It needed to draw on the lineage of nationalist history not just to establish the legitimacy of Zanu(PF) rule, but also to discredit the MDC. A series of oppositions needed to be fleshed out (see Raftopoulos 2003, 2004; Hammar & Raftopoulos 2003; Ranger 2004). Nationalism was still about fighting men and the land. But it was no longer about democracy and rights. Democracy and civil rights were increasingly tarred with the brush of neo-colonialism, cast as an un-African and inauthentic element of an alien and imperial agenda, and ceded to the MDC. They were said to be the terrain of hypocritical former colonial powers who had never genuinely cared for the rights of black men, and of their local stooges – whites and the forces of opposition. Democracy and rights were also associated with the international financial institutions. These institutions wanted, the argument went, to use an empty discourse of political rights and electoral rules in order to deprive Zimbabweans of their economic rights and their material heritage – that is, the land. Even worse, they wanted to deprive Zimbabweans of their very history, as embodied most importantly in the first and second chimurengas, and of their culture as expressed through their relationship with the land. A third chimurenga was needed to finish the fight against foreign and white domination. Calling this process an uprising, a chimurenga, had the additional effect of signalling – and legitimising – the necessity of violent intolerance of dissent and disloyalty, as in previous wars.

Veterans were crucial both in the land occupations and in the escalating use of political violence to enforce patriotic history's exclusions. In the period between the referendum defeat of February 2000 and the national elections of June that year, war veterans spearheaded the occupations, and received logistical support from the security and intelligence services. Veterans everywhere played leadership roles, despite the fact that they constituted only a tiny minority of occupiers, the bulk being drawn from communal and urban areas as well as party youth. They were able to play such a key role because of the organisational and political work of 1997: the committees of the veteran association reached into every rural area, and they were tied by patronage and the declarations of patriotic history to Zanu(PF). Veterans also played a key role in doing the work of justifying the occupations. They were the living symbols of the liberation war, and they proclaimed that they had fought the war in order to give the people the land. Veteran leaders blamed white farmers for blocking the constitutional referendum so as to frustrate land redistribution. This of course was not an accurate account of people's reasons for voting 'no' in the referendum; political accountability had stood at the heart of the 'no' vote. Veterans were also central in popularising a discourse that legitimated the abrogation of the law. Their practices came to be known as *jambanja*, loosely meaning disorder or lawlessness. Unfavourable judicial decisions were met with threats of going to war; whites and the MDC were cast as 'enemies' and sell-outs who would undo the revolution, and hence, as in the war years, as legitimate targets of violence.

As the mid-2000 elections approached, veterans alongside state security forces increasingly used violence in the course of campaigning. The land occupations were intended to appeal to a broad constituency by demonstrating a tangible commitment to land redistribution. They were also used to punish constituencies seen as illegitimately engaged in opposition politics. Initially, white farmers and farm workers were construed as alien and traitorous. White farmers were attacked, and farm workers subjected to political re-education or simply driven from their homes in what would turn into a major humanitarian disaster (Sachikonye 2003; Rutherford 2001, 2003). As the campaign wore on, war veterans, in alliance with Zanu(PF) and the security forces, directed violence against the MDC or those perceived to be MDC much more widely. This encompassed entire social and occupational categories, such as teachers. It was a strategy that worked in the end. Zanu(PF) narrowly, and extremely controversially, won the 2000 elections.

The combination of violent electioneering and the land occupations required something else too: a concerted attack on the state. As noted above, Zimbabwean state institutions were technocratic and bureaucratic to a fault. These were useful attributes where the government wanted to implement a top-down, modernising development programme. They were not useful where the abrogation of the law on a massive scale and for political ends was required. In the sphere of land policy, the relevant ministries with their many experts were shunted aside in favour of an alliance led by Zanu(PF) and veterans, a move that built on the shift to party control of land designations that had occurred over the 1990s, and which had been clearly demonstrated in the 1997 designations.

Other arms of the state were forced into a partisan mould as well. Civil servants in general came under tremendous pressure to support Zanu(PF) and under violent attack where they did not. The judiciary was subjected to concerted pressure; judges were threatened and hounded out, and inconvenient rulings were ignored or overridden. Eventually the government simply changed the law to legalise its actions after the fact and introduced new laws allowing the vast extension of executive power. Zanu(PF)'s parliamentary dominance meant that it could do so with ease. The security forces also came under pressure. The police force was increasingly politicised and manned by new recruits drawn from among veterans and party youth, while the army was drawn into ever more unprofessional roles, a trend that had been under way for some time.[10]

None of this was easily done, and none of it succeeded entirely. The initiation of the third chimurenga was marked by intense struggle within the state. Everywhere civil servants, as well as a significant number of Zanu(PF) politicians and veterans who were uncomfortable with the direction of events, sought to defend a different form of state craft, rooted in an alternative history and set of political ideals. They had a voice in the first few years of the third chimurenga, but over time they were increasingly marginalised where they were not forcibly silenced. This was in part accomplished through the mobilisation of new forces outside the state – the veterans of course, and then the youth militias or 'green bombers'[11] – and increasingly it was achieved through a systematic policy of 'militarising' state institutions by installing senior military men, almost all war veterans, at the top levels of the state's bureaucratic hierarchies, thus allowed the disciplining of the disloyal and the use of institutions for partisan, and increasingly for corrupt, ends (Ndlovu-Gatsheni 2006). More and more, the security forces took a direct hand in areas well outside their remit and areas of expertise, unsurprisingly in the realm of repression but also for example in economic and agricultural policy.

Zanu(PF) proved remarkably adept at adapting itself to ongoing political challenges. Its strategies combined coercive tactics that employed different agents and techniques over time and space, the creation and transformation of state and quasi-state institutions, and the distribution of resources. After the 2000 elections, the vast expansion in permanent land occupations and the far-reaching implications of escalating attacks on state institutions and the MDC brought new changes. Shortly after the elections, the government introduced the 'fast track' resettlement programme, initially designed to settle 5 million hectares. This target was rapidly superseded – under pressure from veterans, Zanu(PF), and popular demands for land, as well as in retaliation against the often successful legal challenges launched by white farmers. By mid-2002 the vast majority of formerly white land had been listed for acquisition and in effect opened up to occupation.

The rapid expansion of fast-track resettlement had important consequences for the political sphere. Among other effects, it gave great latitude to the recently constituted district and provincial land committees. These committees are a fascinating illustration of the creation of institutions in order to circumvent, displace and transform an inconveniently bureaucratic and professional state. Theoretically headed by district administrators and Provincial Governors, their composition was highly variable, and many were dominated by a mixture of veterans and Zanu(PF). The committees spent much of their time attacking institutions they considered insufficiently committed to the third chimurenga. They shut down rural councils and schools, and threatened, attacked and drove out civil servants and elected representatives with whom they disagreed. The effect was to weaken and politicise the state at these intermediary levels. Professionalism, education, and skills were no longer the predominant criteria for holding state posts; loyalty to Zanu(PF) and political and military connections were (see McGregor 2002).

The third chimurenga played into and created a bewildering range of conflicts over both land and political power. The basis on which one could claim authority over the land was in flux, and this uncertainty occasioned a diverse set of disputes between and among veterans, occupiers, chiefs, technocrats and politicians which have yet to be fully resolved. It is nonetheless clear that Zimbabwe's large-scale agricultural sector has been transformed beyond recognition. In the late 1990s, around 4,500 mostly white commercial farmers and a number of multinational companies held private title to their land and employed over 300,000 farm workers. By 2005, white farmers' numbers had dwindled to about 500, while around 200,000 farm workers had lost their jobs and often also their homes and access to services. They were replaced, according to official sources, by over 130,000 smallholders (A1 farmers) and roughly 16,000 new medium and large-scale farmers (A2 farmers). These figures must, however, be taken with a large grain of salt, given the ongoing processes of evictions and movement.

The 'new' farmers held land under unclear systems of tenure; for all, political connections remained important in defending rights to land. Smallholders formed their own committees but these were not clearly linked to the councils and chiefs who theoretically held sway over all fast-track land. For medium and large-scale farmers, tenure was even less clearly defined. Many farms remained unsurveyed and unoccupied years after their allocation. A form of leasehold tenure was proposed but went unrealised. In the meantime, the farms were plagued with poaching and vandalism (see Government of Zimbabwe 2003).

For all settlers there were additional, significant sources of insecurity. White farmers' legal and other claims remained unresolved, while the escalation of large-scale land allocations in 2002 introduced a new dynamic wherein members of the ruling elite competed with earlier generations of occupiers for the best land and infrastructure, largely in the prime lands of Mashonaland (Raftopoulos &

Phimister 2004). Army commanders, ministers and senior politicians employed thugs to evict people who had occupied land in 2000. Clashes between well-connected elites, smallholders, and veterans multiplied, leading to loud protests from veteran leaders, chiefs and others. Finally, most farmers – with the notable exception of those whose connections with the state, party and military allowed them subsidised access to fuel, inputs, tractors and other commodities – suffered under the fast deteriorating economic conditions as the Zimbabwean economy set new records for its rate of contraction. Severe shortages of foreign currency, fuel and other commodities, sky-rocketing levels of unemployment, repeated droughts, and inflation that had crept up from double digits to the hundreds, to the thousands and, in late 2008, to the hundreds of millions, made farming (as well as other productive activities) extremely risky and difficult (compare Mavedzenge *et al.* 2008 and Matondi *et al.* 2008). The failure of many new farmers to invest in the land was both unsurprising and disastrous for the economy, and severely compounded the contraction of the mining, manufacturing and industrial sectors.

These difficulties were compounded in May 2005 by the extraordinary initiative known as Operation Murambatsvina. The name's sanitised translation is 'operation restore order'; its literal meaning is 'operation drive out the filth'. In the name of 'cleaning' the urban areas, Operation Murambatsvina resulted in the destruction of the homes and/or the livelihoods of a conservatively estimated 700,000 people in the midst of winter and an unprecedented economic meltdown. Replacing a lost source of livelihood or a home was a Herculean, and for many impossible, task. For the vulnerable, these losses too often proved lethal.[12]

Operation Murambatsvina was, among many other things, a dramatic demonstration of the ongoing power of the Zimbabwean state to order and discipline its citizens in the name of a political project. The timing was instructive in that it came at a moment when Zanu(PF) had succeeded to a great extent in crushing the MDC's rural committees and ability to mobilise, through a combination of coercion and denial of access to resources including food aid. The cities remained the opposition's stronghold in the sense that they remained disloyal to Zanu(PF), though they rarely offered large-scale protest in this period and when they did they were met with extreme repression. In this context, Operation Murambatsvina encompassed a host of motives and purposes, both political and economic: to control foreign-exchange dealings and the informal economy where the vast majority of urban Zimbabweans made their living in 2005; to undermine the political opposition by disenfranchising its urban constituencies and driving them into the rural areas where they could be more easily controlled; to weaken city governments still loyal to the MDC; and to control veterans and other forces outside the state that were proving too independent, by revoking their role as urban patrons (some of the first houses to be demolished belonged to veteran leaders). Operation Murambatsvina was also something else: a reassertion of the project of modernising development. Its form and public justification owed a good deal to Rhodesian views on urban order and to the state's post-independence commitment to a 'planned' and 'modern' city (Potts 2007; Fontein, forthcoming). Whatever its mixed intentions, Operation Murambatsvina served to centralise lines of even the most meagre patronage and to reduce the ambitions of urban citizens to finding the barest means of survival.

Operation Murambatsvina produced misery and destitution not 'modernity' and order; fast-track resettlement delivered the land from white ownership, but with it came violence, insecurity and economic calamity. Alongside these urban and rural processes the state's capacity to deliver basic social services, notably health and education, was severely compromised, creating a generation of Zimbabweans deprived of education and causing widespread death and suffering as the sick and injured went untreated in hospitals and clinics that were increasingly devoid of staff and basic drugs. These developments cannot be said to embody a realisation of the liberation struggle's goals even as defined by the third chimurenga, and they certainly do not offer the hope of a life of dignity that nationalism had at various moments so eloquently expressed. One of the third chimurenga's most dramatic consequences was the unprecedented scale on which it forced Zimbabweans of all classes out of the country, as political refugees or in search of a bare living. The narrowed and intolerant nationalism embodied by Zanu(PF) created a vast Zimbabwean diaspora which was both essential to the survival of the national economy and a poignant reminder of the failure of the political nation.

Conclusion: Zimbabwe in 2008

The battles of the third chimurenga have been fought out on an ideological and institutional level. Understanding its consequences requires close attention to economic factors – the inheritance of vast inequalities, the costs of structural adjustment, the uses of patronage – as well as to the discursive strategies of elites and the transformations of the state. Though some still await the 'national democratic revolution' (Moyo & Yeros 2005), Zimbabwe's recent history does not bode well for democracy however it is understood – and nor have elections alone offered a remedy, as developments in 2008 illustrated.

The Movement for Democratic Change (MDC) remains the most significant source of opposition in Zimbabwe, but it has suffered deep divisions, born of the unrelenting pressures of Zanu(PF) and its own heterogeneous composition and sometimes self-interested leadership. It is an irony that the party ultimately split in 2005 over abuses of power within its own hierarchy that involved the use of violence and the sell-out language of Zanu(PF) (Raftopoulos 2006). Key elements of the MDC's constituency – the working class, the middle class, students, civics, white farmers, business – have been severely undermined and divided by a combination of political repression and co-optation, emigration, and economic contraction. Despite the desperate need for a united opposition, it seemed that personal enmities and the narrow ambitions of office, alongside a flourishing ethnic politics, placed unity beyond reach.

It was in this parlous state that the MDC entered into SADC-mandated talks, mediated by (the then) South African President Thabo Mbeki, with Zanu(PF) in 2007. Initiated in the aftermath of the vicious beating of Morgan Tsvangirai and other civic and political leaders at a 'prayer meeting' on 11 March, the talks were intended to pave the way for a 'normalisation' of Zimbabwean politics and for creating the conditions necessary for genuinely free and fair elections. Despite the ongoing regional appeal of its third chimurenga narrative, Zanu(PF) needed both to bolster its claims to political legitimacy and to provide a basis for building the bridges necessary to address Zimbabwe's economic woes (see Phimister & Raftopoulos 2004, 2007). The negotiations did not create a level playing field, but they did produce some significant changes, notably the amendment of key repressive and electoral laws (Solidarity Peace Trust 2008). Negotiations were, however, broken off in the face of Mugabe's unilateral setting of an election date in January 2008. There followed a feverish period of campaigning in the run-up to the 29 March elections in which the MDC was able to enter rural areas and to campaign openly to an extent that had not been possible since 2000. The relative lack of violence – due to Zanu(PF)'s 'complacency' (as Mugabe put it) and to the distractions of an intense succession politics within the party that had, not least, led to an alternative presidential candidate in the shape of former Zanu(PF) Finance Minister Simba Makoni – created sufficient space for the MDC to pull off a surprise victory. The two MDCs won a total of 109 parliamentary seats to Zanu(PF)'s 97, while Morgan Tsvangirai won a reported 47.9 per cent of the presidential vote to Robert Mugabe's 43.2 per cent (the remainder going to Simba Makoni). The MDCs swept the urban areas as expected, but also made significant inroads into Zanu(PF)'s rural heartlands (LeBas 2008).

The response of Zanu(PF) to its defeat was at first uncertain, but as the carefully engineered delays in announcing the disputed presidential results dragged into weeks it became clear that Zanu(PF) was regrouping, with the Joint Operations Command – made up of the heads of the security forces – calling the shots. The 'militarisation' of the Zimbabwe polity and state had never looked so clear. A presidential run-off was called for June 27 (because no candidate was deemed to have achieved over 50 per cent of the vote), and there followed a campaign of political violence that evoked the extreme repression of the 1985 elections (see Alexander and Tendi 2008). The security forces were the key organisers and perpetrators of violence, often using party youth, militias and veterans to carry out beatings, intimidation and torture. The targets were overwhelmingly MDC leaders and members. The violence drew heavily on the language of the sell-out once more, casting the MDC as traitorous to the nation, in league with foreign powers, and so beyond the protection of the law. Violence was aimed at punishing, terrorising and re-educating those who had voted 'wrongly'. Liberation war-era *pungwes* or mobilisational meetings were used to punish publicly those charged with betraying the third chimurenga. The worst violence was reserved for those errant voters within the Zanu(PF) heartland. In early July the MDC stated that over 1,500 of its activists, including 20 MPs and parliamentary candidates, were in police custody, over 100 supporters had been killed, 5,000 were missing, and tens of thousands were displaced or in hiding. The MDC was unable to hold meetings even in its strongholds. In the end Tsvangirai withdrew from the poll, allowing Mugabe to claim a one-sided victory.

This result did not provide Mugabe with the legitimacy he craved, even within the southern African region. SADC judged that the election did not represent the will of the Zimbabwean people, and ordered a renewal of the Mbeki-led negotiations. A memorandum of understanding was signed on 21 July and a power-sharing deal ostensibly reached on 11 September in which Zanu(PF) and the MDCs would share out Zimbabwe's ministries, with Mugabe remaining President while a new position of Prime Minister would be occupied by Tsvangirai. These interim arrangements were to persist until a new constitution was agreed upon (within 18 months) and new elections held. Much remained unclear. Critically, the allocation of ministries had not been agreed upon and wrangling over the crucial economic and security ministries created a deadlock amidst a rapidly accelerating economic disintegration in which the Zimbabwe dollar was rendered virtually value-less, as even the pettiest of economic transactions were increasingly undertaken in South African Rands and US dollars, hunger spread across the land, and the country's already much battered hospitals, schools and other state institutions collapsed or closed. Many civil servants simply did not show up to work; the costs of transportation for just a day or two often exceeded their monthly pay packet, which could at any rate not be accessed at the bank owing to government-imposed upper limits on the withdrawal of cash. Civil servants spent their time in the ubiquitous queues for cash, commodities or food aid when they were not engaged in informal sector economic activities. This marked a new and dramatic transformation of state institutions.

Amidst this dearth, retaining control of the commanding heights of the state remained all the more crucial. Access to the state was the means by which the Zanu(PF) elite produced and safeguarded its wealth as well as its coercive and political power. Sharing wealth and power posed a tremendous threat and many of Mugabe's powerful constituents baulked at the implications of the deal. The MDC's constituencies, notably its trade union and civic backers, were also critical. They felt too much had been conceded to a corrupt and criminal Zanu(PF). Civic groups took to the streets in protest at the delays in forming a government and at the dire economic situation, and were met with the language of the third chimurenga and violence once more. Negotiations nonetheless remain the only plausible way forward, given the weaknesses of the opposition, the legitimacy crisis and divisions within Zanu(PF), and the insolubility of the country's dire economic predicament short of external help. But negotiations at the level of elite alliance did not in themselves promise democracy. For that, the messy legacy of the third chimurenga for Zimbabwe's institutions and political culture must be addressed.

Notes

1. See for example the detailed analysis of Kriger (2005). Human rights and election monitoring groups have written extensively on the flawed elections of 2000 and after.
2. See Raftopoulos (2006). The best exemplar of this new work is Hammar *et al.* (2003). For earlier work in a political economy mould see, for example, Stoneman (1981, 1988) and Mandaza (1986).
3. For example, Zapu leader Joshua Nkomo was rehabilitated after the signing of the Unity Accord in 1987, while the single white occupant of Heroes Acre no longer merits a mention.
4. See discussion in Raftopoulos (1999) and Ranger (2003). Terence Ranger's work (2006) on urban violence in Bulawayo provides a fascinating insight into the complexity of social and labour struggles amidst nationalist mobilisation, as does Tim Scarnecchia's study (2008) of Harare.
5. Scarnecchia (2008) provides a detailed analysis of the origins of violent intolerance in the nationalist movements in the early 1960s.
6. See Worby (2003). It is an irony in the light of post-2000 developments that the bureaucratic state of the early post-independence years was criticised for being *insufficiently* politicised. See discussion in McGregor (2002).
7. The most comprehensive human rights report on this period is CCJP/LRF (1997). See also Alexander *et al.* (2000).
8. On the costs of structural adjustment in a wide variety of spheres, see, for example, Bond and Manyana (2003), Raftopoulos (2001), and Gibbon (1995).
9. In this period, JoAnn McGregor and I were involved in interviewing dozens of Zipra veterans and heard many such tales of outrage.
10. The August 1998 intervention of the ZNA in the Democratic Republic of Congo is often seen as the point at which senior army commanders became extensively involved in corrupt practices, but of course the ZNA's Fifth Brigade of the early 1980s was the first and still the most dramatic example of unprofessional behaviour by the army, here in the sense of violent partisanship.
11. On youth militia, see Solidarity Peace Trust (2003). Also see Scarnecchia's careful exploration (2006) of parallels between Zanu(PF)'s political uses of the youth militia and the Fascist *squadistri* of 1920s Italy.
12. For a rigorous discussion of the terrible costs of Operation Murambatsvina for people's lives and livelihoods, see Potts (2006) and the large and growing literature she reviews.

References

Alexander, Jocelyn. 2006. *The Unsettled Land: State-Making and the Politics of Land in Zimbabwe, 1893-2003*. Oxford: James Currey.
Alexander, Jocelyn and JoAnn McGregor. 2006. Veterans, Violence and Nationalism in Zimbabwe. In *States of Violence: Politics, Youth and Memory in Contemporary Africa*, eds. Edna Bay and Donald Donham. Charlottesville, VA: University of Virginia Press.
Alexander, Jocelyn, JoAnn McGregor and Terence Ranger. 2000. *Violence and Memory: One Hundred Years in the 'Dark Forests' of Matabeleland*. Oxford: James Currey.
Alexander, Jocelyn and Blessing-Miles Tendi. 2008. La Violence et les Urnes: le Zimbabwe en 2008. *Politique Africaine*. 111.
Bhebe, Ngwabi and Terence Ranger (eds.). 1996. *Society in Zimbabwe's Liberation Struggle*. Oxford: James Currey.
Bond, Patrick and J. Manyanya. 2003. *Zimbabwe's Plunge: Exhausted Nationalism, Neocolonialism and the Search for Social Justice*. Harare: Weaver Press.
CCJP/LRF. 1997. *Breaking the Silence, Building True Peace: A Report on the Disturbances in Matabeleland and the Midlands, 1980-1988*. Harare: CCJP/LRF.
Fontein, Joost. Forthcoming. Anticipating the Tsunami: Rumours, Planning and the Arbitrary State in Zimbabwe. *Africa*.
Gibbon, Peter (ed.). 1995. *Structural Adjustment and the Working Poor in Zimbabwe: Studies on labour, women, informal sector workers and health*. Uppsala: Nordiska Afrikainstitutet.
Government of Zimbabwe. 2003. *Report of the Presidential Land Review Committee on the Implementation of the Fast Track Land Reform Programme, 2000-2002*, Chairman Charles M. B. Utete. Harare.
Hammar, Amanda and Brian Raftopoulos. 2003. Zimbabwe's Unfinished Business: Rethinking Land, State and Nation. In *Zimbabwe's Unfinished Business: Rethinking Land, State and Nation in the Context of Crisis*, eds. Amanda Hammar, Brian Raftopoulos and S. Jensen. Harare: Weaver Press.
Hammar, Amanda, Brian Raftopoulos and S. Jensen (eds). 2003. *Zimbabwe's Unfinished Business: Rethinking Land, State and Nation in the Context of Crisis*. Harare: Weaver Press.
Kagoro, Brian. 2004. Constitutional Reform as Social Movement: A critical narrative of the constitution-making debate in Zimbabwe, 1997-2000. In *Zimbabwe: Injustice and Political Reconciliation*, eds. Brian Raftopoulos and Tyrone Savage. Cape Town: Institute for Justice and Reconciliation.
Kriger, Norma. 1992. *Zimbabwe's Guerrilla War. Peasant Voices*. Cambridge: Cambridge University Press.
——. 1995. The Politics of Creating National Heroes: The Search for Political Legitimacy and National Identity. In *Soldiers in Zimbabwe's Liberation War*, eds. Ngwabi Bhebe and Terence Ranger. London: James Currey.
——. 2003. *Guerrilla Veterans in Post-War Zimbabwe: Symbolic and Violent Politics*. Cambridge: Cambridge University Press.
——. 2005. Zanu(PF) Strategies in General Elections, 1980-2000: Discourse and Coercion. *African Affairs* 104 (414): 1-34.
LeBas, Adrienne. 2008. 'The Politics of Collapse: Political Responses to Violence and Displacement in Zimbabwe'. Paper presented at the conference 'Political Economies of Displacement in Post-2000 Zimbabwe', Johannesburg, 9-11 June.
Mandaza, Ibbo (ed.). 1986. *Zimbabwe: The Political Economy of Transition, 1980-1986*. Dakar: CODESRIA.
Mandaza, Ibbo and Lloyd Sachikonye (eds). 1991. *The One Party State and Democracy*. Harare: SAPES Trust.
Matondi, Prosper B. and Themba C. Khombe with Norman R. Moyo, Gospel M. Matondi and Manase Chiweshe. 2008. *The Land Reform and Resettlement Programme in Mangwe District, Matabeleland South Province*. Harare: Centre for Rural Development, University of Zimbabwe, and Institute of Rural Technologies, National University of Science and Technology.
Mavedzenge, B. Z., J. Mahenehene, F. Murambarimba, I. Scoones and W. Wolmer. 2008. The Dynamics of Real Markets: Cattle in Southern Zimbabwe following Land Reform. *Development and Change* 39 (4): 613-39.
McGregor, JoAnn. 2002. The Politics of Disruption: War Veterans and the Local State in Zimbabwe. *African Affairs* 101 (402): 9-37.
Moyo, Sam. 1994. *Economic Nationalism and Land Reform in Zimbabwe*. Harare: SAPES Books.
——. 2000. *Land Reform and Structural Adjustment in Zimbabwe: Land Use Changes in the Mashonaland Provinces*. Uppsala: Nordiska Afrikainstitutet.
——. 2001. The Land Occupations Movement and Democratisation in Zimbabwe: Contradictions of Neoliberalism. *Millennium: Journal of International Studies* 30 (2): 311-30.
Moyo, Sam and Paris Yeros. 2005. Land Occupations and Land Reform in Zimbabwe: Towards the National Democratic Revolution. In *Reclaiming the Land: The Resurgence of Rural movements in Africa, Asia and Latin America*, eds. Sam Moyo and Paris Yeros. London: Zed Books.
Ndlovu-Gatsheni, Sabelo. 2006. Nationalist-Military Alliance in Zimbabwe and the Fate of Democracy. *African Journal of Conflict Resolution* 6 (1): 49-80.
Phimister, Ian and Brian Raftopoulos. 2004. Mugabe, Mbeki and the Politics of Anti-Imperialism. *Review of African Political Economy* 31 (101): 385-400.
——. 2007. Desperate Days in Zimbabwe. *Review of African Political Economy* 34 (113): 573-80.

Potts, Deborah. 2000. Urban Unemployment and Migrants in Africa: Evidence from Harare, 1985-94. *Development and Change* 31 (4): 879-910.

——. 2006. "Restoring Order"? Operation Murambatsvina and the Urban Crisis in Zimbabwe. *Journal of Southern African Studies* 32 (2): 273-92.

——. 2007. City Life in Zimbabwe at a Time of Fear and Loathing: Urban Planning, Urban Poverty and Operation Murambatsvina. In *Cities in Contemporary Africa*, eds M. Murray and G. Myers. Basingstoke: Palgrave.

Raftopoulos, Brian. 1999. Problematising Nationalism in Zimbabwe: A Historiographical Review. *Zambezia* 26 (2): 115-34.

——. 2001. The Labour Movement and the Emergence of Opposition Politics in Zimbabwe. In *Striking Back: The Labour Movement and the Post-Colonial State in Zimbabwe 1980-2000*, eds. Brian Raftopoulos and Lloyd Sachikonye. Harare: Weaver Press.

——. 2003. The State in Crisis: Authoritarian Nationalism, Selective Citizenship and Distortions of Democracy in Zimbabwe. In *Zimbabwe's Unfinished Business: Rethinking Land, State and Nation in the Context of Crisis*, eds. Amanda Hammar, Brian Raftopoulos, and S. Jensen. Harare: Weaver Press.

——. 2004. Nation, Race and History in Zimbabwean Politics. In *Zimbabwe: Injustice and Political Reconciliation*, eds. Brian Raftopoulos and Tyrone Savage. Cape Town: Institute for Justice and Reconciliation.

——. 2006. Reflections on Opposition Politics in Zimbabwe: The Politics of the Movement for Democratic Change (MDC). In *Reflections on Opposition Politics in Zimbabwe*, eds Brian Raftopoulos and Karin Alexander. Cape Town: Institute for Justice and Reconciliation.

Raftopoulos, Brian and Ian Phimister. 2004. Zimbabwe Now: The Political Economy of Crisis and Coercion. *Historical Materialism* 12 (4): 355-82.

Ranger, Terence (ed.). 2003. *The Historical Dimensions of Democracy and Human Rights in Zimbabwe. Vol II: Nationalism, Democracy and Human Rights*. Harare: University of Zimbabwe Publications.

——. 2004. Nationalist Historiography, Patriotic History and the History of the Nation: The Struggle over the Past in Zimbabwe. *Journal of Southern African Studies* 30 (2): 215-34.

——. 2006. The Meaning of Urban Violence in Africa: Bulawayo, Southern Rhodesia, 1890-1960. *Cultural and Social History* 32 (2): 193-228.

Rich Dorman, Sara. 2003. NGOs and the Constitutional Debate in Zimbabwe: From inclusion to exclusion. *Journal of Southern African Studies* 29 (4): 845-64.

Rutherford, Blair. 2001. *Working on the Margins: Black Workers, White Farmers in Postcolonial Zimbabwe*. London: Zed Books.

——. 2003. Belonging to the Farm(er): Farm Workers, Farmers and the Shifting Politics of Citizenship. In *Zimbabwe's Unfinished Business: Rethinking Land, State and Citizenship in the Context of Crisis*, eds. Amanda Hammar, Brian Raftopoulos and S. Jensen. Harare: Weaver Press.

Sachikonye, Lloyd. 2003. 'The Situation of Commercial Farm Workers after Land Reform in Zimbabwe'. Report prepared for the Farm Community Trust of Zimbabwe, May.

Saunders, Richard. 2000. *Never the Same Again: Zimbabwe's Growth Toward Democracy 1980-2000*. Harare: Open Society Institute of Southern Africa.

Scarnecchia, Tim. 2006. The "Fascist Cycle" in Zimbabwe, 2000-2005. *Journal of Southern African Studies* 32 (2): 221-38.

——. 2008. *The Urban Roots of Democracy and Political Violence in Zimbabwe: Harare and Highfield, 1940-1964*. Rochester, NY: University of Rochester Press.

Selby, Angus. 2006. 'Commercial Farmers and the State: Interest Group Politics and Land Reform in Zimbabwe'. DPhil thesis, University of Oxford.

Solidarity Peace Trust. 2003. National Youth Training Service: 'Shaping Youth in a truly Zimbabwean Manner'. An overview of youth militia training and activities in Zimbabwe, October 2000- August 2003. Johannesburg, SPT, 5 September.

——. 2008. *Punishing Dissent, Silencing Citizens: The Zimbabwe Elections 2008*. Johannesburg: SPT.

Stoneman, Colin (ed.). 1981. *Zimbabwe's Inheritance*. London: Macmillan.

——. (ed.). 1988. *Zimbabwe's Prospects: Issues of Race, Class, State and Capital in Southern Africa*. London: Macmillan.

Tendi, Blessing-Miles. 2008. 'Zimbabwe's Third Chimurenga: The Use and Abuse of History'. DPhil thesis, University of Oxford.

Triulzi, A. 2006. Public History and the Re-writing of the Nation in Postcolonial Africa. *Afriche e Oriente* 8 (2): 7-35.

Werbner, Richard (ed.). 1998. *Memory and the Postcolony: African Anthropology and the Critique of Power*. London: Zed Books.

Worby, Eric. 2003. The End of Modernity in Zimbabwe? Passages from Development to Sovereignty. In *Zimbabwe's Unfinished Business: Rethinking Land, State and Citizenship in the Context of Crisis*, eds. Amanda Hammar, Brian Raftopoulos and S. Jensen. Harare: Weaver Press.

Yeros, Paris. 1999. Peasant Struggles for Land and Security in Zimbabwe: A Global Moral Economy at the Close of the Twentieth Century. Unpublished manuscript.

——. 2002. Zimbabwe and the Dilemmas of the Left. *Historical Materialism* 10(2): 3-15.

12

Conclusion
The Politics of African States in the Era of Democratisation

LINDSAY WHITFIELD
& ABDUL RAUFU MUSTAPHA

Reviewing the progress of African democratisation in 2001, Herbst (2001: 359) pointed out the difficulty analysts face in characterising the situation in most countries, as some democratic forms have no content and, in some instances, democratic content is found outside of the expected forms. This difficulty persists as we seek to draw together the central lessons from our case studies. Nevertheless, the balance of evidence suggests that our case-study countries can be classified into three broad categories:

(i)   countries in which democratisation is progressing, albeit with some problems (Ghana and South Africa);

(ii)   intermediate countries in which the democratic form is functioning, but is beset by major problems (Senegal, Nigeria, Kenya, Zambia and Mozambique); and

(iii) countries with a distinct authoritarian or militaristic drift, despite the enactment of democratic forms and rituals (Rwanda, Burundi and Zimbabwe).

Such an evaluation tilts our case studies on the side of the pessimists. Addressing the outcomes of African democratisation in this classificatory way, however, may shift our attention away from our emphasis on democratisation as a *process*. An emphasis on process dictates that we look at the ways in which democratic institutions and practices are built or undermined, and the norms and values through which such actions are legitimated. This process-tracing puts the emphasis on trajectories and avoids the static conception implicit in outcomes.

In this Conclusion, we explore the processes in our case-study countries using the comparative method. In the first set of comparisons, we compare our country pairs, for example Nigeria and Ghana, in order to explore similarities and differences. This process should deepen the historical contextualisation of each casestudy. Our second set of comparisons is thematic and addresses the four key questions posed in the Introduction. Looking across the eleven country studies, we explore the answers suggested to our four key questions and how these answers illuminate our understanding of the process of African democratisation. Through this multi-layered comparative process, we intend to give greater depth to our individual case studies.

Comparing Country Trajectories

Comparing our country pairs has the advantage of situating their experiences in a familiar historical and geo-political context that brings into sharp relief the achievements, problems, and failures of each country set against the experience of the other.

Senegal and Côte d'Ivoire

Senegal and Côte d'Ivoire shared a similar colonial experience under the French empire in West Africa. Both gaining independence in 1960, the two countries also shared a similar trajectory in the immediate post-independence period with the establishment of stable one-party states under the *Parti Socialiste* (PS) in Senegal and the *Parti Démocratique de la Côte Ivoire* (PDCI) in Côte d'Ivoire. However, their paths began to diverge in the 1980s and then sharply in the 1990s as Senegal continued on its gradualist approach to political liberalisation while Côte Ivoire faced a succession crisis followed by violent and exclusionary multiparty politics that eventually culminated in civil war. How do we explain this divergence in the trajectories of the countries? The answer can be found in the different formal and informal linkages developed in the post-colonial period to connect the state and society, and the implications of those linkages during the democratisation process. Secondly, the Senegalese political party system was more developed and dynamic than the Ivorian system. Senegal therefore experienced a greater institu-tionalisation of state-society linkages, while in Côte d'Ivoire the linkages were more elitist, ethnic and personalised around President Houphouet-Boigny.

In Senegal, democratisation was a gradual process beginning in the late 1970s when the one-party state was replaced with a limited version of competitive party politics and the independence leader Senghor voluntarily left office. In contrast, democratisation in Côte d'Ivoire was abrupt, with multiparty elections held in 1990, as the result of internal crises (economic crisis and an ageing Houphouet-Boigny) combined with external pressures (demands for political liberalisation from France and the World Bank). While Senegal had been democratising since the 1980s through political liberalisation and competitive elections, the PS remained the only ruling party. Only after the 2000 elections did the country experience an alternation in the ruling party with the victory of Abdoulaye Wade, leader of the *Parti Démocratique Sénégalais* (PDS), and the formation of a coalition government led by the PDS. In contrast, although the PDCI in Côte d'Ivoire won the 1990 elections with a huge margin, the government responded to organised protest over the state of the economy with violent suppression. In the absence of a culture of political pluralism and dissent, the process of democratisation led to a cycle of state-sanctioned violence against protestors and the increasing use of reciprocal violence by protestors. To understand why, we need to look at the different forms of political mobilisation and patronage used to maintain support for the PS and PDCI.

Côte d'Ivoire saw the institutionalisation of a particular type of one-party state. Houphouet-Boigny produced a class of technocratic elites through the provision of educational opportunities for the gifted few from all ethnic backgrounds, and ensured that they supported the PDCI through his regulation of opportunities for jobs and enrichment. He used state-controlled patronage to build an elite loyal to him personally and a national bourgeoisie capable of acting as a class of local investors and entrepreneurs in an economy dominated by foreign capital. This was the post-colonial model of Houphouet-Boigny—an economy that remained open to foreign investment and an administration that still relied on foreign expertise, but a deliberate strategy of building up an indigenous class to partner with foreign capital and to eventually take over from the expatriates. But it was also a model in which he retained personalised control. And while there was a deliberate attempt at ethnic balancing within the emergent elite, this balancing was built on a notion of the hierarchy of ethnic rights. Similar to most African countries, he used the proliferation of parastatal organisations to promote a national bourgeoisie that was at the same time a political client of the ruling party. Thus, patronage structures linked a politico-economic elite to the party-state. Social investments in education and infrastructure were used to maintain the political support of the urban and rural masses, but this investment hinged on the high economic growth experienced in Côte d'Ivoire.

In Senegal, however, the structures that developed to mobilise political support for the PS evolved in a different direction, drawing on the patron-client relations between Muslim brotherhoods (marabouts) and peasant producers, on the one hand, and linking these marabouts to the party through patronage, on the other. In Senegal, therefore, the post-colonial state had a greater rooting in the culture and psychology of the population. The fall of the PS during the 2000 elections was the product of several factors that came together in the right combination at the right time. First, the opposition parties managed to present a unified front. Second, there was massive societal mobilisation for the opposition, especially by the youth in urban areas. Third, the crisis in the groundnut economy combined with economic liberalisation and privatisation under structural adjustment in the 1980s and 1990s to loosen the close relationship between the state, the marabouts and the peasants and weakened the state's capacity to distribute patronage.

Changes in the political economy of both Senegal and Côte d'Ivoire significantly affected the viability of the post-colonial model developed in both countries. Since the decline of the groundnut economy, the Senegalese economy has been restructured around migration, remittances and foreign aid. This restructuring has had contradictory effects. It has reduced the grip of the state on society, at the same time that it has allowed the PDS government under President Wade to rebuild the dominant party rule of the PS era. Economic growth is fuelled by consumption made possible through remittances and foreign aid, while productive sectors decline. This 'de-localisation' of the economy stems from the erosion of the earlier social contract based on the distribution of state resources through patron-client relations and the provision of social services, and its replacement with migration as a social safety-net and as an exit option for young people caught between non-employment-generating growth and the fragility of social services.

In Côte d'Ivoire, the post-colonial model was one of state-run capitalism based on foreign capital (mainly French) and a national bourgeoisie (re)produced through the state. This model produced high economic growth, which became unsustainable when the government continued to increase public investments as the cocoa price declined from 1980 to 1993. The result was a fiscal crisis and a contraction of employment. The patronage structure for the elite came under attack, as elite social mobility, previously guaranteed through education and state jobs, ground to a halt. It is in this context of shocks to the post-colonial model that democratisation took place. Democratisation in 1990 allowed students and other affected urban groups to protest against these effects of structural adjustment, grievances with which opposition political parties aligned themselves. It also allowed dissent against the post-colonial model itself by those who wished to see it reformed or overthrown. These demands, not just for entitlements, but for the reconfiguration of the social contract took place in the context of economic crisis, a succession struggle within the dominant party, and a political system developed around the personality of the President and lacking in institutionalised mechanisms for resolving political conflicts. This combination proved volatile.

In the struggle to succeed Houphouet-Boigny, the explicit politics of ethnic exclusion started during the 1995 elections with the introduction of a new electoral law which introduced the policy of *Ivoirité* or Ivorianness. *Ivoirité* went directly against the post-colonial model of development in which dual citizenship was readily accorded to all West Africans who moved to the country and aided in its development. However, this exclusionary politics does have some origins in the Houphouet-Boigny model, a hierarchical model premised on the idea that some ethnic groups should rule over others because of their alleged superiority. The exclusionary politics continued with the passage of a land law in 1998 stipulating that only Ivorians could own land, revoking one of the pillars of the Houphouet-Boigny model and leading to violent conflict at the local level between native and non-native.

In Côte d'Ivoire, as in Zambia, the ethnic identities of political leaders became explicitly linked to political contestation under democratisation. While in Zambia this only affected Kaunda's qualification to run for office against the incumbent, in Côte d'Ivoire it took on another dimension that raised the stakes of ethnic politics. Northerners in general were discriminated against and declared non-citizens. This linking of ethnicity and citizenship, or the loss of political and economic rights for sections of the population, is similar to what occurred in Rwanda and Burundi and is central to the violence and civil war witnessed in these countries. The civil war in Côte d'Ivoire, which lasted from 2002 to 2007, was a conflict over the definition of rights and the notion of the nation: a war over how to restructure the post-colonial model created by Houphouet-Boigny. The rebels wanted to make the social contract more ethnically inclusive and less hierarchical, while the Gbagbo government only wanted to overturn 'Baoulé hegemony', whilst at the same time narrowing the definition of the nation.

Changes in Senegalese political economy also led to a restructuring of the post-colonial model, but one which saw the transformation of patronage structures rather than their violent overthrow. The coalition that won the 2000 elections quickly fell apart afterwards, and President Wade struggled to re-establish a political bloc under his control. Many parties left the government, so Wade turned to the old PS tactics of co-opting the opposition, which was made easier by the high degree of intra-party factional pressures and the proliferation of parties. Political mobilisation at elections is still based on clientelist relations between PDS leaders and smaller political entrepreneurs with their own following, but allegiances are no longer fixed as under the PS. Dahou and Foucher (Chapter 2) call this situation 'competitive clientelism', where opportunities for patronage are no longer concentrated, due to decentralisation and to aid that flows directly to local organisations and NGOs. Local patrons tap their own resources to mobilise clients, whom they use to bargain for influence and advantage up the political 'food chain'.

President Wade also sought to expand his political support base beyond clients within the PDS and his political coalition allies to include students, the press, and the trade unions, using group-based patronage. He also sought to gain new support in the rural areas by creating rival organisations to the peasant movements that have recently organised as an independent force in conflict with the government over land and agricultural policies. President Wade has also revived the linkage between the state and religious brotherhoods, drawing on a new generation of younger and ambitious religious brokers. In short, the PDS government's strategies for mobilising political support resemble those of the PS, simply under different conditions.

The fracturing of the ruling party and the positioning of the President as the arbiter of factional contests is a long-standing feature of Senegalese politics. It is also one that leads to the centralisation of power around the President and increased personalisation of that power. The French-inspired presidential political system created by the Constitution bequeaths a strong President and a weak Parliament, but this imbalance in the institutional design is exacerbated by the patronage politics of the executive. The fragile political base of the PDS and of President Wade has led to the re-centralisation of state power, to its concentration in the presidency and to increasing authoritarian tendencies such as the suppression of the media. These practices have significant negative implications for government accountability, particularly through the lack of executive oversight.

In sum, political practices in Senegal seem to display more continuity than change under President Wade's PDS government. The case of Senegal illustrates that democratisation does not proceed in a linear, teleological manner, but rather in fits and starts which may sometimes result in steps backward rather than forward. It also provides a theme that re-surfaces in some of the other case-study countries and is taken up in the concluding discussion: the fragility of political support for ruling parties and the effects of the political practices used by ruling parties and of presidents within those ruling parties to ensure their support.

The case of Côte d'Ivoire emphasises the importance of institutionalisation that can survive personalities. It also highlights the importance of a shared minimal conception of the political community. The debates about citizenship, because they define the political community, must be resolved before elections can become peaceful, stable means of elite circulation. Where membership of the political community is itself in doubt, elections may make things worse by highlighting the relative absence of national and cultural solidarity and by reproducing the bitter divisions in this highly fragmented society.

Ghana and Nigeria

Ghana and Nigeria also share a similar colonial experience under the British in West Africa and a similar post-independence experience of political instability at the hands of multiple interventions by the military that resulted in cycles of military regimes and re-civilianisation through the holding of elections. Like Senegal and Côte d'Ivoire, these two Anglophone countries have also taken divergent trajectories under democratisation in the 1990s.

One explanation for this divergence is the different degrees of elite consensus around democratisation and its institutionalisation in the two countries. Both experienced elite fragmentation as a result of the decolonisation trajectory and thus fierce intra-elite rivalry. This situation led to sections of the elites aligning with sections of the military to overthrow the government. Since the inauguration of their Fourth Republic in January 1993, the political elite in Ghana have become more integrated and have built a consensus around the electoral and constitution-based rules of the game, while the political elite in Nigeria have not. This elite consensus in Ghana was not achieved immediately. The first highly controversial election gave rise to an intra-party dialogue, which produced improvements in the 1996 election and again in the 2000 election. The peaceful standing down of

Rawlings at the end of his two terms as President and the peaceful transition of power from one party to another consolidated this elite consensus. In contrast, Nigeria's elections since its democratic transition in 1998-9 have been characterised by the deterioration in their quality as instruments for determining voters' preferences. Obasanjo even made a bid to remove the extant term limitation by asking for a third term. His attempt failed, but his party remained in power through coercive rigging of the 2007 election. The lack of elite consensus has had significant effects on the competence and legitimacy of the Nigerian electoral machinery, while Ghana's Electoral Commission has become a model in Africa.

However, this reading of the relative importance of elite cohesion in Ghana and Nigeria needs to be nuanced further, for while elite cohesion around the rules of the game in Ghana has promoted the institutionalisation of democracy, the *lack* of elite cohesion in Nigeria has also had the beneficial effect of blocking personalised authoritarian tendencies like presidential tenure extension. Disputes between competing factions of the elite have been vital for access to information by civil society organisations in their effort to impose accountability on different sections of the Nigerian state. Lack of elite cohesion has so far proved to be a bastion against authoritarian tendencies in Nigeria.

Another explanation for the divergence of the two countries is the higher level of party consolidation and identification in Ghana compared with Nigeria. In between military coups, multipartyism was revived in Ghana, each time awakening the party networks and loyalties among political elites grouped largely into two historic blocks formed in the period of decolonisation. These two party traditions (Nkrumah and Danquah/Busia traditions) have persisted through to the present day, giving Ghanaian party politics an ideological hue – 'liberal right' against 'populist left' – which is largely absent in Nigeria. The high degree of continuing party institutionalisation in Ghana has led to a more coherent party system and less personalisation in the patronage structure used by both main parties.

In contrast, Nigeria has a fragmented and non-institutionalised party system. The nature of colonial rule and the decolonisation process led to the emergence of competing nationalist movements and leaders centred around three ethno-regional blocs. Ghana also had competing nationalist movements based on ethno-regional blocs, but the cleavages were more pronounced in Nigeria. While Ghana's movements turned into nation-wide political party networks, Nigeria's nascent party networks withered under fifteen years of continuous military rule. The quick democratic transition in 1998-9 gave the political class little time to organise political parties, and the parties that formed were often an opportunistic melange of personalities and local notables referred to ominously as 'godfathers'. Three major political parties contested the 1999 elections, but the party system has disintegrated since then due to serious factionalism within each party, the mushrooming of parties with no social base, and the increased prominence of personal political networks and organisations operating within formal party structures. Parties use both personal networks and appeals to collective identities to mobilise political support. Oil wealth and presidential power have created a more individual patronage system. The stakes are high and the level of political violence and intimidation within the formal party structures is very high.

President Obasanjo attempted to solve the problem of his weak power base in the ruling People's Democratic Party after the 1999 elections by using presidential power to build a personal power base, similar to that of President Wade in

Senegal. Obasanjo manoeuvred between different political personalities and groupings that had come together under the PDP. He sought to secure his power by maintaining and using institutions and rules left over from military rule (a powerful presidency, a weak legislature, the use of force to contain challenges, the use of bribery and patronage to buy support), similar to the way President Wade used the tactics of the former hegemonic party in Senegal. Thus, as in Senegal after *alternance*, Nigeria under Obasanjo's first term exhibited strong institutional continuities with the previous regime that was the target of democratisation. This trend is not totally absent in Ghana, as the marginal victory of the New Patriotic Party after the 2000 elections and factionalism within the NPP led President Kufuor to adopt similar strategies of using presidential power to co-opt parliamentarians and party members in order to consolidate his political base – practices which had negative effects on the independence of Parliament and its role as a check on the executive. Unlike in Ghana, however, the collapse of the party system in Nigeria removed an important institutional restraint on officeholders, compounding the problem of lack of accountability caused by Obasanjo's authoritarian tendencies.

Ghana's democratic institutions are weak in terms of providing a check on executive power. This results from institutional design in the 1992 Constitution and the limited capacity of Parliament as an institution as well as from intentional practices on the part of the NPP and President Kufuor to quell any signs of an assertive, independent Parliament. However, the counterpart institutions in Nigeria fared much worse under Obasanjo, but have shown some signs of recovery since 2007 under President Yar' Adua. President Obasanjo's second term in office from 2003 saw some major institutional changes, but changes not in favour of democratisation. The division of powers horizontally within the federal government, and vertically between federal and state governments, came under severe strain. Furthermore, elected State Governors replicated Obasanjo's centralised and personalised 'military' style of governance at the State level, compounding the accountability deficit within the political system. Accountability at the State and local government levels continues to flow upwards, rather than in the direction of the electorate – but this is something with which Ghana is also struggling. Decentralisation in Ghana has moved government closer to the people, but the institutional design in which the heads of District Assemblies are appointed by the President means that local governments are ultimately answerable to the President.

Again, while Ghana's seemingly successful democratisation still faces challenges of accountable government through effective state-society linkages, Nigeria's challenges in this area are more formidable. In Ghana, patronage between voters and politicians is increasingly impersonal and collective, with voters demanding socio-economic development in the form of generalised benefits for their communities. But citizen-politician linkages are still plagued by a general lack of information about the incumbent party's performance and policies and about the contesting parties' policies and plans. This information deficit stems partly from limited public access to information on the government, partly from poor access to the media in rural areas and small towns (especially in the northern part of the country) and partly from high levels of illiteracy (especially in rural areas). In Nigeria, formal institutional linkages between the state and society atrophied under military rule. Oil rents created a further divide, as the government did not need to legitimise the extraction of taxes and citizens had limited ability to scrutinise the use of state revenue. The erosion of links between governance, representation and accountability in Nigeria led increasingly to a politics of place, ethnicity or religion as a way to gain patronage from powerful individuals and political blocs within the state.

Nigeria has not witnessed much change in its political economy since the discovery of oil in the 1970s. Democratisation has led to greater decentralisation of oil revenue to State and local governments, but although there is now more money, it has not had much impact on social and economic conditions for the majority of the population due to non-accountable governance structures. At the federal level, President Obasanjo's macroeconomic reforms have gone hand in hand with authoritarian politics, with the limited gains of economic reforms being used to justify authoritarian political practices. Furthermore, Nigeria's oil wealth has tended to shield it from external pressure. In the run-up to the bungled 2007 elections, the Independent National Electoral Commission (INEC) deliberately refused to accept grants from some foreign donors so as to protect its independence from them, but apparently not from the incumbent government. Nigeria, with its oil revenue, retains a high degree of policy independence vis-à-vis international donors and agencies.

In contrast to Nigeria, Ghana's political economy has been dominated by aid dependence since the early 1980s to meet its foreign-exchange needs (for imports and debt servicing). Aid dependence has had significant but contradictory effects on democratisation in Ghana. As in Senegal, aid has provided large inflows that have revitalised not only the budget and domestic spending, but also the clientelist politics of the early independence period. Another effect has been the extensive participation of donors in formulating and implementing policies, with the effect of making it more difficult to hold the government accountable for policies and their outcomes and leading governments to cede some responsibility for development strategies and policies to donors (although this appears to be changing since 2006).

In sum, the different political economies of Nigeria and Ghana may also explain their divergent political trajectories. The struggle to gain control of a centralised presidency, backed with large oil revenues and enormous discretionary powers, has undermined tendencies towards consensus building within Nigeria's factionalised elites. In Ghana, by contrast, a significant degree of economic liberalisation, dependence on the approval of aid donors, and the absence of a highly valued, centrally controlled export commodity have lowered the stakes of electoral competition and given elites more incentives to play by the rules of the electoral game.

Kenya and Zambia

Like Senegal and Côte d'Ivoire, Kenya and Zambia are former one-party states, but they prove that, even within the one-party-state typology, patronage structures and state formation differed significantly. Kenya and Zambia are interesting to compare because they also share a similar political trajectory after independence in 1964, but then their trajectories diverged after democratic transitions through multiparty elections in the early 1990s. Cheeseman (2006) has argued that this divergence is due to institutional variations in the one-party state that was constructed in each country. In particular, differences in patronage structures developed to support the ruling party affected centre-local relations and forms of political mobilisation and continued to do so even under multiparty politics.

The personalised and competitive patronage structures that developed in Kenya under one-party rule enabled the President and his advisers to construct a tier of local patrons that could effectively mobilise vast constituencies through the ruling Kenya African National Union. Power resided with individual patrons whose loyalty provided the one-party regime with political stability in the 1970s and 1980s. The one-party system allowed citizens to choose their patrons in elections that regulated competition within the ruling party. This form of political mobilisation around local patrons and the expectations of constituents that their patrons will deliver to the community give electoral politics in Kenya its ethnic flare, as it emphasises one's place or locality and one's links to the local patron. In contrast, the institutionalised and non-competitive patronage structures that developed in Zambia under one-party rule restricted the reach of the ruling United National Independence Party and its capacity for mass mobilisation (Cheeseman 2006). When the party structures in both countries began to atrophy in the absence of multiparty elections, the executive in Kenya responded by relying on personal connections to link the centre to the locality, while the Zambian executive retained centralised control and created top-down structures. KANU party structures survived, but UNIP's did not, and it was forced to rely on the support of urban workers.

The circumstances under which democratisation occurred in Kenya and Zambia differ in ways that are important for the subsequent pattern of political change and continuity in each country. In Kenya, the trigger for the downfall of the Moi state in particular, and the one-party system in general, was due to the defection of senior patrons from the ruling party KANU. The rigging of the 1988 one-party elections undermined the institution which played a major part in legitimising the political system and leading those who lost their seats to join the campaign for multiparty politics. In Zambia in contrast, UNIP party structures were defunct and many prominent leaders had already abandoned the party or had been expelled from it. It was only when organised labour came out in opposition to the one-party state that the game was up. The context for this move by the labour movement was the severe economic crisis and the removal of food subsidies that triggered mass protests in 1990. KANU was therefore better equipped than UNIP to manage the transition to multiparty politics and to win the founding elections. KANU party structures were still able to mobilise support, while UNIP's were not. Thus, the Movement for Multiparty Democracy easily defeated UNIP, while KANU could still draw on its network of local patrons to deliver the support of their constituencies.

Moi and KANU's eventual fall from power flows from the trajectory outlined above. While the political opposition in Kenya was fragmented (around individual political leaders – big patrons) in the 1992 and 1997 elections, the two major opposition parties headed by Kibaki and Odinga formed an alliance (NaRC) for the 2002 elections. At the same time, KANU fragmented around the issue of the succession to Moi. After winning the elections, NaRC split apart because President Kibaki failed to follow through with his promise to distribute power to other factions, in particular Odinga and his party. This fracture solidified around the constitutional reform process and referendum in 2005, with Odinga forming an opposition movement that would become the main challenger to Kibaki and his party in the 2007 presidential and parliamentary elections. However, political mobilisation has changed somewhat under the Kibaki government. Its promise to reform *harambee* has seen the replacement of personalised patron-client networks between MPs and their local constituents with more impersonal patronage mechanisms such as the Constituency Development Fund and the creation of new districts, a tactic also used in Ghana under Kufuor. It remains to be seen if the Constituency Development Fund will lead to a new form of politics and centre-local relationships.

Recent developments in Zambia's electoral politics also follow from the country's decolonisation trajectory and seem to be repeating history, with the MMD party structures in the 1990s suffering a fate similar to that of UNIP. After its victory, the MMD was transformed into a political machine, replicating the methods used by UNIP under the one-party state. It won the 1996 and 2001 elections with a decreasing percentage of the vote (and which was less than 50 per cent), but with the discredited UNIP as its only major opposition. There was no alternative policy platform until the rise of the Patriotic Front in the 2006 elections. The PF espoused a populist, neo-nationalist development discourse, and drew on the same network of mineworkers as the MMD did in 1990. The presidential candidate of this new party gained 29 per cent of the vote and the party won every urban seat. Compared with Kenya, ethno-regional politics overlaps with social and economic grievances, preventing ethnicity from being a dominant form of political mobilisation in Zambia. Urban workers remain the base of any government in Zambia, which has a higher degree of urbanisation compared with other African countries.

Despite these differences, the general structure of the one-party state has left both countries with similar legacies concerning the structure of the state and formal political institutions. Both countries developed what Allen (1995) calls executive-bureaucratic states, but what Cheeseman (2006) has argued are more correctly described as centralised-executive states, because while they share the trait of centralisation of power in the executive, they differ in bureaucratic and party capacity. The new parties that took over from the old one-party-era ones (MMD and NaRC, respectively) both promised constitutional reform while in opposition, but then failed to deliver once in power (and thus in control of the centralised-executive state). In Zambia, the Parliament is not able to act as a constraint on the power of the executive, partly because legally its powers are weak and partly because MPs are unwilling to use the limited powers they do have and can be bought off through appointments. More supervision comes through societal accountability than through institutions of horizontal account-ability, as the successful societal campaigns to prevent Chiluba from seeking a third presidential term and then demands for constitutional reform illustrate.

In Kenya, the Kibaki government intervened in the constitutional reform process to ensure that the draft new Constitution did not reduce the power of the President; thus the 'no' vote in the constitutional referendum was a win-win situation for the government. In the Kenyan political system, the distribution of resources that come from the state is seen by constituencies as coming from the personal largesse of MPs. Thus, there is less societal accountability than in Zambia due to the network of patron-client relations and the norm that MPs are responsible for local development. This patron-client contract, combined with ethno-regional cleavages, crowds out the emergence of alternative forms of political mobilisation and contestation in Kenya.

After the disputed December 2007 election results in Kenya, the opposition political elites decided not to use the formal political institutions, which are mediated by established processes and laws, to solve the conflict. Instead, they sought to use popular mobilisation and even violence to force the new government to listen to their demands, partly because they did not trust the formal political institutions to mediate the conflict impartially in a speedy manner. Both presidential candidates had engaged in fraudulent electoral practices, which reveals a lack of consensus among the political elite to play by the rules of the democratic game. While the failure to reform formal institutions has contributed to political instability in Kenya, the current crisis is also the legacy of the instrumental use of violence in the 1990s. In contrast, even if the next Zambian elections are an extremely close contest between the MMD and the Patriotic Front and if the constitutional reforms do not go through, one would not expect the political instability and violence witnessed in Kenya because Zambia does not share this legacy of institutionalised violence.

As with the other countries discussed so far, developments in political economy have played an important role in shaping the democratisation processes in both countries. In Zambia, sharp economic decline in the 1970s reduced the ability of the UNIP one-party state to deliver patronage, and worsening economic conditions as well as discontent with the structural adjustment policies led to the rise of the MMD. Similarly, the rise of the Patriotic Front stems from discontent with the economy and the government's economic policies, particularly the selling off of strategic assets to foreign companies and the role of the Chinese in the mining sector. Economic decline triggered by the fall in copper prices and a heavy debt burden led to a high degree of aid dependence and the ceding of responsibility for economic policy to donors, thus undermining government accountability. The recent dramatic rise in copper prices is reducing donor dependence and leading to changes in economic policy, at the same time as the rise of real political opposition is pressuring the MMD government to be more accountable to domestic constituencies for its economic policies. In Kenya, low economic growth and the freezing of aid by donors led to the end of the one-party state. But subsequently Moi and Kibaki used resumed aid flows to improve the economy and revitalise the patronage structures. Kibaki's management of the economy, and the impressive growth of the Nairobi Stock Exchange, have won him the support of donors (especially the World Bank), even in the face of the 2007 election controversy.

South Africa and Mozambique

Unlike the paired comparisons so far, South Africa and Mozambique do not share similar colonial experiences and post-independence trajectories. However, their histories are intertwined in that apartheid South Africa supported the rebel group Renamo against the Socialist Frelimo government in a Cold War battle that began only a few years after Mozambique's independence from Portugal in 1975. This 'war of destabilisation' came to an end only with the signing of a peace accord in 1992. South Africa has had a markedly different historical experience, which saw racial segregation under British colonial rule give way to a more staunch form of racial discrimination and exclusion under the Afrikaner National Party from 1948 to 1990. However, a closer look reveals that the two countries share important features. Both held their first ever multiparty elections in 1994, and both engaged in liberation struggles and have ruling parties that were originally armed liberation movements. In both countries, democratisation coincides with a fundamental paradigm shift in the political system: from Socialism in Mozambique and from apartheid in South Africa. The key difference is that Frelimo used democratisation in Mozambique as a strategy to maintain itself in power, while the ANC in South Africa used democratisation to win power through majority rule.

South Africa has a dominant party system, in which there is little chance of opposition parties securing enough votes to oust the ANC in the near future. In contrast, Frelimo in Mozambique did almost lose the Presidency to the opposition leader in the 1999 election and had to ensure its victory in the 2004 election by using fraud and violence. However, the party systems in the two countries have a high degree of party consolidation. Even though opposition parties in South Africa have changed names and shifted alliances, they continue to capture about the same percentage of the vote, and Mozambique basically has a two-party system. This high degree of party consolidation stems from the fact that, in both countries, the liberation movement background means that factional struggles are maintained *within* the ruling dominant party; these parties are essentially coalitions, but the factions hardly lead to splinter parties as in the case of Kenya, Senegal, or Côte d'Ivoire. Frelimo consists of several factions, which have been identified not on the basis of personalities, but rather on ideology and policy. The power struggles within the party over who would succeed Chissano saw the 'national developmentalist' faction come to power, allied with the 'ethical' faction, at the expense of the 'predatory' faction. However, the expected rupture with Chissano's rule, given this adjustment in the ruling party, has not materialised.

In South Africa, the ANC is also a coalition of factions based around different group interests – organised labour, the Communist Party, and black business. The factional politics of the ANC might best be seen in terms of a contest between a 'populist' faction identified with Jacob Zuma, and a 'technocratic' faction, identified with Thabo Mbeki. The interest groups and factions overlap. The populist faction is allied to sections of the trade unions and the Communist Party, while the technocratic faction is allied to black business and top functionaries of the state; both coalesce around the personalities of Zuma and Mbeki respectively. But both factions share key policies such as the commitment to neo-liberal macroeconomic management and black empowerment. The power of different social groups and factions has changed over time and can take different forms, but these groups have tended to articulate their interests through the ANC rather than in a breakaway party. However, Zuma's defeat of Mbeki in the ANC presidential contest in Polokwane in December 2007, the forced resignation of Mbeki from the state presidency in September 2008, and the assumption of that presidency by Kgalema Motlanthe, all mark the supremacy of the Zuma faction within the ANC and the state. Since late 2008, the former Defence Minister under Mbeki, Mosiuoa Lekotu, has been leading moves to form a breakaway party by pro-Mbeki dissidents. While this may contribute to the deepening of democracy, as happened in India with the collapse of the dominant Congress Party, it may also herald a period of instability. It is difficult to be sanguine about the implications of these developments for democracy and political and economic stability in South Africa.

Although the two countries have different political systems as set out in their Constitutions – a strong presidential system in Mozambique and a parliamentary system in South Africa – they both exhibit a concentration of power in the executive branch of government as well as a centralisation of power around the Presidency. This is because the dominant party system in South Africa leads in practice to a hybrid parliamentary-presidential system, as the ANC's dominance undermines checks and balances at the federal level, undermines the autonomy of state and local levels of government, and increases presidential authority. Under

Mbeki, this centralisation of power has occurred alongside an intolerance of opposition both inside and outside the party.

The authoritarian tendencies of Presidents Mbeki and Guebuza might be explained by their backgrounds in the armed liberation movements and these movements' conception of their party as playing a vanguard role. However, the dominant party in Botswana has also shown authoritarian streaks (Good 1996; Taylor 2003), even though it did not engage in a liberation struggle. The Botswana Democratic Party has won every election since independence in 1965, and its dominance is arguably due to the electorate's vote of confidence in its successful management of the economy (despite extreme income inequality), since its elections have been free and fair (Maipose 2009). South Africa seems to be following in the dominant-party footsteps of Botswana, while Mozambique is doing so by force rather than by clear electoral mandates, since the 2004 elections were not free and fair, and the Frelimo government under President Guebuza has used state structures to neutralise the political opposition.

Developments in the political economy of South Africa and Mozambique have transformed the social character of both the ANC and Frelimo from their origins as liberation movements with largely Socialist ideologies. At independence, Frelimo embarked on a Socialist revolution but failed to get material support from the Soviet Union. By the early 1980s, several years into the civil war and in the context of domestic discontent, it embarked on political and economic reforms and then shifted toward the West and signed economic agreements with the Bretton Woods institutions. This shift towards political and economic liberalisation by the close of the 1980s was a strategic choice by Frelimo in order to remain in power. The country experienced high economic growth in the 1990s, but its economic strategy created few jobs and led to significant regional imbalances (with production mostly in the southern part of the country). In the context of unregulated economic liberalisation, factions of the political elite took advantage of new economic opportunities (legally and illegally), while income inequality increased dramatically. The rise of Guebuza and the developmental faction, which emphasised poverty reduction and state engagement in agriculture, was a response to the predatory accumulation tactics of the erstwhile ruling faction and the unmet expectations of the majority. By this time, however, the social character and political base of Frelimo had already been transformed from a party of workers and peasants to a party of the bureaucracy or state-based bourgeoisie (employees of the state and party administration). Perhaps this is why the Guebuza government has so far failed to change the economic dynamics of the country and the resulting patterns of personal and regional inequalities.

Like Frelimo, the ANC has become a party of black business and the black middle class. At first the ANC's economic strategy adopted in 1996 appeared to be pro-business, but by the late 1990s it was clear that it was pro-black business. Organised labour is powerful within the ANC, resulting in large parts of the economic strategy not being implemented, and public sector workers have benefited tremendously from the ANC's policies and actions. But in recent times, it is black business that has benefited most, as a result of ANC leadership and state officials being closely tied to new processes of capital accumulation. Because black capital is dependent on the state (as well as on established white capital), the ANC political elite do not allow much power to the left and would not go the way of Zimbabwe.

Rwanda, Burundi and Zimbabwe

Rwanda and Burundi are like the first pairs of countries: a set of similar cases sharing common colonial experiences and post-colonial trajectories. However, here we want to compare the experience of Rwanda and Burundi with that of Zimbabwe. Like the previous comparison between Mozambique and South Africa, Rwanda and Burundi, on the one hand, and Zimbabwe, on the other, appear to have little in common, but a closer look reveals that these countries share two features which have shaped their democratisation processes.

First, they share a pattern of deep social divisions and exclusionary politics. Under majoritarian rule in Zimbabwe since the end of the liberation war in 1980, the white minority is no longer a political elite, though it remains an economic power. Within the black elite, the only consensus is that 'nationalists' must rule, although there was an intra-black war in Matabeleland to decide which group of nationalists. Elites circulate within the Zanu-PF through periodic party elections, which provide a measure of accountability. Multiparty elections have, from the beginning, been marred by violence and intimidation. Beginning in the 1990s, diverse groups in society began to unite under the banner that the nationalist ticket does not give Zanu-PF the right to rule forever. Faced with mounting economic problems and internal political challenges, Zanu-PF opted for increased exclusion and an alliance with the war veterans. This option was highly contingent on historical factors, but it would probably have been difficult for Zanu-PF to stay on top of a broader political alliance. However, the power-sharing deal between Zanu-PF and the two factions of the MDC in 2008 has raised the possibility of a deconcentration of power within the state.

In Rwanda, Hutu-dominated military regimes from 1961 to 1994 practised ethnic discrimination and exclusion of the minority Tutsi from political power. State-sponsored violence was used to counter demands for greater political representation of the Tutsi population, including massacres of Tutsi by government troops in 1988. This systematic exclusion of the Tutsi only ended with the civil war that led to the overthrow of the Hutu government after the genocide of 1994, the ascendance of the Tutsi-dominated Rwandan Patriotic Front and the establishment of a power-sharing government. However, observers have noted the increasing 'Tutsification' of the current RPF government elected in 2003 amidst charges of intimidation of opponents and electoral irregularities, and Patricia Daley (Chapter 10) argues that the discriminatory state persists in Rwanda despite the post-genocide peace-building and democratisation.

Unlike in Rwanda, the Tutsi minority in Burundi held on to political power after independence through the use of the military. The Tutsi-dominated government used the 'Hutu threat' to exclude the Hutu majority from prominent roles in the political and economic spheres. A single-party dictatorship established in 1966 used violence to quell dissent. Democratic elections held in 1993 saw the election of a Hutu President who was assassinated shortly afterwards. The subsequent power-sharing government was then overthrown in a military coup and the former Tutsi leadership took control again. A long-drawn-out civil war ensued, ending only in 2000.

Despite the fact that ethnicity forms the fault line along which groups divide in Rwanda and Burundi, a substantial part of the political contestation and violence stems from regional and personal differences within each group of ethnic elites. In Rwanda, it was political infighting within the Hutu ruling party and Hutu elite around regional and ideological differences, especially around the democratic transition where some moderate Hutus sought an alliance with the RPF, which precipitated the genocide. There was also infighting within the Tutsi according to their different exile histories, and power struggles and policy divisions have emerged along these lines in the post-2003 government. In Burundi, intra-elite rivalries within the Tutsi population caused coups and counter-coups. In sum, the Hutu-Tutsi ethnic divide is not the only significant cleavage, but ethnic differences are the easiest to articulate and manipulate. In all three countries, deep social divisions and the dynamics of exclusionary politics lead to a process of democratisation characterised as much by force, violence and intimidation, as by formal rituals of electoral choice.

The second feature that this set of countries has in common is that the exclusionist governments have legitimised their political institutions and practices (formal and informal) with reference to history and political ideas. Ideas of patriotism and nationalism – the so-called 'Patriotic History' – define the boundaries of who is included and who is excluded in Zimbabwe. With the nationalist credo determining who rules and all contenders for the nationalist mantle co-opted or defeated, there is no need for multiparty elections to determine elite circulation. The single, narrow historical narrative produced by Zanu-PF addresses real grievances and popular memory, and meets the needs of the ruling party's political project. It also draws on the entrenchment of violent intolerance of dissent and disloyalty within the nationalist movement which is a legacy of the liberation struggle. The idea of liberation struggle is not just against the colonial power, but also against sell-outs among the black population. Similarly in Rwanda and Burundi, histories of oppression and dominance between Hutu and Tutsi during the colonial period are used to legitimise claims to power and for political mobilisation of Hutu and Tutsi populations. Politics is inexplicable in these three countries outside the framework of particular constructions of 'history'.

Thus, in Rwanda, Burundi and Zimbabwe, despite electoral democracy, the state itself became a tool of discrimination against significant portions of the population. In Zimbabwe, Zanu-PF initially had the legitimacy of being the liberation movement and the rightful ruler representing the black majority. The party also inherited a very effective state apparatus and professional civil service and retained its legitimacy through the effective delivery of social services. However, by the late 1990s, and rapidly after 2000, the logic of the Zimbabwean state was radically transformed. With a worsening economic crisis and the strictures of structural adjustment, the state became increasingly partisan as it strove to maintain control. Support for the party increasingly trumped merit as the basis for civil service recruitment. Those already in the public service were increasingly forced to carry out their jobs in a partisan manner. Zanu-PF began using the distribution of food aid, land and public services to maintain party loyalty. But it also increasingly mixed coercion with patronage, such that basic human rights were contingent on supporting the party. Zanu-PF now more closely resembles a totalitarian party where people are ruled through implicit or explicit terror, than one which relies solely on patronage as the key link with citizens.

In Rwanda and Burundi, the lack of political representation as a result of ethnic discrimination undermined the legitimacy of the state and caused political instability. Armed revolt became the only possible means for demanding an end to state repression and political exclusion. Given the history of exclusionary politics and the imbalance in the size of ethnic groups in these two countries, winner-takes-all democracy could not resolve the issues of representation. The democratisation process in the 1990s was highly contested and had violent repercussions, as in Côte d'Ivoire. The peace agreements brokered to end the civil war in Rwanda and Burundi determined the parameters for democratic governance, often balancing majoritarian principles with power-sharing provisions. While it sought to restructure the state to make it more representative, the power-sharing government in Burundi enabled rebel leaders to gain power. But this only provided incentives for the reproduction of insurgent violence as others took up arms to win political leverage. In Rwanda, there was not enough support for the peace agreement among all factions, and the democratisation process was halted by the genocide in 1994, but resumed by the RPF-led government in 1999.

Despite elections, issues of justice and reconciliation remain unresolved. The culture of impunity is a continuing problem. In Rwanda, the increasingly Tutsi-dominated government feels threatened by Hutu rebel incursions and their claims to power on the basis of ethnicity, while the majority Hutu population feels besieged. While Rwanda is trying to bring justice to the victims of the 1994 genocide, it is slowed by a judicial system seriously damaged in the genocide and the slow and costly international process at the International Court in Arusha, Tanzania. In Burundi there has been much immunity and little attempt at justice for fear of implicating current politicians on both sides of the political divide. On the other hand, the significance of ethnicity in Burundi has decreased since the election of a Hutu-majority power-sharing government, and most of the political contestation is within the Hutu elites, while Tutsi elites focus on capturing opportunities from economic liberalisation.

Thematic Comparisons: The Four Key Questions Revisited

Next we use the four key questions identified in the introductory chapter as guides to compare the experiences of all eleven countries and draw attention to common trends.

The Prevalence of Presidentialism

As many of our case studies demonstrate, democratisation in Africa has been marked by the persistence of presidentialism. Power continues to be centralised around the Presidency, and the executive branch of government continues to dominate the political system. Bratton *et al.* (2005: 19) argue along the same lines, suggesting that 'the task of dividing and distributing presidential power has barely begun'. Even where a new ruling party emerged in the 1990s, it tends to consolidate its power rather than be held in check by other institutions or interest groups. Although the degree to which power revolves around the President varies, across all countries discussed in this volume power is concentrated in the executive, and legislatures exercise limited power and thus act as weak checks on executive authority. But despite its pervasiveness, presidentialism often has features specific to each country's political history and culture. President Mbeki of South Africa has been described as a person with an 'egocentric view of his own epic place in history' (Seekings, Chapter 8). Most Nigerians will readily see a striking similarity in personality type with President Obasanjo. Yet the presidentialisms built and sustained under both leaders are quite different. In South Africa, the presidency has a large and resourced Policy Coordination and

Advisory body, along with five clusters of ministers, five presidential working groups and two international working groups. Though the Nigerian presidency has some of these features, it is more personalistic and less technocratic, with the person of Obasanjo at the hub of most government business.

The tendency to have strong executives and weak legislatures holds despite differences in state trajectories before democratisation and despite differences in levels of economic development, urbanisation and past political stability. So what accounts for this presidentialism? The country studies show that presidentialism stems from institutional design. In several countries, new Constitutions preserved the centralisation of power (as in Ghana and Mozambique), or the new Constitution was rushed through by the military just before the democratic transition (as in Nigeria), or a new Constitution was not even created before the democratic transition and the old one concentrated power in the executive (as in Kenya and Zambia). In Ghana and Senegal, lack of legislative capacity and the prerogative of the executive to initiate laws weakened the legislature. In Nigeria, on the other hand, long years of the absence of the legislature because of prolonged military rule undermined legislative capacity. In South Africa, the weak legislature results from a combination of electoral arrangements of proportional representation based on party lists under the control of party leaders and from the dominant party system which in practice undermines the checks and balances built into the Constitution. But in Zimbabwe, when the government failed to change the Constitution to concentrate more power in the executive, it just began to ignore the Constitution and created parallel state institutions.

The centralisation of power in the Presidency has raised the issue of constitutional reform to the top of the political agenda in several countries, resulting in constitutional review processes. In recent years the Constitution has become a focus of debate in Kenya, Zambia, Nigeria and Zimbabwe. Constitutional review is an important issue in these countries because, in paving the way for multiparty elections, KANU in Kenya and UNIP in Zambia resisted calls for radical constitutional change and only implemented very small changes in order to legalise opposition parties. As a result, the democratic transition carried over the Constitution of the one-party state, which conferred extensive powers on the executive. Both NaRC in Kenya and the MMD in Zambia promised to rewrite their Constitutions if they came to power, in order to promote civil liberties, enhance the distinction between party and state, and reduce the powers of the President. Once in power, however, Chiluba and then Mwanawasa of MMD and Kibaki of NaRC recognised the benefits of the powers they inherited and tried to shape the outcomes of the constitutional review processes to their continuing advantage. While Presidents Kibaki and Mwanawasa struggled to impose their will against pressure from mobilised groups in society, neither was forced to adopt constitutional changes that significantly reduce their powers. The tight elections of 2001 and 2006, in Kenya and Zambia respectively, only increased the importance of the advantages that incumbency confers during electoral competition, thus decreasing the ruling party's desire for constitutional reform. The constitutional review process similarly failed in Nigeria and Zimbabwe; in these latter cases, the executive sought, but failed, to re-write the Constitution to its advantage.

But institutional design is only part of the story. The prevalence of presidentialism is fundamentally linked to the structure of clientelist politics, particularly the first tier of elite clientelism. Elite clientelism takes strikingly similar forms across the country studies. Where presidents came to power through a coalition, as in the case of President Kibaki in Kenya and President Wade in Senegal, these leaders use the extensive powers of the President as glue to keep their unstable coalition together. In Nigeria, presidential power was instrumental in enhancing and consolidating the initially weak position of President Obasanjo within the ruling party. Even in the case of an institutionalised party system such as in Ghana, weak or challenged authority within the ruling party can also lead the President to use the distribution of public offices to reward politicians loyal to the ruling party or to a faction of the ruling party and to punish those who are not loyal enough or too independent-minded. Anti-corruption agencies are often turned on uncooperative or recalcitrant members of the elite. Parastatals continue to be a source of prebends and patronage, but privatisation programmes in many countries have reduced the number of parastatals. It is clear that the concentration of power around the presidency still explains why the electoral contest is so tense, often leading to electoral fraud and violence. However, economic liberalisation, foreign aid, and increasing foreign investment have opened new opportunities for economic enrichment and social mobility for elites, and thus have reduced what is at stake at elections. This trend does not hold in oil-producing countries, such as Nigeria, which have even more at stake in elections.

But there are increasing signs that presidentialism is being slowly restrained in many countries. Firstly, limitation of the presidential term seems to be a major achievement of democratisation in Africa. Adherence to that constitutional principle can even be seen as a litmus test for the entrenchment of constitutionalism. While Presidents Nujoma of Namibia, Museveni of Uganda, Idriss Deby of Chad and Paul Biya of Cameroon managed to overturn the term limitations so as to extend their rule, Presidents Chiluba of Zambia and Obasanjo of Nigeria faced opposition which thwarted their ambitions at longevity in office. In several countries, presidents left quietly, as in Ghana and Kenya. In South Africa, Mbeki resigned at the behest of the ANC executive. Although the prevalence of bids for a third term is a worrying sign, the fact that some are being defeated and others restrained reveals the increasing sturdiness of constitutionalism as it confronts the monarchical tendency in African presidentialism. It is also significant that in countries like South Africa and Ghana, incumbent Presidents are not able to dictate who succeeds them. Instituting something akin to life presidencies is becoming more difficult.

A second source of restraint on presidentialism is societal. In South Africa, the trade union confederation COSATU successfully blunted the full implementation of GEAR, while the Treatment Action Campaign successfully used the courts to force the Mbeki government to reverse its position on the provision of anti-retroviral drugs for some categories of HIV/AIDS sufferers. Similarly, the Nigeria Labour Congress (NLC) and its civil society allies have been particularly successful in stopping the Obasanjo government from deregulating petroleum prices. And in Zambia, societal mobilisation in the media and civil society has been instrumental in setting the political agenda, including the defeat of Chiluba's bid for term extension. More recently, the breakdown of social order that accompanied the Kenyan elections of December 2007, regrettable as it is, nevertheless has had the positive effect of forcing President Kibaki to accede to the creation of the office of Prime Minster which he had stoutly resisted earlier. These constitutional and societal constraints are beginning to shape the political culture, and it is not surprising that Bratton *et al.* (2005: 275) found that 'an understanding of democracy that includes procedural constraints on the exercise of power is becoming woven into the popular political culture'. These slow and incremental changes to presidentialism across the continent are just as important as the durability and ubiquity of the institution.

Political Mobilisation and Clientelist Politics

All our case studies suggest that patronage is a significant factor in political mobilisation and the maintenance of party loyalty, but how does this relate to van de Walle's notion of intra-elite clientelism in the authoritarian era discussed in the introductory chapter? The Kenyan case study shows that clientelism in the one-party state could go beyond the elites and incorporate significant sections of society. The other cases reveal the significance of clientelism in building political support under authoritarian regimes. Where access to the clientelist system was more inclusive, it provided a means of social mobility for elites and the regulation of competition for access to public office, and thus a measure of political stability. That is why the one-party regimes of Senegal, Côte d'Ivoire, Zambia and Kenya delivered political stability. In contrast, political instability in countries such as Ghana and Nigeria stemmed from a more exclusionary system of elite clientelism in which the faction of the elite which controlled the state often excluded the other factions or took a disproportionate share of state resources.

But van de Walle over-generalises the intra-elite nature of authoritarian clientelism and underplays the extent to which patron-client networks could permeate the wider society, as in Kenya. We would therefore expand his thesis by emphasising that clientelist politics in Africa often has two levels – one intra-elite and the other societal. At one level, clientelism could bind elites to the political party or ruling coalition, and often directly to the Head of State. At a second level, clientelism could also bind citizens to local patrons. Ken Post (1963) and Chris Allen (1995) described this two-tiered clientelism as the most successful strategy used for winning the elections that were introduced in the terminal colonial period with little notice and required the mobilisation of huge new electorates. Our cases suggest that this two-tier clientelism applied again in many countries that reinstated multiparty elections after years, sometimes decades, of military or one-party rule. Voters were offered collective material benefits (roads, schools, water – modernising development) for their votes, while candidates and local elites were offered individual benefits (cash, access to import licences, credit, land) as well as the opportunity to present themselves as benefactors to their communities.

Van de Walle's thesis is also open to a second type of nuancing when we look specifically at patronage structures in the second, societal tier. The main point here is that different types of patronage dynamics can be used to penetrate society. Cheeseman (2006) argues that, although patronage may begin and end with individuals, the focus in contemporary Africanist literature on the personalised nature of patronage is incorrect. Patronage may be distributed through political parties and general government expenditure as well as through local patrons; it may be received by regions and organisations as well as by individual clients. Therefore, patron-client relations which are a highly personalised exchange relationship are only one particular form of patronage. More diffused or collective forms of patronage need not create direct personalised ties of subordination and dependence. Patronage structures can also be more or less competitive – competitive in the sense that the recipients of patronage are able to choose between, or periodically change, the source of patronage. This feature determines how responsive patrons are likely to be to local needs and demands. Patronage structures are therefore best understood as products of the interaction of these two dimensions – how personalised and how competitive – and can be disaggregated along four ideal types; insulated patron-client (high personalisation and low competitiveness), insulated corporatist (low personalisation and low competitiveness), responsive patron-client (high personalisation and high competitiveness), and responsive corporatist (low personalisation and high competitiveness) (Cheeseman 2006: 46).

Related to the issue of competitiveness is the critical question of the agency of non-elites. This is closely tied to individual and group calculus, sometimes informed by notions of public honour. The extant emphasis on prebends in Africanist analysis has been heavily influenced by culturalist notions of consumption centred on the proverbial 'politics of the belly'. Similarly, 'neopatrimonial' analyses tend to locate agency exclusively with the 'big man'. What is often lost within these perspectives is any notion of agency for the non-elites who are cast as too economically needy or dependent to be able to have any serious say in the terms of their incorporation into the political system. Yet mass engagement in the political system continues to be influenced not just by economic need, but also by calculations of personal advantage and notions of public honour which constrain or structure elite options. That individual calculations matter is aptly captured by Ambrose Bierce who defines patronage as 'the process of creating nine enemies and one ingrate' (cited in Krislor 1974: 5). And demands for 'development' or patronage from below are often framed in the context of specific notions of personal or public honour, the breaching of which puts the 'big man' in peril, as a Nigerian Senator, laden with patronage goods, discovered when he confronted his constituents in 2008:

> Senator Nuhu Aliyu representing Niger North district of Niger State on Monday evening publicly suffered rejection from his people, a development that has occurred twice in the last three months. Aliyu, ... was publicly rejected and booed at Sabuke Square in New Bussa, Borgu Local Government Area by his constituents. ... Aside from this, the people also rejected 40 motorcycles the lawmaker brought for distribution ... The people said that they were not ready to have anything to do with the Greek gift of the Senator.[1]

With these qualifications of van de Walle's understanding of the nature of African clientelist systems, we now turn our attention to the evidence from our case studies. What has been the impact of democratisation on clientelism and political mobilisation? In a multiparty context, competitiveness should be high. Similarly, the extent to which the party system is institutionalised and party identification strong should also determine whether the patronage structure is characterised by high or low personalisation. It is therefore not surprising that countries like Ghana with a consolidated party system and relatively competitive elections have been able to evolve patronage structures that were characterised by low personalisation and a corporatist focus. On the other hand, some former one-party states such as Kenya and Senegal have tended to have patronage structures with a higher degree of personalisation because of the fragmented party landscape that resulted from democratisation and the difficulties in building and maintaining effective coalitions. New parties tend to be strongly associated with particular leaders who personally cultivate a political base either through their own wealth, such as in Kenya, or by bringing their small following under the umbrella of patrons higher up the political order, as in Senegal.

In Nigeria, the combination of personalised power structures, substantial oil rents, and mobilised ethnic communities, has meant that democratisation is characterised by patronage networks with high personalisation and high competitiveness, which disadvantaged and combative ethnic entrepreneurs are trying to shift in the direction of a competitive corporatist model. However, the situation is further complicated by the replication of personalised patronage structures at the sub-national level by these same ethnic entrepreneurs. In Zambia, after the MMD lost its urban political support base, it fell back on using the same rural-based patronage structures of the UNIP from the one-party era, while the new PF has taken over the MMD's base among the mineworkers' trade unions. This spatial dimension of patronage networks – whether they are largely urban or rural-based – which is so discernible in Zambia, is observable to different degrees in other countries, and has influenced the course and outcomes of elections and democratisation.

Van de Walle (2007) argues that democratisation requires a shift from prebendal to patronage-based clientelist strategies, as seen in other parts of the world. We would add that what is required is not just a move towards patronage generally, but a move towards corporatist and competitive patronage structures. These are more likely to put pressure on political parties and leaders to respond to citizens' demands, whereas personalised patronage structures would tend to institutionalise the subordination of the client to party barons, thus reducing the possibility of systematic influence over a party's policy and political agenda.

Restructuring the Social Contract

Democratisation in Africa took place in the context of economic crisis and attempts at economic restructuring. Most countries had signed up to structural adjustment programmes under the tutelage of the World Bank and the IMF. As the introductory chapter made clear, the foundation of social policy changed from the redistributive ethos of universal entitlement which underpinned the nationalist developmentalism of the post-colonial state to a market-driven strategy built around effective demand, cost recovery and user fees, and a safety-net for those without effective purchasing power. While this change was promoted on the grounds of efficient resource use and improved access, in reality it left huge sections of the population with deteriorating access to vital social services. The hypothetical safety-nets were conspicuously inefficient or inappropriate; critics demanded 'adjustment with a human face'. The legitimacy crisis of incumbent regimes was therefore linked to the imperatives of economic restructuring and the changes in the nationalist social contract that such restructuring implied. Democratisation offered the possibility for re-negotiating and recasting state-society relations in the light of increasing societal challenge to the state.

Hyden suggests that this re-negotiation has not happened. He characterises the period between 1955 and 1968 in Africa as the era of the Party state, premised on Order, while the period between 1969 and 1981 is characterised as the era of the Development state, built around the idea of Progress. From 1982 till now, he characterises as the era of the Contracting state, guided by the idea of Control (Hyden 2006: 27). Similarly, van de Walle suggests a problematic relationship between democratisation and economic growth; while Africa witnessed its best economic performance for decades in the years between 1994 and 1997, there was no discernible difference between democracies and non-democracies in terms of their economic performance (van de Walle 2001: 238). What then has happened to the social contract under democratisation?

We suggest that five important shifts have taken place, with implications for the social contract. Firstly, increased aid flows have made it possible for states like Senegal to reconstitute their legitimacy and seek to co-opt some societal groups into their state project. Our Senegal case study even suggests the possibility of the recrudescence of 'urban bias', that malignant emblem of nationalist developmentalism. Increased aid has not only strengthened state budgets, it has also made possible the provision of basic social services like health and education to vulnerable communities, sometimes under the rubric of the Millennium Development Goals (MDGs). Aid-dependent African states are no longer responsible for the social provisioning of significant sections of their population, calling into question the link between the state and the citizen.

Furthermore, by the 2000s, aid-dependent African countries faced a situation where policy conditionalities are negotiated between governments and donors in arenas parallel to formal democratic institutions and largely beyond the reach of organised groups, except where donors and government choose to include them. The relationship that has developed between donors and governments over the past decades in aid-dependent countries like Ghana, Senegal and Zambia (in this volume), as well as in Mali, Rwanda and Tanzania (Whitfield 2009), is structuring the quality of democracy both in terms of how policies are produced and also in terms of the incentives facing politicians to be transparent, open and accountable to their citizens. The observation of Olukoshi (1999: 459) still applies today: the practices of delivering aid undermine the domestic consensus and coalition-building required for sustainable economic reform, and governments' accounting to donors overshadows accountability to their own citizens. While official aid agencies (donors) have since the late 1990s sought to increase the leverage of citizen participation in public policy-making, it is a paradoxical endeavour as donors can sometimes buttress the efforts of non-state actors but at other times block them.

A second shift with implications for the social contract is the windfall profits made by oil-exporting countries like Nigeria and Angola, with oil prices rising above $100 a barrel in 2008. In these countries where the rentier state has proved particularly difficult to tame by the population, more resources have made no significant change in the extant problematic relationship between the state and the citizen. Democratisation has failed to reverse the unaccountable logic of the rentier state. The third shift is in states like Zambia, where resource hunger in China and India has made possible the reactivation of previously abandoned mines. The renewed profitability of the copper mines in Zambia is leading to the resurgence of neo-nationalist development ideas as claims to entitlement are being articulated, but within a socio-economic context that is unfavourable to such claims. In Zambia, therefore, we have increased conflict between the government and Chinese mining interests, on the one hand, and societal groups, on the other. The fourth shift is the massive expansion and societal deepening of the stock exchanges in countries like Kenya and Nigeria. Closely related to this are fundamental changes to pension systems which increase the role of some individuals in the management of their retirement funds. These processes have generated a 'popular capitalism' that has penetrated every nook and cranny of urban society and shifted expectations and orientations. Whether this will lead to the emergence of a class akin to the state-assisted black capital in South Africa remains to be seen.

The fifth shift is in the increasing significance of migration and the rise in prominence of diasporic communities. States like Senegal, Somalia, Ghana and

Nigeria obtain billions of dollars annually in remittances which finance the consumption needs of large sections of the population, thereby easing the subsistence demands placed on the state. Furthermore, some diasporic communities have sought to alter citizenship and political rights to improve their marginal rights in these areas and make them commensurate with their increasing economic roles. In Nigeria, for instance, citizenship rules have been changed to the advantage of the diasporic community. The right to vote in Nigerian elections and even stand for office while still resident outside the country, and the right to be appointed to high offices of the state, are now demanded by the Nigerian diaspora, leading to legal and constitutional battles with different state authorities. This process of re-defining the rights and obligations of citizenship in many African countries will only become more complicated as the so-called 'Afrosaxons' and the 'Afropolitians' become a more pronounced element in the African diaspora in the West. These are usually second-generation, often highly educated, Africans who live and work in various professional capacities in the West, but continue to maintain symbolic or practical ties with their original African countries. Through their increasing economic role and their constant pushing of the boundaries of political and citizenship rights, the diasporic communities may change countries such as Senegal and Ghana into 'diasporic states', a status already conferred on Eritrea (Iyob 2000).

How are these trends likely to intersect with the democratisation process? Aid flows and windfall profits, while meeting vital subsistence needs, nevertheless pose serious challenges of achieving accountability. Resource vents and deepening capital markets, on the other hand, raise the possibility of demands being put on the state by sections of the population with legitimate interests to advance – workers, trade unions, civil society organisations and budding capitalists. This has the potential of contributing to the much needed negotiation between the state and society. The diaspora are likely to have a benign influence on the democratisation process. With perceptions sharpened by separation from home and above-average levels of skills and resources, they have a potential not only to contribute directly to their natal countries, but also to mobilise opinion in their adopted homes in support of democratisation in Africa. The Kufuor government in Ghana insisted on passing a law to allow the Ghanaian diaspora to vote in Ghanaian elections precisely because the government expected that diaspora to be critical of the opposition NDC party associated with Rawlings' military authoritarianism.

Democratisation in Africa will remain tentative until it is rooted in the lives and aspirations of important segments of the population. This is a far from completed process in many African countries, but democratisation has changed the nature of the public sphere. African countries have generally witnessed an expansion in civil and political rights guaranteed by constitutions, and increased freedom of the media as well as an expansion of the private media. However, these changes have not been uniform across the continent and they have been reversible, as some of our case studies show. Furthermore, this expansion has largely been limited to urban areas, and large sections of the population in rural areas are still disadvantaged. Non-governmental organisations have increased the representation of individuals in the public sphere and mediate their participation, but most NGOs are not mass-based organisations. In some countries, such as in Senegal, Nigeria and Zimbabwe, religious organisations have taken up this role. Zambia, South Africa, and to a lesser extent Nigeria, are the only countries where trade-union participation in the public sphere is strong, and this is linked to the degree of urbanisation in these countries.

The Meaning of Elections

There was a certain naivety about the transformative efficacy of elections at the beginning of the 1990s in Africa. There was a feeling that if multiple parties were allowed and competitive elections held, voters would assert choices consistent with democratic aspirations. All that was left was for the incipient democratic regimes to be consolidated. This rationalistic approach concentrated on building the 'hardware' of democratisation, institutions such as political parties, electoral institutions and parliamentary capacity, to the neglect of the 'software' needed to run the 'hardware' effectively: the perceptions and values of important social actors (cf. Shin & Tusalem 2007). For example, introducing multiparty elections to Côte d'Ivoire with no culture of political dialogue invariably precipitated political violence and civil war. The rational-choice perspective on elections also ignored important asymmetries of power in the process of democratisation. Voting never took place in a power-neutral environment. Ruling groups often embraced democratisation as a survival strategy. As Morier-Genoud (Chapter 9) points out in the case of Mozambique, Frelimo, the party of militant nationalism and independence, and of the one-party Socialist state, turned towards liberalism and multipartyism as a way to end the civil war *and* to remain in power. Frelimo shaped the emergent democracy narrowly to serve its own interests.

Similarly, in Ghana, the military-bureaucratic regime headed by Rawlings, a long-standing critic of representative democracy, took an unexpected turn in 1991 and embraced representative democracy in order to rejuvenate the legitimacy of his rule (Whitfield, Chapter 4). More often than not, even international and local observer teams – the standard-bearers of electoral good practice – become participants in the power calculus surrounding African elections.

As a result of the power play surrounding many elections, discredited individual leaders may have been thrown out, but it has been much more difficult to change fundamental practices or to restructure formal institutions and informal practices. Elections have not always led to a renewal of elites, but rather in many countries the individuals competing for high office are part of a relatively narrow circle that has been at the political apex for decades (Chabal 2005: 32). Elections, in and of themselves, remain problematic as the main instruments for changing existing political logics and institutions. Although they may lead to improvements in civil liberties, elections have yet to bring vast improvements in the quality of governance in Africa (see Gyimah-Boadi 2004: 22).

Chazan (1979) has also argued that too many functions have been attributed to elections, which cannot address larger problems confronting the political system: (i) the gaps that persist between leaders and the majority of the population; (ii) the inability to find acceptable answers for political participation; and (iii) the lack of consensus on the framework of politics and the values necessary to legitimise the government of the modern state. She argued that the ballot box is an appropriate mechanism only for selecting the people who will solve these problems. Elections are not the emblematic seal of democratisation in Africa; instead, they should be properly understood as the opening moves in a long-drawn-out drama in which different social forces seek to control the state. The extent to which the 'software' of rules is commonly held and applied will determine the efficacy of elections to serve the important functions of representativeness and accountability.

None of these qualifications should be taken as a diminution of the importance of elections in the process of democratisation. Prior to the era of democratisation, authoritarian regimes often fused the party and the state together, creating a party-state in which the state is subordinated to the party. Multiparty elections have been instrumental in triggering a separation between the party and the state. Though dominant parties are a prominent feature of the democratisation process, it is now generally taken for granted that parties must justify themselves to the electorate. Even authoritarian parties like the RPF in Rwanda and Zanu-PF in Zimbabwe now find themselves confronted by the embarrassment of electoral contests.

Conclusion

Since 1990, African countries have engaged in a multi-faceted process of democratisation that has fundamentally transformed the politics of many African states. Comparing the Freedom House categorisation of African countries in 1989 with those of 2007, we get an idea of the transformation under way (see Table 12.1).

Table 12.1 Freedom House Categorisation of Sub-Saharan Africa, 1989 and 2007 (%)

| | 2007 | | 1989 |
	World (208 entities)	Africa (49 entities)	Africa (44 entities)
Free	44.2	22.4	6.8
Partially free	30.8	46.9	25.0
Not free	25.0	30.6	68.2

There is clearly a movement away from more authoritarian forms of governance, and towards more democratic forms. This conclusion is borne out by similar trends in the enjoyment of political and civil liberties. The average rating for sub-Saharan Africa on political rights and civil liberties has moved from about 6 and 5.5 respectively in 1990, representing high levels of repression, to just below 4 on political rights and precisely 4 on civil liberties in 2006. However, comparing Africa's performance with the rest of the world in 2007 through the objective criteria of Freedom House indicates that the continent still lags behind by having a smaller percentage of free entities and a higher percentage of the not-free category. If we use evidence from opinion surveys, however, we get a different picture of Africa's performance in this global process. Shin and Tusalem (2007) argue that, in most countries in the world, a clear majority now endorse democracy as the best system of governance. However, democratisation depends, not on this generic and vague support for democracy, but on the level of 'authentic support' by committed democrats, 'when ordinary citizens show they view democracy as the only political game by endorsing it always and rejecting its undemocratic alternatives fully' (2007: 22-3). Africa scores high on the level of 'authentic support', compared to other parts of the world involved in 'third wave' democratisation: 14 per cent in Latin America, 35 per cent in East Asia, 38 per cent in New Europe, and 44 per cent in Africa. No country in Latin America or East Asia has reached the 50 per cent threshold for authentic support, while three countries each in New Europe and Africa have (Kenya, Senegal, and Zambia) (ibid.: 23). Bringing the objective indicators in line with these subjective indicators, in other words, making the institutions of governance more accountable to their various constituencies, is the great challenge before African democratisation, despite the great advances since 1989.

Note

1. 'Kinsmen reject Senator Aliyu's gifts', www.thenationonlineng.com, 26/03/08.

References

Allen, Chris. 1995. Understanding African Politics. *Review of African Political Economy* 65: 301-320.

Bratton, Michael, Robert Mattes and Emmanuel Gyimah-Boadi, 2005. *Public Opinion, Democracy and Market Reforms in Africa*. Cambridge: Cambridge University Press.

Chabal, Patrick. 2005. Power in Africa Reconsidered. In *The African Exception*, eds Ulf Engel and Gorm R. Olsen. Aldershot: Ashgate.

Chazan, Naomi. 1979. African Voters at the Polls: A Reexamination of the Role of Elections in African Politics, *Journal of Commonwealth and Comparative Politics*, XVII(2), (Summer): 135-58.

Cheeseman, Nicholas. 2006. 'The Rise and Fall of Civil Authoritarianism in Africa: Patronage, participation and political parties in Kenya and Zambia'. D.Phil. thesis, Department of Politics and International Relations, University of Oxford.

Good, Kenneth. 1996. Authoritarian Liberalism: A defining characteristic of Botswana. *Journal of Contemporary African Studies* 14(1): 29-51.

Gyimah-Boadi, Emmanuel (ed.) 2004. *Democratic Reform in Africa: The quality of progress*. Boulder, CO and London: Lynne Rienner.

Herbst, Jeffrey. 2001. Political Liberalization in Africa after Ten Years, *Comparative Politics*, April: 357-375.

Hyden, Goran. 2006. *African Politics in Comparative Perspective*, Cambridge: Cambridge University Press.

Iyob, Ruth. 2000. The Ethiopian-Eritrean conflict: diasporic vs. hegemonic states in the Horn of Africa, 1991-2000, *Journal of Modern African Studies* 38(4): 659-682.

Krislor, Samuel. 1974. *Representative Bureaucracy,*, Englewood Cliffs, NJ: Prentice-Hall Inc.

Maipose, Gervase. 2009. Botswana: An African Success Story. In *The Politics of Aid: African strategies for dealing with donors*, ed. Lindsay Whitfield. Oxford: Oxford University Press.

Olukoshi, Adebayo. 1999. State, Conflict and Democracy in Africa: The Complex Process of Renewal. In *State, Conflict and Democracy in Africa*, ed. Richard Joseph. Boulder, CO and London: Lynne Rienner.

Post, Ken W. J. 1963. *The Nigerian Federal Elections of 1959*, Oxford: Oxford University Press.

Shin, Doh Chull and Rollin F. Tusalem. 2007. The Cultural and Institutional Dynamics of Global Democratization: A Synthesis of Mass Experience and Congruence Theory, *Taiwan Journal of Democracy*, 3(1): 1-28.

Taylor, Ian. 2003. As Good as it Gets? Botswana's 'Democratic Development'. *Journal of Contemporary African Studies* 21(2): 215-31.

van de Walle, Nicolas. 2001. *African Economies and the Politics of Permanent Crisis, 1979-1999*. Cambridge: Cambridge University Press.

—. 2007. Meet the New Boss, Same as the Old Boss? The evolution of political clientelism in Africa. In *Patrons, Clients, and Policies: Patterns of democratic accountability and political competition*, eds. Herbert Kitschelt and Steven Wilkinson. Cambridge: Cambridge University Press.

Whitfield, Lindsay (ed.) 2009. *The Politics of Aid: African strategies for dealing with donors*. Oxford: Oxford University Press.

Index

Abacha, Sani 71-2, 74, 80, 82, 85, 91
Abubakar, Abdusalami 71
Abubakar, Atiku 79-80, 88
accountability xii, 6, 8, 23, 53, 56-9, 66, 68, 73, 76-8, 83, 85, 90, 100-2, 104, 106, 111, 115-16, 126, 128, 131, 134, 138, 189, 192-3, 206-9, 211-12, 215, 223-5
African Growth and Opportunity Act 16
African Union 44
Afrobarometer xiv, 4-5, 54, 59, 61, 86, 90, 103, 106, 112, 129
agriculture 14, 16, 18, 89, 121, 137, 144, 158, 161, 175, 192, 214
aid dependency 52
Akan 32-3, 36, 40, 42, 44, 63
alternance 15-16, 20, 22-3, 25-9, 208
Annan, Kofi 44
anti-corruption 24, 81, 89, 123, 162, 219
apartheid 7, 134-5, 137, 139, 140-1, 144-8, 150, 154, 88, 212
Arap Moi, Daniel 96-8, 103-8, 210, 212
autocratic rulers xii

Babangida, Ibrahim 71, 74, 81-2, 90
Baoulé 32-3, 36-42
Bédié, Henri Konan 38-42
Bemba 117, 124
Bete 32, 38-40
Bizimungu, Pascal 176
black business elites 142, 189
Black Economic Empowerment (BEE) 142, 149

Bomas Draft 108-9
Bongo, Omar 44
Bosnia xiii
Botswana xi, 163, 214
Brazil xiii
Bretton Woods institutions 29, 36, 214
Buhari, Muhammadu 71, 82, 88, 90
bureaucratic state 188
Burkina Faso 32, 40, 44-6
business community 67, 86, 121; business elite 122, 142-3
Buyoya, Pierre 171, 174, 177

Casamance xvi, 14, 22
centralisation of power in the executive 137-8, 188, 206, 211, 213, 218
centralised-executive state 211
CFA Franc 14, 16, 38
chiefs 21, 61, 148, 151, 195-6
Chiluba, Fredrick 116, 118-27, 129, 211, 218-19
Chimurenga 185-8, 190, 192-5, 197-9
China 19, 223
Chissano, Joachim 155-8, 160-4, 213
Chona Commission 128
Christianity 63, 167, 175
churches 126, 188, 192
citizenship 32, 34, 39, 42, 44-6, 48, 102, 205-6, 224
civil liberties 1, 3, 11, 51, 94, 97, 123, 218, 225-6
civil society 4, 6, 15, 23, 28, 59-60, 85-7, 94, 97, 114-15, 119-20, 123, 125-9, 131, 134, 173-4, 182, 207, 219, 224

civil war xiii, 31, 42, 48, 50, 153-4, 203, 205, 214-15, 217, 225

class xii, 1, 13, 24, 32-4, 53-4, 60, 63, 79, 82, 97, 117, 122, 129, 134-5, 139-40, 142-3, 145-6, 148-50, 153, 169-71, 175, 182, 188, 190-1, 197, 203, 207, 214, 223

clientelism xv, 8-9, 16, 19, 22-3, 26, 28, 34, 67, 81, 205, 218, 220-1

Cold War xiii, 1, 212

colonialism xiii, 9, 33, 45, 72, 167, 186, 193

Compaoré, Blaise 44-6

comparative method 4, 6-7, 202

Constituency Development Fund 95, 104-6, 211

constitution 8, 21-2, 25, 38, 43, 54, 56-7, 59, 61-2, 73, 76, 80, 85-7, 90, 95, 108-10, 117, 127-9, 135-6, 155-7, 168-9, 172-8, 188-9, 198, 206, 208, 211, 213, 218-19, 224; constitutional change 2, 87, 124, 189, 218; constitutional referendum 100, 105, 109-10, 128, 177-8, 192-3, 210-1; constitutional reform 107-8, 114-16, 128-9, 131, 174, 210-12, 218

corruption 27, 51, 53, 57-8, 73, 75-8, 81, 84-5, 89, 94, 103-6, 117, 123, 127, 148-9, 158, 160-4, 175, 188-9, 219

COSATU 144-6, 151, 219

Côte d'Ivoire xi, xii, 2-3, 7, 18, 26, 31-50, 72, 203-6, 209, 213, 217, 220, 225

coups 2, 33, 40-2, 45, 50-4, 71, 91, 97, 119, 163, 167-8, 171, 174, 177, 180-1, 207, 215-6

debt 19, 38, 55, 84, 117-19, 125, 127, 129, 130-1, 191, 209, 212

decentralised power 62, 95, 179

decentralisation 23, 52, 54, 61-2, 67, 95-6, 109-10, 161-2, 177, 205, 208-9

decolonisation xi, 31, 35, 54, 192, 206-7, 211

democracy xi-xiii, 1-7, 11, 13, 15, 20, 36-7, 44-5, 47, 51-6, 59, 62, 64, 66-8, 71-3, 79, 82, 83, 85, 90, 96-103, 109, 114-16, 118-20, 122-3, 126-30, 134-5, 138, 141, 148, 150, 153-5,

157, 159-64, 168, 172, 175, 181-2, 185, 188, 193, 197, 199, 207, 210, 213, 216, 220, 223, 225-6

democratisation xi-xiv, 1-11, 13-17, 20-4, 27-9, 31, 33, 36, 38-42, 44-5, 47-8, 50, 59, 71-81, 83, 85-8, 90-1, 99-100, 107, 114-15, 120, 129, 156, 158, 166, 168, 172, 175-6, 82, 202-13, 215, 217-19, 221-7

democratisation school 3-4

dependency 52, 121, 147

development state 146-7, 222

Dhlakama, Alfonso 156, 158-9

Diouf, Abdou 13, 14, 15, 22, 26, 27, 29, 30

discriminatory state 167-8, 176, 215

disorder and insecurity xiii

divided societies xiii

donors 14, 15, 19, 20, 23-4, 43, 54-5, 57, 59-60, 62, 64-7, 98, 104-5, 116-21, 123, 125, 126, 130, 163, 174, 179, 192, 209, 212, 223

dos Santos, José Eduardo 44

East Timor xiii

Eastern Europe 2, 119-20

economic crisis 10, 14, 16, 35-6, 53, 118, 141, 203, 305, 210, 216, 222

economic decline 10, 50, 68, 79, 117, 130, 185, 191, 212

economic development 9, 64-5, 68, 116, 144-6, 157-8, 160, 208, 218

economic elite 162, 204

economic liberalisation 14, 115, 119, 120-1, 123, 125-7, 129, 182, 204, 214, 217, 219

economic nationalism 189

economics 9, 120, 137, 140

ECOWAS 43-4

education xiv, 9-10, 13, 19, 29, 33-5, 52, 61-2, 117, 120, 134, 137, 148-50, 169, 188, 192, 194-5, 197, 204, 223

elections 1-2, 4-6, 8-11, 14-15, 20, 22-3, 25-6, 29, 36, 39-41, 45-6, 50, 52-7, 61-8, 72, 79-80, 87-90, 96-8, 103, 109-11, 115-16, 118-19, 123-3, 126, 128-30, 134-5, 138-9, 146, 149-50, 153, 155-9, 161-4, 168, 172-8, 180-1, 185, 189, 193-5, 197-8, 203-12, 214-22, 224-6

electoral commission 46, 55-7, 111, 115, 135, 173, 176, 207, 209
electoral democracy 7, 181, 216
electoral institution 15, 87, 225
elite circulation 52, 54, 206, 216
elite consensus 55, 67-8, 90, 171-4, 206-7, 209, 212
elite fragmentation 52, 55, 206
elites 4, 7-9, 13, 17, 28-9, 52, 54-5, 60, 62-3, 67, 72, 74-5, 89-90, 99, 106, 111, 115, 119-20, 125, 131, 141-2, 149, 167-8, 170-1, 173, 177, 182, 188-90, 192, 196-7, 203, 206-7, 209, 211, 215, 217, 219-21, 225
ethnic militias 72, 79
ethnic mobilisation 41, 94, 117, 124-5, 211
ethnic parity 173-4, 176-8
ethnic politics xiii, 100, 124-5, 197, 205, 209
ethnicity 1, 34, 40, 42, 63-4, 74, 77-8, 99-104, 106-7, 111, 124, 156, 160, 167-70, 182, 205, 209, 211, 215, 217
European Union 16, 18, 111, 119
exclusionary politics 168, 203, 205, 215-16
executive power 135-6, 149, 194, 208

factionalism 21, 26, 83, 160, 207-8
farmers' organisations 121
federalism 72-3, 81, 86, 93
Forces Nouvelles 42, 46-7
foreign investors 32, 116, 121, 126, 130, 203
France 31, 33-4, 43, 45-6, 175, 203
Freedom House xi, xii, 3, 112, 226

Gacaca courts 179
Gbagbo, Laurent 36-47
GEAR 138, 141-6, 157, 219
genocidal ideology 167, 169, 170-1, 181
genocide xii, 167-81, 215-17
Ghana xi, xii, 2-3, 7, 10, 40, 43-4, 50-68, 71, 81, 87, 103-4, 156, 202, 206-9, 211, 218-25
globalisation 17, 29, 130
governance 14-15, 20, 22, 27-8, 37, 40, 50, 53-4, 62, 65-6, 73, 75-8, 81, 84, 98, 101, 114, 123, 127, 129-30, 153,

168, 172, 177, 179, 208-9, 217, 225-7
Guebuza, Armando 160-4, 166, 214
Gur 32
Guyana xiii

Habyarimana, Juvenal 169, 171, 173-5
Haiti xiii
harambee 94-5, 102-7, 111, 211
Hausa/Fulani 74, 82
health xiii, xiv, 9-10, 19, 26, 28-9, 35-6, 62, 79, 89, 109, 115, 117, 120, 136-8, 142, 150, 188, 197, 223
Heavily Indebted Poor Country 19
hisbah 76, 79
HIV/AIDS 120, 136, 138, 219
horizontal accountability 6, 8, 56-7, 211
Houphouet-Boigny, Félix 26, 31-42, 44-48, 50, 203, 205
human rights 1, 43, 56-8, 80, 100, 157, 168, 174, 179-80, 216
Hutu 167-82, 215-17

Igbo 74, 82
IMF 10, 37, 53, 118, 125, 127, 130, 141, 155, 157, 161, 222
immigrants 35-6, 45
immunity 28, 123, 179, 217
impunity 10, 42, 178-9, 217
independence struggles xiii, 212
individual agency 5-6, 8, 221
Indonesia xiii
industrialisation 157
industry 16-17, 83-5, 116, 118, 121, 127, 141, 146
inequality 117, 119, 129, 150, 158, 161, 170, 188, 214
infrastructure 19, 34, 62, 80, 95, 121-2, 146, 179, 188, 195, 204
institutional change 78, 81, 130, 208
intellectuals 15, 33, 60, 118, 124, 167, 178, 188
interahamwe 181
International Criminal Tribunal for Rwanda 179
International Crisis Group 47, 170, 176
international observers 15, 56, 88, 123, 130, 172, 174, 178, 180
Islam 25, 32, 75-6,
Ivoirité 205
Ivorian miracle 33-4

journalists 15, 27-8, 59, 141, 159
judiciary 19, 56, 71, 81, 83, 111, 134-5, 156, 188, 194

Ka, Djibo 14, 21, 26
Kagame, Paul 171, 176-7
Kalenjin 109
Kaunda, Kenneth 116-20, 122-4, 128, 205
Kenya xi, xii, 2-3, 7, 10, 27, 72, 94-111, 115, 117, 122-5, 181, 202, 209-13, 218-21, 223, 226
Kenyatta, Jomo 27, 95-8, 103, 105, 107, 110
Kibaki, Mwai 94-5, 98-9, 104-5, 108-11, 210-12, 218-19
Kikuyu 96-8, 109
Konaré, Alpha Oumar 44
Krou 40
Kufuor, J.A. 44, 50-1, 58, 62, 67, 208, 211, 224

land 8, 24-5, 36, 39-40, 42, 44, 48, 59, 72, 89, 105, 138, 147-8, 150, 157, 185-99, 205-6, 216, 220; land reform 24, 147-8, 189
leadership recruitment 2
legislature 21, 57-8, 79-81, 83, 86, 96, 107, 135-7, 188, 208, 217-18
legitimacy 1, 4-5, 9-10, 20, 25, 27, 32, 36, 40, 53-4, 57, 62, 73, 76, 79, 81, 87, 90, 97, 101, 103, 106, 111, 116, 131, 148, 157-8, 163, 173, 181, 186, 188-9, 193, 197-9, 207, 216, 222-3, 225
liberal autocracy 7
liberal democracy 7, 54, 68, 116, 153-4, 159, 160, 163-4
liberation movement 134, 186-7, 212-14, 216
liberation war 154, 159, 185-91, 193, 198, 215
Linas-Marcoussis accords 42-4, 46
local government 23, 61-2, 67, 72, 77-8, 83, 116, 135, 208, 221
Loum, Mamadou Lamine 20
Lozi 124
Luo 96, 98, 109

Machel, Graca 161

Machel, Samora 154-5, 161
macroeconomic reforms 83-4, 209
Makonde 160-1
Mande 32
Mandela, Nelson 134-5, 137, 139, 141-2
Manuel, Trevor 137, 141-2
marabouts 13-4, 17, 25-6, 28-9, 32, 204
Mauritania xi
Mbeki, Thabo 43-4, 137-9, 141-2, 146-7, 149-50, 197-8, 213-14, 217, 219
media xiii, 6, 15, 23, 28, 38, 43, 50-3, 57, 59, 65, 67, 68, 71-6, 75, 78-83, 85-7, 89, 90-1, 115, 122-3, 126, 157, 169, 174-5, 186, 191, 206, 208, 219, 224
migration 13, 15-18, 29, 35, 139, 204, 223
military dictatorship 1, 85
military xii, 1, 9, 33, 37, 40-1, 43, 45, 47, 107, 154, 160, 168-73, 175, 177-8, 181, 187, 194-6, 206-8, 215, 218, 220, 224-5
moodu-moodu 16-17
moral ethnicity 99-104, 106-7, 111
Movement for Multiparty Democracy 18, 134, 152-3, 230
Mozambique 2-3, 7, 10, 153-5, 157-9, 161-4, 202, 212-15, 218, 225
Mugabe, Robert 190, 197-9
multi-ethnic 98, 102, 177
multiparty elections 1-2, 4, 9, 36, 50, 68, 97-8, 119, 134, 156-8, 163-4, 168, 172, 174-7, 203, 209, 210, 212, 215-16, 218, 220-1, 225-6
Murids 17-18, 25
Mvunga Commission 128
Mwanakatwe Commission 128
Mwanawasa, Levy 95, 114, 123, 125-31, 218
Myanmar xiii

national reconciliation 42-3, 46, 169, 178-80
nationalism 27, 33, 35, 160, 186-7, 189, 193, 197, 216, 225
nationalist movement 54, 72, 114, 187, 207, 216
nationality 39-40, 43, 45, 48, 99
Ndadaye, Melchior 177
Négritude 14

neo-liberalism 126, 141, 143, 146, 182
neo-patrimonialism 8, 99, 131, 221
NEPAD 18-19
newspapers 27, 59, 126
NGOs 6, 23, 59-60, 62, 65-6, 157, 169, 205, 224
Niasse, Moustapha 14, 20
Niger 43
Niger Delta 72, 74-8, 86, 89
Nigeria xi-xiii, 2-3, 7, 10, 18, 27, 34, 44, 56-7, 71-87, 89-91, 156, 202, 206-9, 217-24
Nkrumah, Kwame 9, 50-3, 64, 114, 207
non-elites 8, 221

Obasanjo, Olusegun 71, 73-5, 77-91, 207-9, 217-19
Odinga, Oginga 98
Odinga, Raila 98, 109-10, 210
Ojukwu, Chukwuemeka 90
one-party state 9-10, 13, 33-4, 37, 96, 98, 114, 116-18, 122, 130-1, 163, 188, 203, 209-12, 218
opposition parties 37, 50, 55, 109, 121, 126, 138, 140-1, 176-7, 180, 204, 210, 213, 218
Ouattara, Alassane Dramane 37-42, 45

parastatals 14, 22, 32, 34, 57, 74, 107, 116-18, 171, 204, 219
parliament 50, 56-8, 66-7, 107, 109, 111, 115, 117, 123, 125, 128-9, 135, 137, 140, 156, 159, 175, 180, 188, 206, 208, 211
parliamentary accountability 128
partisan identification 139
party identification 63, 207, 221
Patriotic History 186-7, 190, 193, 216
patronage 8-9, 14, 19, 23-4, 32, 35, 51-3, 57, 60, 64-5, 67, 77, 82-3, 94-5, 97-108, 110-11, 116-17, 123-5, 130, 149, 185, 192-3, 196-7, 203-12, 216, 219-22
patronage networks 9, 24, 52, 60, 95-8, 101, 107, 211, 220, 222
patron-client 9, 24, 84, 94-6, 98-9, 101-4, 107, 111, 204, 211, 220, 221
peace agreements 168, 172-5, 177-81, 217
personal rule 8

personalisation of power 26-7, 29, 81, 206
political accountability 115, 131, 193
political community 39, 173, 206
political culture 27-8, 34, 71-2, 99-101, 114, 199, 219-20
political economy xi, 16, 32, 122, 141, 185, 204-5, 209, 212, 214
political elites 17, 29, 52, 55, 99, 115, 149, 207, 211
political instability 50, 52-4, 67-8, 167, 206, 212, 216, 220
political liberalisation 1-2, 14, 23, 54, 98-9, 115, 130, 203
political mobilisation 7-9, 22, 51, 65, 94, 117, 124, 203, 205, 210-11, 216, 220-1
political parties 9, 20-1, 36-7, 44, 52, 54-5, 63, 65, 68, 82, 114, 124, 137, 130, 153, 176, 171-5, 177-8, 180, 204, 207, 220, 222, 225
political pluralism 29, 203
political representation 5, 181, 215-16
political rights 2-3, 45, 68, 94, 97, 135, 189, 193, 205, 224, 226
political tribalism 99-103, 111
political violence 9, 36, 38, 41-2, 47, 81, 91, 96, 167, 193, 198, 207, 225
popular movement 114, 121, 126, 130
poverty 24, 38, 56, 76, 85, 89, 101, 105, 120-1, 125, 147-8, 150, 161, 190, 214
power-sharing 63, 99, 135, 168-70, 172-6, 180, 192, 198-9, 215, 217
praetorianism xiii
prebendalism 9
prebends 8, 219, 221
presidential term limits 2
presidentialism 7-8, 21, 26, 28, 52, 56, 67, 156, 217-20
privatisation 14, 17, 19, 24-5, 60, 84-5, 116, 119, 121, 125, 127, 129, 143-5, 158, 204, 219
PRSP 125, 127

radio 59, 157
Ramaphosa, Cyril 142
Rawlings, J.J. 50-1, 53-5, 58, 62-4, 207, 224-5
redistribution 34-5, 138, 141, 147-8,

150, 187-8, 192-3

regionalism 39, 41-2, 45, 72, 156, 171

religion xii, 1, 25, 75-8, 137, 154, 156, 209

religious organisations 1, 154, 157, 224

representative democracy 51-4, 56, 64, 66, 68, 134, 225

revenue allocation 77-8, 107

rule of law 56, 81, 89, 148, 174

rural 12-13, 16, 23-5, 39-40, 52-3, 59, 60, 62-5, 76, 108, 116-17, 120, 125-6, 128, 130, 135, 142, 150-1, 158, 187, 189, 191-6, 198, 204-5, 208, 222, 224

Rwanda xi, xii, 2-3, 7, 39, 48, 167-82, 202, 225, 215-17, 223, 226

Sata, Michael 128-30

Seck, Idrissa 25-9

Senegal xi, xii, 2-3, 7, 13-23, 26-9, 31-6, 43, 56, 62, 64, 67, 115, 202-9, 213, 218-21, 223-4, 226

Senghor, Léopold Sedar 13-5, 27, 34, 203

September 11th 19, 75

settlers 7, 116, 134, 186, 195

Sexwale, Tokyo 142

Shangaan 161

Sharia 74-6, 79

social contract 8-10, 14, 18, 53, 195, 204-5, 222-3

socialism 7, 146, 153-5, 160-1, 163, 188, 212

societal accountability 6, 211

soldiers 24, 37, 41, 90, 180

Somalia xi, 223

Soro, Guillaume 46-7

South Africa xi-xiii, 2-3, 7, 39, 44, 48, 104, 134-5, 138, 140-1, 143-5, 147-51, 154, 156, 158, 186, 188, 202, 212-15, 217-19, 223-4

Sovereign National Conference 73, 86

Soviet Union 97, 146, 154, 214

Sri Lanka xiii

state xi-xiv, 1-2, 4-6, 8-11, 13-29, 31-41, 43-7, 50, 52-5, 57-60, 62, 64-8, 71-84, 86-8, 94, 96-104, 107-11, 114, 116-31, 135, 137, 142-3, 146-50, 153, 155-64, 167-72, 174-82, 185-99, 202-4, 206-18, 221-6

state accountability 73, 189, 192

state bureaucracies 21, 62, 169, 192

Straw, Jack 87

structural constraints 6, 61, 154

students 1, 17, 20, 23, 35, 37, 41, 60, 111, 118, 188, 190, 191, 197, 204-5

Sub-Saharan Africa xi, xiii, 1-3, 6-7, 19, 107, 118, 120, 123, 226

subsidies 117-21, 210

Sufi brotherhoods 25, 76

taxation 76, 126

Thiam, Iba Der 21

Third Term 85-7, 116, 123, 127, 107, 219

Togo 43-4

trade unions 119, 144, 148-9, 188, 199, 219, 224

traditional authorities 154

Treatment Action Campaign 136, 150, 219

Tsvangirai, Morgan 192, 197-8

Tutsi 167-80, 182, 215-17

Twa 167, 170, 177,

United Nations 43-6, 85, 105, 122, 155, 168, 178-80

United States 16, 19, 75, 87

unreformed autocracy 7

Upper Volta 32, see Burkina Faso

urban 9, 13, 15-16, 23-5, 28, 39, 52-4, 59-61, 63, 122, 124, 130, 135, 150, 189, 193, 196, 198, 204, 210-11, 218, 222-4; bias 23, 223

vertical accountability 6, 8

veterans 185, 189-96, 198, 215

vigilantes 76, 88

virtual democracies 3

voters 14, 46, 55-6, 62-5, 88, 90, 95, 98, 103, 105, 109, 134, 138-40, 156, 176, 178, 192, 198, 207-8, 220, 225

Wade, Abdoulaye 14, 15, 17-29, 203, 205, 207

Wako Draft 109

welfare state 53, 147-8, 150

white farmers 191-7

women's organisations 1

World Bank 10, 35, 37-8, 53, 107, 118-

19, 125, 127, 130, 141, 155, 157, 161, 203, 212, 222

Yar' Adua, Umaru 71, 79, 84, 88-90, 208
Yoruba 74, 79-80, 82, 89
'Young Patriots' 45-6, 48
youth 29, 63, 76, 122, 142, 190, 193-4, 198, 204

Zambia xii, 2-3, 7, 94-6, 103, 114-30, 181, 188, 202, 205, 209-12, 218-20, 222-4, 226
Zimbabwe xi-xiii, 2-3, 7, 10, 18, 29, 48, 121, 149, 181, 185-99, 202, 214-16, 218, 224, 226
Zuma, Jacob 149-50, 213

Lightning Source UK Ltd.
Milton Keynes UK
UKHW022213240122
397636UK00004B/224